The North Marston Story

A History of the Village

Compiled and Edited

by

Sue Chaplin and John Spargo

NORTH MARSTON HISTORY CLUB

Published in 2014 by the North Marston History Club

Sue Chaplin and John Spargo

Copyright © North Marston History Club

northmarstonhistory.org.uk

ISBN: 978-0-9929089-0-4

All rights reserved. No part of this publication may be reproduced, stored in a retrieval system, or transmitted in any form or by any means, electronic, mechanical, photocopying, recording or otherwise without the prior permission of the copyright holder.

Printed in Spain under the supervision of MRM Graphics, Winslow, Bucks

www.mrmgraphics.co.uk

CONTENTS

	Foreword	5
	Acknowledgements	6
	Introduction	7
One	Roman Times	9
Two	St Mary's Church	12
Three	John Schorne, North Marston's Saint	38
Four	John Schorne's Well	44
Five	Windmills	49
Six	The Great Fire of 1705	54
Seven	Open Fields and Enclosure	58
Eight	The Methodist Churches	66
Nine	Sunday Schools	74
Ten	The Housewife and the Miser	82
Eleven	Doctor Samuel James	87
Twelve	Schorne College 1876-1910	92
Thirteen	The Victorian Village	101
Fourteen	H J Holden and the Tailors	110

Fifteen	The Great War 1914-1918	120
Sixteen	Shops	128
Seventeen	The Post Offices	138
Eighteen	Trades and Occupations of the Past	145
Nineteen	Pubs and Ale Houses	181
Twenty	Events and Celebrations	194
Twenty-one	Clubs, Societies and Charities	221
Twenty-two	Village Sport	236
Twenty-three	The Second World War 1939-1945	256
Twenty-four	Farming Part One: The History of Farming from 1778	269
	Part Two: Farms and Farming Families	294
Twenty-five	The School 1835-1968	350
Twenty-six	Gypsies on the Doorstep	388
Twenty-seven	A Walk Through the Village in 1901	398
	The Origin of Street Names	424
	Field Map and Field Names	426
	Bibliography	430

FOREWORD

It is unbelievable that until now a book has never been written about North Marston, a Buckinghamshire village with an unusual and rich history.

When John Spargo, a keen local historian, moved to the village in 2009, he decided to rectify the situation and started by forming a History Club. Sue Chaplin, who was born and raised in North Marston, as were many previous generations of her family, offered to help John with the research, writing and production of a village history book.

In 2010, Sue started to interview the older village residents.... published as *Memories Shared* in 2011....and it became evident that there was a fascinating story just waiting to be written.

A number of factors combined to give John and Sue the impetus to fulfil the project: a local survey had highlighted a wish for information about the village history to be made accessible; the availability of the Victorian village magazines provided an amazing insight into the daily workings of North Marston at a time it was going through huge changes; the discovery of the School Log Books and Admissions Registers from 1900 helped to provide a picture of the social history of the village; and the response to requests for photographs and documents was overwhelming. In fact, North Marston has a treasure trove of information.....the sheer volume of *The North Marston Story* speaks for itself!

Sue Chaplin and John Spargo

ACKNOWLEDGEMENTS

This book would not have been possible without the help of many others to whom we are truly indebted. Many of the chapters in the book have relied on information gathered by other people and generously made available to us.

In particular, we acknowledge the research and advice from local historian Michael Finnemore. In the context of studying the history of this village, it is difficult to over-estimate the importance of the research and the information he has amassed over the years, particularly in relation to the village enclosure, property deeds and land ownership. His research enabled him to produce a meticulous plan of the 1778 enclosure of the village and a detailed map of the open fields prior to this, both of which future local historians will find invaluable. It is fitting and gratifying that we have been able to bring his work to a wider audience through this book.

We also acknowledge the previous work done by local resident John Wright which helped greatly in the writing of the chapter on *Windmills*, and we are indebted to Colin Price for writing six of the chapters in this book and for serving on the Editorial Committee. We are also extremely grateful to Rosemary Morton for the thorough and lengthy research she carried out on the village farms, and for her support as a member of the Editorial Committee. We thank Eddie O'Keefe for all his help with finding information on village football, and Barbara Harwood whose previous research provided us with many useful starting points. Janet Gowin's impressive and important family archive of letters, photographs and village magazines has proved priceless; she and Jennifer Heffer have been dedicated and valued members of the Editorial Committee.

We acknowledge fellow History Club members and all the people, living both in the village and far afield, who have loaned photographs and documents, given us information or allowed us to look inside their homes as part of the process of compiling a history of North Marston, and we are very grateful to North Marston Church of England School for their loan of old Log Books. We are especially indebted to the twenty-three village residents (past and present) whose memories, published as *Memories Shared* in 2011, proved invaluable in the writing of this book.

We are very grateful to our proof-readers: Valerie Newby, Valerie and Colin Price, Alex and Rose Matthews, Susie and Simon Kelly, John Tate and Stuart Chaplin.

We thank the Heritage Lottery Fund for their sponsorship towards the cost of publication, and Keith Allison and his colleagues at MRM Graphics for their help and support in guiding us through the technical maze from desktop to the published volume.

Finally, we thank our spouses, Fran Spargo and Stuart Chaplin, to whom this book is dedicated, for their patient support, help and encouragement.

John Spargo (Chairman NMHC)

Sue Chaplin (Secretary NMHC)

April 2014

INTRODUCTION

Recorded as *Merstone* in the Domesday Book (a name meaning *marshy estate*), North Marston has for centuries been the place that thousands of people have been proud to call their home. At first glance it is not a particularly remarkable place: just a small, agricultural village in North Bucks nestled between Whitchurch and Winslow. However, its history tells a very different story.

This book, produced by the *North Marston History Club*, tries to capture that story by incorporating the traces left from centuries past with words, photographs and documentation. It is through the memories and shared experiences of its residents, whether written or recorded, that we feel the real essence of this quiet, dignified village. It evokes the picture of a community at one with itself.

Virtually self-sufficient for much of its history as a farming community, North Marston was in balance with the seasons and with nature. Over the years it has suffered set-backs and tragedies but has also celebrated great achievements and historic events.

Many of the old family names run like a thread through the generations, with marriages weaving a tapestry between them. Some prospered, some fared less well, but all survived.

Tracing our local history helps us to understand our village and to appreciate the *linear* process and the role played by individuals and events in shaping what we have today. Some of these were high-profile while others were almost invisible; yet all had a contribution to make.

One of the fascinating things about looking at the village's history is to discover how events of the past still have an effect today. Some are quite obvious: for example, the Enclosure of the village in the late eighteenth century gave the village its shape and explains why some buildings are where they are; the founding of the Holden tailoring business brought a host of families to the village, many of whose descendants are still here today. Further back in time, the pilgrimages to John Schorne's shrine and his "Holy Well" created great prosperity for the village, leading to the substantial enhancement of the parish church and probably saving the village from being abandoned after The Black Death.

Gathering together a local history is a community effort and many people have contributed very generously to the making of this book by giving us access to old family photographs, letters and other documents. The personal memories of many village residents which, in 2011, were recorded and published in the *Memories Shared* booklets paint a vivid picture of the life of North Marston in the past and have provided us with a valuable source of information. Quotes from these booklets have been used extensively throughout the book (and are presented in bold font).

One of our most precious historical resources is a collection of parish magazines published during the late Victorian period. North Marston's parish magazine first saw the light of day in January 1870. It was entirely due to the efforts of one man, the Reverend Samuel Benjamin James, who was appointed vicar here in 1869.

Samuel James was an industrious and methodical editor, not afraid to scold and sermonise his parishioners through the pages of his monthly publication called *The Schornian*. Each edition carried a section he called *The Parish Chronicle*, a detailed diary of events in and around the village. This provides a unique and rich source of information about the village during a period of unprecedented change: the arrival of the village post office and telegraph; the first bus service to Aylesbury; the modernisation of water supplies and drainage; the creation of the parish school; the formation of the parish council and the building of some of the village's most iconic houses.

The Schornian is therefore a precious gift to us from a time when village life was radically different from nowadays. In the early years of its publication, James wrote about a community that was virtually self-sufficient, and where a cluster of ancient families provided the employment and labour in respective roles that had remained constant for generations.

Yet all was to change. The upheaval of progress and technology that swept into the village in the latter quarter of the nineteenth century meant nothing was to be the same again. North Marston became connected and interdependent with a wider community. The historic framework of social order was eroded. In the space of a generation the population was presented with opportunities that had been once available only to the wealthy. Communication technology, public transport, local councils, state education and the rising influence of the middle-class were to transform rural England and to give shape to much of today's village.

Rev Samuel James's *Parish Chronicles* assemble, piece by piece, the story of this change as it happened. Many of Rev James's personal comments have been included in this book.

One of our tasks in compiling this book has been to select which information to use and which to leave "for another day". This book is therefore a subjective picture of North Marston`s history as seen through *our* eyes; future generations might create a different but equally valid interpretation.

Some of the book's chapters, such as *Open Fields and Enclosure,* have information rooted firmly in the past; other chapters, such as *The School,* end at a strategic date; others come up to the present day.

The key achievement is that for the first time we have an *accessible* account for all to share. Advances in information technology have enabled us digitally to capture words and images which are all safely archived by *The North Marston History Club* for future generations.

We hope you enjoy reading this book and, through these pages, understand and appreciate the legacy left to us by those who have been here before.

North Marston History Club
April 2014

One
ROMAN TIMES
Colin Price

The Buckinghamshire County Museum has in its collection part of a Roman roof tile found in the grounds of the vicarage in North Marston. We also find Roman roof tiles incorporated into the fabric of the church walls. Stonemasons building the church would have used any suitable local material and no doubt found the tiles lying in the vicinity of the church albeit eight centuries after the Romans departed. So we have some evidence of buildings in North Marston at the time of the Roman occupation of Britain.

Further evidence is provided by an early Anglo-Saxon loom-weight found in the village (also in the collection of the Buckinghamshire County Museum) showing that people were making textiles in the village soon after the Roman period. This is all the evidence we have for a community in North Marston at that time but we do have two outstanding legacies from the days of Roman occupation: the Roman Road and the Roman Burial Cist.

Roman Road

Carters Lane follows the course of a Roman road which, during the Roman occupation of Britain, was a major route linking the important towns of Fleet Marston and Thornborough. The way that it fits into the network of major Roman roads is illustrated in Figure 1 which shows how close North Marston was to three well known routes: Watling Street, Akeman Street and the Icknield Way.

Watling Street was a paved Roman causeway running from Richborough in Kent to Holyhead. It passed through Canterbury, London, St Albans and Chester providing a vital link between these major centres. Akeman Street linked the two major towns of St Albans and Alcester. The Icknield Way, on the other hand, was an ancient Celtic route connecting Yarmouth with Land's End. It passes through Buckinghamshire in the shadow of the Chilterns from Ivinghoe to Princes Risborough.

Not only did we have well-known Roman roads in our area but there were also many sites of Roman occupation of which the most significant were Fleet Marston, Thornborough and Magiovinium.

Fleet Marston was an important posting station for imperial couriers travelling along Akeman Street towards the garrison town of Bicester and it was large enough to be called a town.

Magiovinium was a major town located east of Fenny Stratford at a site close to Bow Brickhill. Its location was important as it straddled Watling Street. Magiovinium was a posting station and remains have been found of a Roman fort.

Thornborough was an important religious centre. Two large burial mounds can still be seen. They have been excavated and found to contain glass, bronze and pottery providing evidence of a Romanised culture. In addition, there is a third century Romano-Celtic temple nearby at Bourton Grounds.

From Figure 1 it can be seen that, during the Roman occupation, North Marston lay alongside a very significant road. The road linked the town of Fleet Marston with the religious centre at Thornborough from where it continued to the garrison town of Towcester. It is believed that much of the traffic on this road would have been military personnel heading towards Towcester as well as civilians going to Thornborough.

To this day the Roman road marks the parish boundary between North Marston and Quainton.

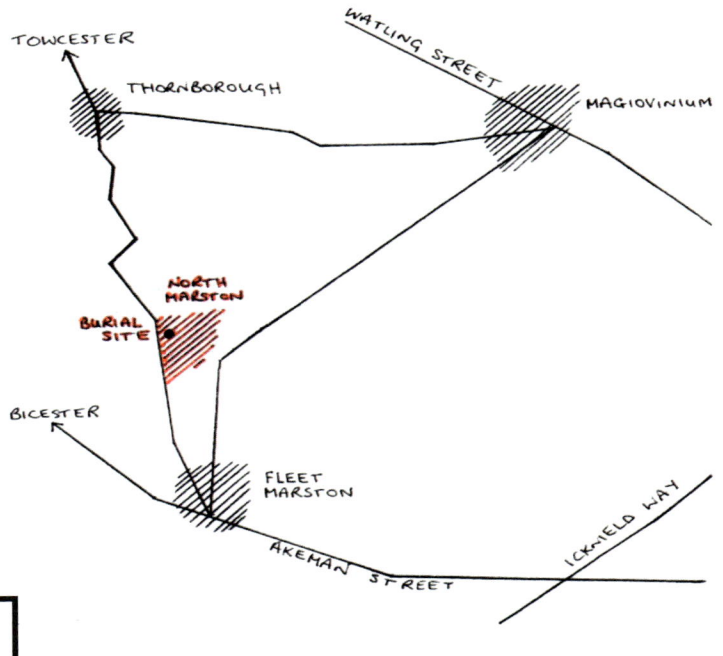

Figure 1

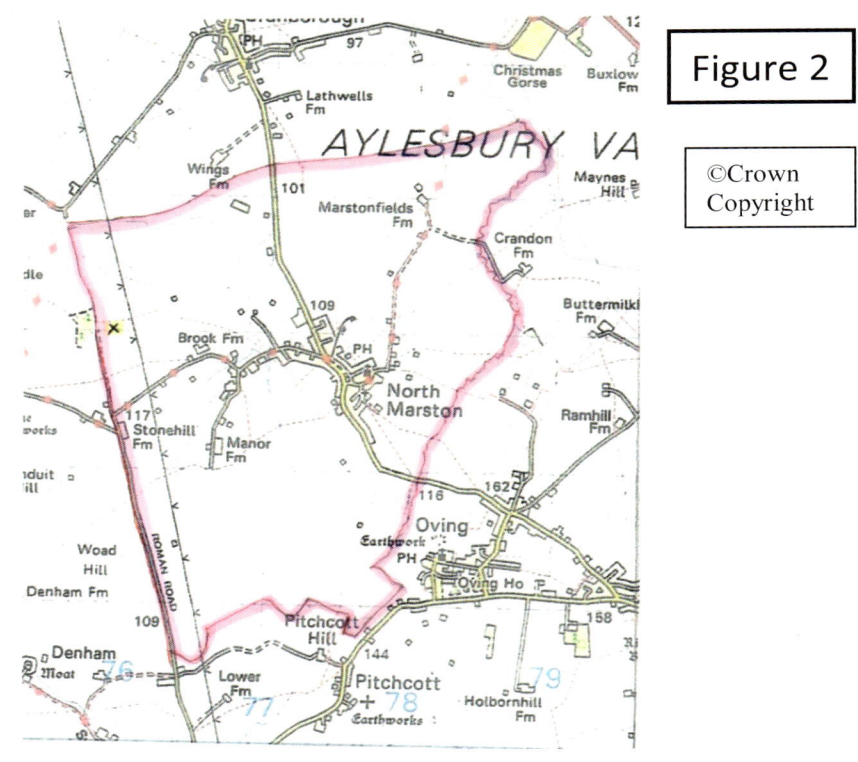

Figure 2

©Crown Copyright

Figure 2 is a modification of the current local Ordnance Survey map showing the location of the Roman road. It can easily be visualized as it runs along Carters Lane and into Deadman's Lane but from that point it peters out as a hedgerow eventually disappearing altogether.

Roman Burial

In 1973, Buckinghamshire Archaeological Society excavated a Roman burial cist in a field to the east of Deadman's Lane as marked on Figure 1. This site is only seventy metres from the Roman road. It is undoubtedly a Roman cremation burial site and has been dated to the late Third Century AD.

Despite finding that the site had been disturbed at sometime in the past, much of value was revealed by the excavation. The cist was composed of limestone slabs laid horizontally with walls of upright slabs. The structure was rectangular in shape and would originally have measured 1.4 metres by 1.5 metres, with the long axis north-south. The walls of the cist were 0.4 metres high.

The main pottery find was a thin-walled, orange-coloured bowl. It had broken into thirty pieces but nonetheless four-fifths remained and were restorable *(see following photograph)*. A few fragments of three other similar bowls were found. Amazingly, these have been firmly identified as products of a group of kilns near Headington in Oxfordshire. In addition, shards of four other pottery vessels were found. The only metal object found was referred to as a bronze *brooch spring*.

The Roman burial at North Marston is of particular interest to archaeologists because Roman cist burials, although common on the continent, are very uncommon in Britain and this is the only one found so far in Buckinghamshire.

The isolated position of this solitary burial is hard to explain as Roman burials were usually associated with settlements or religious centres such as the burial mounds further up the road at Thornborough. Could there have been a significant Roman settlement in North Marston of which we are unaware? It is interesting to note that a field further to the North is called "Deadman's Ground", a name which may indicate earlier discoveries of burial sites in this area which have gone unrecorded. Could there be more Roman artefacts buried in these fields?

The Roman bowl excavated from the North Marston cist burial in the collection of Buckinghamshire County Museum (Museum Number AYBCM: 1973.163.1

Two
ST MARY'S CHURCH
John Spargo

North Marston Church, officially the Church of the Assumption of the Blessed Virgin Mary, is by far the largest and oldest structure in the village.

In the year 1185 North Marston (which was called *Mereston* by the Saxons) lay on the edge of King Henry II's great hunting forest, Bernwood Forest. Henry had a summer palace about eight miles away at Brill.

The church, which was Catholic, as all churches were in England at that time, was in the patronage of the Order of the Knights of St John, also known as the Knights Hospitallers. In common with a number of churches in the area, it was endowed to the Knights as a source of income. But the Order was not concerned with attending to the spiritual welfare of the village so in 1185 they commissioned Dunstable Priory to assume care of the church.

Dunstable Priory Church

This meant that the Priory was to supply the church with secular canons to act as rectors. In return, the Priory was allowed to retain one pound a year *pension* from the local church taxes (called *tithes*) with the balance going to the Knights.

The Church in 1185

The church at this time would have been tiny by today's standards, a simple rectangle the size of the modern central nave; it had no aisles, no tower and a much lower roof. The chancel (the altar end of the church) is likely to have been half the length of the modern chancel.

As a small, stone Norman church, it was probably built very early in the twelfth century on the foundations of a wooden Saxon church which is likely to have served the community on this site for centuries before-hand.

Sometime during the early 1200s a north aisle was added for processions. The pillars in the arcade of the north aisle are completely different in style from those of the south aisle built a century later.

The arcade of the north aisle with "Early-English" pillars

At about the same time as the north aisle was constructed, a small Lady Chapel was added as a lean-to at the south-east end of the nave. It was dressed with a pretty *decorated-style* window which would have flooded the little chapel with light. The light on the left of the Lady Chapel window was blocked by the later addition of a buttress outside.

The east window in the Lady Chapel

It was later in that same century that North Marston welcomed its new Rector, Master John Schorne (*see Chapter Three*). He had been Rector at Steppingly in Bedfordshire for about seven years before coming to North Marston in 1282. Schorne was probably a Doctor of Divinity and was titled *Master* John Schorne or *Magister* John Schorne thus indicating a man of learning and seniority. He was said to have been a very pious man and the story goes that during a terrible drought in the village he struck the ground with his staff and a spring gushed forth. The spring became a well, the water from which was thought to have miraculous healing qualities about which word quickly spread.

When Schorne died in 1314, and in common with the practice at the time, he was buried in the floor of the chancel in front of the main altar.

Soon, pilgrims began to arrive in the village to seek cures from his holy well-water and to venerate Schorne's resting place in the church. The pilgrims brought votive offerings: small gifts of money and goods.

A pilgrim

No doubt having witnessed this, the Abbot of Dunstable Priory asked for consent fully to *appropriate* the church from the Knights of St John; this was granted in 1330. The Priory immediately commissioned the construction of a new south aisle incorporating the existing Lady Chapel and also built on a south porch so that the church would look more fitting as the resting place of a man who had become venerated to saintly status.

The south aisle

The Church in 1353

Although there was now a new south aisle and south porch, the church in 1353 had no tower and it had a much lower roof than in modern times (*you can see this by the height of the original roof brackets, or 'corbels', at back of the church at the end of the nave*).

A corbel from the original roof support at the south west corner of the nave

The floor was un-paved; it was a packed earth floor which for most of the year was strewn with straw or bean haulms. It was relatively dark inside as, apart from the window in the Lady Chapel, the rest of the church had small lancet windows that do not let in as much light as the later Gothic windows. An example of an early lancet window can still be seen at the west end of the north aisle.

The lancet window at the west end of the north aisle

The venerated John Schorne still lay buried in the chancel floor and, as was the custom at the time, his burial place will have been marked by an incised slab. Across the chancel arch there was a *rood-beam* or *candle beam*, on which was a large painted figure of Christ on the cross. Beside the cross were figures of Mary Magdalene and John the Evangelist. This collective group is known as the *rood*.

An example of a rood-beam spanning a chancel arch

Crude candles, or *lights*, usually made from animal fat (tallow) would have burned along the rood beam all the time, hence the term candle-beam. A partition rising up from the floor spanned the chancel arch and so divided the chancel from the nave; this was known as the *rood screen* and it would have been covered with pictures of saints (s*ee the example pictured*).

An example of a rood screen covered with pictures of saints

The walls of the church were also covered with brightly coloured paintings of biblical stories or saintly deeds. About us we would have seen many flickering *lights* dotted around the nave. These marked small shrines or *nave altars* to particular saints and each would have been tended by particular people of the village for whom that saint had a special meaning. The church had no heating in winter. Outside in the churchyard there were no gravestones (they did not appear until the 1600s) but there were trees and a large stone cross to the south east of the church where a processional mass would have been held on Easter Sunday.

A medieval religious procession

The church had no seating so everyone had to stand. Those who were frail leaned against a wall or a pillar, hence the expression "the weakest go to the wall".

The church was built from stone taken from Oving Quarry a couple of miles away. It is a soft limestone that weathers poorly so it was lime-rendered to protect it; the rough stone now exposed on the outside walls was never supposed to have been seen.

The original patronal dedication of the principle altar, probably in Saxon times, is not known but it may have been connected with the church's location in Bernwood Forest (for example, it might have been dedicated to St Giles or St Lawrence, these being "forest saints").

St Giles, a forest saint

To us, one of the noticeable things about the interior of the church of 1353 would have been the organic smell of damp earth, crushed vegetation, tallow smoke, incense and possibly animal dung or smelly people!

It was probably a noisy place during daylight hours, with the sound of trading, conversation, devotions and chanting from behind the rood screen. Being the biggest building in the village, it was an obvious place to gather in numbers, to trade, to get one's livestock blessed or to shelter from bad weather.

This was a poor church in a poor village; the church's income in 1291 was six pounds thirteen shillings and four-pence a year (by contrast, neighbouring Quainton church's income at the same time was twenty pounds a year).

The lay population of 1353 would have been *very* pious and spiritual because they had just survived the Black Death, or *Great Pestilence*, of September 1349. It wiped out nearly half the population and had the most devastating consequences:

- With so many fatalities, there was no labour for working the fields, harvesting or for tending the livestock. As a result, many small rural communities ceased to be viable and the surviving population migrated to other settlements. Abandoned villages could be found throughout the county.
- People stopped travelling around unless it was a matter of life or death. The advice given to those who could afford to go to a safer place was "run away quickly and walk back slowly".
- Many of the clergy died: offering the final sacrament to people dying of the plague proved a risky occupation! This led to dumbing down of the clergy.
- People sought their own interpretation of what had happened; they believed that such a momentous tragedy was God's punishment for sinfulness and as a consequence people became far more pious and religious.
- There was a breakdown of law and order. Squatting and property theft were rife. The immediate post-plague era saw violent and lawless times. Small communities were virtually in a state of siege and strangers were treated with great suspicion.

In the years immediately following the Black Death, people understandably had three chief concerns: illness, sudden death and the fate of one's soul after death in *purgatory*. Purgatory is defined as "*a state or place in which the souls of those who have died are believed to undergo suffering to become purified of the remaining effects of mortal sin*" so it was not a benign waiting-room and one would not want to stay there a moment longer than necessary!)

Any help the saints could offer to speed the passage of one's soul through purgatory was much sought-after.

In all these areas, saints became everyone's great allies. Saints had a number of important roles:

- a) **For the living** they could cure illness and disability, cure sick animals, or act as a talisman against sudden death (for example, St Christopher). There were *specialist condition* saints: St Barbara and St Katherine for childbirth; St Sebastian for protection from the plague; St Erasmus against intestinal disorders; St Petronilla for the ague (malaria); and North Marston's John Schorne for the ague and for gout (though Schorne was never formally canonised as a saint).
- b) **For the dead** saints were believed to be able to intercede on behalf of the soul in purgatory. *Virgin martyr* saints were particularly powerful in this regard because it was believed that being so pure they were closer to God.

The Virgin Mary intercedes for souls suffering in the fires of purgatory

People specified in their wills provisions for paying for lights at shrines and for masses to be said for their souls; bequests to specific saints were thought to offer an assurance the saint would look favourably on them and intercede on their behalf when their soul entered purgatory.

Saints and Symbols

Walls and rood screens, as mentioned earlier, would have been covered with pictures of famous saints. To help identify the saint each was given a unique icon or symbol: Peter had his keys, St Giles a wounded doe, St Agnes a white lamb, St Catherine of Alexandria a wheel (*see picture*) and North Marston's John Schorne ..... a devil in a boot.

Saint Christopher

St Catherine of Alexandria

An image of John Schorne with the devil emerging from a boot

Images were crucial and themselves became shrines at which people lit candles and left votive offerings. Dedicated *gilds* were formed to look after the lights for specific shrines. Most parish churches in the country would have had many *lights*; they burnt before the rood, before the sacrament and before each of the sacred images in the church.

At North Marston in 1519, Joan Ingram left bequests in her will for *"the rood light, and the lights of St Katherine, St Christopher, St John, St Margaret, St Anne and 1 lb wax each for Master John Schorne's lights and the sepulchre light"*: in other words, six shrines or altars not counting the Lady Chapel and any others.

Life in medieval times was *completely* regulated by religious festivals and saints' days. Over fifty days a year (apart from Sundays) were solemnly dedicated to saints; these were feast days when all but the most essential agricultural work was forbidden. There were almost seventy days in a year when adults were obliged to fast…no meat, eggs or cheese. No-one could marry during the four weeks of Advent or the six weeks of Lent. Even for those who were married, conjugal activity was discouraged during Advent to reduce the risk of childbirth at harvest time, when everyone would be needed to work in the fields.

The labour-intensive harvest

Calendar dates were meaningless. Specific days were defined by adjacent saints' days; thus, for example, 25th June would have been described as "the morrow of St John the Baptist and the eve of the disciple saints, John and Paul".

Many people would have attended a daily mass, a short ceremony celebrated at one of the nave altars, but the lay population would only have received Holy Communion once a year, on Easter Sunday.

Changes in the 1300s

As mentioned earlier, when Dunstable Priory appropriated the church from the Knights Hospitallers in the 1330s they set about changes to the building. One of these was to enlarge and upgrade the Lady Chapel and incorporate it into the south aisle. This was consistent with the Marian cult that was sweeping the country and is illustrated by the elaborate stone carving to the window mouldings, pillar capitals and other exposed stonework in the chapel.

The flowers seen here are a Marian symbolic flower, the mystic rose

On the wall of the chapel is an elaborate piscina, a small sink with a drain where the officiating priest would have rinsed the chalice after mass.

The Lady Chapel piscine

A corbel for the original Lady Chapel roof (seen here on the right next to the later rood-loft door)

This also tells us that the rood door in the wall above the Lady Chapel was pierced through *after* the roof of the Lady Chapel was raised, which in turn means the chancel arch is likely to have been much lower than it is today.

You can see the arch to the Lady Chapel is lower than its neighbouring arches in the south aisle; that tells us the construction of this arch pre-dated the creation of the south aisle.

The south arcade showing the Lady Chapel arch (on the left) as being lower than the subsequently installed south aisle arches

Mindful of the pilgrims and their money, the Priory also installed a very unusual, ornate little shrine at floor-level in the Lady Chapel. This would have housed a boot, John Schorne's icon (*see picture below*).

The shrine would have had a grill of iron bars with a small aperture into which gout-sufferers could insert a troubled foot.

From the Lady Chapel, there was a *squint,* or *hagioscope,* looking to the central altar (the squint is now blocked).

The blocked squint from the Lady Chapel looking to the chancel altar

Even more unusual, there appears to have been a *second* squint in the Lady Chapel and this is looking through to a point at the east end of the nave, against the south chancel pillar to the altar of the *Holy Rood*.

The unusual second squint in the Lady Chapel

By the chancel arch is an *aumbry* (a locked cupboard for the sacramental silverware). From the evidence of former chapels, it appears there were at least three canons working here and accordingly there are three very ornate *sedilia* (stone seats for the priests) set in the south wall of the chancel.

The three ornate sedilia in the chancel with the chancel piscina beyond

In the early 1350s (as the Priory at Dunstable had already spotted) there was a noticeable surge in the number of people going on pilgrimage.

Why did people go on a pilgrimage?

a) *Penance* (either in person or by proxy) which removed some of the stain of sins on their soul.

b) *Cure* from disease or impairment.

c) They had made a *pact with God* in return for being spared death or injury in some calamitous event or illness, such as the Great Pestilence, and were giving thanks for being spared.

The Church in 1478

The year 1478 was in the Late Medieval Period and Edward IV was the king. Pilgrimages were now at their most popular and *very* big business indeed.

The pilgrimages to North Marston were the *third largest* in the country, behind those to Thomas Becket's shrine at Canterbury and Our Lady of Walsingham. The church's income had now reached a staggering five hundred pounds a year.

The church building of 1478 would have looked more familiar to us. The chancel had been enlarged to its modern length and height, a tower had been added to the west end of the church, the nave and chancel roof had been raised and a line of upper windows called a *clerestory* had been installed.

The clerestory above the arcades

Minstrels and choristers were carved into the roof-supporting timber brackets around the nave; most of the narrow lancet windows had been replaced with larger windows.

One of the nave minstrels

To brace the walls (which would have been put under greater weight-stress by raising the roof and weakened by being pierced for larger windows) buttresses had been built against the external walls.

Inside, the church had become much bigger and brighter. The font cover was locked to prevent the theft of holy water for sale as a charm.

Another security measure was a squint on the north chancel wall that was pierced through from an upper priest's room to monitor Schorne's shrine (*see picture below*).

By now, the remains, or *relics*, of the venerated 'saint' had been placed in a raised tomb called a *reliquary*: a receptacle for housing relics (*see example below*).

A simple medieval reliquary shrine

Reliquaries were designed to enable supplicants to get as close as possible to the relic to gain the maximum supernatural power. In other words, Schorne's remains had been exhumed from the floor of the chancel where they had lain since 1314 and put in a fancy tomb, befitting his status as a saint and miracle-worker. The chancel squint in the north wall is there so that canons in the upper priest's chamber (the *watching chamber*) can guard against the theft of offerings left at the shrine.

All around the chancel were ornately carved stone corbels depicting winged choristers or mythical flying beasts.

A chancel angel with a scroll

The three priests on duty were kept busy and had a liturgical rota of masses or *hours* to be said throughout the day at exactly prescribed intervals.

The rood lights were kept burning on the candle beam that spanned the chancel arch. Young boys would have been used to go up on to the rood loft (through the narrow rood loft door over the Lady Chapel) to tend to the lights on behalf of benefactors.

The country was gripped by pilgrimage mania and the cult of saints was at its height. Pilgrims meant money; poor folk could not afford to leave their land and go on pilgrimages but North Marston benefited through providing refreshments and accommodation for these more affluent visitors. It is probable that some of the oldest buildings in Church Street once provided pilgrims with sustenance and shelter.

Attempts to draw in the pilgrims sometimes led to desperate measures: in 1448 an entrepreneurial vicar of North Marston called Walter Budde was summoned before the Bishop of Lincoln's court on a charge of blasphemy. In an attempt to boost income, he had added to the attractions of the site by exhuming a skull from the churchyard, sprinkling it with blood, and claiming it to be the head of John Schorne. Allegedly, he assaulted the bishop's representative who came to present him with the charges, which probably did not help his case. He was to be in trouble again a couple of years later when he appeared in another court over unpaid debts.

In the midst of pilgrim-mania, things in North Marston were about to change: the Dean of Windsor (the Bishop of Salisbury) had designs on Schorne's lucrative shrine. With papal consent given in 1478, Schorne's relics were taken to the newly-built St George's Chapel at Windsor to draw pilgrims there.

St George's Chapel, Windsor

Dunstable Priory was 'bought off' by being given another church and, at the King's request, the Dean and Chapter of Windsor appropriated North Marston church. It is likely at about this time there was major embellishment of the chancel and the church's exterior stonework *possibly* as compensation by Windsor Chapel to the village; but it was more likely to have been commissioned by Dunstable Priory shortly *before* Schorne's remains were moved, using some of the pilgrim money it had amassed. This was high quality and expensive work and left the church one of the most ornamentally lavish parish churches to be found anywhere (*see following picture*).

One might have assumed the canons in the church at the time of King Edward's removal of Schorne's relics would have been furious with the king that their local saint was being transferred to Windsor but, cleverly, one of them left us a message seeming to contradict this notion. High on the chancel arch, on the chancel-side chamfer (so as not to be visible from the nave) one of the clerics has scratched in Latin:

"EDWARDE ERAM HONEORR"

It is believed this is a mis-spelling of *"Edwarde Eram Honorer".* Translated to modern English, this broadly means "Edward behaved respectfully".

The cleric, crouched on the rood-loft scratching away at the stone of the chancel arch with a nail, must have been strongly motivated: the desecration of such a holy place would not have been tolerated. He had obviously heard views of discontent expressed concerning Edward's removal of the Schorne relics from the chancel below to St George's Chapel Windsor and decided to make his own opinion known. The fact that a personal message has remained apparently unnoticed or un-recorded for five hundred years is truly remarkable as so much of the history of a church is based on inference from what we know from other churches.

Edward IV surrounded by his courtiers

We *know* Schorne's remains were taken from this church with papal consent in the late 1470s. We *know* Schorne was venerated as a saint (though never canonised) and North Marston was once a hugely popular place of pilgrimage. But these covertly scratched words high on the chancel arch are a hitherto undisclosed history of the *feelings* of someone who was actually here in North Marston at the time. Understandably, he did not sign his name so we will never know for sure if it was John Middleton, the canon who was vicar until 1489, or one of his assistants.

Of course, pilgrims continued to come to North Marston's holy well and probably to the church too as it had a sacred association with the great man. Probably the most famous pilgrim to visit North Marston after Schorne's remains had been taken to Windsor was none other than King Henry VIII who visited twice.

However, by the 1530s, the cult of John Schorne had almost run its course and, within a couple of decades, Henry VIII's Reformation would change the way the village worshipped forever. Many of the traces of its earliest medieval Catholic heritage were erased, but not all.

Scratch Dials

If you leave the church through the south porch and turn to the left you will see the priest's door in the side of the chancel. If you take a closer look at the stonework close to the door you can make out the faint remnants of odd-looking holes and patterns etched in the stonework. These are medieval *scratch-dials* or *mass dials* created by the canons from Dunstable Priory.

What were they for? Scratch dials were *service markers*. Before the age of clocks, the actual time of the day was almost meaningless. Scratch-dials helped to measure the *intervals* between a sequence of services that made up the canonical *hours*.

How did they work? The central hole is generally deeper than the other marks (which is why it is sometimes the only trace left). This was made for a dowel or peg called a *gnomon* to be inserted. Gnomons may have been wood or metal. If the sun was shining, the gnomon would cast a shadow across the *arc.* When the shadow neared one of the *hour* lines scratched in the lower segment of the dial, it told the priest it was approaching the time for the next mass or *hour*.

One of North Marston's many scratch-dials

The Victorian Make-over

The story of North Marston church does not stop in the medieval period: more was to come. In 1852 a very wealthy local landlord called John Camden Neild died and left his entire fortune of two hundred and fifty thousand pounds to Queen Victoria.

She and Prince Albert used the money to re-build Balmoral Castle to the Prince's design, but not before she had commissioned a leading architect of the day to re-furbish North Marston's chancel and to install a very grand east window and an ornate *reredos* (the panel behind the altar).

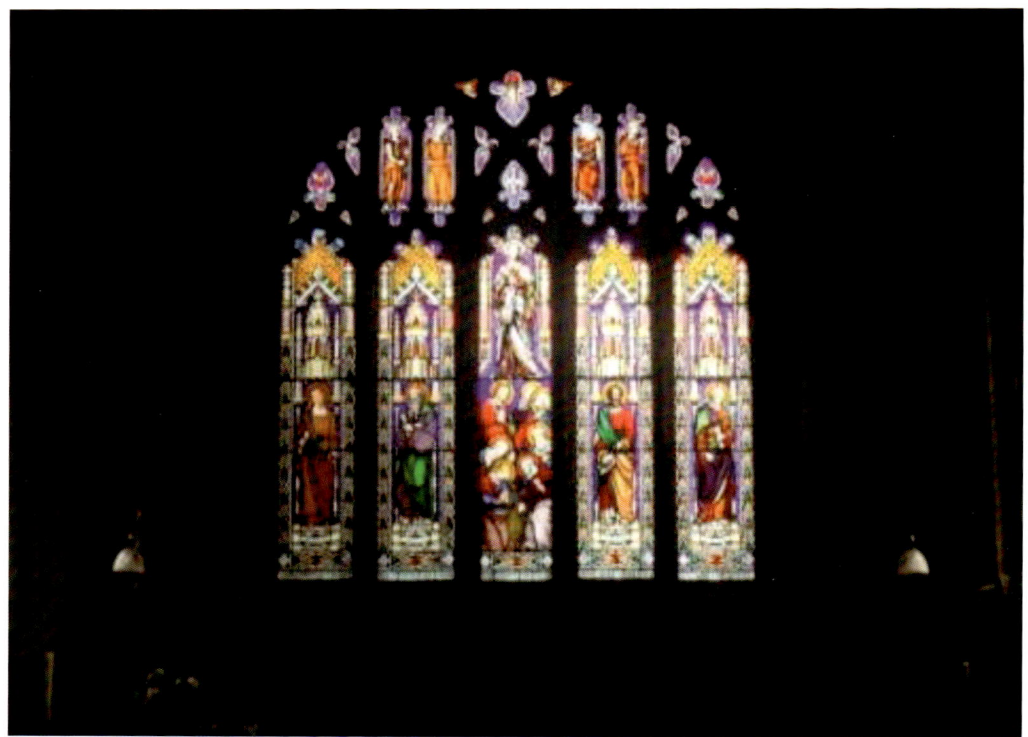
Camden Neild's memorial window commissioned by Queen Victoria

The plate marking John Camden Neild's burial place in the floor of the chancel

On Queen Victoria's instruction, *and against his wishes*, her benefactor John Camden Neild lies buried in the floor of the chancel at a spot marked by a plate (*see above*). The story of the bequest and Victoria's commissioning of the improvements to the church made national news briefly putting North Marston church back in the spotlight again after four hundred years.

The West Gallery

The practice of installing galleries in parish churches is likely to have resulted from an Act of 1644 banning organs from churches. Galleries were generally erected against the west (tower) wall and were to accommodate choristers and musicians who were collectively described as *church bands*.

A nineteenth century church band

However, many of the west gallery bands were eventually driven out by Victorian clergy who considered them vulgar and irreverent. Subsequently, a harmonium or organ was then installed in the church.

A typical church harmonium

For a while, galleries continued to be used for seating but by the latter part of the nineteenth century, west galleries were being removed from parish churches, and the west gallery at North Marston (described as "unsightly" by the vicar) was taken out on 4th December 1873 by the village blacksmith, John White.

Its removal was not without complaint as, by removing the gallery, the tower arch was exposed leading to draughts being felt by the congregation at the back of the church. Others found themselves displaced from their favourite gallery seat and forced to find another seat. Writing in *The Schornian* nearly twenty years later, Dr James looked back on the removal of the gallery and wrote:

"Following the removal of the unsightly gallery many years ago….some people said they would never enter the church again and one person said they would not even be buried in the churchyard."

At about the time of the removal of the west gallery, during a restoration of the church, a wall painting was discovered over the tower arch and reported in the Records of Buckinghamshire:

"A fresco was discovered immediately above the pointed tower arch. This consists of a crowned fleur de lys, the emblem of the Virgin Mary, to whom the church is dedicated. The fleur is executed boldly and with admirable proportion, as it is quite four feet wide, and more than that in height. The tower was built in the fifteenth century, and it is probable that the fresco was executed at the close of that century..."

A typical west gallery in-situ

The Heating System

In June 1887 work began on a new heating system which was a "formidable undertaking" according to Rev James:

"Mr Grundy's men commenced work in church....two furnaces of 16cwt. each being let under the floor, two coal cellars to match being made also under the floor (one in nave, the other in chancel), chambers running along (again underneath) to let in cold air from north and south doors, pipes under middle aisle and out of north wall of chancel, iron chimney, and altogether a most elaborate and gigantic undertaking, well worth £90."

It appears that in the process of excavating under the church floor to accommodate the new heating system there were unearthed a number of skeletons from medieval burials. In an article in The Schornian in 1888 Rev James refers to these as being:

"Giant's bones....denoting the vast height of Marstonians of the olden time and type. Nowadays we are mostly little men; those former Marstonians must have been very different, eight or nine feet high in fact."

The heating system was later updated when the coal cellars were removed and, most recently in 2011 a new central heating system was installed by Steve Gates.

The Church Organ

By way of contrast, the protest that met the removal of the west gallery seems not to have been a problem when the church installed its first organ in 1895, although according to The *Schornian* the exact location of the organ within the church was not without some debate.

The church had enjoyed the accompaniment of a harmonium for many years when, in 1894, the piano tuner declared it impossible to tune the harmonium again without a thorough renovation and restoration. That set in train a major fund-raising exercise spearheaded by the churchwarden, Henry John Holden, and culminating in the purchase for forty pounds of an "American Organ" that was installed in the east end of the south aisle and dedicated in October 1895. As this was before electricity was supplied to the church, the organist needed someone to pump the bellows (*see below to the right*).

The newly- installed organ being played

Subsequently, an electric blower was installed (the church was electrified in 1935 as a thanksgiving offering by the churchwarden, Henry Cheshire, on the event of his Golden Wedding) and the organ was later re-located to its current position at the west end of the south aisle.

Parishioners who provide many years of dedicated service to the church are not especially unusual, but one parishioner who invested a great many years of her life as organist at St Mary's was Mrs George Holden (nee Annie Dickens from Granborough).

By June 1970, when Mrs Holden was the organist at the service of institution of a new vicar (which was conducted by the Bishop of Oxford), she had been organist for thirty-five years.

The local newspaper article reporting the event (*see following picture*) shows Mrs Holden meeting the bishop.

In fact Mrs Holden continued to play the organ occasionally at St Mary's for a few more years. Her successor, who had actually taken over as the lead organist in 1964, was Ann Cheshire who herself played the organ at the church for sixteen years. Subsequent organists have included Jim White and Jennifer Heffer.

Commemorative Windows

The popular practice of commissioning commemorative windows stems from Victorian times, and the prime example at North Marston is the grand east window, mentioned earlier, which was commissioned by Queen Victoria to commemorate her benefactor, John Camden Neild. There is also a beautiful, albeit smaller, commemorative window in the north aisle at the east end. This was commissioned by the local businessman Henry John Holden in memory of his wife Matilda who died in 1914.

Matilda Holden's memorial window

Directly opposite in the south aisle is a window dedicated to the memory of Henry John Holden himself who died in 1926. Concealed within this window are various symbols of his tailoring trade.

Memorial window to Henry John Holden

Wool symbol in Holden's window

Scissors in Holden's window

Weavers' shuttles in Holden's window

One window in the church has two commemorations. The left hand *light* commemorates the major renovation of the church and the right hand *light* is to the memory of two brothers who lost their lives in the Great War, Bernard and Gilbert Cheshire. This window was dedicated in 1923 by the Bishop of Buckingham and can be seen in the north wall at the tower end.

The 1923 window to Bernard and Gilbert Cheshire

The John Schorne Panel

On 10th December 2006 a service was held to dedicate a new panel (*see picture below*) in the Lady Chapel window above the Cheshire altar.

This panel, designed by village artist Lauren Isherwood and researched by village historians Alison and Michael Finnemore, retells the legend of John Schorne and was inspired by the seven rood screens featuring John Schorne in churches in Norfolk, Suffolk and Devon. It depicts John Schorne holding the devil in a boot in front of a green and gold lattice background. The Schorne Well is shown as an illuminated letter on the scroll at the bottom of the panel while an ox is depicted as an illuminated letter on the scroll at the top. The panel was presented to the church by the three villagers at the service and a new hymn *In Praise of John Schorne* (written by Alison) was sung.

The Bells

At North Marston there were originally five bells and a small Sanctus bell, the origin of the bells being:

1. James Keene 1627 (Woodstock)
2. James Keene 1627
3. James Keene 1627
4. Richard Chandler 1699 (Drayton Parslow)
5. Lester & Pack 1763 (London)
6. Unknown Founder c 17th Century (Sanctus Bell)

Between 1911 and 1924, the bells at North Marston had fallen into disrepair: three of the bells were cracked and all five of them were out of tune. Experts were called in and they recommended that all five of the bells should be recast and a new treble added to make a ring of six bells.

In 1924, the church launched the Bell Repair Fund, its committee comprising the vicar, T B Biggs, H W Cheshire, A E Cheshire and F M Holden. They started with a sum of one hundred and eighty pounds.

The bells were eventually taken away to the Whitechapel Bell Foundry in London where they were recast and the new treble was also cast. The lightest four of the old five bells had some extra weight added to them to put them in harmony with the tenor. After the bells had been rehung, the vicar (Rev A H James) said that the bells have *"beauty of music and beauty of tone"*. A local newspaper reported:

"The village now boasts of a peal, second to none in beauty of tone and ease of manipulation."

In the dedication service to the bells in December 1925, the Bishop of Buckingham spoke in his sermon about many different bells including *"Winslow's Shrove Tuesday bell reminding townsfolk to use up all the butter before Lent."*

The bells were re-hung in a cast iron frame with modern fittings and the second bell was hung in the second tier of the bell frame. The Sanctus bell was hung up high in the belfry on an old beam of the original bell frame.

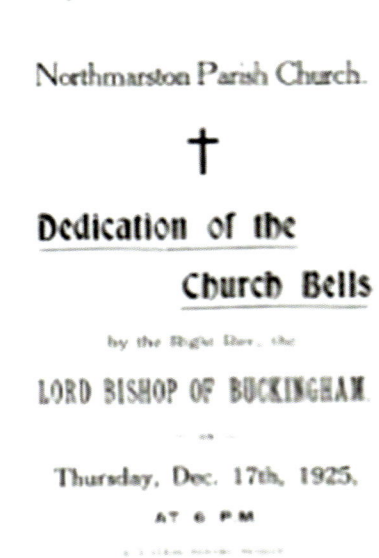

Throughout the years, the bell ringing teams have been made up of local people, sometimes more than one from the same family. The regular team during the 1950s and 1960s comprised Felix Gregory, Olive Gregory, William Woodford, Douglas (Jack) Ayres, Clifford Cheshire, Clarence Cheshire and Norman Newman from Granborough (whose son, Malcolm, continued in his father's footsteps and is still ringing today). Clifford Cheshire taught Peter Morton to ring in the 1970s and Peter has been ringing ever since, thus preserving the continuity of the team.

New bell-ropes were fitted in 1972 for the sum of £42.50 and the bells were overhauled in 2010 by Whites of Appleton, Church Bell Hangers.

The Church Clock

Until the 1970s the church clock was an antiquated mechanism that required regular winding to keep time. John Carter wound the clock in 1930; his son, Basil, took over from him and his son, Brian, took over from *him* (three generations!) until 1961 when Neville Morton took on the job. This is an account by Neville Morton of the task involved:

"I had the job of winding the Church Clock for about nine years until 1970 when I married and moved away. The mechanism can be described as loosely fitted and ancient. I know that, if it was not allowed to stop, it kept good time but that was difficult for a lad in his late teens and early twenties, who, surprisingly, had a social life. Once wound, it required winding every 'one day, twenty-one and three-quarter hours'. So, unless it was wound daily, no routine could be established.

As I worked in Aylesbury, it got wound either first thing in the morning, or in the evening, often after the pubs shut, or once I had taken my future wife home. I had a key to the West Door and the door to the spiral steps, the clock was situated in a cupboard on the floor above, in the room below the bells.

There were levers and lengths of wire connecting the striking mechanism to the bell. There were also two pulleys, which each lifted a weight about thirty feet from floor level, operated by a handle slotted on the barrel attached to the cord. The heavy weight, of lead, operating the striking mechanism, weighed about thirty kilograms, while the weight for the clock was iron and only weighed about eight kilograms.

I was paid, from the rents collected by the Clockland Trustees, about eleven pounds a year, which was quite a lot. I got to know those spiral steps, and trotted up and down them in the dark. If there were any ghosts there in the middle of the night, they did not come near me.

All did not go well, however. Villagers will no doubt have been woken, as I was, by the clock striking continually. This was caused by a screw with well-worn threads, dropping out, resulting in it taking about half a minute for the hands to go round an hour. This would have been disconcerting for anyone walking up Church Hill after downing a pint or three at the Bell. I was able to make it strike thirteen in that way. I had to keep tightening that screw."

In 1985 the old clock mechanism was lowered from the tower. The present clock mechanism is in a box that is no bigger than a standard Bible. The new electric clock was donated and installed by Michael Finnemore and Neil Tuckett when the church tower was renovated in the year 2000. The old clock mechanism is on display at the back of the church, (*see picture*). The bell hammer, however (to strike the hours on the tenor bell) is still in the tower but no longer in use.

The clock movement was probably made locally, circa 1700, and must have replaced a previous clock since the Clockland, which produced income to support the clock, was in existence before 1587.

The likely maker of the clock is a member of the Chandler family who were also bell-founders in Drayton Parslow. A similar earlier clock by Anthony Chandler, dated 1673, is in Whaddon church. It is also interesting to note that Richard Chandler made a bell for North Marston church in 1699.

Churchyard Gates

The beautiful wrought iron gates that greet visitors to the churchyard on the south side were made and donated to the church in 1887 by the village blacksmith, John White, who was a Methodist. They replaced the unsightly wooden gates that had stood there previously. At the time they were hung, the gates were valued at fourteen pounds and were painted bronze and gold. The pillars on each side were donated by two churchmen, Mr John Price and Mr Henry Cheshire. The vicar, Doctor Samuel James, wrote in *The Schornian* at the time: "*Those gates will stand for a century as memorials of a nonconformist's goodwill and of parochial prosperity and success.*"

The gate-pillars were replaced in 2012, but the gates are the original 1887 creations, and so have already out-lived Dr James's prediction by twenty-five years!

The church pre-1887 with wooden gates

The 1887 gates and pillars

BBC Broadcast Appeal

In 1968 Sir Evelyn Hone, the churchwarden at the time, broadcast an appeal in *The Week's Good Cause* on BBC Radio to raise money for St Mary's Church Restoration Fund.

Sir Evelyn received over one hundred replies, and the total contributions amounted to about two hundred pounds, the smallest being just sixpence.

Some of the donations came from as far afield as Belfast; many of the givers were anonymous and many were elderly people who recalled old associations with North Marston. One read:

"Your appeal reminded me of the time when I lived at North Marston and knew the lovely church well. I was head teacher of the school for some years."

Sir Evelyn Hone KCMG, CVO, OBE

Sir Evelyn Hone had served as the last Governor of Northern Rhodesia from 1959, and his wise counsel had greatly smoothed the path to independence which Zambia achieved in 1964. He retired to North Marston, living at the Mill House in the High Street, but continued to act as Adviser to the West Africa Committee. He died in 1979, aged sixty-seven, and The Evelyn Hone College in Lusaka, still flourishing today, was named after him.

Restoration of the Church Tower

One of the striking things about the external appearance of the church today is the clean and smooth face of the tower. This is the result of a major programme of renovation spear-headed by Nikki Day. Nikki explains what happened:

"The sixty-foot west tower part of the Grade I structure of St Mary's North Marston was built in its present form in the fifteenth century using soft local Oving limestone, and it has been the subject of much conservation during its lifetime.

In the Victorian period iron ties had been inserted to hold some of the stone together; this had been found necessary as the stone for the tower had been laid incorrectly on its side. These ties had subsequently rusted and adversely affected the joints.

Evidence gained from photographs showed that, in the twentieth century, the whole structure had also been coated in cement render which had caused the stones to erode.

In early 2000, pieces of the parapets had fallen from the tower and a survey showed that in some places the walls had deteriorated so much that they were only five centimetres thick!

With the help of English Heritage and other benefactor funding, including a programme of local fundraising, the stonemasons Boden and Ward were contracted in 2002, under the guidance of the architect Pam Ward, to conserve the structure.

This was carried out in two phases. Unusually, and because the top of the tower was most precarious, work began there by re-facing the stone on the east wall down to the nave roof and the other three walls down to the Belfry string.

As the Oving stone quarry is no longer in use, some stone was preserved from the structure whilst other was obtained from Stoke Ground. Windows were replaced with ones made of oak. This work was supported by a stone bridge constructed at Belfry level inside the structure.

The part-renovated tower

This first contract cost around £245,000. Later, English Heritage supported the second stage, and resurfacing of the bottom of the tower was carried out this time under the guidance of architects from the Victor Farrar Partnership.

The second stage was completed in 2006 and comprised re-facing the stone from the Belfry string course down to ground level; buttresses were rebuilt and two decorative window hood stops were fixed.

Because the original designs of these stops were difficult to determine, it was decided to fashion them as the heads of Camden Neild and John Schorne: two characters who had been highly influential in the fortunes of both the church and the village in the past (see picture)."

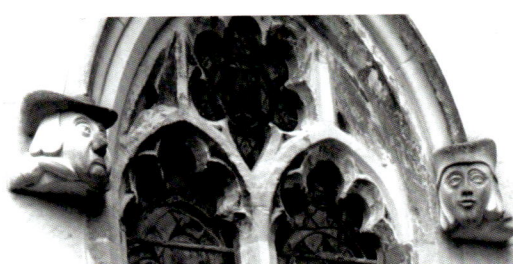

Neild on the left and Schorne on the right

Clergymen Since 1900

At the start of the twentieth century the highly influential **Dr Samuel James** was the rector at North Marston (*see Chapter Eleven*).

Rev Samuel James in the pulpit in 1901

On his death in 1909 he was succeeded by his son, **Arthur Harold James**, who was the last vicar to reside in the Old Vicarage.

The Old Vicarage

The Rev Hugh Waters arrived with his family in 1929 and his son, Basil, recalled:

"When my father was offered the living, the old vicarage was in a desperate state and was found to be in an advanced condition of dry rot, as well as in a poor structural state, and it was decided that it should be pulled down and replaced by a new house. The old vicarage had stood close to Glebe Farm and

it was decided to re-site the new one in another part of the grounds. While this was being built we lived in Vine Cottage, next to the church and almost opposite the vicarage."

Rev Waters (left) standing for the National Anthem outside The Bell before the 1937 Coronation Parade

Rear view of the vicarage erected in the early 1930s

Rev George Robertson followed as Rector in 1938, and saw North Marston through the war years. He was of Canadian descent and came from British Columbia on the west coast. He had three sons, David, Bede and Chad. Tommy Gray, an evacuee in the village at the time said:

"He would give talks at the guild meetings at the Methodist chapel and spoke at length on the varied wild-life to be found in the forests...it all sounded like heaven on earth."

Rev Robertson

When **Rev Ronald Martin** took over as vicar in 1948 he ran the Sunday school in the afternoon. Janet Gowin, one of his pupils at the time, says:

"All I remember learning were the Catechism and the Ten Commandments."

Another pupil, Jimmy Tattam, remembers running away from the Methodist Sunday School (where he was in trouble for misbehaving):

"We didn't dare go home so we went up to the Church Sunday school and joined in that. Rev Martin welcomed us with open arms."

Rev Ronald Martin in 1954

In 1956 a new vicar, **Rev Stanley Keene**, was inducted and lived with his parents in the vicarage. During his time in North Marston he ran a youth club in the village school-room for the young people of the village.

Rev Stanley Keene with his parents

Rev Dennis Daly became the vicar in 1959 and was in the village for only eighteen months before he died tragically, aged sixty-three, at the altar during an Evensong service in February 1961. People remember him as a very gentle, kind man; during his life-time he had devoted twenty-five years of his life working for the Mission for Seamen for which he had been awarded an MBE. His gravestone lies on the right by the church door.

Rev Dennis Daly and his family in front of the vicarage in 1960
(Stone from the old demolished vicarage was used in the end wall of the new house as can be seen in the photograph)

Rev John Charrington, inducted in 1962, was a member of the Charrington brewery family and it is said that meetings at the vicarage would usually be followed by a glass of beer!

Rev John Charrington

Mrs Charrington was very instrumental in running the Mothers' Union and, during their time in the vicarage, many memorable Church fetes were held in the beautifully-kept garden and orchard.

Rev William Watt, a single man, became Priest-in-Charge in 1970. He had started his ministry in Liverpool and then moved to Oxford, acting as full-time chaplain of the Radcliffe Infirmary after which he was the vicar of Long Crendon for eight years. On leaving North Marston he retired from the ministry.

Rev William Watt in 1970

Rev Watt was succeeded in 1974 by **Rev Peter Lawrence**, a much-loved and respected vicar who with his wife, Molly, was to stay in the village for eighteen years. In 1981 he became Team Rector of the newly-formed Schorne Team Ministry which included Granborough, Hoggeston, Dunton, Oving, Whitchurch, Quainton, Hardwick and Weedon. Later, Waddesdon was added.

Co-operation between the churches increased. Rev Lawrence was closely involved with helping church people of all kinds through the Cottesloe Christian Training Programme of North Bucks. In 1990 he was closely involved with the celebrations to mark the Seven Hundredth Anniversary of the year since John Schorne became Rector of North Marston.

*Rev Peter Lawrence pictured on the steps of the former vicarage with his wife, Molly, and children **(L-R)** Stephen, Mary and Tom (Dale Photos, Winslow)*

Rev Brian Kyriacou continued to work for the Team Ministry as Team Vicar when he took over from Rev Lawrence in 1992. His wife, Jenny, ran the Sunday school at the vicarage which was by then combined with the Methodist Sunday school.

Rev Brian Kyriacou in 1993

Rev Andy Bell arrived with his family in the village in 1998 and continued as Team Vicar to the Schorne Team Ministry. He lived in Elmers Meadow for seven years whilst the old vicarage was being demolished and a new one built. It took a long time as there was much local opposition to the development of the site. The old orchard that had belonged to the vicarage was sold to add longer gardens to the barn conversions at Glebe Farm next door. After a year or so it was becoming apparent that the village congregations could no longer support both a church *and* a chapel so, with the help of David Heffer, Rev Bell started the move towards setting up a local ecumenical partnership. This meant that Anglicans and Methodists could share a building and a minister, with all services from then on taking place in St Marys Church.

Rev Andy Bell

The former vicarage just before it was demolished in 1998

The latest vicarage

In 2011 an historic step forward was taken in the village when **Rev Christopher James (Jim) Gorringe**, formerly the Methodist Minister at Stewkley, was appointed as the new Team Minister in North Marston.

Although the Anglican and Methodist congregations had been worshipping together since 2004, having formed a Local Ecumenical Partnership (LEP) when the Methodist Church in Schorne Lane closed for services, it was the first time a Methodist minister had been licensed to the, now, ecumenical church of St Mary's in North Marston.

Rev Jim Gorringe

Janet Bayly moved from London to North Marston in 1973 living for the first seven years at Prune Cottage in Quainton Road. She then lived at Crandon Farm, Marston Fields for the next twenty-nine years before moving to Granborough Road in 2009.

Whilst still teaching at Whitchurch School, Janet started training as a Licensed Lay Minister in the Church of England and, after completing her studies in 2004, began work with the Schorne Team Ministry.

Rev Janet Bayly

Janet later felt called to Ordination and was ordained as a Deacon in 2008 and a Priest in 2009. She is widely travelled in the area having taken services in all eleven churches of the Schorne Team. She now (in 2014) works closely alongside Jim Gorringe, sharing meetings, pastoral care and services, mainly in North Marston, Granborough and Oving. It is unusual that, having lived in North Marston for the past forty years, Janet is now ministering in the village among her friends and acquaintances.

Three
JOHN SCHORNE, NORTH MARSTON'S SAINT

John Spargo

It is difficult in today's modern age to picture how the arrival of a pious monk in the village in 1282 could lead to momentous events involving thousands of people and bringing great wealth and fame to North Marston for more than two centuries. Yet that is the story of Master John Schorne who was rector here until his death in 1314. It is a story set in times when the country was devoutly Catholic, very superstitious and when a belief in the supernatural power of saints, omens and miracles was at its height.

Who was he?

We believe that John Schorne attended Oxford University where he obtained a Master's Degree. Being, therefore, a learned man he was often referred to as *Master* John Schorne or *Magister* John Schorne and pictured in screen paintings wearing an academic hood or cap which suggests he later became a Doctor of Divinity. Richard Marks (2002) wrote that John Schorne *"spurned the opportunities offered by his education for advancement and remained in his parish serving his flock."* He seems to have been a very pious priest and was said to have had horny knees from constant praying.

Before John Schorne came to North Marston the church here was in the care of Dunstable Priory.

Dunstable Priory Church

It is certain the rectors of all the churches in the Priory's care would have been appointed from amongst the secular Augustinian Canons in its Order. Schorne was made rector, in the year 1273, of the Priory's parish church at Steppingly in Bedfordshire and transferred to North Marston nine years later.

Steppingly Church, Bedfordshire

Here he would have found a small stone church in a poor village that provided precious little income to the priory. An ecclesiastical tax assessment of the church at North Marston in 1291 revealed its annual income was six pounds, thirteen shillings and four-pence; one pound a year went to Dunstable Priory. (At the same time, Quainton church had an income of twenty pounds, and Whitchurch over thirteen pounds).

John Schorne's Miracle

Sometime during his ministry at North Marston the village was experiencing a terrible drought. The story goes that Schorne struck the ground with his staff and, like the story of Moses, a spring gushed forth that was to become Schorne's Holy Well and the principal source of water for the village for centuries.

Moses gets water from a rock

Perhaps Schorne was a water diviner? Tales of this miracle would have spread quickly. As time progressed, the miracle was enhanced by stories that the water had remarkable curative powers especially for the *ague* (malaria which was rife in medieval England) and *gout*, a painful condition that affected the joints of the foot.

Schorne died in 1314 and, in accordance with his will and the custom of the time, he was buried in front of the principle altar at North Marston church. Local pilgrimage to the holy well is likely to have started soon after his death as word of his 'miracle' was spread. Aware of this, Dunstable Priory took the far-sighted step of appropriating North Marston church, with papal consent, in 1332, thus securing *all* the money generated by the church and not simply a one pound a year pension.

As it turned out, this was remarkably good timing by The Priory as events were about to take an extraordinary turn.

The Black Death

In the autumn of 1348 the Black Death arrived in North Bucks. Entire families and communities were wiped out. Fields lay fallow and crops un-harvested. Many small rural settlements that had been eking out a feeble existence in poor soil were abandoned. The map of Buckinghamshire is littered with such deserted villages and it is likely North Marston could have suffered such a fate but for a form of divine intervention….

The enormity of the impact of the Black Death is hard to imagine. It is estimated that over a third of the entire population was killed by the plague, profoundly transforming the lives, attitudes and beliefs of those left behind. The Black Death was a stark reminder of man's mortality, the fragility of life and the uncertainty of the future. People sought sanctuary and comfort in a more profound religion which manifested itself in intense devotion and self-sacrifice, with a life-long obsession in preparing one's soul for death.

From this backdrop, the cult of saints emerged. Powerful saints like the Virgin Mary could intercede as advocates for souls in purgatory being cleansed for heaven; some, like St Christopher, could act as a talisman to protect against unexpected death, or they could perform miracles of healing. Some saints developed a reputation for being particularly effective at curing specific diseases or impairments (similar to John Schorne).

The Blessed Virgin Mary

The Pilgrims Arrive

Steadily over the period from the late fourteenth century until the early sixteenth century, increasing numbers of people took part in pilgrimages to the shrines of powerful saints, the three most popular pilgrimages in England being to the shrine of Thomas Becket at Canterbury, the shrine to Our Lady of Walsingham and the shrine of John Schorne at North Marston. The impact on the village must have been immeasurable.

A contemporary picture of a pilgrimage

We know the pilgrims started to arrive within a few years of the Black Death but *how do we know this?* En route to North Marston, the pilgrims (many diseased and disabled) would have stopped at churches they passed on their way to say a prayer and leave a small offering to the talisman St Christopher. A custom at the time was to make a pledge to the saint and to mark that pledge with a small votive cross scratched into stonework within sight of the saint`s image (which was nearly always painted on the north wall opposite the south door so as to be visible from the south doorway or at the west end of a south aisle).

At Whitchurch, pilgrims travelling to North Marston left their votive crosses and other graffiti on a pillar at the west end of the south aisle; but at Quainton the pilgrims who were preparing to cross Quainton Hill to North Marston carved their votive crosses on the south door jambs in the south porch, apparently not entering the church, albeit within sight of the image of St Christopher on the wall opposite the open doorway.

Votive crosses at Quainton's south door

Why should this be? The reason was that for many years from the mid-fourteenth century Quainton church was not accessible to lay persons as it had become endowed as a religious college by Thomas de Missenden in 1353, just five years after the Black Death had arrived. This tells us the pilgrimages to North Marston are likely to have started quite early in the second half of the fourteenth century and we know that people were still visiting his shrine almost two hundred years later!

As the numbers of pilgrims increased, North Marston would have benefited from the income through providing lodgings and refreshments. Rumour has it that some of the older buildings in Church Street such as Pilgrims Cottage formerly had a role in this context. The church clearly made money from offerings to Schorne's shrine. This shrine

A Whitchurch votive cross

would have been erected in the centre of the chancel and is likely to have taken the form of a reliquary, a stone box tomb raised on a plinth with openings underneath.

An example (from another church) of a simple medieval reliquary containing the remains of a saint.
The bones would have been housed inside the raised tomb. The openings underneath allowed pilgrims to leave gifts or lights.....

...or even climb inside to get as close to the dead saint as possible!

Pilgrims Mean Money

Pilgrims would have been wealthier than most of the people in the village, few of whom could afford to leave their land to wander about the country.

The scale of the gifts left by pilgrims at Schorne's shrine in the church would have been considerable; it is likely to have sponsored a significant rebuild including a watching chamber with a piercing of the chancel's north wall to create a *squint* so that a priest in a watching chamber could keep an eye on the shrine in the centre of the chancel as a security measure.

The gifts left at the shrine and in bequests would have been considerable; the church's income was transformed from six pounds a year to five hundred pounds! This equates to over two and a half million pounds in today's values!

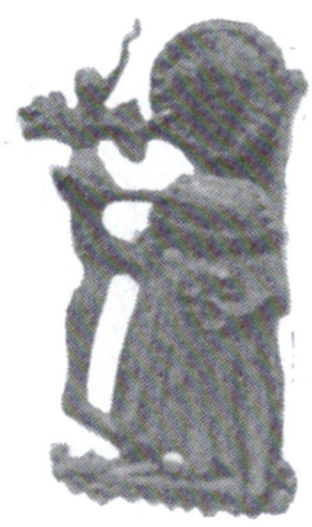

A John Schorne token worn as a badge to identify the pilgrim to others

The window from the watching chamber at North Marston church

And so the cult of John Schorne was born. Although never formally canonized, he was regarded as a saint by the hundreds of pilgrims who visited his shrine and sought the healing powers of his holy spring-water.

The Devil in the Boot

As John Schorne's fame spread across southern England, his image began to appear on painted screens and as wooden or stone effigies. Iconographers needed to give him a 'trademark' or symbol to differentiate him from other saints' images. The curative power of his spring water was to provide the answer, and in particular its efficacy in curing gout. In medieval art, pain was generally represented as a devil or imp. Gout, an affliction largely of the foot, was thus a devil in your boot, and Schorne's ability to cure the pain of gout was illustrated as a devil being drawn out of a boot. This image was misinterpreted as Schorne capturing the devil *in* a boot and so was born another enduring legend. There is also a story that Schorne's devil in the boot was the concept behind the "Jack-in-the-Box" toy.

A rood-screen portrait of John Schorne with his trade-mark boot and devil

The money-generating effect of his shrine and holy water continued to impact on the village:

"In 1448 an entrepreneurial incumbent of North Marston was arraigned before the bishop of Lincoln's court on a charge of blasphemy. No doubt in an attempt to augment the income, he had added to the attractions of the site by exhuming a head from the churchyard, sprinkling it with blood, and claiming it as the head of John Schorne". (Marks, 2002)

Schorne Moves to Windsor

Towards the end of the century, however, the success of his shrine in attracting pilgrims came to the interest of higher authorities, and in 1478 Schorne's remains were removed from North Marston and transferred to purpose-built shrine at Windsor in the new St George's chapel, so as to draw Schorne's pilgrims and their offerings there.

What did the canons of Dunstable Priory think about their loss? We know that Dunstable Priory was given another church in exchange, and graffiti found in North Marston church suggests there were no hard feelings harboured against Edward IV (*see Chapter Two*). Pilgrims would have continued to come to the village to seek a cure from the holy well. In 1501 the church at North Marston was appropriated by the Dean and Canons of Windsor.

"Although Schorne's cult had enjoyed remarkable longevity, the modest offerings at the Windsor shrine in 1533-34 indicate that by then it had run its course." (Marks, 2002*)*

There are still papers associated with John Schorne's shrine at St George's Chapel at Windsor, held in the archives there. A copy of the Papal Bull authorising the transfer of his relics can also be seen at Windsor and a copy is held at North Marston Church.

North Marston's Late Medieval Status

Of course, pilgrims would have continued to come to North Marston for the curative power of Schorne's holy spring. Indeed, no less a person than King Henry VIII made two pilgrimages to North Marston, one in 1511 and one in 1521, despite having easy personal access to the St George's Chapel shrine housing Schorne's actual relics!

This throws light on the status of the village that seems to have risen from the early years of the fifteenth century, no doubt directly associated with it having become a major centre for pilgrimage.

By the mid-fifteenth century, with the church becoming increasingly wealthy through pilgrim gifts and bequests, the status of the village approached its zenith as is reflected in the fact it became the location for important hearings more generally associated with county towns.

One such example was an Inquisition (Enquiry) held at North Marston on 20th October 1461. This was conducted by the *escheator,* a royal official whose jurisdiction is likely to have covered Bedfordshire and Buckinghamshire, and whose job it was to determine the ownership of land in the event of the death of the tenant-in-chief or if the land-holder or their heir had forfeited the rights to the land due to a felony. In a sense, the escheator was the King's (Henry VI) County Land Agent and on receipt of a writ from the King's Chancery the escheator would have *empanelled a jury* to hold an inquisition or *inquest of escheat*.

The 1461 North Marston *Inquisition* concerned land in Aylesbury, Bierton and Burcott owned by a man named William who owed two hundred marks (over one hundred and thirty pounds) to a Ralph Verney, a mercer (draper) of London. Although the outcome of the Inquisition is not known, the fact it was held in North Marston is noteworthy.

The medieval period was drawing to a close with the coronation of Henry VIII in June 1509. Twenty years later Henry VIII declared Aylesbury the county town of Buckinghamshire, possibly to curry favour with Thomas Boleyn who held the manor of Aylesbury (amongst other properties) and whose daughter (Anne) Henry wanted to woo. Henry would have been familiar with the area as a result of his previous visits to North Marston.

The dissolution of the monasteries during Henry VIII's reign meant escheators were busy allocating the land and property previously held by religious orders to those feudally favoured by the King, typically the local lord of the manor.

Surprisingly, North Marston was again the setting for a hearing concerning the manorship of Wingrave in Bucks which had originally belonged to Woburn Abbey in Bedfordshire. The Inquisition was held on 21st October 1539. The escheator, Thomas Deacons, granted the manor to John Gostwyke and his wife Joan. The manor was assessed to be worth four pounds thirteen shillings and fourpence a year (ie four pounds and one mark). But why was the Inquisition held in the village of North Marston rather than the nearby county town of Aylesbury?

The answer is probably based on logistics. The escheator would have had a retinue of clerks and aides assisting him with the Inquisition. His needs would have been for adequate accommodation with reasonable access for all those involved including the jury. He may also have had previous contacts in the village. One presumes the venue would have been a manor house, quite possibly the medieval manor that once stood on the site of Manor Farm in the High Street, with a hall large enough to house a temporary court.

Schorne's Legacy

The legacy left to us by John Schorne in North Marston, nearly seven hundred years after his death, is a uniquely elaborate chancel of very grand proportions, a small shrine set into the east wall of the south aisle (*see following picture*), an unusual squint on the wall of the chancel and, of course, a well which was to remain the main source of water in the village until the twentieth century.

However, given the ravages of the Black Death, perhaps Schorne's most important legacy is the village itself: the fact it survived extinction and prospered throughout the Middle Ages is almost entirely due to it becoming a major centre for pilgrimage at a time when rural settlements all around were struggling for survival.

The "boot shrine" to John Schorne in the east wall of the Lady Chapel

Four
JOHN SCHORNE'S WELL
John Spargo & Sue Chaplin

Whether or not we believe the Schorne miracle, the well in Schorne Lane was for centuries the village's prime source of water and was called the *Town Well*.

Famed for its medicinal qualities to which some attributed longevity in the village, the water was analysed at St Thomas's Hospital London in 1868 and found to contain lime carbonate, magnesia and iron carbonate, chlorine, sulphuric acid, silica, lime-sulphate and magnesia sulphate (Epsom Salts).

In her book *Buckinghamshire* published in 1950 Alison Uttley wrote:

"The water of Sir John Schorne's spring was so strongly impregnated with iron that the taste was too strong for ordinary drinking and after the days of miracles and pilgrimages were past, that is after the Dissolution of the Monasteries, troughs were placed round it and the water kept for cattle. After the year 1835 the spring was used for the town supply, and now the water is only slightly different from ordinary spring water."

In the early nineteenth century the well comprised an open stone-lined cistern with four stone steps leading down to water several feet deep. There is evidence that, in about 1800, a building was placed over the well with walls composed of brick and stone, about five feet high and a roof of boards covering it. This would have replaced a previous well-house known to have existed before 1700.

Not surprisingly, it claimed at least one life. In July 1861, a forty year-old lace-maker, Jane Watson, drowned in the well. The inquest was held at The Armed Yeoman pub in North Marston and the coroner said that steps should be taken to make the well safer. The building was subsequently locked and a hand-pump installed outside. This was in use until mains water arrived in the village in the early 1930s.

The 1800s saw people come to North Marston from all around carrying bottles to fill with the 'precious' water to cure their ailments.

The hand-pump stands by a timber building close to Well Cottage

The picture above, taken in the 1920s, shows Emily Young (and friend just visible) pumping water into a pail. This scene had hardly changed for over half a century. Robin Harwood recalls:

"The Holy Well in Schorne Lane, which the farmers used for their animals, produced water from 6am to 10pm and was always full again the next morning."

When the ponds were low, most of the farmers would come to the well with their horse and cart, bringing churns to fill; some of them, such as Albert Franklin, brought along a tank on wheels.

Back in the 1970s Ewart Dancer recounted some of his memories of the well:

"At the end of the decade of the 1930s, the village pump was sunk into the six feet deep Schorne Well which was something of a meeting place. A few houses had their own well but, for the most part, it was 'fetch and carry'. A woman named Mary, who lived at the bottom of Quainton Road, had never had a job, as I remember, because she was unable to do normal woman's work but she earned part of her living by fetching two buckets of water which she carried on a shoulder yoke for the sum of three-pence. She made the mile and back journey for possibly six customers twice a week. I was lucky as I drove a pony and cart with two churns which I fetched twice a week. Mary walked with her yoke, others made barrows of bicycle wheels to which they fixed a churn and handles whilst those near the well fetched a single bucketful at a time. The pleasant part of the exercise was that there was always somebody about."

With the arrival of mains water in the 1930s the pump was no longer needed so it was removed. All that then marked the site of the well was a concrete cover with an iron pull-ring (*see below*).

The well pictured in the 1960s

By the late 1960s, however, there was an interest in making the well a more attractive village feature and a renovation programme was started. Local builders Laurence Young and Norman Higgins were set to work building a brick housing for the well and re-instating the hand-pump.

Laurence Young (left) and Norman Higgins at work on the well in 1970 with onlookers Christopher Tompkins, Stephen Wright and David Tompkins

The newly-renovated well in 1970

Once completed, there was an official opening in 1970 by the Chairman of the Parish Council, Graham Ward.

North Marston residents drink the well water at the opening ceremony

Graham Ward (right) ladles out water for a young Tommy Dancer

From time to time over the years, and to celebrate specific anniversaries or feast days, the well has been decorated.

Pilgrim Weekend 1978

The photograph above shows the well decorated for the Pilgrim Weekend in 1978 when the village raised much-needed funds for St Mary's Church by holding a weekend of celebration centred round the idea of the by-gone religious travellers. Over one hundred 'pilgrims' took to the hills on a sponsored walk.

The 1970 well design had unfortunately created a flat top which did not allow rainwater to run off and the wooden well-covers started to rot away. It was therefore decided to raise the back of the well surround to create a gradient. The resultant changes, made in the 1990s, created a well which became known as the "coal bunker".

The "coal bunker" design

By the year 2000 John Schorne's Well had fallen in to such disrepair that it was becoming quite an embarrassment when visitors to the village came to view it, as Alison Finnemore relates:

"Some keen Japanese tourists arrived. They descended from their coach, cameras at the ready, and all agog to see the miraculous well. How quickly their enthusiasm turned to disappointment when they viewed the murky water beneath the ugly coal-bunker-like structure! How sadly and politely did they thank the 'Keeper of the Key' before climbing resignedly back onto their coach! He felt profound embarrassment that John Schorne's well should have such an adverse effect on modern pilgrims! However it had the salutary (or was it miraculous?) effect of galvanizing into action a small committee of six who took on the task of restoring John Schorne's holy well to something of which villagers could be proud, and tourists/pilgrims would enjoy."
(Buckinghamshire Countryside 2005)

The new well was the brain-child of village resident Michael Finnemore who chaired the Committee, acted as Project Manager and, along with John Wright, voluntarily carried out most of the work. It was restored with historical and environmental concerns in mind using natural or reclaimed materials and employing traditional skills. Village builder, Mark Gurney, was employed to build the rear wall and help to lay the slab floor, and Guy Davies (the only person from outside the village to work on the project) tiled the roof. John Schorne's image, fashioned from clay by village craftsman, Vincent Lilley, stands in the alcove in the back wall of the well-house.

Work in progress 2004

The devil emerging

The blessing of the new well in 2005

When water is drawn into a stone trough via the pump a little red devil rises from the lead boot at the edge (*see picture above*) and as the water drains away he subsides into the boot. A pierced stack-pipe ensures that a little water is always available for birds and animals to quench their thirst. The 2004 renovation followed a fund-raising effort which raised £8,000. In May 2005 a Celebration and Re-dedication Service took place at the well, conducted by Rev Andy Bell.

The restored well in 2006

The report from the local newspaper

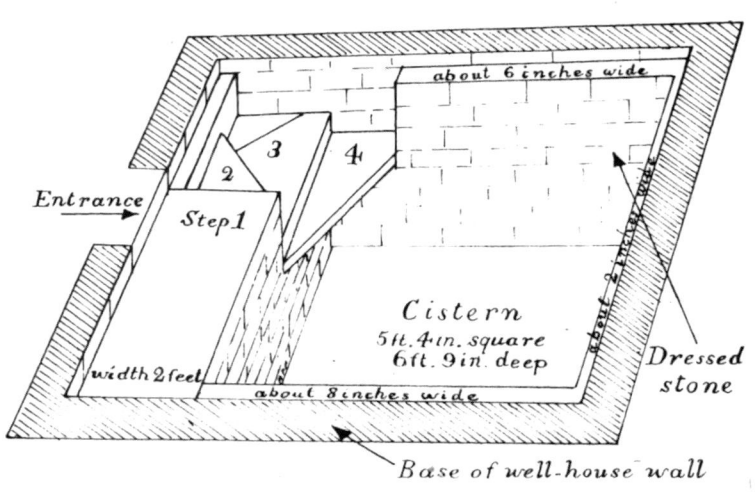

The above drawing shows the plan of the well in the mid-1800s. When the well was restored it was not practical to expose the open well but the layout of the floor today shows the 1859 well-house and cistern in plan form. Large blue bricks define the position of the well-house with its entrance, York stone has been cut to represent the four steps descending into the water and thin blue bricks show the outline of the well cistern and edge of Step 4.

Five
WINDMILLS
Colin Price & John Wright

Harvesting the power of the wind to grind grain is believed to have originated in Persia and the knowledge brought to Britain by returning crusaders in the twelfth century. A windmill was in existence at Stone by 1190 and was one of the earliest in Britain. The value of windmills to the local community, especially in those parishes without a suitable stream to drive a watermill, was soon recognized and by the end of the thirteenth century most parishes had at least one windmill.

In the days before the industrial revolution the local miller was a key person in rural communities. It was only through the miller that local grain could be converted to flour to create bread, the main component in the diet of the population. He was a crucial part of a supply chain from field to plate and upon him, farmers, carriers and bakers depended for their livelihood as much as householders depended on him for food on their tables. The miller was at the mercy of mixed fortunes: in a traditional rural society, and in times of a good harvest, a miller was often wealthier than ordinary peasants, which led to jealousy and to millers being targeted in bread riots at times of famine when the harvest failed.

The miller would charge for milling grain equivalent to a twelfth or sixteenth of its value, according to the quality of the grain. Typically, the miller would take his payment in kind and use the grain for his personal use or sell it perhaps as flour or bread (some millers were also bakers). Storage of this grain led to successful millers constructing tithe barns for the safe storage of their share.

We have definite records of a windmill in North Marston in 1272 in the deeds of St John's Manor which are held by Magdalen College, Oxford. From this date through to the North Marston *Inclosure Act* in 1778, windmills played a vital role in the parish milling the wheat, barley and oats which were the principle crops of the Open Fields. The enclosure of land into clearly defined fields in 1778 allowed land to be set aside for grazing which was better suited to North Marston's poorly drained soil than the growth of cereals. So grain production fell rapidly in the years following enclosure (*see Chapter Seven*) and the need for milling decreased proportionately. However, milling continued on a reduced scale through to the 1880s when industrialization closed the last remaining mill in North Marston.

Surprisingly, there is some evidence that there might have been a medieval watermill in North Marston. Watermills do not need a large or powerful stream of water; what is essential is a steady, continuous flow. Documents from 1291 refer to a mill on the North Marston/Oving border on the brook which marks the border between North Marston and Oving known as the Washbrook. Early documents refer to fields bordering the brook as "Mill Ditch" and "Little Mill Ditch" and more recent valuations of 1812 and 1816 refer to "Mill Ditch Ground" and "Hither Mill Ditch". The most likely location on the Washbrook is to the very north of the parish (*as shown as Mill A in Figure 1*).

Windmill Hill

The windmill referred to in the 1272 deeds of St John's Manor was located at Windmill Hill (*as shown as Mill B in Figure 1*). The deeds state that:

"Adam of Northmerstone, miller, is bound in an annual payment of 8d to the Hospice of St John Oxford, for a mill "Chuvaleres" which he made in Northmerstone, and for which presentation was made at the great court before Michaelmas 1272 that it was an injury to the tenants of the Hospice; the Hospice having consented to accept that payment as compensation."

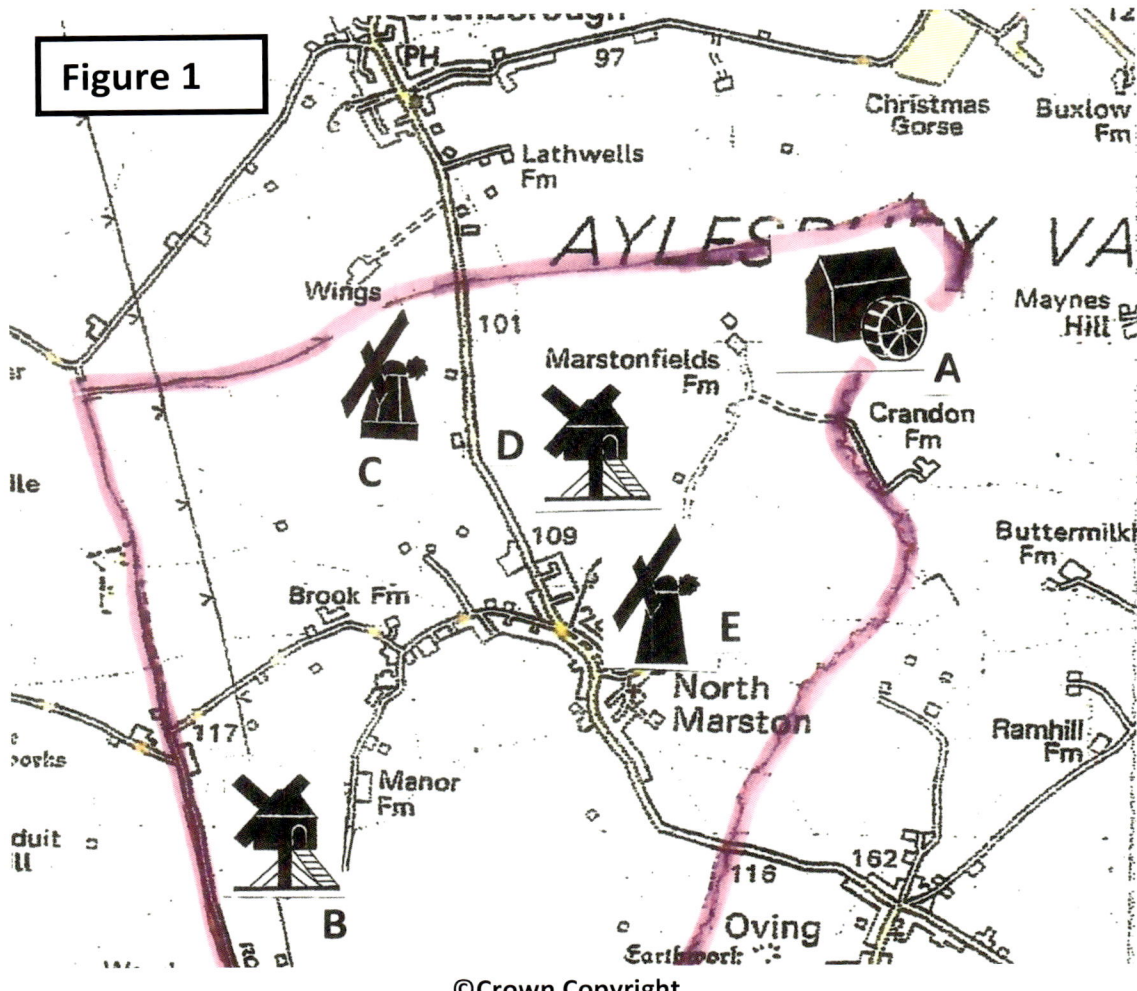

Key: A: There is some evidence for a watermill on the Washbrook in this area
B: Windmill Hill: Location of the earliest windmill in the parish
C: Hearthill: Location of a smock mill during the eighteenth century
D: Old Mill Knob: A windmill was recorded here in 1776
E: Mill House: Location of the last windmill in the parish

There is a further reference to this mill in 1472 in a *"lease from Magdalen College to John Cowley of Dodune (now known as Denham) in the parish of Queynton, yeoman, of all their lands and tenements in Northmerstone, together with a windmill there, for the term of 21 years at an annual rent of £4."*

The location of the mill can still be clearly identified today by two *tumps* (man-made mounds on which windmills were constructed). There is no explanation for the presence of two tumps.

Undoubtedly there would not have been two windmills so closely side by side so, presumably, when the original windmill was damaged it was dismantled and a new mill built nearby re-using the mill stones and machinery.

The earliest windmills were post mills, so named because the whole structure was built around a central wooden post set into the ground and supported by a trestle. The machinery and sails could be rotated about this immense post by the miller so that the sails were always facing the wind.

Old Mill Knob

Old Mill Knob is a hill on the right hand side of the road from North Marston to Granborough. A windmill on this hill was recorded in the North Marston quality book of 1776 which is the only record we have of this mill. Its location is shown in *Figure 1* (Mill D).

Hearthill

Hearthill (also spelt *Harthill*) is the hillock to the left of the road from North Marston to Granborough (*see Figure 2*) and there was a windmill on the hill as early as the sixteenth century.

Figure 2: *Hearthill: the site of a medieval settlement and the location of the parish's principle windmill for over a century*

Hearthill is believed to be the site of quite a large medieval settlement called *Hoertshill* dating back to the tenth century. A windmill mound (tump) is still visible marking the site of the mill but all evidence of the earlier settlement has disappeared. The early mill at Hearthill would have been a post mill as described above, but in 1700 it was converted to a smock mill. Smock mills were a great improvement on post mills. Instead of rotating the whole body of the mill to face the wind, smock mills had a fixed wooden body containing the milling machinery above which there was a rotating cap on which the sails were mounted. By rotating just the cap, the body of the mill could be much larger than in a post mill. Most smock mills were eight-sided and the tower was clad in weatherboard.

Following its conversion to a smock mill, the Hearthill mill was the principle mill in the village for over one hundred years. The first owners that we have records for were Elizons Clarke and his wife Sarah. They sold the mill in 1750 to a millwright named William Sutton. Nineteen years later he sold the mill with cottages, outbuildings and land to William Stimpson, a miller, for eighty pounds. Immediately after the enclosure of land in North Marston, in 1779, it was sold to Samuel Southam for one hundred and forty pounds.

For the next thirty years, the records are confusing. What we *are* certain about is that the mill at Hearthill was dismantled and rebuilt in the centre of the village behind the present day Mill House; by the time of the 1832 North Marston valuation there was no record of the mill, cottages or outbuildings at Hearthill.

Mill House

The millstones, gears and machinery from the Hearthill mill were transferred to the new site and the mill was rebuilt as a smock mill. At the time of the move, the only building on the site was a small house adjacent to the road (the Mill House of the present day was built in 1889) and in the deeds the plot was referred to as 50 Broad Street.

Mill House

The miller at the time of the move was a colourful character called Zachariah Southam. "Old Zac" is described as:

"..picturesque with a felt hat of the Quaker pattern, conical crowned but with turned down brims which almost hid his features. He wore knee breeches, hose and buckle shoes, and over all a frock wonderfully smocked."

After Zac, the mill passed to the Baker family. William Baker was the proprietor in records of 1832 and is referred to as a miller in documents of 1814. His son, Denchfield Baker, mortgaged the mill in 1850 to John Camden Nield who left his entire estate (including the mill) to Queen Victoria (*see Chapter Ten*). This greatly inconvenienced Baker and, as the result of a petition, Her Majesty then made over the windmill to him for life.

William Baker seems to have been the miller in 1854 and the misses Jane and Elizabeth Baker appear in the 1864 directory, although the mill had actually been disused for some little while by that time.

Charles Burton restored and reopened the mill on 25th March 1864. He converted it from a smock mill to a tower mill. It was built with a stone base and a brick tower and the sails were mounted on a cap which was the only part that rotated into the wind. We have a clear record of the appearance of the mill after its conversion, from a photograph (*Figure 3*) and a sketch (*Figure 4*) of the mill both made in 1876.

The Burtons were a large family and Charles' son Ben took over in 1872. He kept the mill at North Marston until 1876 when he left for Singleborough. He then moved to Slough in 1878 where he had a distinguished career and his opinion on milling matters was always accepted as final. He won The Miller Challenge Cup and Gold Medal in 1913 for the best English flour. Benjamin Burton, an uncle of Ben's, was famed for his strength and is described as being able to carry two and a half hundredweight under each arm!

Keeping a mill was a hazardous business and the diary of Thomas Ward records that *a "great wind on 7th January 1839 about three o'clock in the morning blew the top of North Marston mill down."*

Figure 3: *Photograph of the windmill behind Mill House taken in 1876. This is one of the earliest photographs we have of North Marston*

Figure 4: *A pencil sketch of the windmill behind Mill House drawn by Oliver Rudolph Wheeler in 1876 with a note that, at that time, the mill was worked by Ben Burton, a relative of Wheeler's*

There are several alarming incidents recorded in the time of the Burtons. On one occasion *"the brake lever snapped while the cloth sails were tearing round at a great pace in a gale; and before they could be checked, a sack of barley had been ground faster than ever before! Mr Charles Burton, with great presence of mind, loaded the stones down with grain, and rushing outside the mill, pulled it out of the wind as fast as he could with the wheel and chain gear with which it was then fitted, and saved the day."*

On another occasion *"the mill became tail-winded, and before they could wind it round by the chain, three cloths had been ripped off, one of them winding itself round the windshaft."*

There were some very rough winters when Ben Burton was in charge from 1872 to 1876, and he often ran the mill with bare sail-frames (that is, with no sail cloths at all). On one occasion, two sails crashed down shaking the whole mill, one falling nearby and the other being hurled away.

One day during a storm, Ben Burton had a millstone fly to pieces owing to the speed it was running. The brake was not very efficient and some times it was necessary to pull the mill out of the wind and get a heavy prop in the way of a sail during a lull in the wind. The sail-cloths could then be removed one by one. Being a miller clearly required a lot of daring! But it could also be a great joy.

Towards the end of his life Ben Burton recalled his days in North Marston when he would *"often take a walk over the hills to Quainton, and when I stood on the hill and saw Mursley and North Marston, and Stone and Waddesdon mills all swinging along. Then a little further on I used to stand and watch the old post mill near Quainton station. It was a delightful sight to watch the sails of all these old mills working away."*

With the coming of the industrial revolution, the importance of wind as an energy source declined particularly because of its unpredictability and it was gradually replaced by steam power (as at Quainton). More and more grain was being imported and processed by steam driven port mills. Windmills which had served parishes for centuries became unprofitable and redundant.

It is not certain when the mill in North Marston ceased to function but the photograph taken in 1876 shows it to be in operational condition and it is assumed that the mill closed down when Ben Burton left in that year. In 1888 it was sold at an auction held in the Bell Inn to Mr Watkins for an amount in excess of three hundred and fifteen pounds which was considered at the time to be more than it was worth!

In 1892 the mill was demolished. The bricks were cleaned by boys who were paid one shilling per day, and used to build the back wing of the Mill House. Only the stone-built base was left in place.

The picture below on the left shows the remnants as they were in the 1930s. At this time it was used for carpentry classes run by the owner Mr Rogers. Robin Harwood remembers attending these classes and he recalls that Sam Lambourne, Cecil Walker and Archie Higgins also attended.

The remnants of the mill base in the 1930s

In the early 2000s the remains of the mill were modernized to create the attractive building we see today

Six
THE GREAT FIRE OF 1705
Colin Price

A terrible fire swept through North Marston in August 1705. We are fortunate to have two accurate records of the event: the Order Book of the Michaelmas Magistrates Session 1705 and the record of the Reverend Richard Purchas entered in the North Marston Churchwarden's Book. The two records vary a little in their detail but they create a vivid picture of a catastrophic event for the village.

The Reverend Richard Purchas recorded in The North Marston Churchwarden's Book:

"1705 August 11. A terrible fire happened in this village of Northmarston. It began at twelve of the clock in the day and burnt till night, the wind being extream high; it consumed 25 dwelling houses, besides all Mr Saunders and Mr Burnabys outhouses."

The Magistrates Order Book tells us that:

"..upon Saturday the 11th Day of August last past about tern (turn) *of the clock in the forenoone there happened a sudden and lamentable fire to break forth in the Towne of Northmarston in this county which in three hours tyme burnt downe and consumed the Houses Barns Stables and Outhouses of Robert Cuthbert, William Gyles, Mrs Saunders, Robert Ward, James Foster, John Hitchcocke, William Anderson, John Francklin, John Denchfield, Richard Stanbridge, Mrs Burnaby, Thomas Grace, Richard Denchfield, Edward Oviatt, Henry Foster, Joseph Rickard, John Lucas, John Symonds, John Ward, Edward Waddington (Clerk), Christopher Foster, Henry Foster and Anne Whittmill Widdow".*

The Court Order Book (see extract below) then goes on to list those who had lost *"Household Goods, Hay, Wood, Corne, Grayne and other Goods and Chattells".* In addition to the above, it names William Parnell, John Coker, Edward Virgin, Henry Symonds, Martha Denchfield Widow, Thomas Tattam, Thomas Spranks, Anthony Moores, John Blackett, Widow Hind, William Smith, Martha Ingram Widow, Ralph Cooper, Ruth Purchase Widow, John Blackett and Widow Foster.

At that time it was necessary for those seeking charity to obtain a certificate from the Magistrates Court (referred to as a *patent*) confirming the circumstances of their loss before financial relief could be sought. The Court record tells us that:

"..the loss susteyned by the said fire amounted to the value of three thousand four hundred sixty five pounds eight shillings and two pence and forasmuch as the said poore sufferers by the said dreadfull fire have this present Session's Assembly desired the assistance of this Court for theire obteyning theire Magistrates most gracious Letters patents to collect the charitable benevolence of well disposed people towards theire said Great Losses . It is therefore Ordered by this Court that the following Certificate of her Majesty's Justices of the Peace now report to the Right Honourable Sir Nathan Wright Lord Keeper of the Greate Seale of England be fayrely engrossed by the Clerke of the Peace and delivered to the said poore sufferers".

The Reverend Richard Purchas recorded that *"the country was extraordinary kind and sent in moneys to the reliefe of the sufferers"* and went on to list the generous donations of forty-six parishes and benefactors totalling over three hundred and seventy-six pounds, an enormous amount for that time.

The largest single contribution was from the parish of Quainton which donated over twenty-eight pounds. (To put this into context that was equivalent to a year's income for a skilled builder at that time). Perhaps this generosity was remembered, as North Marston was to repay the debt to Quainton over the years in many relief collections for tragedies in that neighbouring village.

Extract from the order book of the Michaelmas Sessions 1705.

Michas Sessions 1705

Justices sitting in Open Court, afterwards by the Oathes of John ffuller Thomas Statham Carpenters of Thomas Richard James Grant Masons able & experienced Workmen duly sworn & examined in open Court as also by the others Concurring testimony of Robert Ward...? Coventry Robert Cutlbert Richard Statham John Dousefield Drury ffoster Edward Virgin Joseph Richard Joseph Symonds John ..? Thomas Graw John ffranklyn Drury Symonds John Blackett W..? Smith John Bonwell Joseph Richard & Ralph Cooper That upon Saturday the 11th day of August last past about Noon of the Clock in the forenoone there happened a Sudden & Lamentable fire to breake fo[rth] in the Towne of Northmarston in the County aforesaid which in the short tyme burnt downe & consumed the houses Barnes Stables Outhouses of the said Robert Cutlbert William Gyles Samuel Wild Robert Ward James ffoster John Pitcroft W[illia]m Anderson John ffranklyn John Dousefield Richard Stanbridge ...? Burnaby Thomas Graw Richard Dousefield Edward Wyatts Drury ffoster Joseph Richard John Lucas John Symonds John Ward ..? Waddington Clerk Christopher ffoster James ffoster and Anne Wil... And also the Household goods Hay Wood Corne Graynes & other good[s] and Chattels of the said Robert Cutlbert Robert Ward John Dousef[ield] Drury ffoster Joseph Richard John Symonds Richard Dousefield John Lucas Thomas Graw Withinall Wild John ffranklyn W[illia]m Anderson Saunders Wild And of W[illia]m Parnell Joh[n] Cobb Edward Virgin Drury Symonds Katherine ffoster Wid[ow] John Ward Martha Dousefield Wid[ow] Thomas Tattham William Anderson Thomas ffranks Anthony Moores John Blackett Lund... James Lucas W[illia]m Smith Martha Ingram Wid[ow] Thomas Anderson Benjamin Ingram John Bonwell Thomas Alday W[idow] Pris.. Stevens Wid[ow] John Stevens Ralph Cooper Richard Purchas Clerk J... Blackett James ffoster & ffrancis ffitkyn Wid[ow] Amounting to the value of Three Thousand Fowre hundred ffifty five pounds Eight Shillings & two pence. So that the poore sufferers with the ffamilyes are totally Impover[ished] and not able to Subsist but must inevitably perish unless tymely relieved by the Charitable benevolence of well disposed people In Wittnesse w[hereof] as well us the said Justices sitt[ing] att the said Gaoll Quarter Sessions as also others of her Maj[es]t[ie]s Justices of the peace for the said County wh[o] are sufficiently Certifyed of the truth of the p[re]misses have hereunto set o[u]r hands & Seales this 4th day of October in the yeare of o[u]r Lord God [One] thousand seaven hundred & five.

Extract from the Magistrates Order Book

Rev Purchas's handwritten note of benefactors

Figure 1 is a plan of the village as it was in 1705 with contemporary streets added to aid orientation. Shown in green is the Village Green which was vast three centuries ago. The church, the well and The Bell Inn are shown in black. The approximate locations of houses destroyed in the fire are in red; we cannot be sure exactly where they were situated but Figure 1 gives a clear picture of the extent of the fire.

At the time of the fire, the Manor House was occupied by Mrs Elizabeth Saunders, widow of Thomas Saunders who had died in 1702. The house we now call Burnaby House was occupied in 1705 by Mrs Burnaby. There is no mention of anyone by the name of Burnaby in the Parish Registers of baptisms, marriages or burials, so we have no more information about her. We can only guess at the residences of the others listed in the Court Records. The Reverend Purchas tells us of the *"wind being extream high"* on the day of the fire. It is reasonable to assume that an extreme wind, both hot and dry, in August would be from the west, in which case the fire would have started at the Manor House and spread from west to east finally engulfing Burnaby House. With so many houses packed together, the wind would have carried sparks from thatched roof to thatched roof with alarming speed. It is likely that most of the men and many of the women would have been working in the open fields at the time that the fire broke out and this may have been a factor in allowing the fire to take hold. Once it was raging it would have been unstoppable until it ran out of thatched roofs to ignite. This is presumably why it stopped at Burnaby House and the top of School Hill.

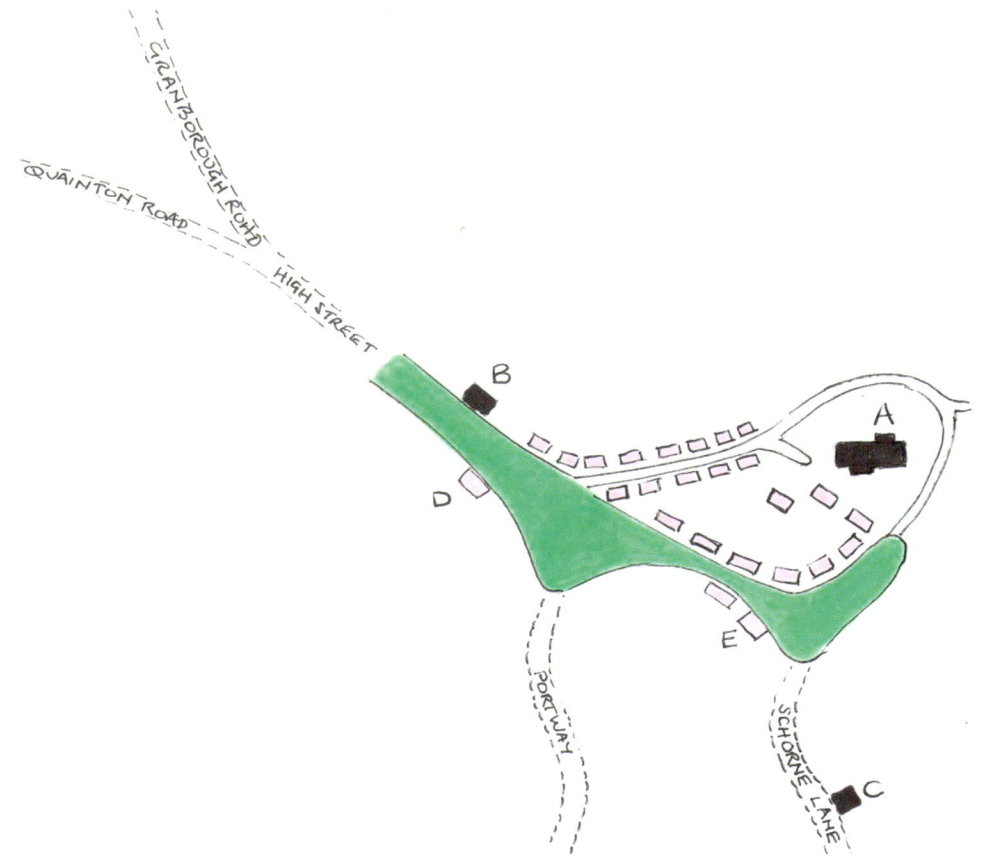

Figure 1   The Village in 1705

A Church
B Bell Inn (renamed The Pilgrim in 2010)
C The Well
D Manor House
E Burnaby House

There are minor discrepancies between the two records. The Reverend Purchas refers to twenty-five dwelling houses being consumed by the fire whilst the court records list the names of only twenty-three people, but it is always possible that some owned more than one house. Also the Reverend Purchas refers to property owned by Mr Saunders and Mr Burnaby whereas the court records name Mrs Saunders (Widow) and Mrs Burnaby; as stated above, the church records show that Mr Thomas Saunders was buried in 1702.

Apart from these minor discrepancies, we are fortunate to have a vivid picture of the tragedy. It is clear that North Marston was devastated by an overwhelming fire during the day on 11th August 1705 which in a few hours destroyed twenty-five houses as well as barns, stables and outhouses, that the Magistrates Court assisted the *"poore sufferers"* in the *"dreadfull fire"* by issuing patents to collect *"charitable benevolence"* and the country was *"extraordinary kind"* in donating surprisingly large amounts for the *"reliefe of sufferers"*.

To this day, in some cottages in the village, there remains evidence of fire damage, quite possibly from the huge fire of 1705.

Seven
OPEN FIELDS AND ENCLOSURE
Colin Price

It is often wondered why some of the older buildings in the village, such as Manor Farm, Home Farm, The Wheatsheaf and The Sportsman, are set back so far from the road and why there are farmhouses situated in the village itself rather than in surrounding farm land.

Did you know that North Marston once had a huge village green? But where has it gone and why has this village, unlike Quainton, now nothing more to show than a few tiny strips of green in the High Street?

Until relatively recently and for centuries North Marston has been essentially a farming community. It is therefore not surprising that much of the village's shape relates to its agricultural history. This chapter seeks to explain how North Marston would have looked in the late eighteenth century, and how its appearance changed dramatically as a result of the *North Marston Inclosure Act* of 1778.

Open Fields Prior to 1778

It is hard for us nowadays to envisage the village as it would have been before 1778 for it was so different from the village we know today. It is hard to imagine an open-field system with no farms and no fields (as we see them today) and only a very few hedges; the entire parish would have had the appearance of one vast open space.

Most of the land was cultivated by being ploughed into long narrow strips but large areas were uncultivated and left as village green and common land where the villagers grazed their livestock.

Michael Finnemore's meticulously researched map of the village at this time shows the location of the green, the commons and between two and three thousand ploughed strips (*see Figure 1*).

The ploughed strips were located in Three Great Fields named Churchill Field, West Field and Hill Field which were not physically divided from each other. The *Three Field System* was the basis for a three-year crop rotation cycle: year one, wheat or barley: year two, oats or beans: year three, fallow or grazing: and all the strips in a particular Great Field would be in the same phase of the rota.

Figure 2 is a sketch map of the village before 1778 and is a simplification of Michael Finnemore's map with present day roads and landmarks added to facilitate orientation. The sketch illustrates the location of the Three Great Fields, and the village green is outlined in green.

The strips of land were ploughed using a technique referred to as "Ridge and Furrow". Traditional ploughs turned the soil over in one direction (to the ploughman's right) and were not reversible. Consequently the ploughman would work along one side of the strip, lift the plough from the ground, move across the end of it and work back along its other long side. As the plough was moving in opposite directions along each side of the strip, the plough would always be turning the soil towards its centre.

The movement of soil year after year gradually built the centre of the strip up into a ridge, leaving a dip (or furrow) between each ridge. The raised ridge offered better drainage in North Marston's heavy soil. The furrow served as a division between one ridge and its neighbour.

Figure 1

Michael Finnemore's map of the village prior to Enclosure.

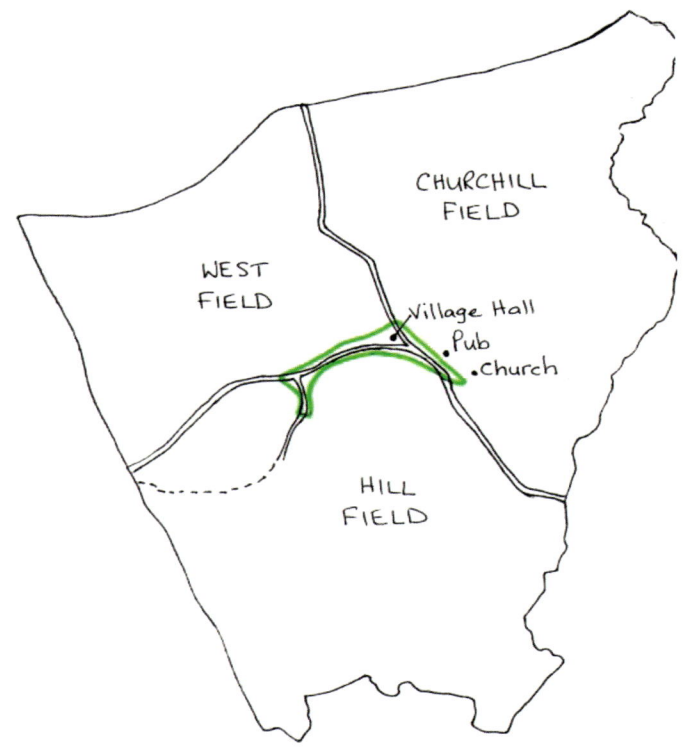

Figure 2

The photograph of a modern day ploughing competition illustrates the way that the plough always turns the earth towards the centre of the strip, thus building up the ridge (*see picture below*).

Strips would traditionally be a furlong (a "furrow-long") in length (approximately two hundred and twenty yards) and between five yards and a chain (twenty-two yards) wide, giving an area of between a quarter and one acre. The length of the furlong was not a fixed length but was a length to suit the terrain but no longer than the point where a plough team would need a rest. Hence, in heavy clay a furlong was shorter.

There are areas of the village today where the soil is so poorly drained that it has not been ploughed and cultivated for centuries, with the result that the ridges and furrows from the old furlongs can still be seen, especially with the sun low on the horizon. If you look to the fields on your left as you drive up Oving Hill you can make out the old ridge lines (*see picture*).

The ridge and furrows on the Oving hillside, as seen from Marston Fields, and made clearer by a light snow

Even more fascinating is to look at the village on *Google Earth*; in many areas of the village, the pattern of ancient ridges and furrows is still clearly visible from the air and exactly as identified on Michael Finnemore's map.

Hard as it is to visualize the village before 1778 with two to three thousand separate strips of cultivated land and no fences, hedges or ditches dividing them up, it is even harder to appreciate that an individual land owner would own many strips of land dotted around the village in an apparently random and haphazard way.

One of the major land owners was Magdalen College, Oxford which owned two hundred and seventy-eight strips in one hundred and forty-two different locations throughout the village. The only consistent feature was that every landholder, irrespective of the size of their holding, held approximately one third of their land in each of the Three Great Fields to allow crop rotation.

This arrangement seems pretty chaotic to us and it is hard to see how it worked. In fact, the open field system had been in existence since medieval times and the farming patterns had been laid down by custom over very many generations so they were well understood and an accepted way of life. Furthermore, it was easier to implement than we might imagine because the rotation system meant that all strips were planting the same crops as their neighbours.

The North Marston Inclosure Act 1778

All this changed in 1778 with the *North Marston Inclosure Act*. (The eighteenth century spelling of "Inclosure" has long since passed out of use). The parish had petitioned parliament for the Act in order to tidy the complex land distribution outlined above.

The intention was that the scattered holding of multiple strips in the common fields would be consolidated to create an individual farm that could be managed independently. The Act states that:

"...whereas the several lands and estates ... in North Marston lie intermixed and dispersed in small parcels ... and in their present situation are incapable of any considerable improvement it would be very advantageous .... if the open and common fields ... were divided and inclosed and .... shares thereof allotted to the several proprietors thereof in lieu of and in proportion ...to their respective Lands, Tithes, Common-Rights, Interests and Properties therein."

Commissioners for dividing and allotting the land were appointed, as were land valuers and surveyors. The main surveyor for North Marston was Westcott-born John Fellows. The valuation was done in 1776 in anticipation of the Act. Work was carried out with great urgency and the Act required that a survey listing *"the number of Acres, Roods and Perches belonging to each Proprietor"* be produced by the first day of September 1778. The land they were measuring and valuing was owned by forty-five landowners, who leased land in the open fields to farmers both large and small, some of which had been passed by father to son over many generations. The principal land owners were Magdalen College Oxford, The Dean and Canons of Windsor, Christchurch College Oxford, and private individuals such as Charles Watkins, Ralph Stevens, Henry Tattam and John Tattam.

The Commissioners then divided up all the Great Fields (which included the commons) into parcels of land and land owners were awarded a plot of the same area and similar quality as that owned before enclosure. There was no appeal against the Commissioners' allocation and the Deeds had to be signed within six months. The owners were required to *"inclose, hedge, ditch or otherwise fence"* their land within twelve months of signing.

It is remarkable to us today to see the speed and efficiency with which such a major social change was brought about. By the end of 1779, the newly allocated parcels of land were enclosed by hedges and ditches, creating a pattern of fields very much as we see them today.

So we can see that, by Act of Parliament, the Open Fields were fenced off and divided with deeds awarded to private owners, ending the centuries-old traditional common rights. Overall, there was a redistribution of wealth in favour of the landed sector of society which left the small-holder and wage-labourer in a very difficult position.

To add to the labourers' problems, once the land had been enclosed there was a marked decline in arable farming and most of the land would have been grazed. Prior to enclosure, cereals would have been the major crop providing employment: weeding, reaping and threshing etc. With the change to pasture land there was a dramatic reduction in available farm work for landless labourers.

Enclosure created a more efficient way of managing the land but was of greater benefit to larger farmers and land owners than the subsistence farmer. Combined with an increase in the rural population towards the end of the eighteenth century (the population of Buckinghamshire rose by twenty-two per cent between 1750 and 1800) this led to spiralling demands on Poor Relief in rural communities. As a consequence, the poor rate levied on freeholders rose dramatically. In the period 1783-1803 the average poor rate in Bucks rose by ninety-five per cent! It will be explained later that there were charitable attempts by the parish to assist the increasing number of poor people in the village *(see Poors Piece below)*.

Highways

The commissioners were required to lay out *"highways"* which were approximately in the same position as today's roads except that there was no highway through the centre of the village. The Act stipulated that the highways were to be at least *"forty feet broad"* but in practice they were at least fifty feet broad in all but the most restricted places. This seems amazingly wide but roads would initially have been un-surfaced so the highway needed to be wide enough to allow detours around impassable stretches that developed during the winter. When properly surfaced roads were made, only a relatively narrow width would have been surfaced with stone and the remainder was left under grass. Outside the village the width of fifty feet still remains today, but within the village the wide verges have disappeared.

To understand the disappearance of the wide verges it is necessary to appreciate that each parcel of land over which the highway ran remained in the ownership of the villager whose land it crossed. The land owner was entitled *to "inclose, hedge, ditch or otherwise fence"* his land and *"shall have liberty to … erect and set up … over and across any roads … any gate made to swing both ways between the posts … so every such gate shall be six feet wide at the least between the posts"*. So, as long as the land was fenced and gated to allow passage along the highway, the verges could be used by the landowner for grazing and hay-making.

It is not really surprising that with the passage of time the verges have been incorporated into the agricultural land of the owner and their designation as "highway" overlooked. Quainton Road is a good illustration. On the south side (ie the Shepperds Close side) the very wide verge of 1779 has completely disappeared along the whole length of the road. This is illustrated by The Sportsman and The Wheatsheaf which were previously only a few metres from the edge of the highway and are now set back twenty metres.

Also, in many parts of the village it is easy to

identify strips of land by the side of today's roads (with or without houses on them) that would have been designated as "highway" in 1779; for example, all the houses along Portway have been built on land acquired in this way.

The gates marked the point where the highway crossed from one plot of land to another and many remained well into the next century, causing great inconvenience to travellers. *The Schornian* records the particular annoyance caused by gates across the Granborough road close to the Granborough border which were such an irritation that they were referred to as "*those botheration gates*". After repeated appeals to the Ecclesiastical Commissioners, they were eventually removed in 1888.

The gates across Carters Lane were still in existence in 1896 when the vicar wrote in *The Schornian*: "*We hope the gates in Carters Lane will be done away with shortly by Magdalen College, Oxford*". They did go eventually as did most others, but Marston Fields remains a "gated" road to this day.

The Village Green

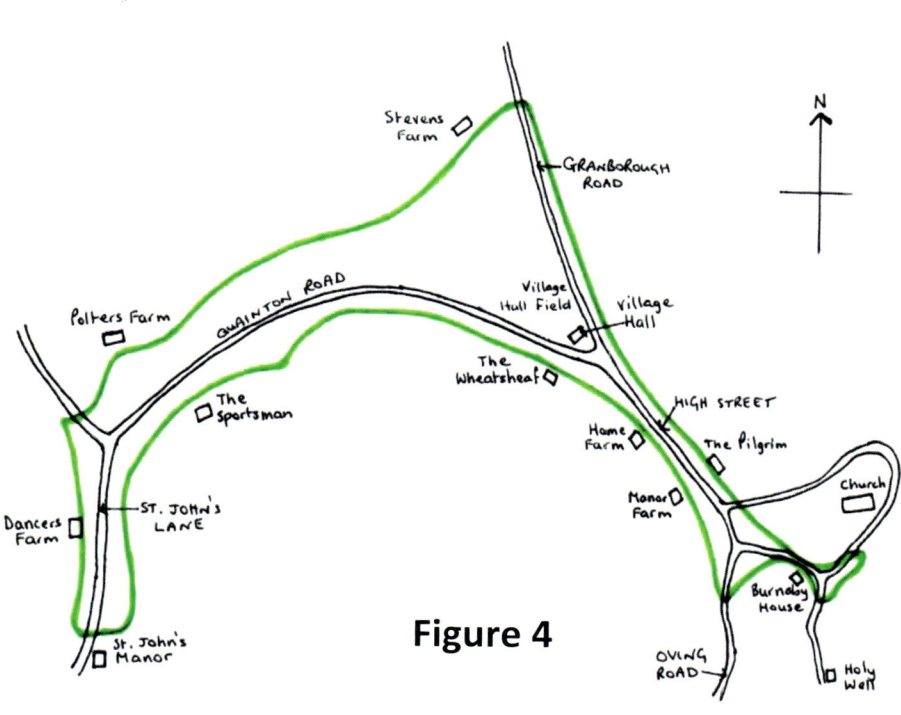

Figure 4

The village green prior to Enclosure (with superimposed contemporary roads and buildings)

Figure 5

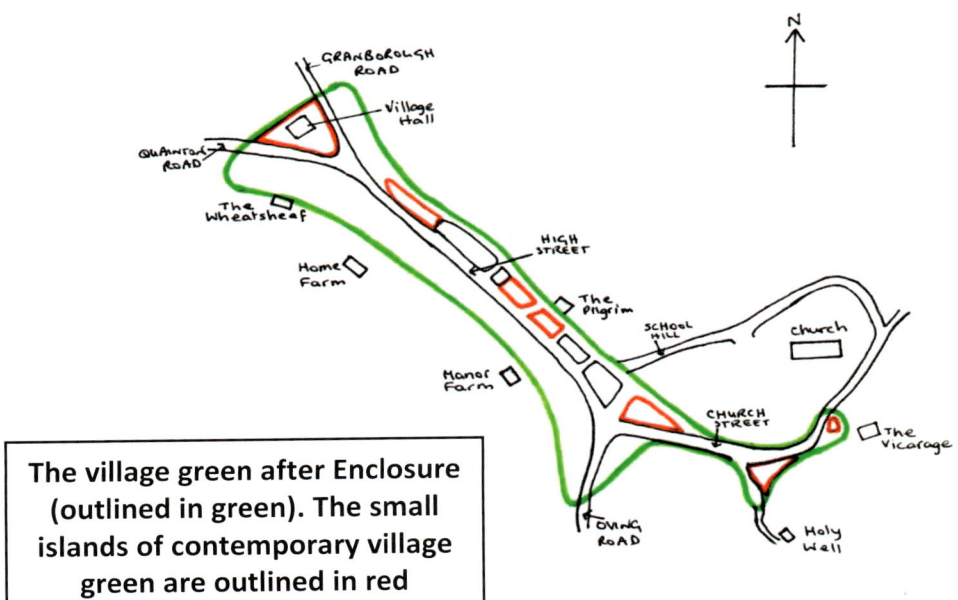

The village green after Enclosure (outlined in green). The small islands of contemporary village green are outlined in red

In Figure 4 we can see the village green as it was for many centuries prior to enclosure (with contemporary roads and landmarks added to facilitate orientation).

It can be seen that the area of village green was vast. Beginning south of the church, it extended in a very wide swathe through the centre of the village almost as far as the Sports Field in Granborough Road, and along Quainton Road and St John's Lane towards St John's Manor. This enormous area of grassland was common land which everyone used by tradition.

All of this changed in 1778. Approximately two-thirds of the village green was re-allocated as agricultural land under the *North Marston Inclosure Act*. All the village green around the present day Granborough Road, Quainton Road and St John's Lane was enclosed and no longer common land.

The much reduced village green of 1779 is outlined in green in Figure 5 whilst, outlined in red, are the small parcels of land still owned by the parish today. It can be seen that ninety-five per cent of the village green had been lost in the intervening years. How had this happened?

Firstly, landowners to the south-west (ie opposite the pub) have appropriated land all the way up to the road as it is today; Manor Farmhouse, Home Farmhouse and The Wheatsheaf would have been on the edge of the Village Green in 1779. Subsequently, all the land in front of them has been appropriated, shaving approximately twenty metres off the village green to the south-west.

In a rather more haphazard way, land owners to the north-east (pub side) have incorporated islands of land into their holdings. A great deal of enclosure on a small scale went on unrecorded so that we can only guess at when and how this happened. The loss of the village green was almost complete by 1832. The Parish Valuation of that date was produced by the same John Fellows who was surveyor to the enclosure of 1778 and detailed the changes that had taken place since 1778.

Interestingly, the Parish Valuation shows that by 1832 there were already buildings on the islands of land at the top of the High Street on which Shakespeare House, Forge House and The Old Forge were subsequently built. On the other hand, it would appear that there have never been buildings on the pockets of land in front of the Mill House although they were taken into private ownership by 1832 (and probably by 1810).

Therefore it can be assumed that the land-grab took place between 1779 and 1832 and, as a consequence, all that is left of the vast village green of the many centuries leading up to 1778 (and the reduced but still substantial village green after 1778) are the small islands (as shown in red on Figure 5) in front of the Village Memorial Hall, The Pilgrim Pub, The Red House, The Elms and Abbotts Cottage.

Farmhouses

It is an interesting feature of the village that the majority of farmhouses are situated in the village itself and very few are to be found in the outlying farmland.

The locations of some of the farmhouses in the centre of the village before 1778 are shown in Figure 4 where it can be seen that Manor Farmhouse, Home Farmhouse, Stevens Farmhouse, Potters Farmhouse, Dancers Farmhouse and St John's Manor were all located around or close to the village green as it was prior to enclosure. When land was allocated in 1778, the commissioners drew up the boundaries in such a way that farms were created around the pre-existing houses so that the farmhouses lay within or abutting their allocated plots of land.

So for the farms listed above there was no need to put up new buildings when land was re-allocated and the farmhouses remained at the heart of the village. In fact, the only farmhouse to be built in the surrounding fields at this time was Marston Fields Farm.

Poors Piece

As already mentioned, prior to enclosure, there were large areas of common land and village green throughout the village, where the poor of the parish were allowed to collect fuel and graze geese etc. These privileges had been established for many hundreds of years and were regarded as 'of right'.

As a consequence of enclosure, the major part of the common land and much of the village green were now allotted for agricultural use and with them had gone the ancient privileges of the poor. To compensate, a piece of land was allocated to the poor of the parish and named Poors Piece. This land was to the north of the parish close to the Granborough border and totalled just over twelve acres. The piece was leased and on 24th December each year the proceeds were given *"in Fuel, Meat, Corn or Apparel to … the most necessitous, industrious, and honest poor of the parish."*

The land was subsequently used as allotments and the Charity Commissioners Report for 1832 states that by that year the land was *"divided into 84 gardens which are cultivated by the poor, who receive the produce."*

Poors Piece remains today exactly as it was in 1779. It is currently managed by the Poors Piece and Clocklands Charity, the income from tenancy being to the benefit of the most needy in the parish.

Clockland

By the end of the sixteenth century, many villages were installing a parish clock. The clock would usually have been in the church tower where it could be seen most easily by the villagers. It is not clear exactly when the clock was installed in North Marston and we know nothing about its appearance. In the year 1600 (the forty-second year of the reign of Queen Elizabeth I), in order to finance the clock, various parcels of land in the parish were allocated as Clockland. The land was to be leased and the income used for the purpose of repairing the clock, maintaining the church and for the *"relief and sustentation of the poor"*. In 1779, under *The North Marston Inclosure Act*, the Clockland was re-allocated as approximately fifteen acres next to Poors Piece in the north of the parish. The Clockland is managed today by the Poors Piece and Clockland Charity for exactly the same purposes as stipulated in 1600.

Eight
THE METHODIST CHURCHES
John Spargo

The non-conformist movement that swept across the country in the late eighteenth and early nineteenth centuries resulted in most villages having at least one alternative place of worship to the parish church. Numerically, the principle non-conformist denomination was Methodism and this led to the building of two village churches: the Wesleyan Methodist Church in Schorne Lane and the Primitive Methodist Church (Chapel) in Quainton Road. Although they were both Methodist places of worship, there were quite distinct differences between the two branches of Methodism. As it happens, non-conformism was not new to the village: records show there were *Anabaptists* here in the late seventeenth century. The roots of Methodism lie with the brothers John and Charles Wesley.

John Wesley (1703 – 1791) was an Anglican cleric and Christian theologian. Wesley is largely credited, along with his brother Charles Wesley, with founding the Methodist movement which began when he took to open air preaching. Methodism was a highly successful evangelical movement that encouraged people to experience Jesus Christ personally. Wesley evaluated and approved men who were not ordained by the Anglican Church to preach and do pastoral work. This deployment of *lay preachers* was one of the key factors in the growth of Methodism. The movement did not form a separate denomination in England until after John Wesley's death in 1791 with the early Methodists acting against perceived apathy in the Church of England, preaching in the open air and establishing Methodist *societies* wherever they went. Wesley himself was a prolific preacher and travelled all over the country to conduct open-air meetings that became extremely popular. There is an anecdotal account that he once preached in Oving.

The original body founded as a result of Wesley's work was later known as the *Wesleyan* Methodist Church. Schisms within the original (Wesleyan) Methodist church, and independent revivals, led to the formation of a number of separate denominations calling themselves "Methodist". The largest of these was the *Primitive* Methodist Church which split from the Wesleyans in 1810.

Methodism in North Marston

It seems the Wesleyan influence was felt in the village from the earliest years of Methodism. The beginnings of Methodism in North Marston were marked by the licensing of William Buckingham's house in 1788. The Buckinghams were a major influence on Methodism in North Marston for generations.

North Marston began to receive Methodist preachers in October 1812 when Mr H Tattam opened his house for Sunday services. He later joined the Anglican Church and eventually became Archdeacon Tattam (*see Chapter Ten*).

From the early days of meeting in private houses the Wesleyan Methodists then used an old malting house in Schorne Lane (formerly Holy Well Lane) in the 1820s. This was demolished and a small chapel was built on the site which opened in August 1833. This was subsequently replaced in 1864 by the building that stands today (*see below*) which, according to the *1899 Kelly's Directory*, had capacity for two hundred.

Schorne Lane Methodist Church built in 1864

Consistent with the ideals of the movement, the North Marston Methodists established a school in the village which drew the attention of an anonymous individual who wrote a letter to *The Times* in July 1946 bemoaning the apathy to the needs of the village shown by the Dean and Chapter of Windsor (who were responsible for the parish church at the time).

In the letter, the writer describes North Marston parish as *"a large and important one, and a wilderness of dissent."* The writer goes on to criticise the failings of the church school in the village (which had been opened in July 1835) saying: *"The Wesleyans have established an excellent school near it….and are educating and converting the rising generation."*

This means that by 1846 Methodism was well on the way to becoming a strong and established movement in the village. An Ecclesiastical Census in 1851 highlights this point: village church attendances at the end of March (ie all daily services on 30th March) show that, whilst the Anglican Church was attended by two hundred and thirteen worshippers, the combined total for both village Methodist Churches was six hundred and seven. Allowing for some worshippers attending more than one service on the day, it speaks volumes that, in a village where the population was six hundred and ninety-two, the Methodist Churches witnessed six hundred and seven attendances.

The Primitive Methodist Church in Quainton Road had been opened in November 1839, six years after the Wesleyan Church, and was subsequently enlarged in 1872 to accommodate three hundred (*Kelly's Directory 1899*).

Given that the population of the entire village in 1870 was less than seven hundred, for there to be seating for a total of five hundred in the two Methodist churches in the village is a measure of the profile of Methodism at that time.

Primitive Methodist preachers and communities differed from their Wesleyan counterparts: although the Wesleyans tended towards 'respectability', Primitives were poor and revivalist. Primitive Methodist preachers were plain speaking in contrast to Wesleyan services *"embellished with literary allusions and delivered in high-flown language."* Primitive Methodist preachers were plainly dressed and poorly paid.

There was also a disparity between the wealth of their congregations. The Wesleyan congregations were more likely to be from a lower middle class or artisan background than the Primitive Methodists who were most likely to be small farmers, servants, labourers or manual workers.

A visit of the Gospel Car to Church Street in 1913
(probably organised by the Primitive Methodists)

The North Marston Primitive Methodist preacher Mark Price (local labourer and brother to John Price the village builder) who later became one of the first North Marston parish councillors

One of the key figures in North Marston Primitive Methodist Church was Mark Price. He was an agricultural labourer who, for over fifty years, worked for farmer Tom Biggs at Marston Fields Farm but his main interest was the Primitive Methodist Church in Quainton Road. His obituary records an association spanning more than sixty years:

"He was Sunday School Superintendent for half a century and organist. He usually conducted the service and furthermore was a trustee, society steward and chapel-keeper. For many years he was a Circuit Steward of the Aylesbury Primitive Methodist Circuit....So attached was he to Marston Chapel that to many people it was known as Mark's Chapel."

After the death of his wife, Mark Price lived at Prune Cottage with his daughter, Mrs T Cox, who later opened a shop on the premises (*see Chapter Sixteen*). It was his express wish that he should be buried in the small burial ground behind the Primitive Chapel in Quainton Road, next to his wife. It was the last grave available (*see picture*).

The Primitive Methodist movement exalted its poor congregations by glorifying plain dress and speech. They promoted it for two reasons: firstly, they thought plain dress was encouraged by the Gospel and, secondly, because it made them distinctive. At a time when Wesleyans sought assimilation and respectability, the Primitives wanted to stand out as 'peculiar' people, making a virtue out of their difference.

An exciting two-day event for the "Prims" in 1908

The Primitives (or *Prims* as they became known) were more likely to go against society's norms: they were visible and noisy and made use of revivalist techniques such as open-air preaching. It is likely that it was the Primitive Methodists in North Marston who facilitated the visit of the Gospel Car (*pictured earlier*). Despite these differences, the Wesleyan Methodists also had much in common as they were both initially very anti-Catholic.

There were many poor Wesleyans; it was in *influence* rather than in numbers that middle-class Wesleyans dominated the movement. In official policy and outlook the two movements also had much in common as they both based their teaching on the Bible and shared similar views on society and morality.

Although the Primitives were generally more radical than the Wesleyan Methodists, both promoted the doctrine of self-help within the working class.

The Anglican vicar of the parish for the latter part of the nineteenth century was Dr Samuel James (*see also Chapter Eleven*). His attitude to the Methodists, as expressed in frequent references in *The Schornian* magazine, was probably intended to read as being benign and benevolent, despite the obvious success of the Methodists in attracting large numbers of villagers to their services.

However, one is eventually led to the conclusion that his attitude to the Methodists was like that of a Victorian explorer meeting an indigenous tribe: they were an amusing sub-species, but not 'proper' people. As an example, Rev James once attended a Primitive Methodist Club dinner (somewhat arrogantly, he only agreed to attend if they first sat through one of his sermons at the parish church) and was surprised to discover they liked the same food (roast beef and plum pudding) as members of the Church of England!

Rev Samuel James

One feels he believed the Methodists to be well-intentioned but misguided and, patronisingly, he puts them in the same category as 'the deserving poor'.

Finally, however, the Rev James's true colours emerged in a piece he wrote in *The Schornian* in December 1887. His patience with the Methodists had been worn down by the thinning of his own congregation whom he perceived had been lured away by the Salvation Army, Wesleyans and Primitive Methodists. He berated the Methodists for stealing his congregation rather than "*seeking to win souls from Satan*." He ends by saying:

"*We fully believe the Church of England is the recognised representative of Christ and Christianity in England.*"

The fact he was hopelessly out of touch in attitude and style of worship (and had thus alienated two-thirds of the village) did not seem to occur to him.

The Methodist Societies were formed of members who were given membership tickets on a quarterly basis.

Attendance at Sunday school was recorded and prizes awarded for good attendance. People like William Buckingham who provided long service to the Methodist Church were also given awards.

William Buckingham's recognition for forty years of service as a preacher

A Wesleyan Methodist ticket, March 1934

A 1995 ticket

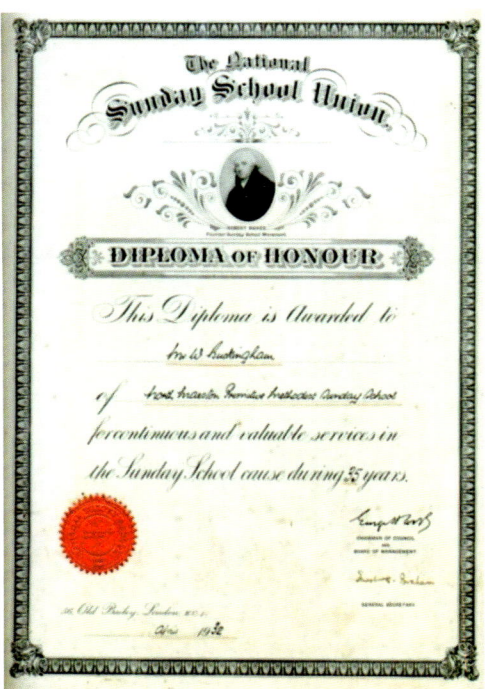

William Buckingham's Diploma of Honour for thirty-five years as a Sunday school superintendent

The Quainton Road Primitive Methodist Church, past and present

The Methodist church played an important social role in the village with clubs, guilds, social events and Sunday schools. Methodist Guild membership was extensive and there were Junior and Adult Guilds and a Guild Committee.

Methodist Guild Junior Members 1940-1

Junior Members:
Arthur Bevan, June Edwards, Rita Franks, Madeline Heath, Roland Linnell, Iris Higgins, Doris Higgins, Lionel Linnell, Douglas Lambourne, Alice Hassell, Betty Battram, Margaret Woodison, Barbara Wood, Norah McGee, Stephen McGee, Charles Petty, Kenneth Coates, Audrey Edwards, John Edwards, Peter Battram, Guy Holden, John Holden, Wilfred Cumberland.

Methodist Guild Adult Members 1940-1

Adult Members:
Miss E. Price, Miss D. Price, Mrs. E. Lambourne, Mrs. A. Price, Miss P. Price, Miss C. Seaton, Miss E. Seaton, Miss L. Bates, Mrs. A. J. Franklin, Miss H. Lambourne, Miss A. Wall, Miss A. Seaton, Miss I. Baker, Mr. F. Price, Mr. P. Bates, Mr. A. Price, Mr. J. Wilkins, Mr. E. Price, Mr. S. Lambourne, Mr. C. Walker, Mr. A. Higgins, Mr. N. Higgins, Mr. D. Rawlins.

Methodist Guild Committee 1940-1

North Marston Guild 1940-1941 Session

President: Mr. F. Price
Secretaries: Mr. P. Bates, Miss E. Price
Treasurer: Mr. P. Bates
Committee: Mr. A. Price, Mrs. E. Lambourne, Miss L. Bates, Mrs. A. Price, Miss P. Price, Mrs. Franklin.
Meetings each Thursday at 7 pm.

Methodist Guild brooch

North Marston Methodist ladies in May 1930

Throughout the early years of the twentieth century, the Wesleyan Church building was enhanced: in 1911 it was registered for marriages; in 1934 electric lighting was installed; in 1957 a new kitchen was fitted; in 1972 funds were raised for a new organ in memory of Harold Carter, the village milkman; in 1992 the building was re-roofed.

A young Jennifer Harwood

In 1956, Jennifer Harwood, aged fourteen, played the organ in the Wesleyan Methodist Church at the funeral of her grandfather, William Buckingham (whose long-service certificates were featured earlier). She was to continue playing at services there until 2004 when the Wesleyan Methodist Church closed for services. As Jennifer *Heffer* she is now the organist at St Mary's Church.

Village Methodism Today

The Primitive Methodist Church in Quainton Road closed in the late 1940s. It was sold for six hundred and fifty pounds and converted into a residence, the first family to live there being a Captain Tattam and his wife. The Primitive Methodist burial ground was sold as a plot in 1978 for three hundred and fifty pounds. The Wesleyan Methodist Church in Schorne Lane finally closed its doors for Methodist services in 2004.

For more than a century Methodism had been an influence on many aspects of life in North Marston. Its legacy is now an unusually strong ecumenical partnership between Methodists and Anglicans which would have been unthinkable in years gone by. Methodism also left a fine church building in Schorne Lane which, it is hoped at the time of writing, will eventually be renovated.

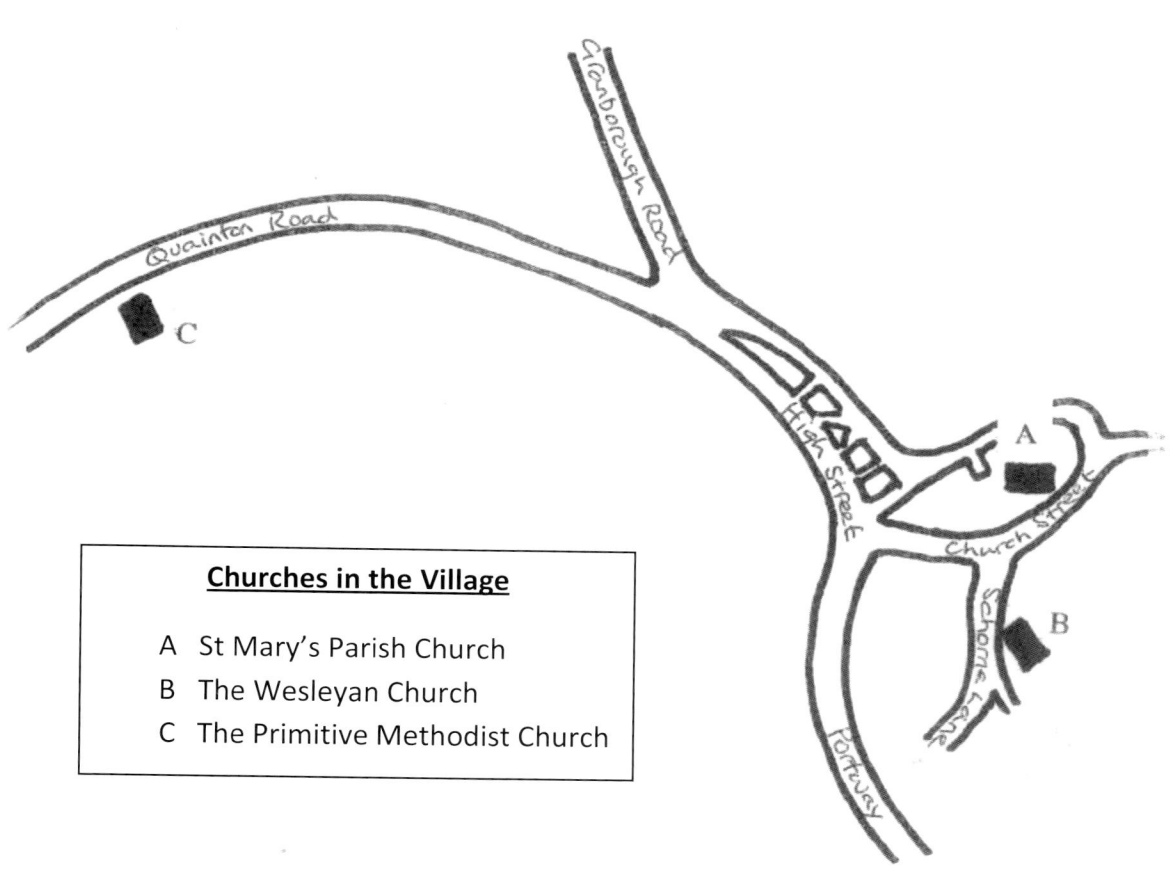

Nine
SUNDAY SCHOOLS
John Spargo & Sue Chaplin

In today's secular society it is hard to imagine that, once, every child (and some adults) attended Sunday school as their only source of education and that the Sunday school had more teachers than the day school.

For the origins of Sunday schools we must travel back to the 1780s when Sunday schools were set up to provide working children with an education in literacy and bible knowledge. This was a time when, as soon as they were able, children were set to work to earn their keep, and there was no compulsory universal education. North Marston had many children working as lace-makers: their nimble fingers and keen eyesight would have been a real asset, so it is likely they would have formed the bulk of the pupils at the earliest village Sunday school. The first Sunday schools were pivotal in the basic education of village children and pre-dated state education by about ninety years.

The Sunday School Movement was cross-denominational; it was funded by subscription and initially Sunday schools could be attended by adults as well as children. In North Marston, where the Methodist movement had gained a significant following in the first half of the nineteenth century, both the Wesleyan and Primitive Methodist Churches founded their own Sunday school to teach and promote their own style of worship.

Meanwhile, the Anglican Church (through the National Schools for Promoting Religious Education Society) had created a *National School* in the village that acted both as a Sunday school and day school. Day school teachers were expected to assist at Sunday school. From 1833 the state began to pay annual grants accompanied by inspections which examined literacy and religious knowledge; this triggered a programme of school building across the country.

North Marston's National School, which opened in 1835, served two functions: prior to the 1870 Education Act it provided an Anglican Sunday school for working children and a day school for infants. The creation of the village National School cemented the link between the church and primary education which is still evident to this day; most village schools, as in North Marston, are described as "Church Schools" (*see Chapter Twenty-five*).

After the implementation of the 1870 Education Act, all children were supposed to attend school during the day and inspectors monitored the schools and the children who were supposed to be attending. The village school, however, was in crisis in the mid-1870s for want of a schoolmaster, and the Sub-Inspector of Factories wrote complaining to the vicar, the Rev James, in 1875 about the *"large number of little lace-makers"* in the village who really ought to be at school but said: *"Am I justified in ordering these children to attend a school where there is no proper teacher?"* This means that, in light of the day-school staffing problem, it is possible the Sunday school continued to be the only source of education in the village for many little lace-makers.

The Anglican Sunday School

The link between the day school and the Anglican Sunday school was further reinforced when, in 1870, the vicar wrote:

"The Schoolmaster and Schoolmistress are responsible for the management of the Sunday school and are required to sit with and take care of the school children at Church."

This expectation might have had to be relaxed due to problems in finding staff as, by 1872, the Sunday school had become the responsibility of unpaid *superintendents* and teachers from the village community, albeit assisted by day school staff.

Sunday schools were administered by Superintendents, sometimes with two people sharing the duties. In the late Victorian period, North Marston's Superintendent duties were shared between Miss Susan James, the vicar's daughter, and Reuben Cheshire, the Post Master.

The Sunday school teaching rota for 1880 shows there were ten teachers and six classes of pupils grouped according to age. By 1883, and with fifty-three children on the roll, the volunteer Sunday school teachers were being augmented by teachers from Schorne College.

Sunday school prize-giving became a big event with dozens of children being awarded cash prizes for attendance and effort.

Writing about the prizes awarded in 1872, Rev James was of the opinion that:

'The coins will do for a little pocket money for sweets if the parents are not poor."

Eleven years later, and writing on the same topic, he said:

"The richer children will no doubt view their money prizes as pocket money (like the Schornians) and the poorer as something towards shoes, or handkerchiefs, or something of that kind; we are pleased to see the Sunday School is not confined to the poor."

For most, if not all, children in the late 1800s, attendance at Sunday school would have culminated in Confirmation.

Lily Dudley's Confirmation Certificate 1897

Following the implementation of compulsory state education for all children (in which religious education formed an integral part of the national curriculum) Sunday schools were gradually being displaced in their core purpose and attendances started to fall. They needed to create incentives for children to attend and one of the schemes adopted was the *Sunday School Stamp*, whereby children attending were given, at the end of each class, a brightly-coloured attendance stamp to stick into a personal album or Sunday Book.

For generations of children who regularly attended Sunday school, the Sunday stamps remain a treasured and abiding memory.

Peter Morton's Sunday stamp album from 1950

The beautiful 'art nouveau' cover of Eveline Young's Sunday Book from the late 1920s

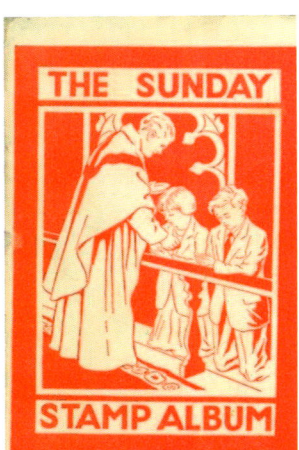
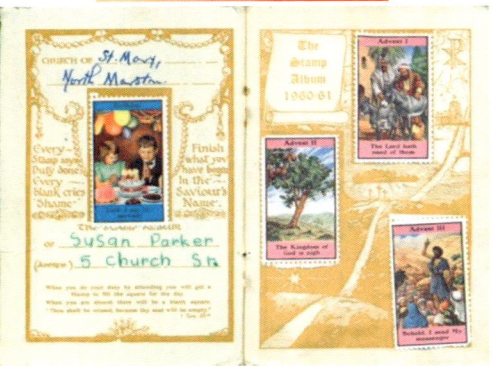

A Sunday stamp album from 1960

Some Sunday schools also offered prizes (generally religious books) for attendance and attainment further to encourage participation and endeavour. Sunday schools broadened their activities to include sport, and Sunday school sports leagues (usually denominational) were formed in which Sunday schools competed against each other. Picnics, parties and day trips also became part of the list of attractions although religious education remained at the core. The notion of the Sunday school 'treat' was nothing new; they appear to have started in the 1870s or earlier and by the 1880s were a well-established tradition, with Sunday school teas and parties held each year in the vicarage garden.

The tradition of members of the local community acting as Sunday school teachers extends back to the 1870s. For each generation of children, volunteers provided a range of activities and annual events. The teachers from the day school continued to play their part too: Mrs Dora Ayres (teacher of Infants at North Marston School from 1917 to 1959) taught voluntarily at the Sunday school until 1963 after which the local potter, Jim Cross, took over for two years, followed by Miss Worrall from Granborough.

Joint Anglican and Methodist Sunday school outing to Littlehampton in 1965

Janet Gowin, whose grandfather Henry Cheshire had been a Sunday school teacher for many years, recalls the years during which she too had fulfilled that role:

"I started teaching Sunday school with Miss Worrall from Granborough in January 1965. In 1966, Susan Linnell (later Cobbold) joined me and we operated a rota system with various local people including Gill Dancer and Janice Deung. When Susan Linnell married in 1974, the last one to join the rota was Tracy Swain (later Brown). Mrs George Holden would come and play a hymn at the end of each Sunday school during which we took the collection. We used to make an Easter Garden, often with help from Ewart Dancer, and we also did a Sunday school Harvest Corner. On Rogation Sundays Ewart or Tommy Dancer would collect us in the pony and cart and take us to the service at the farm.

Jim Cross in 1964

The Sunday school's Easter garden in 1972

Sunday School pupils at the Rogation Service in 1976

We sometimes had a summer party at the vicarage and a Christmas party at the village hall or a trip to the pantomime at Oxford. We also did 'wreathing' at the church every December, as introduced by Miss Worrall before the creation of Christingle.

The Sunday school meetings had always been held at the church but I moved the Sunday school to my home at Winkfield House in the mid-1970s as everything got damp in the church!"

Janet continued to run the Sunday school from her home until she 'retired' at the end of 1978 after which children who wished to continue with Sunday school were welcomed at the Wesleyan Methodist Church in Schorne Lane. When she finished as Sunday school teacher, Janet was given a touching certificate of thanks on behalf of all the children she had taught (*see below*).

> You've given up each Sunday morning
>   and devoted many precious hours
> to teach us children, sometimes naughty
>   a little of God's wondrous powers.
> Whatever our age, whatever our skills
> You've shown us all kindness
>   and love and goodwill.
> Thank you from all of us
>   from now and the past
> We're sorry you feel you must retire at last.
> But for 14 years we've been pleased
>   by your teaching
> Your new ideas — not just conventional preaching
> But during this time we've always been knowing
> that you Janet have always been Gowin!
>
>   Thank you from all friends,
>   parents and pupils for being
>   our Sunday School Teacher.

Joint Sunday school Christmas party in 1967 with Rowland Linnell as Santa

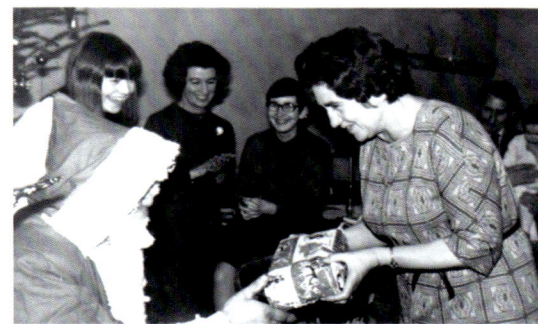
At the joint Sunday school Christmas party in 1968 Mrs Charrington, the vicar's wife, receives a present from Santa

The Methodist Sunday Schools

Records show there have been Methodist Sunday schools in the village since the early nineteenth century. Remarkably, a *Wesleyan Sunday Book* still exists which contains a historic record of Sunday school attendances from 1843 to 1952. The register shows that in 1843 there were thirty-eight boys and thirty-two girls in attendance. The superintendents in 1843 were John Price and John Ward and there were also eight male and six female teachers! William Buckingham served as a superintendent from 1897 until 1932 and received a Diploma of Honour for his work (*see Chapter Eigh*t). During the 1940s and 1950s two memorable and long-serving Sunday school teachers were Mrs Alice Franklin (known as "Mrs A J") and Miss Ethel Price.

The Sunday school at the Primitive Methodist Church in 1890

The Wesleyan Sunday school in the early 1900s

The Wesleyan Sunday school's anniversary, 21st May 1929

The Wesleyan Sunday school in 1964

Many of the records for the Primitive Methodist Sunday school are held at the Centre for Buckinghamshire Studies in Aylesbury. These offer information about Sunday school classes from 1821. Interestingly, the records for that year show the clerk to the class was one William Pinnock who also just happened to be the *Reverend William Pinnock,* the vicar of St Mary's Church!

Rev Pinnock's interest and engagement with the Methodists was well documented and it is known that he often preached at their meetings. As a Classical and Mathematics scholar it is also recorded that Rev Pinnock was tutor to two sons of Rev Charles Wesley, so his Methodist connections were of the highest order. Pinnock's personal identification with the movement was in stark contrast to the attitude of a later incumbent, Rev Samuel James, who wrote in The Schornian in 1875:

"Mr Pinnock was a friend of Charles Wesley and was also a Wesleyan class-leader at the same time he was incumbent of North Marston. This was an extraordinary line of conduct, and it is not because the Church has grown strong since those days that the present incumbent thinks it was altogether a (well-meaning) mistake."

The records of both the North Marston Methodist Sunday Schools offer a fascinating insight into the scale, longevity and importance of these village institutions. They also confirm that they were highly structured, democratic and self-regulated organisations that kept meticulous records and were, for well over a century, hugely important in the lives of a large number of village families.

Until the late 1980s Ted Price had been the Wesleyan Sunday school superintendent for over forty years.

We know that the Methodist Sunday school still had seventeen children in attendance in late 1987 when the children from the Anglican Sunday school joined with the Methodist children and were taught jointly in the Methodist school-room. At this time the teachers were Kathryn Warner, Benjamin Heffer and his sisters, Kate and Estelle.

Ted Price

In 1992 the vicar's wife, Jenny Kyriacou, took over the running of the combined Sunday school and the classes moved to the vicarage. As we write in 2014 the Sunday school is held, once again, in the Methodist school-room and afterwards all the children join with the adults at the end of the Communion Service in St Mary's Church.

Ten
THE HOUSEWIFE AND THE MISER: MARTHA NEAL AND JOHN CAMDEN NEILD

John Spargo

Martha Neal (nee Pinnock)

Martha Pinnock arrived in North Marston in 1806 from the tiny Bucks village of Great Woolstone, now part of Milton Keynes. She had been baptised in April 1805 in Fenny Stratford. Her father, the Reverend William Pinnock, had been appointed as the perpetual curate (ie parson, not rector or vicar) at North Marston and Oving by James Neild of Chelsea, a Quaker jeweller, wealthy land owner and penal reformer who had been the High Sherriff of Bucks in 1804.

James Neild held the lease for the rectory in both parishes giving him not only the right to appoint the parsons, but also responsibilities towards the upkeep of the churches. Neild was also the patron at Great Woolstone where Pinnock had been parson at the tiny church since 1786, and probably knew him well.

Holy Trinity Church, Great Woolstone

Fifty year-old William Pinnock would have assumed this would be his last appointment and settled down in North Marston with his wife Sarah (nee Tall) and children: Martha, Ann, William, John and George. In 1810 another son, Charles, was baptised followed four years later by a daughter, Henrietta. The family would have lived in a glebe house (a house provided by the patron of the church). William's salary would have been less than thirty five pounds per annum.

However, in the year of Henrietta's baptism, their sponsor James Neild died without leaving a will and his huge two hundred and fifty thousand pound estate and responsibilities passed to his son, John Camden Neild.

John Camden Neild

This was not good news for the Pinnocks. Unlike his father, John Camden Neild was not known as a philanthropist and indeed soon developed an infamous reputation as a miser. People must have despaired at John Camden Neild's penny-pinching as the church steadily fell into disrepair for want of him spending money. It was said he once ordered the leaking church roof to be repaired with strips of calico rather than spend money on lead.

Such was the concern about the general dilapidation of the church that many years later (July 1846) it prompted a letter to *The Times* lamenting its poor state. Although the letter was principally addressed to the Dean and Chapter of Windsor (who held responsibility for the repair of the chancel) it bemoans the state of the church and church school in general:

"I feel that the bullets of Cromwell's soldiers in its roof did not work its ruin more effectively than the hands into which it has fallen in these latter times…"

Neild the Miser

John Camden Neild's preoccupation with saving and making money was legendary. It is said he chose to walk from his home in Chelsea to North Marston to collect rents rather than pay a carriage fare. He travelled in winter without a coat because he refused to buy one. At a time when much of the population lived in extreme poverty, it must have been scarcely believable that an immensely wealthy man should choose to live like this.

Neild's frugality extended to his unwillingness to repair the glebe house where the family lived which had been declared *"unfit for the residence of the Minister"* until a parliamentary grant helped towards the cost of improvements to the property.

The Rev William Pinnock died in March 1825 in his seventy-fifth year. A commemorative tablet to him and wife Sarah, who died in 1832 aged sixty-five, can be seen in North Marston church just to the right of the chancel arch.

The tablet was commissioned by Archdeacon Henry Tattam presumably by way of thanks to William Pinnock, his erstwhile tutor, but unfortunately he neglected to pay for it so the burden fell on the impoverished and bereaved Pinnock family!

Martha married William Neal, a local farmer. They married in North Marston under licence (as opposed to Banns). This may have been for speed, Martha being pregnant. Parental consent was required because Martha had not yet reached the age of twenty-one. One of the witnesses at Martha's wedding was her brother William (Junior) who seems to have been a regular witness at weddings: he formally witnessed seventeen ceremonies between 1812 and 1825!

We have no information about young Martha's life after marrying William. It is possible she was employed as a housekeeper or domestic servant by one of Neild's tenant farmers. Perhaps this was John Tattam at "Church Farm" whose son, Henry, had been privately tutored by Martha's late father and went on to become Archdeacon Tattam? In January 1826, the first-born child of Martha and William Neal was baptised. He was named William Pinnock Neal after Martha's father. A second son, Thomas Charles, followed in September 1827, but sadly he died before his second birthday.

Neild Attempts Suicide

Life must have been hard for the curate's daughter, recently bereaved of her father and with a baby and a toddler to care for. It is likely she struggled to make ends meet.

You can imagine Martha's dismay, therefore, when she opened the door one day in 1828 to find the unkempt figure of John Camden Neild standing there.

As usual, he expected to be housed and fed rather than have to stay at an inn or hotel. (The story goes that Martha even used to darn his underwear and stockings when he had gone to bed). To cap it all he seemed particularly morose and remote. He had fallen into a depression brought about by some failing investments.

We do not know what Martha thought of John Camden Neild: perhaps she despised him for the way his miserly obsession had allowed the church and glebe house to fall into disrepair and possibly made her father's last years unhappy ones; perhaps she pitied him as a sad and lonely creature who, despite his great wealth, had never known love and kindness; perhaps she feared him because of the total power he held over her family's welfare.

Accounts are unclear exactly what happened while Neild was at Rectory Farm in North Marston that time. It appears he went to an outbuilding and attempted to kill himself by cutting his throat but his life was saved by the prompt intervention of Martha Neal.

Neild's Bequest

Was John Camden Neild grateful to Martha for saving his life? When he eventually died of natural causes in August 1852 he left her nothing in his will. He left virtually his entire estate, eventually valued at two hundred and fifty thousand pounds, to Queen Victoria.

There was huge publicity about this before probate was granted, with many press articles speculating that his bequest was worth as much as five hundred thousand pounds! An article in The Times described Neild as *"possessed of an immense fortune, but...of eccentric and penurious habits."*

Although the bequest was initially declined by the Queen, she eventually accepted it after none of Neild's family had come forward to make a claim following a notice in The Times asking relatives of Neild to communicate with a London-based lawyer.

This came at a good time for Victoria. She and Prince Albert had acquired the ancient Balmoral Castle in Scotland and they had plans to build a much grander building on the site. Neild's bequest would easily provide the money they needed to do it.

Balmoral Castle

However, despite her authority, the Queen was unable to prevent the publication of *The Poor Relations of the Late Miser Neild* by John Wright in 1855.

As for Martha, things may not have been how they were reported. Most of the press reports about Neild's will claimed he had ignored Martha. This was consistent with the 'super miser' image that had been built up around him. Without doubt, Neild was spectacularly penny-pinching, but did he *never* really reward Martha for her timely intervention that day in 1828?

Neild's Quiet Benevolence

A letter which appeared in *The Morning Chronicle* on October 12th 1852 cast doubts about Neild's ingratitude to Martha. It appears that, when the executors of his will started going through his mass of private records, a different picture began to emerge. The letter explains:

"It has been said that the persons who found him at North Marston when he cut his throat some 25 years since, and but for whose interposition he must have perished, were not rewarded by him. This, it transpires, is incorrect inasmuch as in his life-time, the family were from time to time assisted and some of them were by his aid enabled to emigrate."

Neild's discreet acts of benevolence were substantiated by George Lipscomb in his *"History and Antiquities of the County of Buckingham"* (1847). He described John Camden Neild, whom he knew through their mutual friend Henry (Archdeacon) Tattam, as:

"..a gentleman of great opulence, who, amongst other instances of benevolence and patriotism, has considerately made allotments to numerous labourers, of small portions of land here, and in many other counties, to encourage industrious occupiers in spade husbandry, and to whom he also dispenses rewards in proportion to the quantity of product raised."

John Camden Neild's cash and stock books, which are archived at the Centre for Buckinghamshire Studies in Aylesbury, bear out this description. They also show that Neild was meticulous in recording every single transaction and that, in addition to renting out five farms in North Marston (which in 1840 totalled four hundred and eleven acres), he also farmed in North Marston himself. He employed a farm manager called Joseph Chew who furnished him with regular audits of his stock.

Other records confirm his reluctance to spend money. In 1832, he was served with a summons to appear before the magistrate at Quainton for non-payment of the Poor Rate concerning various North Marston properties belonging to him, including *"the farm of his own occupation"* on which he owed one hundred and ten pounds! However he paid his debts on the day he was due to appear.

In his will, Neild had made a specific request *"to be interred in Battersea Church, and in a vault as near as may be to my beloved father, James Neild."* In fact, both of Neild's parents were buried at Battersea.

Yet this request appears to have been ignored. The Queen is reported to have ordered that he was to be buried in the chancel at North Marston, as indeed he was, on 9th September 1852.

A commemorative tablet in the floor of the chancel marks the place of his interment (*pictured below*). Neild's executors are hardly likely to have opposed this as they were handsomely rewarded by the Queen.

St Mary's Church, Battersea

The commemorative tablet in the floor of the chancel

One of the executors was Archdeacon Henry Tattam, who also had conducted Neild's funeral service and who happened to be one of the Queen's chaplains. As a farmer's son, this North Marston lad had benefited from help and advice from Neild (and private tutoring from Rev William Pinnock) which got him through university and into holy orders. Perhaps it was he who wrote the *Morning Chronicle* letter which painted Neild in a more favourable light?

The Queen Rewards Martha

The Queen sought to make amends for Neild's *alleged* lack of gratitude to Martha Neal and granted her a pension of one hundred pounds a year, the equivalent today of £76,000! She sponsored a major renovation of North Marston church's crumbling chancel by one of the country's leading architects, Matthew Digby Wyatt. She commissioned a beautiful east window as a memorial to her eccentric benefactor.

Local opinion about the window appears not to have been all positive. The night before the window was to be dedicated by the Bishop of Oxford, and possibly as a way of embarrassing the very unpopular curate who was in office at the time, considerable damage was done to ornamental trees in the churchyard. For a while the bright light of public attention shone on North Marston, much being written about the Queen's charity in the major newspapers.

But was this just a clever bit of spin? At the end of the day, the Queen was left with a *huge* fortune which was easily enough to build the new Balmoral Castle with cash to spare. The £3,000 she spent on North Marston church and the settlements on Neild's executors, servants and his life-saver Martha were dwarfed by the enormity of Neild's bequest. Yet Victoria came out of the whole business looking generous.

Martha after North Marston

But what became of Martha? The last official record of Martha and William Neal in North Marston was the baptism of their son, Thomas Charles, in September 1827, a year before Martha intervened in John Camden Neild's suicide attempt. There is no reference to the Neal family anywhere in the censuses of 1841, 1851 or 1861 for North Marston.

However, years later, writing in his *Parish Chronicles*, the then vicar of North Marston, Rev Samuel James, sheds some light when he refers to Martha as *"wife of farmer and innkeeper."* Elsewhere he writes about an old parishioner, Joseph Neal, *"brother-in-law of Martha"*. The *Robson's Commercial Directory* for 1839, fifty years earlier, shows a Joseph Neal as *Innkeeper* at The Bell Inn, Winslow.

Martha certainly had left the area by the time of the 1871 census. By then widowed, sixty-five year old Martha was to be found living with her nephew Reginald Pinnock, an insurance clerk and son of Martha's brother, Rev George Pinnock (who followed in his father's footsteps to become a clergyman and died in 1880). They were living in Cheshunt, Middlesex, and Martha's occupation is described as *Annuitant*.

Martha must often have reflected on how different the outcome might have been if she had not prevented John Neild from taking his life in 1828, twenty years before he wrote his will and nine years before Queen Victoria came to the throne: no grand chancel at North Marston church, no life of comfort in her own final years and for the Queen and her successors.......no Balmoral Castle.

The Queen's commemorative window at North Marston was pictured in an article in The Illustrated London News of September 29th 1855

Eleven
DOCTOR SAMUEL JAMES
John Spargo

The Rev Samuel James arrived in North Marston in 1869 from Winkfield in Berkshire where he had been the rector for eleven years. Born in Colchester in 1830, he was married with a young family and determined to make his mark. This was his fifth benefice and he was to remain the vicar of North Marston for thirty-nine years. He soon found the village needed his firm handling to get things in good order. A year after his arrival he conducted a wedding (on Christmas Day 1870) and had this to say about it:

"The most orderly wedding ever celebrated in Northmarston Church. In former times weddings and funerals were so utterly devoid of all solemnity, and so noticeable for little else than rude and rough horseplay, that people were almost afraid to be married. We were solemnly assured by one respectable parishioner that she would never have been married here in those days. Till this wedding, order had not fully established itself, a churchwarden even of our own time having felt himself constrained to interfere on one occasion."

Rev Samuel James

Within a short time of his arrival he began to publish a parish magazine which he was to continue to do for most of the next thirty-four years, and through which he preached, scolded, cajoled and praised his parishioners. He was a man of strong opinion and robust Victorian (Anglican) ethics which he articulated through the pages of his magazine every month. His attitude to the people of the village was on the whole benign, although he was capable of waspish ridicule if he felt someone was unworthy of respect or was 'getting above his station'. He was also quite prepared to go into print to air his prejudices, which to modern eyes sometimes come across as extremely arrogant, as the following reference to The Red House (1882) illustrates:

"…Mr Brazier's Red House, ugly but substantial….It is not 'half a bad house' if it did not stand in the middle of the village, where no gentleman would live by choice, but where it is convenient to be able to live for want of a house nearer College."

As the parish clergyman, he was concerned about the morality and behaviour of people in the village and was quick to admonish anyone who over-stepped the line, but there was one person who seems to have been far beyond redemption and when she died, she drew an unusual tirade of invective from him (1875):

"Died, a woman who was formerly one of the most desperately and deplorably wicked women that ever led souls to ruin, and whose history was a history of the vilest and most awful character……Years ago, hopes and opportunities of amendment were defiantly thrown away, and if some sad and terrible things could be added, our tale would seem too awful to be true; it is nevertheless all

fact…..this is written for the admonition of the living who knew this once child of Satan."

In common with the policy of the church at the time, Rev James held censorious views about illegitimate births and refused to baptise children born *illegitimately* in the same service with legitimate children and, furthermore, was clearly reluctant to recognise the father of an illegitimate child as one of its sponsors. He writes in *The Northmarston Magazine* in 1873:

"*Baptism, after the service, of an illegitimate child, there having been one during the service of a legitimate child. The vicar accepted the father of the illegitimate child as one of the sponsors, on his promise, given solemnly in God's sight within Church walls, that he would marry the mother, and care for the religious training of the child. If he should fail in a promise given in these circumstances, evil will assuredly, sooner or later, overtake him. The vicar would not be at all sorry to receive a monition from his ecclesiastical superiors forbidding him to admit such sponsors, as he would then be relieved of a very unpleasant responsibility."*

Rev James clearly considered himself the village patriarch and, although nowadays his views seem unbelievably elitist, he was a product of his time and his unquestionable function was to be the shepherd of his flock.

By today's standards, Rev James was *politically* outspoken and not in the least afraid to air his views in print. British politics in the late Victorian era were dominated by two political parties: the Liberals and the Conservatives. Rev James was a staunch Liberal and often aired his Liberal doctrine on national and local matters. Another village Liberal was John White, the blacksmith. When White completed his new brick-built forge in 1891, the scale surpassed Rev James's expectations. In a tongue-in-cheek reference to White's liberalism, Rev James named the new construction "Liberty Hall":

"*We did not do justice to Mr White's new Hall, which (when we wrote) looked as if it was only going to be a blacksmith's shed, but which now has risen into what might be called a sort of 'Liberty Hall', in which public meetings might well be held, and Liberty of speech indulged….We respectfully take off our hat to Liberty Hall, hoping that it will be also (non-politically) Liberality Hall, Loyalty Hall, Love and Good Neighbourhood Hall…."*

Throughout the 1870s there was a tension between Rev Samuel James, the self-appointed patriarch, and a local man called Thomas Biggs, a wealthy farmer and land-owner who clashed with Rev James on a number of issues. It is likely tensions arose as soon as Rev James arrived in the village as he promptly assumed responsibility for chairing the Parish Vestry (effectively, the fore-runner to the Parish Council) in a role he described as being the "village mayor". Despite having been elected to this role a number of times prior to Rev James's arrival in North Marston, Biggs was relegated to other less prominent roles on behalf of the Parish Vestry throughout the 1870s whilst Samuel James was the "mayor". Biggs only recovered this status in 1880; thereafter Biggs chaired the Parish Vestry for most of the following decade.

In 1876, and in the midst of his term as "village mayor", Rev Samuel James founded an exclusive private school in the village which he called **Schorne College** (*see Chapter Twelve*) apparently modelled on Rugby School. He suspended publication of the parish magazine for two years whilst he was setting up the school. When the magazine reappeared in 1878, it was as *The Schornian*, a combination of a school record and a parish chronicle. Thereafter, it combined both functions.

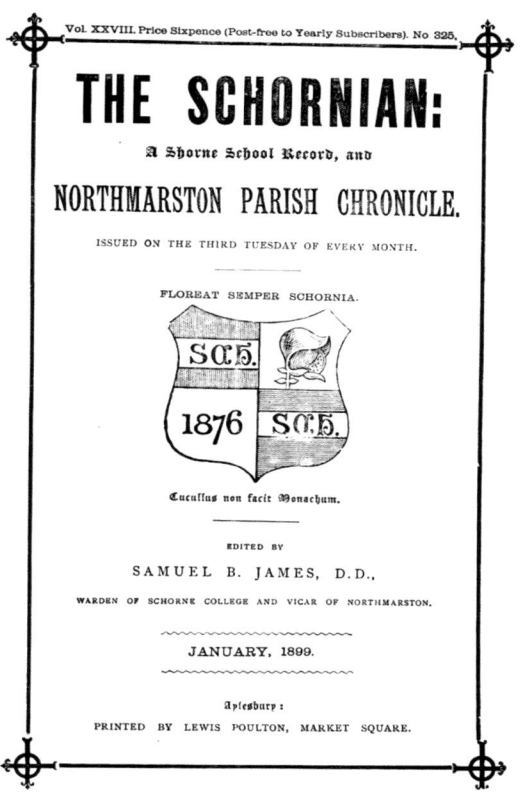

Thomas Biggs

In 1882, Samuel James was awarded a Doctorate of Divinity from Trinity College, Dublin, thereafter entitling him to be known as *Doctor* Samuel James.

Once Thomas Biggs regained his influence in the 1880s, there followed an extraordinary resolution at the Parish Vestry of March 1881, effectively accusing the Rev James of abusing his position and parish funds. *Tellingly, Rev James makes no reference to this in his Village Chronicle.*

The animosity between the two men climaxed in a court case brought by Biggs following remarks about him published in *The Schornian* to which he took strong exception. When Rev James refused to apologise or retract his words, Biggs sued him and won. It is likely the case split the village into two camps. Rev James chose not to print anything about the outcome in *The Schornian*.

Thomas Biggs went on to become the Chairman of North Marston's Parish Council, a District Councillor, Chairman of the District Council and a Justice of the Peace. Clearly, however, the animosity prevailed: as late as 1900, Biggs summoned four 'Schorne Boys' for damage and trespass. The case was dismissed by the magistrates as trivial and unproven but the prosecution may have been intended simply to provoke or embarrass Dr James ….who took delight in printing the full story of Biggs's defeat.

In his private life, Samuel James had been distressed by the sudden death of his nine year-old daughter, Evelyn Blanche, in August 1873. Her unexpected loss clearly affected him greatly. Then twenty-three years later it was the equally sudden death of his wife Susan that devastated him and left him depressed and deprived. Thereafter his writing in *The Schornian* became perfunctory. His bouts of depression impacted on his ability and willingness to engage in the social aspects of his role. His eyesight deteriorated with cataracts which fortunately he was able to have treated to preserve a measure of sight.

Meanwhile, two of his sons had followed their father into the church: one of his sons, St John James (*pictured*) was awarded the joint benefice of Pitchcott and Oving and was a frequent preacher at North Marston;

another son, A H James, was to succeed his father as vicar at North Marston.

St John James

There was also a daughter named Susan Katherine who was born in 1870. Later in life, Susan was to become a stalwart of the parish church's Sunday school, effectively taking over its administration. She was also responsible for a scheme whereby London children were 'fostered' by village families to give the children a summer holiday in the countryside, presaging the wartime evacuations that were to take place forty years later. The scheme ran from 1893 to 1903. "Miss James", as she was always known, never married.

Miss James in the High Street in 1920s

Ivy Wheeler remembers Miss James well:

"My grampy John Carter used to take out Miss James in her wagon and he always wore a top hat. Miss James went to live on her own down the bottom of Quainton Road but in the end she turned to drink and couldn't look after herself. She was a cultured lady though and when my dad died she wrote a letter to my mum in a 'lady's' handwriting. Miss James used to paint and she painted my portrait when I was a girl – it was lovely with pink satin and ivy leaves round it."

Chris Holden also has memories of Miss James:

"At the very bottom of Quainton Road facing you on the bend was where Miss James lived. She was a very pleasant lady, very elegant, and always wore black. She put an umbrella through her arms at the back to keep her back straight and upright as she walked. She was a 'lady'."

Eveline Parker recalled how Miss James's life ended (in 1943):

"When Miss James died in her cottage at the bottom of Quainton Road, my husband Sid and Uncle Ted Dudley, the undertaker, went down to collect her body and they became covered in fleas. It was so sad, as she'd been such a refined lady and such a very good artist. Several of her works now reside in various homes around the village. She just didn't know how to look after herself when she lived on her own."

Following his wife's death, and progressively towards the end of the 1890s, Dr. James was visibly losing the energy and enthusiasm that had driven him for almost thirty years. He finally ceased writing *The Schornian* in February 1904.

Samuel James had previously written a number of times about his depression and sense of his own frailty. His final demise was dramatic. In August 1909 he was found dead in a garden pond. The public explanation was that he had suffered a heart attack whilst trimming a hedge and had fallen into the water but it is a possibility that, overcome by depression, he decided to end his life. We shall never know for certain.

Strangely, nearly forty years earlier, when a local woman had committed suicide in a pond in the village, Rev James had written in *The Chronicle*: *"We have a theory of our own that every village pond of a certain age is a murderer, so to speak....has killed its victim, so to speak."*

We shall never know the true meaning of this cryptic and chillingly prescient comment. What we *do* know, however, is that the legacy of this strong and influential man was felt in North Marston for many years after his death.

Rev James's final resting place near the south door of the church

Twelve
SCHORNE COLLEGE 1876-1910
John Spargo

*Schorne College which stood adjacent to St Mary's Church
(the site is now part of the churchyard)*

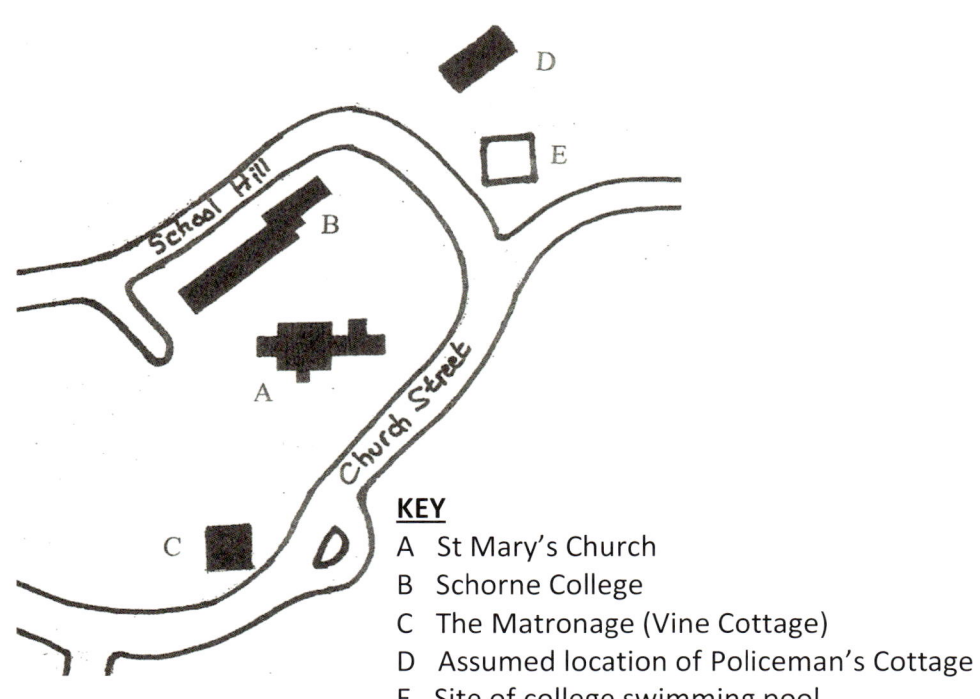

KEY
A St Mary's Church
B Schorne College
C The Matronage (Vine Cottage)
D Assumed location of Policeman's Cottage
E Site of college swimming pool

Arguably, Rev Samuel James's greatest achievement during his years in North Marston was the creation of **Schorne College** which occupied a large sweep of the landscape to the north of the church and several adjacent properties (s*ee location plan*).

It seems more than likely he had the building of the college in mind when he first arrived in the village in 1869 as he wasted no time during the next few years in acquiring the site from a private owner.

The College Plot

In 1869, when Rev Samuel James arrived in the village, the land on which the college would eventually be built was owned by Mr John Holden and Mr John Price.

At this time the overcrowding of the churchyard was a significant problem. In 1871 the vicar wrote that *"offensive mortal remains are frequently being dug up….the churchyard surely needs enlargement."* However, the barrier to enlarging the churchyard seemed to be cost, as the vicar wrote: *"The obstacle seems to be the very high price asked by the owners of the two contiguous pieces, Mr John Holden and Mr John Price."*

In this same year Rev James acquired the land *himself* (he stresses in the parish magazine that the land was owned by him in his *private* capacity) and he was petitioning the Bishop of Oxford for the land to be consecrated as he was donating it to the church *"for the Interment of the Dead of the Parish of Northmarston."*

He then set about establishing a fund for the churchyard enlargement and in 1872 the appeal was in full swing: a donation of thirteen shillings and two pence was made to the fund by the Wesleyan Chapel, and Penny Readings in the parish schoolroom raised one pound five shillings and four pence.

The combination of the *naming and shaming* of the land owners and the public generosity towards the fund-raising seems to have been effective.

By 1875 the plot which Samuel James had acquired had been transferred by deed for use as a churchyard and was fenced and consecrated. However in 1876 the newly built Schorne College would open on that very same site!

One can only speculate as to the outcry which must have arisen amongst the donors to the churchyard extension when they discovered that a large area of the plot was now set aside for the building of a private school!

In fact, only a small area of ground in the churchyard was left available for new burials in the end (the first interment taking place there in 1875).

There are a number of interpretations of Samuel James's actions, some charitable and others less so. A charitable interpretation is that Samuel James *genuinely* intended the land to be used as an extension to the churchyard and his plans for a college on the site emerged subsequently. However, this is highly unlikely for we know that the College was operational by 1876 (with five boys to start with) and, as the planning, financing and building of Schorne College together with recruitment of staff must have taken *at least* three years and possibly four, preparatory planning must have started in about 1872. This raises the following two questions: why did Samuel James give away to the church the land on which he wished the college to be built and how would the church benefit from this?

Being realistic, there were clearly incentives for assigning the land to the church with his future college in mind:

a) Building on land owned by the church (and he may have made this a conditional covenant in the deeds of assignment to the church) perhaps offered solutions to local planning concerns or gave financial advantages to the college, equivalent to charitable status?

b) Politically, the income derived by the church from any rent paid for the lease of the land could take the edge off accusations that he was profiteering or that the college represented a conflict of interest with his clerical duties.

c) He almost certainly acquired the land at a very cheap price *on the assumption it was going to be used by the church* and he was confident he would be able to persuade the Diocesan authorities to permit the building of a college on it, especially one that would bring income to the church, raise the church's profile and offer bespoke education to clergymen's sons.

Despite this, it seems the vicar considered himself to be out of pocket through the donation of the churchyard ground, even though it had been made to appear as a charitable gift at the time.(He had obviously hoped that the donations towards the 'churchyard extension' would match his initial outlay in purchasing the land!)

In summarising (in 1888) what the parish owed him he refers to *"the loss of £200 by the Churchyard enlargement"* amongst other debts. The amount he felt he was owed for the churchyard had increased by fifty pounds in a couple of years as, in 1886, he had written:

"Bye the bye, some day when we have the time and inclination, we may as well start a subscription to cover the £150 which that Churchyard enlargement cost us over and above the subscriptions we obtained."

Interestingly, he makes no mention of the fact he built a successful private school on the land within a year of 'giving' it to the church!

The source of the extensive capital investment for the college building (by local builder John Price) was never disclosed but it is probable James had partners in the venture. Once operational, the college continued to expand quickly with James gradually buying neighbouring properties as they became available. In fact, the first buildings were purchased before the college was built and were referred to as "Policeman's Cottages" (as the village constable was housed there before Garfield House was built). These cottages became known as "Masters' Lodges" and were eventually painted red and thatched. They were later demolished and replaced by a house named "Schorne Lodge" (now re-named "College House") which was built on the site in the early 1900s.

Schorne Lodge in the 1920s

In 1882 the Vicar bought 11 Church Street, a detached house next door to the church, for two hundred and five pounds. This building was to house the younger pupils attending Schorne College as well as acting as a sick bay (matronage). For most of its history the house was officially known as "Vine Cottage" but, in all references in *The Schornian*, Dr James referred to it as "The Matronage" since this was its function for Schorne College. (The house is known by this name today).

Samuel James was clearly pleased with the healthiness of Vine Cottage as in an open letter to parents of boys at Schorne College in 1884 he wrote (following a local outbreak of Scarlet Fever):

"Our isolation, ventilation and attention in the Sanatorium at Vine Cottage is perfect; the rooms there are scarcely half full ….you know what our air and water are... and nine years' freedom is the best guarantee of the healthiness of our buildings and our village."

In 1887, Samuel James assigned the property to his son, Harold James. In 1891, John Julian James (who was then Headmaster of Schorne College) was living at Vine Cottage. Harold James subsequently assigned it, in 1894, to his brother, Samuel Frank Gerard James who, in 1905, assigned it to his brother, the Rev St John B James. In 1905 the property was leased to Susan Katharine James, Samuel James's daughter, for a period of seven years at an annual rent of sixteen pounds. Thus Vine Cottage was either owned or occupied by a member of the James family for a period of

Vine Cottage in 1898

The holes for washbasins in Vine Cottage attic

about thirty years. The 1891 census shows there were twelve pupils boarding at Vine Cottage on the night of the census, the youngest being ten years of age and the oldest nineteen. They originated from all over the country, the most distant location being North Yorkshire. There remains to this day evidence of the house's former function; in the attic one can still see traces of the wash-basins for the small boys in the dormitory (*see picture above*). At about the time of this considerable expansion of the college's footprint, there were concerns about the vicar's priorities and, in 1881, extraordinarily, he was called to account by the Vestry Meeting, the fore-runner to the Parish Council, which raised a number of issues and concerns about his actions:

> A resolution passed unanimously at the Vestry. That this Vestry is of opinion that the Vicar ought to be further called upon to give some information with respect to the paths through the Churchyard. The expenditure of the money he has collected in the name & on behalf of the Church & Parish and of the ground & buildings for which he begged the money to pay, with the avowed desire of building a Reading Room Library &c. for the benefit of the parish And this Vestry considers it to be the duty of the parish Churchwarden to use every lawful means in his power to obtain such information and secure justice for the parish
>
> for the Vestry – Joseph Gregory Chairman

We do not know how the vicar responded to this call to account. Needless to say, *The Schornian* carries no mention. Samuel James was very particular about the type of pupils welcomed at Schorne College: they were exclusively the sons of clergymen or the sons of senior military officers.

The sons of tradesmen, however wealthy, were *not* accepted. Rev James sets the tone when he says in his introductory remarks about the college at the front of *The Schornian* that parents of boys attending Schorne School: "*are mostly from Harrow, Eton, Winchester, Rugby, Charterhouse, Marlborough and other public schools.*" With a concentration on sporting prowess as well as academic achievement, it is probable the College embodied James's personal ethos in the pursuit of excellence through competition. The College prospectus promoted the School by saying it "*prepares boys for the Universities, Public Schools, Army and Navy, Examinations and Commercial Life.*"

In *The Schornian* of 1881, Rev James wrote:

"*Very small boys (for whom the School was originally founded, but parents were reluctant to remove them as they grew older) are especially well grounded, before they are allowed to advance; thoroughness and completeness being considered of the utmost importance. Domestic care and home culture, with systematic religious instruction, both in College and at daily Choral Service in Church, supplemented by Sunday Afternoon Lectures in Church and Hall, have been altogether satisfactory to parents of the boys who have spontaneously and with the utmost kindness expressed much warm approbation; as also in regard to Diet, Matron's care of Wardrobe and other such matters, sometimes neglected.*"

The school's prospectus described the buildings as consisting of "*good class-rooms, studies, three very large dormitories and several smaller ones, bedrooms, matron's rooms, master's rooms, prefect's study, library, large dining-hall, bath-rooms, gymnasium, lavatories, bathrooms, kitchen offices etc.*" There was also a "*Swimming-Bath (used in winter for skating), Cricket-Shed, Football-Field and Athletic Bar.*"

Towards the latter years the fees for attending Schorne College were eighteen guineas a term, with an extra fee of one guinea per term payable for extra lessons such as Greek, German and Music.

Pupils would have travelled to the College mainly by railway, alighting at Winslow, Granborough Road or Aylesbury Stations.

SCHORNE SCHOOL, Winslow, Bucks.

Prepares Boys for the Universities, Public Schools, Army and Navy, Examinations, and Commercial Life.

RAILWAY STATIONS:

WINSLOW:	GRANBOROUGH ROAD:	AYLESBURY:
L. & N.-W. Railway.	Metropolitan & Gt. Cent. Railways.	Midland, Gt. Cent., L. N.-W. & Met. Railways.

Principal - - JOHN F. C. KNIGHT.

Head Master - S. H. WHITHAM, (Royal Academy and Guildhall).

ASSISTED BY A STRONG STAFF OF RESIDENT MASTERS.

A page from the College Prospectus from its latter years

*Schorne College from the south-east
(the church is just out of view to the left and the village school is behind)*

The school curriculum included English, Scripture, Latin, French, Mathematics, Chemistry, Shorthand, Book-keeping and Drawing. Optional extra subjects were Greek, German and Music.

The school operated a Code of Conduct and infringements in school rules resulted in the loss of conduct marks. For example talking at meals was punishable by the loss of between one and fifteen conduct marks. School hours were from 9.00am to 4.15pm; Wednesdays and Saturdays were half-holidays; prayers were held in the Great Hall morning and evening.

The school masters (there was one master to every eight boys) also had a set of rules such as not smoking or reading a newspaper in front of the boys.

Samuel James designed a school crest and cypher "*Cucullus non facit Monachum*" which translates as "The cowl does not make the monk" presumably alluding to the unusual choice of the monkshood flower that forms part of the college crest. It is to be supposed that what he was saying is "never judge a book by its cover" or "don't rely on appearances", perhaps a message to those who might have looked down on his rural academic enterprise?

Two un-named Schornian boys

The school crest

Writing in 1885, Dr James (as he was known by then, having received his Doctorate in 1881) described the college as *"having wide roots for so young a school"*. He forecast that *"three hundred boys will have entered Schorne from its commencement to Christmas this year"* including nineteen from India, two from Australia, one from New Zealand and eighteen from Wales.

Samuel James was the Principal of the College and, although often claiming in *The Schornian* to being impoverished, he is likely to have drawn a healthy salary from the fees to the College as well as receiving royalties on the sale of his publications *and* his stipend as a clergyman.

In 1893 he handed over control of Schorne College to his son Samuel Frank Gerard James who had formerly been the *Mathematical Master* there. Later, "SFGJ", as his father referred to him, also became the Chairman of the Parish Council.

Steadily from its inception in 1876, the college thrived and expanded: corner-stones for a new wing were laid by two of Samuel James's sons in October 1878 and an external swimming bath created in that same month; the dining hall and the swimming pool were enlarged in 1880; by 1886 the College had thirty rooms; in 1890 a college laundry was built in Schorne Lane adjacent to the Wesleyan Church. The vicar described it as *"a building about 50 feet long by about 15 wide, substantial and neat-looking."*

The college 'swimming bath' (*see location map*) which officially opened in October 1878 appears to have started life as a fresh-water pond, and must have been quite large: in January 1879 it was being used as a skating rink on which *"about nine boys learned to skate"*. Writing in *The Schornian*, Rev James described it as:

"...a great source of amusement; some fish have been put in and live bravely there, cleansing the water but testifying to its healthiness; boats are sailed and general resort is had to water side."

The pool was enlarged in 1880 and upgraded with changing facilities. By March 1886 the College boys had to make an annual payment of ten shillings to use it.

The dining hall

In addition to acquiring village buildings, the College also used a local field as a cricket pitch. The protective 'hoof slippers', worn by the horse used for mowing and rolling the cricket pitch, were found in the workshop of Ted Dudley, the local builder.

no way of knowing for sure. After its closure the building was bought by Ted Dudley who demolished part of it and used the material in buildings around the village (one of which was named "Schorne Stones").

The protective shoes worn by the horse when working on the college's cricket field

Although it was not without its critics, the College was a major employer and brought considerable business to the village. Ivy Wheeler remembers:

"Schorne Stones" cottages in Quainton Road

"My granny Julia Carter....lived at the bottom of School Hill at number three and her husband, John, was the groom at the College then and Julia's sons all went to Vine Cottage (the Matronage now I think) every night to clean their shoes to earn a few pence. The boys lived there and they were all gentlemen's sons; it was an annexe to the College. My granny Julia had a shop in her front room at the bottom of School Hill and the college boys used to go there to buy their sweets from her."

A woman stands at her garden gate with the college looming behind her

The College finally closed its doors to boys in 1910, shortly after the death of its founder. Rumour has sometimes abounded that its closure was due to a typhus epidemic though we have no evidence to support this. It is possible that, after the death of its founder, and with the impending outbreak of world war, the school became non-viable. We have

The section of the college building nearest the top of School Hill remained in use as tenanted accommodation until the early 1930s and was lived in for a time by the Harwood family.

Robin Harwood remembers:

"I was born in 1924 in the cottage near the Holy Well; then I lived with my family in part of the old Schorne College until I was six years old. Most of the old building had been pulled down by then and there were lots of shrubs and trees growing on the site in the ruins. We lived in the end bit nearest the top of School Hill. Ted Dudley, the builder, had bought it and we had to pay him rent of 2/6d per week. I remember going down the road and giving the rent to his wife, Mrs Dudley, who had been the headmistress of the school. Apart from the bit we lived in, there were still left standing twelve of the old boys' toilets – just wooden seats with holes in - along the side of the road opposite what is now the school. We used to keep our milk cold by hanging it down the well behind the College."

Eventually this remaining part of the college was also demolished and the site subsequently appropriated by the church for an extension to the churchyard removing all traces of Dr James's imposing establishment that had influenced North Marston for over thirty years.

The church with the college buildings visible on the right hand side and two college boys posing nonchalantly by the churchyard's boundary hedge

Thirteen
THE VICTORIAN VILLAGE
John Spargo

Introduction

By the 1870s, barely one hundred years after "Enclosure", the shape of the village had changed to something we would recognize today. The plan of the village from an Ordnance Survey map (surveyed in the late 1870s) shows the village green had all but disappeared and that a significant reduction in the width of the highway had resulted from residents 'appropriating' the highway verges and, in places, building property on what had been the village green (*see Chapter Seven*).

The highway at the top of Quainton Road, where the village hall now stands, was re-routed to form a new junction thus freeing up land subsequently used for Garfield House and Melba Cottage. (The original road still runs alongside Eleanor Cottage towards The Wheatsheaf). A small cottage stood on the plot of land at the top of the High Street that within a few years would be the controversial site for Henry John Holden's new building, Shakespeare House.

Shakespeare House (in centre of picture) circa 1900

An extract from the Ordnance Survey map of North Marston based on a survey of the late 1870s

The village enjoyed the spin-off benefits of the private Schorne College which stood in the north shadow of the church on land that now forms part of the churchyard (*see Chapter Twelve*).

The windmill, in what was to become the garden of Mill House, was still standing, as marked on the map, before its collapse in a violent storm (*see Chapter Five*). Portway was virtually building-free and the site where the village hall now stands was an empty field.

Village life in those times was, for many, very hard indeed. With no welfare state, illness was dreaded as only the wealthy could afford to pay for a doctor or a hospital bed. Benefactors would sometimes donate infirmary 'tickets' to be used by the poor at The Royal Bucks Infirmary in Aylesbury, which itself was built using money from subscription and donations. (A proportion of the collections taken at North Marston Church was given to The Royal Infirmary). If people became too frail to support themselves they relied on the Parish Board of Guardians for food and fuel; as a last resort they might be sent by the Board to the Winslow Union Workhouse where husbands and wives were segregated and conditions would have been very grim.

The former Winslow Union Workhouse

For most villagers there was no inside toilet or running water; the village had no gas or electricity so lighting came from oil lamps or candles. The roads were rough tracks covered with broken stones and in winter they would have become muddy and rutted. Homes were often draughty and damp with leaking roofs; some even collapsed in bad weather. Keeping warm in the winter must have been a constant struggle.

However, all was set to change. The last decades of the nineteenth century were to see an unprecedented boom in commerce and building throughout the village, reflecting the growth in the national economy and the economies of all European countries.

By great fortune, we have a remarkably full account of village life in the latter quarter of the nineteenth century through the writings of the vicar, Dr Samuel James, who published a monthly parish magazine called *The Schornian*.

Dr Samuel James
Vicar of North Marston 1869-1909

The Schornian is a gift to us from a time when village life was radically different from nowadays. In the early years of its publication, James wrote about a village that was virtually self-contained, and where a cluster of ancient families provided the employment and labour in respective roles that had remained constant for generations. But the progress and technology that swept into the village in the latter decades of the nineteenth century meant nothing was to be the same again. North Marston became connected with a wider community. The historic framework of social order was challenged. In the space of a generation, the population was presented with opportunities previously only available to the wealthy.

Public transport, compulsory state education, communication technology, local government and the rising influence of the middle-class were to transform rural England forever.

The Victorian Village Building Boom

Schorne College built in 1876

The first sign of change in North Marston was the building of Schorne College in the mid-1870s. The brain-child of Dr Samuel James, this elite private college was to dominate the landscape to the north of the church for over half a century and provide an income for many villagers.

Within a short space of time, North Marston then saw the building (or extensive renovation) of dozens of new properties: Winkfield House, The Laurels, The Elms, Camden Villas, Garfield House, Glebe Farm, The Red House, The Mill House, The Gables, Marston House, Forge Cottage, Gordon Cottage, Bankside, Brook Farm, Prune Cottage and Holden's Shakespeare House….the grandest of them all.

Gordon Cottage, after extensive renovation, in 1905

He was sure that the advent of Schorne College marked a turning point in the welfare of the village. In 1884 he wrote:

"The death-rate in Northmarston has materially diminished since Schorne College was started. We put it down to the removal of unhealthy cottages, the good example of sanitation set by Schorne, the better wages and consequently better food of labourers…..The death rate, which when we came was two per cent per annum, is now at the lower rate of one per cent per annum."

He praised householders who sought to smarten up their properties. In 1885 he wrote:

"We note improvement after improvement in our village. Mrs Webb's cottage is having its

Winkfield House in 1905

Dr James took a paternalistic pride in village "improvements" (as he called them) and assisted in the naming of properties such as Gordon Cottage and Winkfield House.

railings enlarged; Marston House is having ornamental gates added by Mrs Tattam; Mr Watkins palings are looking bright with new and tasteful-coloured paint; and Mr John Holden's Shakespeare House with its new inscriptions so well lettered and not erroneously punctuated or badly spelled would have pleased the bard himself."

The Gables

Camden Villas in 1896

Dr James returned to this theme of village improvement regularly. In July 1888 he wrote:

"The village is looking up in the building way, as evidenced by the erection of "Brook Cottages", "Garfield House", and above all "Camden Villas". The Vicar is answerable for the pulling down of various wretched cottages, and yet there are some persons, possibly, who would pretend to think that the tumble-down hovels which stood where Camden Villas stand, dangerous and uninhabitable though they were, are a loss!....The practice we have introduced of naming houses is very useful, and we have now, greatly to public convenience and private advantage, "Ivy Cottage", "Clare Cottage", "Shakespeare House", "Rose Cottage", "Marston House", "Red House" and various others."

Samuel James was still praising villagers for their modernizing and development into the Edwardian era. In September 1902, when he wrote *"Young Mr. Dudley's house is nearing completion we observe: and a very pretty cottage-villa sort of dwelling it looks"*, he was referring to The Gables built by the village builder, Ted Dudley, in readiness for his forthcoming marriage.

Dr James saw improvements to the village as a barometer of village morality. He wrote:

"We hope our people will go on building, and improving, educating and being educated, becoming independent and outspoken for God and His Truth, for order and quietute and peace...."

Miss Tattam's Marston House

Further words on the subject of housing in the village appeared in *The Schornian* in January 1902 where Dr James wrote:

"When we came here it was difficult to get a house or cottage; now it is easy enough and the difficulty is rather to find tenants. But there are also some twenty new or as good as new houses and enlarged houses, and cottages, enlarged or newly-built or much improved since 1870."

"Botheration Gates" Removed

In 1888, the village saw the removal of the gates across the Granborough Road at a place called Hagditch, which themselves were a remnant from the enclosure of the village in the late 1700s. *The Bucks Herald* carried a report of the event:

*"The Ecclesiastical Commissioners have at last removed two gates which blocked the way and made it necessary for passengers between Winslow and North Marston to dismount at both ends of a piece of land called "Hagditch", on the Winslow side of Marston….The numerous and frequent visitors to Schorne College….will be gainers by the change being now approachable from both Aylesbury and Winslow without having to open those "botheration gates". But the village children will lose a good many pennies and half-pennies, and an occasional sixpence and three-penny piece by the removal of the said obstruc*tions."

Those last decades of Victoria's reign saw huge improvements in hygiene and sanitation, including the improved access to water throughout the village. Up until the 1890s, water was drawn from Schorne's Well or from private wells sunk by householders. Typically, tenants would have had no private well and so would have had to walk to the well in Schorne Lane and then carry the water in pails on a yoke to their houses. With the arrival of the Parish Council, this state of affairs was reviewed. At a Parish Council meeting on 11th January 1897:

"..the Chairman of the District Council submitted plans for the conveyance of Holy Well water to the Lower End of the village where a pump will be erected for that part of the population, to save them the walk of half a mile or over to fetch their water." (The Schornian)

A cistern was dug at a cost of twenty pounds at the top of Quainton Road and a water pump was fitted. This was repeated in the High Street and outside Abbotts Cottage in Church Street. In a slightly whimsical account in The Schornian, Dr James writes:

"Yes, all of you "down-towners" will be glad and gratified, and we hope will find the water good and abundant".

The private wells and street pumps were to be the source of domestic water in North Marston until the late 1920s and early 1930s when mains water was piped into the village. In his Pastoral Review of 1895, Dr James looked back on his twenty-five years at North Marston and summarised the changes seen in that time:

"An enlarged Vicarage House, an enlarged and altogether improved Parish School and new playground. Our secular progress as a parish has been very great in the matter of charities, sanitation, improved and multiplied house-building of the better class, seeping away of gates on the public road, a Post Office in place of a pillar box, two deliveries and dispatches, a telegraph and money order office, PO Savings Bank etc, the commodious Labourers' Barn, the growth of healthy public opinion…."

The water pump in Quainton Road being use by a "down-towner" circa 1900

Two women at the High Street water pump circa 1905

Most of these improvements resulted from a plethora of national reforming statutes that sought to provide all people, irrespective of wealth and status, with an acceptable standard of living and, above all, access to opportunities for self-betterment. Yet all these changes relied on an effective and *accountable* administration. This was to be the Age of Committees, where an astonishing array of bodies was formed to ensure representation in decision-making. One of the final pieces of the jigsaw to fall into place was the *Parish Council*.

The Way the Village was Managed

To understand the role of the Parish Council we need to look at what it replaced: the *Parish Vestry*. Until the creation of the North Marston Parish Council in 1894, most of the administration of the village was done by the Parish Vestry. Parish Vestries were governing bodies responsible for raising a rate, helping the poor, repairing the highways and electing village constables. Any *male* ratepayer could attend the Vestry Meeting and vote on issues, principally the election of the village officers. Vestry Meetings were generally chaired by the vicar and held in the church vestry, hence their name.

Throughout most of the Victorian period, the parish Vestry Meetings had to decide which local men were to be Guardians, Constables, Surveyors (for road maintenance) and Overseers of the Poor. These were not paid functions and so responsibilities were rotated annually amongst a 'pool' of potential candidates who were elected by those who owned land or property (thus requiring them to pay the Poor Rate). Some men undertook the same role for years on end.

From time to time, the Vestry was also called upon to deal with a parishioner where the conduct of that individual was against the parish's interest. In a small village that led to battle lines being drawn and old scores settled. The Vestry Meetings empowered local people to challenge even the most influential of residents.

As the note from the Vestry Book shows, the Vestry Meeting of 20th March 1884 clearly had concerns about the scale of John Holden's development that became Shakespeare House at the top of the High Street (*see below*).

Sometimes a village dispute might be beyond the Vestry Meeting to resolve and could end up in court such as one celebrated case in North Marston involving the vicar and a local farmer. (*This is covered more fully in Chapter Eleven*).

> 20th March 1884
>
> It is the unanimous opinion of this Vestry that the Enchroachments by Mrs John Holden be brought and laid before the Magistrates by the Surveyors.
>
> W. Hood
> John Clarke
> Ralph Tattam
> Joseph Gregory
> John Chapman
> W. A. Clarke
> Jno. Geo. Clarke
> H. Clarke

Overseers of the Poor were elected every Easter and their main job was collecting the Poor Rate. This was a local tax paid by all householders and land-holders and was the source of revenue for the welfare of the poorest in the community *and* for the maintenance of public roads.

Overseers continued to be elected until the formation of the Parish Council in 1894. In the era before state welfare, the Vestry monitored the village's most impoverished residents and collected a local tax to pay towards their needs.

Surveyors were required to be appointed by each parish from 1836 to keep parish roads in good order. Then, in 1862, counties were divided into Highway Districts governed under a Highway Board. Each parish had an elected representative on the Highway Board. The state of the highway and the demarcation of responsibility for road maintenance were thereafter to be a constant source of dispute.

Guardians were annually elected and were the parish's representative on the Poor Law Union responsible for the administration of the local work-house.

Parish Constables were law enforcement officers, usually part-time, serving a parish. In North Marston, in most years the village had six constables. On the 6th February 1857, when the Buckinghamshire Constabulary was established, it marked the eventual end of the long tradition of the locally elected parish constable.

However, progress in the county constabulary's policing of rural parishes appears to have been slow as in North Marston the Vestry continued to appoint parish constables until 1877, twenty years after the County Constabulary was established.

We are fortunate that the Vestry Book for the village spanning the years 1863-1894 has survived, so we can see all the key decisions it made during this pivotal time as well as the names of all the men co-opted into the roles listed earlier.

The Parish Council inherited a tiny residue of the civic responsibilities that systematically had been lifted from the Parish Vestry with the creation of regional and national institutions to deal with Education, Health, Poverty, Roads and Local Policing.

However, tensions sometimes arose between North Marston's Parish Council and the next tier above it, South Winslow District Council, concerning responsibility for road and footpath repairs. These will have been sensitive issues as the Chairman of the District Council was the local (North Marston) farmer Tom Biggs. As an example of the feelings aroused by these issues, the account in *The Schornian* of the parish council discussion in March 1897 is illustrative:

"Mr. W. Tattam proposed a strong resolution threatening the District Council with an appeal to the County Council, if the former body did not repair paths and act impartially with regard to roads….Mr. Albert White spoke out respecting the contempt meted out to the parish council by the district council and noted the absence of the parish District Councillor from the meeting."

By the time the parish council was getting into its stride, Dr James had become an elderly, frail man and no longer a driving force behind village *improvements*. His private college was to survive into the first years of the twentieth century, but the Great War was to sweep away the spirit of enterprise and initiative that had been the impetus for an unprecedented thirty-year period in Victorian times that transformed North Marston forever.

A plan showing many of the new Victorian buildings

1. Shakespeare House
2. Site of Schorne College
3. Winkfield House
4. Camden Villas
5. The Red House
6. Garfield House
7. The Laurels
8. The Elms
9. The Gables
10. Marston House
11. Forge House
12. Gordon Cottage
13. The Mill House

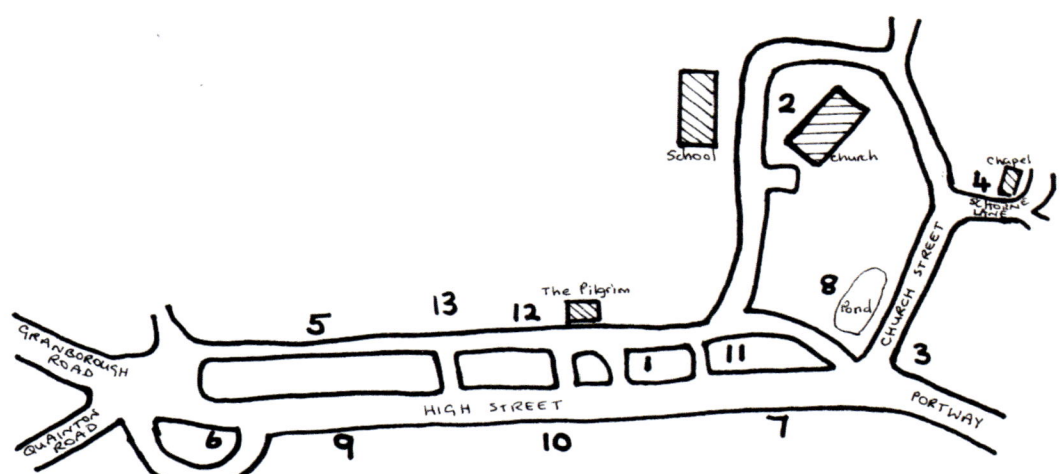

Fourteen
H J HOLDEN AND THE TAILORS
John Spargo

Holden's tailoring premises in the early twentieth century

Have you ever wondered about that large building at the top of the High Street near the pub? Why does it occupy such a huge plot right in the middle of the village? Who and what was it built for?

While Rev James was attending to the structural and moral improvements in the village, one of his closest colleagues, and another Victorian patriarch, was attending to his own empire. Through his efforts the basis of the village's economy shifted away from farming. His name was Henry John Holden, known as "John" Holden to his contemporaries (presumably to differentiate him from his father who was also called Henry), and it was he who drew tailors to North Marston. If you look at the roll-call of his tailors, you realise that many of their descendants still live in the village to this day. But how did it all begin?

Henry John Holden was a near-contemporary of Rev Samuel James (he was seven years his junior) and became a friend and ally of the vicar, latterly helping to raise substantial funds towards repairs and improvements to the church. Both men shared a passion for self-improvement and propriety and both were a product of the time.

Matilda Holden (nee Buckingham)

Henry John Holden was born on 20th November 1837, the year Queen Victoria came to the throne, and entered the tailoring trade under his father, Henry Holden, *when only ten years of age*! In March 1863 he married North Marston girl Matilda Buckingham (*pictured*), daughter of the butcher, Matthew Buckingham, and they soon started a family which eventually numbered thirteen children. He took over the tailoring business from his father (who, according to his son, *"was more interested in sporting pursuits than tailoring"*) but in 1870, at the age of thirty-three and with four young children, disaster struck and he became critically ill.

In his memoirs, written in 1915, he describes how, when close to death, he had a revelation. On recovering from his illness, he set about honouring his pledge of gratitude to God to be a better Christian, vowing to cease doing business on Sundays. He took his first communion in February 1873 aged thirty-six.

By 1882, the Holdens had nine children and the business was prospering. In that year, and in the face of much local consternation, Henry John Holden built a substantial new house, workshop and retail shop right in the centre of the village (called Shakespeare House) which Rev James described as *"equal to anything of the kind in Winslow or Aylesbury."*

Holden's shop in the High Street, North Marston, in the early 1900s

Holden's shop in Kingsbury Square, Aylesbury

With his business flourishing in North Marston, it was not long before Holden sought to expand his empire, opening a shop in Kingsbury Square, Aylesbury (*see picture above*). As the doyen of the local tradesmen and by far the biggest local employer, Holden was a very influential man in North Marston and he appears to have enjoyed his status in the community. He also had a special relationship with Rev James and many of Holden's children were baptised privately.

Fanny Holden's wedding to Mr Goodwin

The previous picture is iconic; it shows a very self-assured Henry John Holden and his family seated in front of Shakespeare House, the model of middle-class affluence in late Victorian England. The occasion is the marriage of Holden's daughter, Fanny, to Mr Goodwin, the organist at St Mary's Church Aylesbury, in September 1902. Holden's wife Matilda sits primly next to her son-in-law and surrounded by her daughters, all bridesmaids. The man standing in the doorway is Frederick Holden, the bride's brother.

On their Golden Wedding Anniversary in 1913, Henry and Matilda were presented with a specially-made ink-stand by Lord Rothschild, one of Holden's wealthiest customers for whom the tailoring firm made hunting wear.

The ink stand presented by Lord Rothschild of Waddesdon Manor to Mr & Mrs H J Holden on their Golden Wedding Anniversary in 1913

Mona Dumpleton remembers the Holdens:

"There were ever so many tailors in the village who all worked for H J Holden: Nathan, Fred and George Gowin, George, John and Will Woodford, Joe Holden, Ezra Rawlings, Alfie Wilkins, Jim and Harold Chapman, John Young and Arthur Hughes, to name a few. They used a middle room in Holden's shop for the cutting out. Mr Rowe from Pitchcott was the main man for all the cutting out. My dad used to go round in a pony and trap in the 1930s delivering coats for the hunt. There was also a Holden's shop in Kingsbury Square in Aylesbury. My dad was working there towards the end of his life. Sam Holden had a tailoring shop in Winslow too."

Robin Harwood also recalls:

"One voting day all the tailors were called to the central courtyard and given half a pint of beer so they'd vote for Bowyer whom Mr Holden supported. They'd never been given anything by him at any other time! Some of them (like Fred Gowin) specialised in trousers while others eg George Woodford were 'coats'. They used to draw the thread through beeswax to strengthen it."

An invoice from H J Holden dated January 1890 (note the spelling of Shakespeare House)

After his first communion, Henry John Holden became involved in church affairs and eventually became a church-warden, a position he held for forty years. He was also to become a School Manager and a Trustee of Poors Piece Allotments.

It is said that behind every great man there is a good woman. Holden's wife Matilda was a great influence on him. In his memoirs he says that he never made a major decision in his business without first seeking her advice. However, he expected his wife to play her part in keeping costs down. One story tells how he sent her to Aylesbury *on foot* to buy cotton. On returning with the wrong colour he promptly sent her back again to change it - a round trip of over thirty miles!

When Matilda died at the age of seventy-three, a year after their Golden Wedding Anniversary, he commissioned a stained glass window which can be seen in the north wall of the church. It is one of the most beautiful windows there.

The window commissioned by H J Holden after the death of his wife

When Holden became one of the Managers of the village school, the school logs show he visited the school from time to time to reward good achievement. The headmaster's entry in the school log of 18th December 1902 is typical:

"Mr H J Holden paid a visit to the school. He expressed himself pleased with the regular and punctual attendance of the children as shown by the registers and gave a shilling to be divided between the top two children in each department."

Holden's memoirs, written the year after his wife's death, are a summary of his moral principles rather than an account of his life; he also talks more about his achievements than his feelings. His family gets no more than a cursory mention yet his efforts on behalf of the church warrant several pages!

One gets the sense he was a man for whom wealth and appearances were by far the most important things in life. His attitude to his work-force was cynical and dismissive; he was highly critical of Government attempts to introduce a half day in the six-day working week. He thought labourers should work for six days. He wrote:

"If I was to send my tailors out on Thursday dinner-time it would be the worst thing I could do, as I should probably not get them in again for the rest of the week."

Young lads apprenticed to him faced five years of strict discipline. Not surprisingly, at least one ran away. Ivy Wheeler (nee Hughes) recalls:

"My dad was a tailor but he suffered ill health and died from consumption in 1930. He came from Botolph Claydon and Sir Harry Verney paid for him to do an apprenticeship with Holden's the tailor's shop. He was very young when he first went there and they half-starved him. They only gave him bread with grease on it. He ran home back to Claydon but his mother sent him straight back again."

Arthur Hughes, Ivy's father

Mona Holden remembers:

"My father was Alan Ernest Holden, though he was always called "Joe". We were distantly related to Henry John Holden the tailor. I remember old H J Holden once gave my father a sixpence and my dad drilled a hole through it and nailed it to the doorpost as it was so unusual for Mr Holden to give away anything—he was a tight old devil!"

"Joe" Holden in the 1920s seated on his tailoring bench

It is said that if one of his wealthy customers gave one of his lads a tip (perhaps for holding a horse or opening a gate) Holden would take it off the lad and put it in his own pocket!

Henry John Holden was a product of his time: a self-made man who, through effort, application and an obsessive work-ethic, rose above his contemporaries. He was a pillar of the community. He was a wealthy businessman, churchwarden and the highly successful fund-raiser behind some of the most substantial renovations and improvements made to the church: heating installed, the church roof completely repaired and a new organ bought and installed,

After Henry John Holden died in 1926, his family sponsored a memorial window placed in the south aisle of the church commemorating his forty years as a churchwarden (*see also Chapter Two*). The service was led by the Bishop of Oxford.

The window commissioned by the family of Henry John Holden following his death

Henry John Holden's last big fund-raising effort was just before the Great War. He managed to raise two thousand pounds for essential church repairs, a staggering sum in those days.

But perhaps Holden's most striking legacy is Shakespeare House which, even today, dominates the centre of the village and seems to characterise Holden's assured and forthright personality, standing defiantly in the centre of the road looking down the High Street and dwarfing neighbouring buildings.

Holden's death did not mark the end of his tailoring business which continued to be run by the Holden family and kept tailors employed in North Marston for many years.

The sights, sounds and smells of tailoring remain clear to many people. Rosemary Woodford recalls:

"Somewhat reluctantly Dad followed into the tailoring profession for H J Holden. I can well remember seeing him and his colleagues sitting cross-legged on the workbench in the room which always smelt of tobacco, beeswax and hot pressed serge."

Another of the tailoring families was the Gowin family, and Fred Gowin was still working independently as a tailor in the late 1970s. His daughter Janet also has vivid memories of tailoring:

"My father, Fred Gowin, was one of the many tailors in the village, as was his father, grandfather and four uncles - always very handy for me as I hated sewing! He trained at H J Holden's, along with many others. He worked from his tailor's workshop in the garden, which had been his father's before that. Previously he had a workshop on the corner of Church Street.

Unfortunately, in 1990 the shop was moved down the sports field for use as storage and got set light to, by whom I never knew - boys, matches, cigarettes maybe. It must have scared the living daylights out of them as it would have gone up like a tinder box because he put a coat of creosote on it every year! I used to spend many hours watching him sew, sitting cross-legged on a cushion on his board. Both his ankles had corns on them from many years of contact with the board. His thread used to hang on a line behind him, ready cut into lengths and graded by colour. He would then pull it through a lump of beeswax and sew the smallest stitches I have ever seen. He was trained as a trouser maker though could turn his hand to most things.

Fred Gowin in his workshop

No-one ever got charged more than a few pounds despite the hours of work he put in, but it still took most of them months to pay. He had big, heavy irons which he heated on a small paraffin stove, some of which I could hardly lift. There was a huge tin of buttons, various zips, hooks, eyes, and boxes of threads etc. Of many of the 'off the peg' clothes he would say 'put together with a hot needle and burnt thread'. As true now as it was then."

Mention of Fred Gowin's tailoring workshop reminds us that many village tailors worked from home. The tailor's main requirement was for somewhere dry where he could heat up an iron, and preferably somewhere with good light, although sometimes this might have been in short supply. Janet Gowin puzzled at how one of her relatives could see to sew:

"Dad's Uncle George – also a tailor – lived in Rose Cottage, now demolished, which stood next to The Laurels. Many are the times I used to go in there and wonder how he could see to sew even though his board was right by the window. There was a big holly tree standing right outside; he had no electricity and no running water and an old range for heat and cooking."

Rose Cottage(now demolished) at the top of the High Street

Fred Gowin's tailoring workshop in his garden

Another tailoring family were the Chapmans (father and son, Jim and Harold).

Jim Chapman as a young apprentice

Sue Chaplin, Jim's great-niece, remembers the shed in which they did their tailoring:

"Harold and his father, my Uncle Jim, had both worked as tailors for H J Holden. Their old tailoring shed which stood in Chapman's Field, just behind their Portway cottage, still had in it, in the Sixties, an old treadle sewing machine and boxes of cottons, threads, scraps of material, beeswax and tailors' chalk. The houses on the left (on entering Portway from the High Street) are all built on the site of Chapman's Field."

Jim Chapman of East Claydon was the son of a tailor, Joseph Chapman, and was indentured (*see Indenture Agreement below*) to H J Holden for a five-year apprenticeship in 1897 partly sponsored, like a number of apprenticed tailors at Holden's, through a charitable trust which was established by the late Honourable Elizabeth Verney.

One of the effects of the development of Holden's business in the village, as previously mentioned, was the way it attracted tailors and their families here from all over the country. The village census of 1901 reveals there were fourteen tailors working in the village at that time and they came from eight different places, the farthest away being Staffordshire. In 1891 there were tailors in the village including some from Surrey, Derbyshire and Devon. With tailoring running in families, it was not unusual for there to be three generations of tailors resulting in a continuity of over fifty years or more.

Fred Gowin was probably the last living tailor in North Marston and when he died in 1983, one hundred years after Shakespeare House was built, it brought to an end a special connection between the village and tailoring that had lasted from the early years of Queen Victoria's reign.

Jim Chapman's apprenticeship indenture

Telephones:  Telegrams:
7, North Marston   "Holdens, North Marston"
10, Aylesbury   "Holdens, Aylesbury"

H. J. Holden & Sons

F. M. HOLDEN   A. E. HOLDEN

Civil, Military and Hunt
Tailors and Outfitters

Breeches Makers

Ladies' Tailors & Costumiers

SHAKESPERE HOUSE
NORTH MARSTON

25, KINGSBURY SQUARE
AYLESBURY

HEATH'S HATS   DENT'S GLOVES

Fifteen
THE VILLAGE AT WAR
THE GREAT WAR 1914-1918

John Spargo

The Edwardian Era had hardly begun to impact on North Marston before something devastating befell it…..the Great War of 1914-1918. The resultant slaughter of young men touched every corner of the nation and hit small communities like North Marston particularly badly.

In the space of four years, sixty men left the village to fight across the seas and, of those, twenty-two young men were never to return. Scarcely a family in the village was not touched by the loss of a father, son, brother or uncle; an entire generation disappeared and it cast a long shadow over the village for many years afterwards. They are remembered on a plaque on the wall at the back of the church and another over the fire-place in the village hall (the village hall itself being a memorial to the dead of the First World War).

Fred Walker (left) and Edward John ("Jack") Tattam both died in the Great War

These soldiers also left us other sad reminders in the form of the numerous photographs taken before they went off to war: look at these proud and confident young men (*above*) in their new uniforms, specially photographed so their family or sweetheart would have a keep-sake while they were away. On studying these pictures, taken before they left these shores, one can see faces of fresh innocence, totally unaware of what lay ahead.

We have many of their letters too, sent home from the trenches. As poignant as the photographs, they tell of minor matters and trivia, for these homesick young lads, many perhaps away from home for the first time in their life, were struggling to inject a sense of normality into the frightening mayhem of war. Perhaps the saddest letters of all, however, are those from commanding officers notifying parents of the deaths of their sons.

The village appears to have dealt with the news of each death with quiet dignity as households all over the country reeled from the impact of loss. And such a loss! Twenty-two young lads from North Marston who had grown up together, played together, gone to school together… and died together.

The Cheshire Brothers

Perhaps the best way to understand the effect of the Great War on village families is to look at the stories of Gilbert and Bernard Cheshire, the only sons of Henry Cheshire, the village baker and churchwarden.

Gilbert Nelson Cheshire was born in 1891 and he was joined by a brother Ashley Bernard (whom everyone called Bernard) four years later. Their parents, Henry and Edith, were to have twelve children of which Gilbert was the fifth and Bernard the seventh. As the only boys in the family, they were doubtless loved and idolised by their parents and sisters.

On leaving school, Gilbert got a job as a gardener on the Cliveden Estate in Berkshire. As a result, when war was declared, he enlisted in the Fifth Royal Berkshire Regiment while his brother Bernard enlisted in the Oxfordshire and Buckinghamshire Light

Infantry. Before leaving for war they visited a Winslow photographic studio to have their picture taken in uniform.

Bernard stands on the extreme right with a group of fellow soldiers outside a mess hut

Gilbert and Bernard

Gilbert also had a picture taken of himself with his sweetheart, "Nance" Lightfoot

The boys were sent to military training camps to prepare them for life as a soldier. There, too, photographs were taken for family and loved ones at home.

In November 1914, still at his training camp on the south coast, Gilbert wrote to his sister 'Syb'. He was clearly concerned about what lay ahead and his thoughts were about his girlfriend Nance. In his letter he says: *"I'm going to give the Mrs a ring before I go so she'll have something to look at if I don't come back, but I feel confident enough that I shall."* He asks Syb for her help in getting a ring: *"Would you send Nance a book for her to choose one?"*

By 1915 the brothers were in France and getting closer to battle. Bernard wrote home in June 1915 and said he'd seen Gilbert: *"..he was just off to the trenches for the first time."* But it wasn't long before Bernard found himself in the trenches too. In his letter home in September 1915 he says: *"We are out of the trenches at last for a day or two after having sixteen days without our boots off. This month has been a great improvement on last although the nights are very cold."*

Gilbert too was in a bad situation. Writing to his parents in October 1915 he describes how *"of late we have been in the thickest of the fray more especially during the last eight days."* He had experienced a heavy bombardment from his own artillery and was almost buried alive: *"I hope for the sake of humanity this terrible affair will soon be over"* he wrote. But, unknown to the Cheshire brothers, much worse was to come the following year.

In July 1916 Henry and Edith received the news in North Marston they must have been dreading. Gilbert, their oldest son, had been wounded by a shell in the Battle of the Somme on 3rd July and had died of his injuries two days later. A memorial service was held for him in North Marston Church on 30th July. Gilbert was buried at Heilly Station Cemetery in France and in 1927 his parents had an engraved headstone erected over his grave (*pictured below*).

Meanwhile, within a month of his brother's memorial service, Bernard was struck down but, unlike his brother, he survived and was brought back to England, initially to the Derbyshire Royal Infirmary and then for seven weeks he was cared for at the Red Cross Hospital at Ashbourne in Derbyshire.

The Red Cross Hospital in Ashbourne, Derbyshire, September 1916 (Bernard is seated front right)

He was discharged on 19th October and after ten days sick leave posted to Ireland for light duties, where he died unexpectedly of heart failure on 15th November 1916 at the age of twenty-one. He is buried at North Marston, the Cheshire's last son. Unsurprisingly, Edith Cheshire suffered a nervous breakdown following the death of her sons and was never to be the same again.

Bernard Cheshire's gravestone in North Marston churchyard

In 1921, Henry and Edith were sent their sons' medals (three medals each colloquially known as "Pip, Squeak and Wilfred") and large bronze memorial plaques accompanied by scrolls from King George V acknowledging the brothers' sacrifice for their country.

Gilbert Cheshire's memorial plaque

"Pip Squeak and Wilfred"

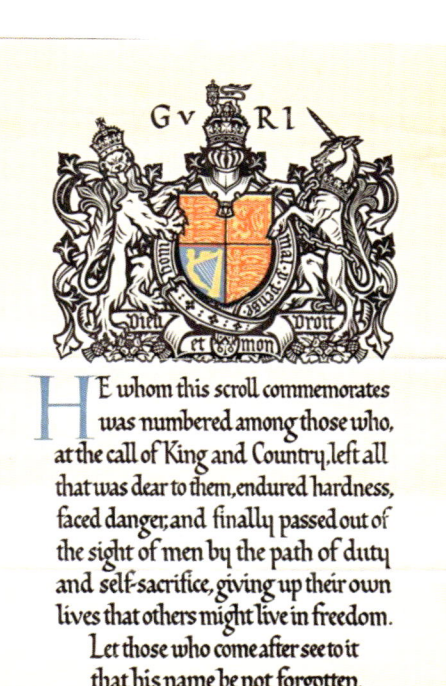

After the War

Henry and Edith's grief at the loss of their only sons must have been matched by the sorrow felt in dozens of families throughout the village.

Soon after the end of the war, communities everywhere sought ways of creating a permanent reminder of those that had made the ultimate sacrifice: memorial plinths, memorial gates and parks, even memorial hospitals began to appear through the 1920s.

In North Marston, fund raising began for a Memorial Hall and this was opened by Lord Cottesloe, Lord Lieutenant of the County, on Monday 21st April 1924 (though the date on the stained glass window is 1923). The building cost one thousand two hundred and ninety pounds. It was designed by Mr H Cripps of Winslow and built by Mr A Thorne of Weedon.

A builder (possibly Mr Thorne) sits on the first brick-courses of the Memorial Hall with Quainton Road cottages in the background

A view looking down Quainton Road just before the Memorial Hall was built (the builder's hoarding can be seen on the extreme right)

The newly- built Memorial Hall in 1924

Guests at the Opening Day of the new Memorial Hall on 21st April 1924

Windows in the Memorial Hall

There is also a plaque in the church (*see below*) and another in the Memorial Hall as constant reminders that, almost one hundred years ago, nearly an entire male generation from this village gave their life for their country.

The plaque in the church to those who died in the Great War

More of our brave soldiers....

Harold Chapman

Tom Biggs (front) with a passenger

Harold Tattam

William Jarrett

Alfred Dancer and colleagues in 1916

Cyril Holden (second from right) in the Royal Flying Corps

Samuel Henley who died in the war

Alfred Cheshire

Sixteen
SHOPS
John Spargo & Sue Chaplin

Village shops hold an important place in the lives of a community. Their evocative sights, sounds and smells, the shopkeepers who ran them and the experiences of using them, all leave an indelible imprint in villagers' memories.

From time long forgotten, North Marston would have enjoyed the services and facilities of a wide range of traders and dealers and it is probable there have been 'shops' in the village for hundreds of years.

In 1869 a Joseph Price is mentioned as being a shopkeeper and we know from *The Schornian Parish Chronicle* that, in 1881, North Marston supported at least half a dozen shops belonging to *"Mr Reuben Cheshire, Mrs Gregory, Mrs Henley, Mr Davis and others."*

They clearly flourished as, six years later, the Rev Samuel James again reported in the *Parish Chronicle*:

"Our village is so prospering and progressing, that we are ambitious of shops, a blacksmith's, a book-sellers, a baker's and a butcher's. We already have a tailor and draper's that cannot be matched nearer than Oxford, and we are persuaded that shops make custom."

Some of the shops had 'shop windows' and the Rev James observed in 1890:

"Even in our own village we see people gazing into Mrs Gregory's shop window, and Mr Holden's, though there is nothing wonderful in those windows; they cannot look into Mr R Cheshire's, except from a respectful distance, as the iron railing prevents."

Rev James became quite preoccupied with access to these shops and wrote at great length about it:

"Mrs Gregory's is the easiest of access; at Mr Holden's you have to rap with a big rapper, at Mr Cheshire's you have to open an iron gate, down at Mrs Mark Henley's you tingle-tangle a little bell which startles you, whereas at Mrs G's you are almost as welcome as you are at the blacksmith's, where we believe, discussions political, theological, social, sporting (football etc) are exercised in a sort of debating style."

Trading premises in those days would have fallen into three main types:
- The "Parlour Shop" set up in someone's front room (by far the most common type)
- The shed in the yard
- The purpose-built shop

There were clearly more shops and traders than were *officially* recorded. Kelly's Trade Directory of 1899, for example, lists the village as having three butchers, two grocers, a baker, a post-office, a boot-maker and a draper's; yet we know there were many others that would have been in business at that time but perhaps chose not to pay for an entry in the Trade Directory? Clifford Cheshire says:

"The house where I live now, 5 High Street, used to be a shop. As you come along the front path you can see where the door was blocked up."

5 High Street today

This little shop at 5 High Street, which sold general provisions, was run by Thomas Ward and his wife, Mary Ann, who were married in 1870. Thomas Ward was also a carpenter (*see Chapter Eighteen*).

The following invoice shows provisions which were bought for their shop from an Edward Glaisyer, a "Provision Merchant" in Leighton Buzzard.

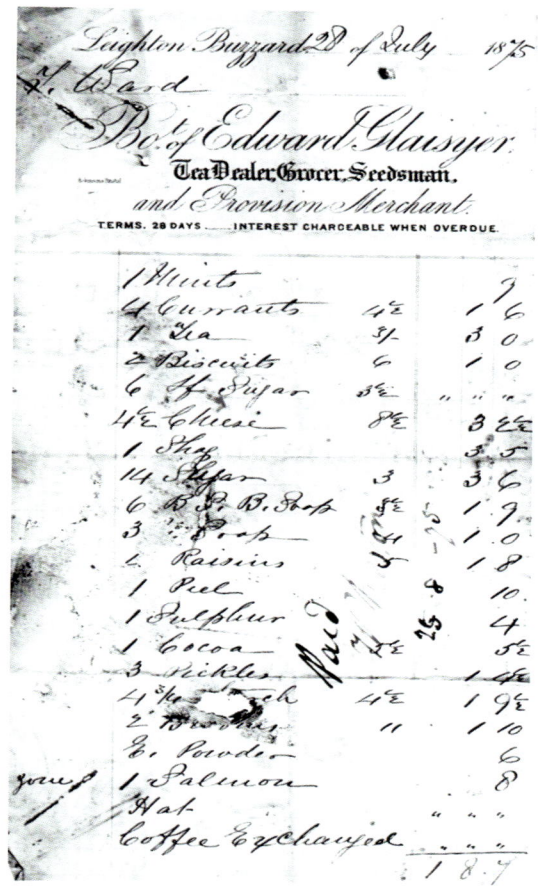

There is also evidence of a grocery shop run on the same premises by a Mr and Mrs Ward before this time.

It seems hard to imagine but for hundreds of years North Marston was virtually self-sufficient: up to the first half of the twentieth century the village blacksmith was also an ironmonger selling oil and paraffin; there was a village post office, a petrol garage and a number of shops selling sweets; milk and bread produced in the village was delivered daily to households (*see Chapter Eighteen*).

The shops also supported other village businesses such as carriers. Anything not available locally was brought in by travelling salesmen. In the 1930s we know of a trader from Stewkley who travelled the villages on his bike selling vests, pinafores and such-like garments. At this time there were also a greengrocer from Oving, a coalman from Quainton, a steam-laundry and a man who sold cakes from Aylesbury. Mr Brown's fresh fish van came to North Marston most weeks after the war and, in more recent years, Mr Slade continued this tradition.

In the days before most homes owned a refrigerator, daily access to fresh food was important. Without refrigeration, food such as meat and dairy products did not remain edible for long especially in the summer months. The village shops were therefore a vital part of the community particularly in the days before the motor-car. Most of the people who have owned and managed shops in North Marston were born in the village; and, in some cases, businesses were passed down through the generations.

Home Sales

Many things sold in the village could be bought in people's front rooms. One enterprising villager in School Hill, Julia Carter, ran a tuck shop in the early 1900s for the boys from Schorne College but also sold home-made wine as a side-line. It appears to have been a popular tipple as her grand-daughter, Ivy Wheeler, recalls:

"My granny Julia Carter (who was a Dudley by birth) lived at the bottom of School Hill at Number Three and her husband, John, was the groom at the Vicarage for Dr James. She had a shop in her front room and the college boys used to go there to buy their sweets from her. She'd do anything to earn money. She used to make lots of home-made wine and many people from the village went there and bought a shilling's worth".

The site of Julia Carter's shop at 3 School Hill (pictured in 2011)

Mrs Elmer's Sweet Shop

Mrs Elmer's sweet shop circa 1900

Mrs Elmer's Sweet Shop was situated in Melba Cottage at the junction of the High Street and Quainton Road, between the Police House (Garfield House) and the Wheatsheaf Pub. The sweet shop was in one of the front rooms and was run by Helena Elmer, wife of Henry (Harry) Elmer who had previously run Baker's Stores with her brother, James Baker.

The shop was certainly still trading during the First World War but it is likely to have closed shortly after as Helena died in 1920. Her son, St John Elmer, and his wife, Kathleen continued to live at Melba Cottage until Kathleen's death in 1949.

Miss Cox's Shop

This shop was situated in Prune Cottage in Quainton Road in the small room to the right of the property. It was run by Miss Lizzie Cox and her sister Elsie who took the shop over from their mother, Mrs Louise Cox, and continued to run the little shop up until the early 1960s. They sold such commodities as biscuits, sugar, tinned goods, paraffin, sweets and cigarettes from behind a large wooden counter.

Smoking was much more common in the 1950s and Miss Cox's shop, it appears, did a good trade in cigarettes as Rod Abbey remembers:

"I bought Players Navy Cut, Players Weights, and Woodbine cigarettes there for my grandfather."

Prune Cottage showing the old shop window of Cox's shop on the right

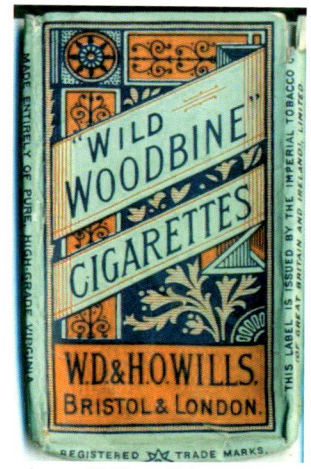

A packet of Woodbine Cigarettes

Baker's Stores

Baker's Stores was founded in 1897 by Mr James Baker and his sister, Helena. James was the son of Denchfield Baker, a village butcher. They bought the business from Mrs Annie Gregory, wife of Jeremiah Gregory, the village carrier, who had kept a grocery and provision store in the village for at least thirty years.

James Baker died a relatively young man in 1906. In living memory the shop was run by two spinster sisters, Emily and Vida (known as Ida) who were his daughters.

Forge Cottage and Baker's Stores in the High Street

As the sisters would have been only six and seven years of age when James died, Baker's Stores continued to trade under the management of a young Albert J Franklin until the Baker sisters were old enough to take on the business. Valerie Little (nee Richardson) remembers Baker's from when she was a small child in the 1930s:

"I would finally reach my destination – the sweet shop run by the Miss Bakers. You had to go up two steps to get in the door and they would peer at you over the tops of their glasses."

Customers were served from behind a fine wooden counter. The walls of the shop were lined from floor to ceiling in shelving on which stood the commodities on sale, including large glass jars of sweets. Most of the village children would buy their sweets at Baker's. In the Forties and Fifties popular varieties were sherbert dabs (or fountains), liquorice sticks, lollies (four for a penny), black-jacks and sticks of barley sugar. Mona Dumpleton remembers:

"Baker's shop catered mainly for the kiddies. When it was the Oxford and Cambridge Boat Race they used to sell sherbert fountains with a pale blue or dark blue feather on them."

It appears that the two Miss Bakers wasted nothing: broken biscuits and crisps were bagged up and sold cheaply, as Susan Cobbold recalls:

"I clearly remember buying 'penny crisps' which were basically bags of broken crisps which couldn't be sold for the full price. They

were so popular that the Miss Bakers rationed them and we were only allowed to have one bag each."

The shop was situated in a prime location at the centre of the village, adjacent to the Forge and opposite Malcolm Holden's Garage.

Ida Baker on the steps of her shop, probably in the 1920s

Baker's Stores was also a popular place to purchase cigarettes. Miss Baker would sometimes sell just five Woodbine cigarettes and wrap them in newspaper to be taken away. Janet Gowin recalls visiting the shop even when it was closed:

"I went to Miss Baker's shop to get dad his Players cigarettes. If he ran out and they were shut I used to go to the back door. I don't know that they were always too pleased, but they never refused."

Graham Ward (whose parents ran Franklin's stores) says:

"Ida and Emily Baker were quite eccentric, strange ladies really. One was tall and the other really short. The shop was like something out of Dickens! It had an atmosphere all its own and was very unusual; *it certainly added to the village but I think they struggled a bit."*

Ida Baker as a teenager and in old age

When Baker's shop closed down for good it became a residential property but the original shop facade and doorway remain (*see below*).

The old Baker's Stores today

Franklin's Stores

Perhaps the most significant of the village shops in people's memories was Franklin's Stores. Tucked away behind H J Holden's large red-brick building was Flora Villa, an impressive Victorian house built by the village builder John Price for his family home.

When Albert J Franklin ceased being the manager of Baker's Stores (*see earlier*) he bought Flora Villa and converted it into a shop.

Franklin's Stores seemed to have been a popular village meeting place. One young Marston lad, writing to his family from the misery of the trenches in the First World War, was dismissive of the self-professed 'experts' whom he pictured chatting at Franklin's Stores about the rights and wrongs of the conflict while he himself was out in France. Pictures (like the one below) of groups of men clustered on the steps of Franklin's Stores in the 1930s suggest that it continued to have a role as a gathering-point long after the First World War.

Men gathered outside the door of Franklin's Stores in the 1930s

The site of the entrance door to Franklin's Stores (now blocked up)

Before the Second World War sugar was delivered straight from Tate and Lyle and kept in a zinc-lined sugar store; and a large refrigerated meat store was built which the local slaughter-man, Clarence Cheshire, kept stocked with fresh meat.

Clarence Cheshire

The slaughter-house itself was situated near the entrance to Portway (from the High Street) but closed down after the war. Franklin's provided the village and beyond with a full range of groceries and fresh meat all year round.

Mr Franklin bought a van and provided a delivery service to neighbouring villages. Clifford Cheshire remembers:

"Franklin's used to deliver groceries to all the villages around: Oving, Whitchurch, Granborough, Winslow and even Aylesbury. During the war they supplied Oving House, which was an evacuee children's home at that time, as well as the canteen at The Firs* in Whitchurch." (*A wartime weapons research establishment)

The slaughter-house in Portway was behind this red brick store (viewed from the garden of Winkfield House in 1978)

Albert J Franklin

When Albert J Franklin finally retired in the early 1940s the business was taken over by his daughter, Ida, and son-in-law, Bill Ward, who ran the shop until they retired in 1969. Graham Ward (A J Franklin's grandson) recalls the shop as a child:

"I remember as a child during the Second World War when my grand-father "A J" was serving in the shop, mostly on a Saturday afternoon; there would be a shop full of customers including a few local characters. One of these was Jim Buckingham who was a great friend of my grandfather and from my vantage point sitting on one end of the counter I was enthralled by the bustle and conversation taking place there.

Of course in those days we sold almost everything but shoppers were only allowed to purchase food by means of a ration book. Although, officially, the shop shut at 6pm, people were forever calling at the door after hours and were never turned away and this highlights the community spirit which existed in so many ways."

After the war and throughout the 1950s and 1960s, Franklin's shop provided the villagers with virtually everything they needed including meat, ham and cheeses. Nothing was pre-packed; ham was sliced to the thickness required on a large slicing machine; cheese was cut to size with the 'cheese-wire' and joints of meat trimmed on the huge wooden butcher's slab.

Grocery items were stacked up on the shelves surrounding the walls and, if a customer wished to purchase something from a high shelf, it would be reached using the special long-handled 'grabber' with pincer-like ends specially designed for the purpose. The freezer selection in the Sixties comprised mainly ice-cream and *Birds Eye* products, such as fish-fingers and peas.

Franklin's was easily the prime shop in the village. Regular customers had an order book and kept an account with Franklin's which was paid in instalments. Bill Ward continued to deliver to all the villages in the surrounding area as well.

A customer account book from the 1960s when Ida and Bill Ward were the proprietors of Franklin's Stores

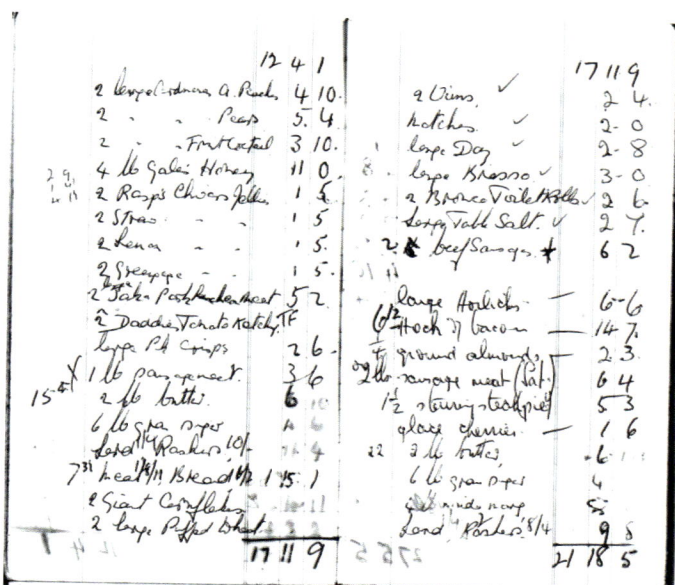

*Shoppers ordered items for delivery and settled their account weekly or monthly.
This account is from 1967 (note this is before decimal currency so the prices are in shillings and pence)*

When Ida and Bill Ward retired from the business in 1969, it was taken over by Jim and Doreen Sharp. Franklin's Stores eventually closed in about 1978 after which the shop was incorporated into the house.

He also ran a very successful antiques shop from the premises. When Willy Woodford's shop closed in the early 1980s, it ended an unbroken tradition of village shops stretching back for well over a century.

Bill and Ida Ward on their Golden Wedding Anniversary

Willie Woodford in the window of his antique shop looking down the High Street

Willie Woodford's Shop

After the closure of Franklin's, villagers in North Marston were served by a small shop run by Willie Woodford in his home premises of Shakespeare House (formerly the site of H J Holden's tailoring business)) close to The Bell public house. Willie Woodford ran the post office from here and sold general groceries.

Willy Woodford in the inner courtyard of Shakespeare house

The Village Shop Reappears

With the arrival of the family car, supermarkets, home freezers and TV marketing, shopping habits changed forever leading to the steady decline of village shops. A few villages retained a convenience store, but their commercial viability was precarious and by the 1990s these had become a rarity.

After a while, many rural communities came to realise the lack of a shop deprived a village of something important. Gradually, the notion of a community owned enterprise (ie not-for-profit and volunteer-staffed) gained favour and, after considerable planning and fundraising, North Marston saw the opening of the North Marston Community Shop in the car park of the village hall in July 2011 (*see also Chapter Twenty*).

For the first time in many years, North Marston again had somewhere in the village to buy staple foods and local delicacies. It also reminded people that a village shop is a social hub where people stop for a chat and to catch up with local news.

Following in the footsteps of Franklin's, Baker's and Cox's, "The Shop" is creating a new set of memories for village youngsters to recount to future generations, thus completing the cycle once again.

Shop Manager Eddie Parsley with the banner celebrating the "Community Shop of the Year" award in February 2012

Buckingham MP John Bercow and Shop Chairman Alison Finnemore at The Shop opening in July 2011

The High Sherriff of Buckinghamshire (in hat) calls in at The Shop in September 2012 as part of a sponsored horse-ride around the county

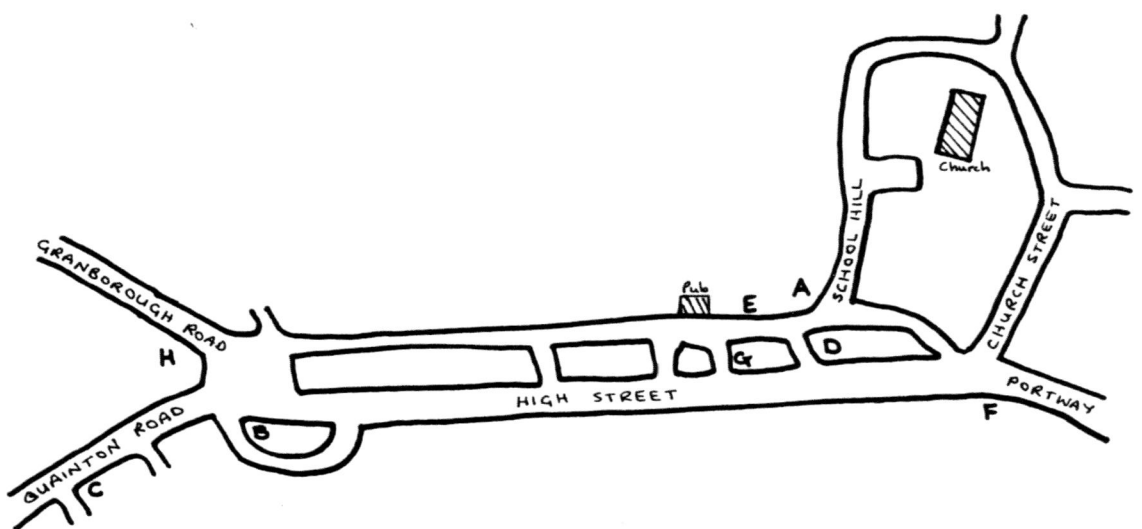

KEY TO VILLAGE SHOPS
A   3 School Hill
B   Elmer's
C   Cox's
D   Baker's
E   Franklin's
F   Portway Slaughter House
G   Woodford's
H   Community Shop

Seventeen
THE POST OFFICES
John Spargo

The arrival of the post office and the telegraph transformed the village, connecting its residents and businesses with the rest of the country and the world. It was the Victorian equivalent of the internet and in a large part we have the efforts of one man to thank for its arrival in North Marston: Reuben Cheshire.

Dr Samuel James

Reuben Cheshire

The First Post Office

Reuben Cheshire was born in North Marston in 1833 and was clearly a bright lad who was fortunate to have received an education which equipped him for the numerous roles that he undertook later in life: parish clerk, sexton, poor rate collector, Sunday school superintendent, church sidesman and postmaster. He was neat, ordered and literate: the archetypal administrator, though he started his working life as a gardener and agricultural labourer.

The vicar, Samuel James, relied heavily on Reuben Cheshire's facilitation and administration in both church and secular capacities.

In the two-party British political system that prevailed at the time, the two men were diametrically opposite, with Reuben a lifelong Conservative and the vicar an ardent Liberal.

In several references in *The Schornian* alluding to Reuben Cheshire, he is described by Rev James as *a labourer*. Later in life, and by then with a more elevated status in the community, Cheshire clearly took exception to this description as, in his personal collection of the bound copies of the village magazine, he has vigorously inked out the word *labourer*.

To modern sensitivities, we might interpret Samuel James's use of the term *labourer* as demeaning, but a more charitable explanation lies in the way Victorian society assessed an individual's social status. In Rev James's world, men fell into one of four classes: *labourer, tradesman, farmer* and *gentleman*. Professionals such as doctors and clergymen fell into the latter category. Because of the paucity of the definitions available there simply was not a definition that was more appropriate to an administrator like Reuben Cheshire and so, having started his working life as a gardener, he was thereafter defined as *a labourer*. Doubtless, Rev James was playing a game because of Cheshire's political leanings.

In 1855, Reuben married a Maids Moreton girl, Sarah Newman. She was to bear him thirteen children. Through successive generations of large families and inter-marriage with other village families, Reuben's descendants were to become a key proportion of the village population; many of today's residents are able to trace their lineage back to Reuben Cheshire.

Sarah Cheshire

Reuben was a poor rate collector in Maids Moreton (a role he had also previously undertaken in North Marston) but in March 1881, a year after the birth of Alfred Ezra (his ninth child), Reuben Cheshire opened a parlour shop in North Marston in the row of cottages between The Bell and School Hill. A couple of years later he was formally proposed to the Postmaster General as Village Postmaster.

The vicar lost no opportunity to score political points by pointing out in *The Schornian* that Reuben Cheshire's sponsor in parliament was a Liberal (whilst Reuben Cheshire was a Conservative). With surety bonds placed by Dr James (the vicar) and Miss Lines (a village resident) the application was endorsed and so, in 1883, Reuben Cheshire's little shop became North Marston's first Post Office.

The opening of the village Post Office would have been a feather in Reuben's cap and one can imagine his clerical skills suited him well to the role of the village postmaster. The villagers must have been delighted as, prior to Reuben's enterprise, they would have had to travel all the way to Winslow or Whitchurch to send and collect their mail, or pay a carrier to do it for them.

According to an article in *The Schornian,* Dr James had been paying ten pounds a year for his post to be delivered from Winslow to North Marston.

Alfred and Cissie Cheshire standing on the doorstep of the first Post Office (the sign can be seen on the wall)

The first village Post Office as it looks today

Initially the Post Office in North Marston would only have handled letters but later that year Samuel James wrote in *The Schornian*:

"We hope our Post Office will soon become a Money Order Office, and if so, the Vicar and Miss Lines will be Mr Cheshire's sureties."

Sure enough in July 1883, and barely three months after it had first opened, Reuben's Post Office was given the approval to become a Money Office, issuing Postal Orders and managing savings accounts in addition to basic postal services.

The following year Rev Samuel James (probably with his business interests at Schorne College in mind) began lobbying the Postmaster General for a telegraph extension to the village from Whitchurch via Oving but he was told it would only be carried out with a guarantee of twenty-nine pounds from North Marston which the vicar declined to underwrite from his own pocket. It seems he was trying to encourage co-investment from village businessmen like Henry Holden and John White. The lobbying continued and eight years later Dr James wrote:

"We should of course like telegraphic and telephonic communication, but we have refused to pledge ourselves for more than a twelfth of the cost and only for that if it does not exceed £2.00."

The Village Telegraph

In 1893 Dr James finally got his wish and reported accordingly in *The Schornian*:

"On Wednesday May 3rd our telegraphic communications was formerly opened, the first message being sent by Dr James to his nephew, the Rev J C James, curate of Chard, Somerset."

Reuben Cheshire lost no time in building up this side of his business and by November 1893 he was employing a telegraph boy cyclist *"who also now and then fetches second delivery letters and brings them to Marston earlier by an hour."*

The young Alfred Ezra Cheshire

Reuben Cheshire retired in 1901 and died ten years later. He passed the post office to his son Alfred Ezra Cheshire who was to become the longest-serving village postmaster as well as undertaking a host of other functions including being the chairman of the parish council, newsagent, churchwarden, parish clerk and wartime evacuee billeting officer. (It would seem that community service ran in the family).

Alfred Cheshire setting off on deliveries at the Post Office gate

The Second Post Office

After taking over the Post Office, Alfred relocated it to larger premises at 18 High Street. His son Howard was employed in the Post Office and one of his jobs was delivering telegrams. Rod Abbey recalls:

"I remember one day Howard had to deliver an urgent telegram; he always wore a crash helmet but for some reason he left it behind and, of course, he had a bad accident on the Granborough Road. He was in a coma for quite a few weeks."

18 High Street as it looks today

The village newspapers were also delivered from this Post Office.

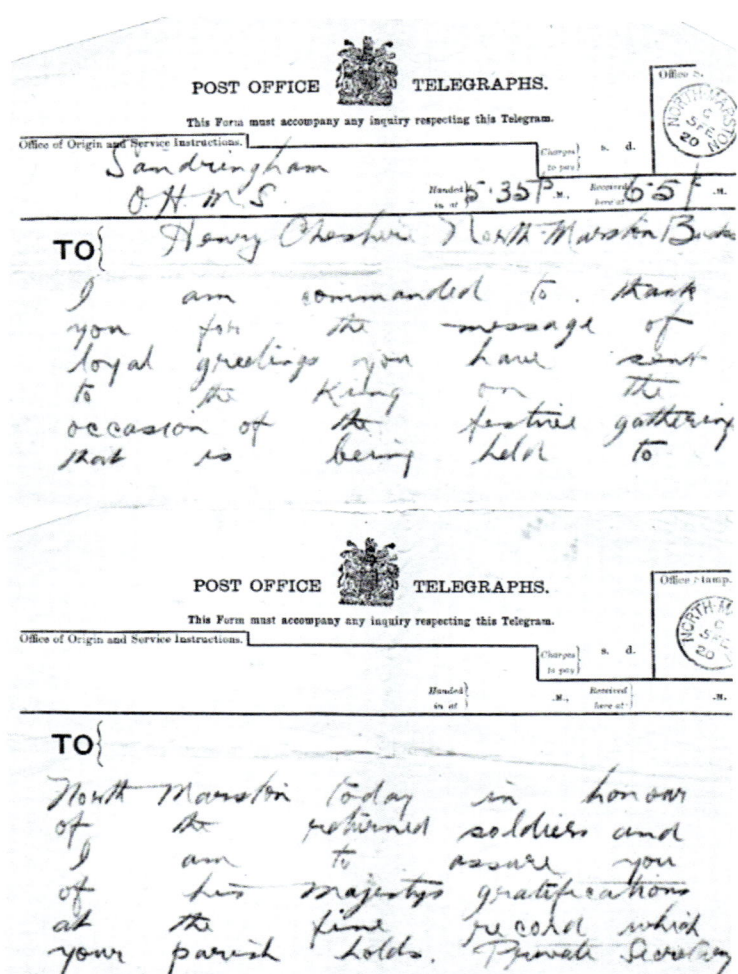

A telegram from the King at Sandringham to North Marston Post Office in 1920

A North Marston Post Office Book dated 1954 which was opened by Alfred Cheshire himself with a gift of five pounds to the newly-born Susan Parker

In 1954, Alfred was awarded the British Empire Medal *"for services to the Post Office and community"*.

There is a slight air of mystery surrounding this high-ranking award being given to a civilian. On the rear of the photograph (*below*) taken that day are hand-written the following words: *"1954 Alfred Cheshire with four of his siblings having just received the BEM for his services at Bletchley Park in WWII."*

As all work relating to Bletchley Park was shrouded in secrecy, it is impossible that anyone at the time would have known of Alfred's work and it is unlikely that we shall ever find out the truth or even when this note was put on the back of the photograph. Alfred retired and died in 1958 and was succeeded by his son Howard who ran the Post Office until 1959.

Alfred Cheshire (centre) and his family on the day he was awarded his BEM (his son, Howard, is on the right of the picture)

THE HEAD POSTMASTER OF BLETCHLEY

requests the pleasure of the company

of _Mr and Mrs F. N. Gowin_ on

the occasion of the presentation of the British Empire Medal to

Mr. A. E. CHESHIRE, of NORTH MARSTON POST OFFICE,

at 3 p.m., on Friday, 27th August, 1954, in the Memorial Hall, North Marston.

The presentation will be made by
MAJOR SIR HENRY AUBREY-FLETCHER, Bart. D.S.O., M.V.O.
Lord Lieutenant of the County of Buckinghamshire

POST OFFICE,
BLETCHLEY.

R.S.V.P.

The Third and Fourth Post Offices

After the Cheshires, and from 1959 to 1971, the "Post Office Stores" was run by Paddy and Stan Gurney from their home at Marston House (near the top of the High Street). They also sold cards, stationery, toiletries, cigarettes, sweets and tinned food. Stan drove a van around the locality to make deliveries of bread and cakes (which were brought to North Marston from the "Snowwiss" bakery at Leighton Buzzard). However, he delivered the post on his bike. When Stan started a new job with Balfour Beatty (who had moved into the village) the post was delivered by Hazel Barton (*see later*).

With concerns about impending decimalisation (or "new-fangled foreign" as Paddy called it) Paddy and Stan Gurney sold the business to Jim and Doreen Sharp who had taken over Franklin's Stores in 1969 (and which they continued to run until the late-1970s). After its closure the following words of appreciation were written in the Parish Magazine:

"All of us in North Marston have been served, with courtesy and consideration, by Mrs Gurney and her assistants at the Post office for the last twelve years. The Post Office has been a place to leave messages, hear the news, sell the raffle tickets and have a chat, as well as do business".

Marston House as it looks today

The site of the former Post Office entrance door (now a window)

The sign that Stan Gurney attached to his van

Stan and Paddy Gurney with their first-born son, Robert

Hazel Barton, the Village Post Lady

After Stan Gurney stopped delivering the post, a local woman, Hazel Barton who lived in Schorne Lane, became the village post-lady. After the Post Office had transferred to Franklin's Stores, Hazel would go there early every morning to sort the post, which she usually did on the butcher's block at the back of the shop; history recalls how village letters were sometimes delivered with blood on them! When Franklin's finally closed in the mid-1970s, Hazel sorted the morning post at her own house.

The last village post-lady, Hazel Barton (the site of Alf Cheshire's Post Office can be seen over her shoulder)

Hazel's commitment was celebrated when she was awarded, in 1991, a medal by the Post Office for twenty-five years loyal service; and the following year she was presented with a Christmas hamper at Winslow Post Office in recognition and appreciation of her service to North Marston.

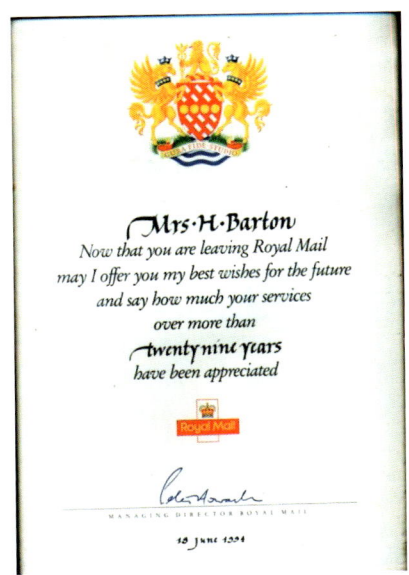

Hazel Barton's's Retirement Certificate

Hazel took final retirement in June 1994 after twenty-nine years' service. A great deal of money was raised in the village and on the evening of her last day her friends gathered in The Bell to present her with a large array of gifts.

The Fifth Post Office

It appears the village may then have been without a Post Office for a while until, at the suggestion of the vicar Rev Peter Lawrence, one was opened at the general stores run by Willy Woodford (based in H J Holden's former tailoring premises near the pub).

This was to be North Marston's last Post Office and when it closed it marked the end of village Post Offices spanning a century.

At about this time, Freda Holden had applied for (and was given permission) to run the post-office from her home in Schorne Lane, but she eventually decided against it as she was not to be allowed to sell any goods unrelated to the postal service, a condition which made the business non-viable.

Eighteen
TRADES AND OCCUPATIONS OF THE PAST
Sue Chaplin

For hundreds of years North Marston, like most other villages, was a self-sufficient community. Businesses, sometimes passing down from father to son, provided the village with builders, carpenters, blacksmiths, tailors, bakers, butchers, dairymen, undertakers and a whole host of others. The village had all the services any community would need: shoe-makers, barber, dress-makers, carriers, chimney-sweep and petrol pumps. It was not unusual for an individual to have two or three jobs: Ted Dudley was both a builder and undertaker; Thomas Ward was both a carpenter and a shop-keeper.

A very early reference to a 'trade' in North Marston concerns that of a thatcher named John Hartnoll who was sent in 1654 as a messenger to London to attend a meeting of an association of General Baptist Churches – a considerable distance to travel in those days! In the late 1600s, the Baptists or *anabaptists* are likely to have met alternately in local villages including North Marston and Winslow (where Keach's Meeting House, dating from that period, still stands).

With improvements in communication and transport during the latter part of the 1800s, some of the local businesses prospered and spread further afield (following in the footsteps of the most successful of the village entrepreneurs, Henry John Holden).

Other chapters of this book describe the village millers, tailors, religious ministers, schoolteachers, shopkeepers, publicans and farmers. *This* chapter, however, explores other occupations and trades, some lowly but all important, which have served the needs of this village and from which many legacies are left with us to this day.

THE CENSUS IN 1851 AND 1901

The trades and occupations listed in the Census of 1851 make interesting reading and are worthy of a mention: dress-maker, midwife, straw-bonnet cleaner, grazier, school mistress, agricultural labourer, dairy maid, miller, baker, tailor, horse-dealer, sawyer (one who saws timber), drover, cattle-dealer, victular, grocer, carrier, wheel-wright, carpenter, blacksmith, butcher, farmer, lace-maker, boot-maker, cordwainer (a shoe-maker), shoe-binder, higgler (itinerant pedlar), eggler (dealer in eggs and poultry) and bricklayer.

In 1901 we see some additions: journeyman tailor, tailor's cutter, dress-maker, nurse, slaughter-man, gardener, bread-maker, laundress, police constable, groom, roadman and publican. The tailors would have been employed at Holden's (*see Chapter Fourteen*). In other records we come across needle-maker, whitesmith (a worker in tin or white iron), street organist and watch-maker. Many girls marrying in the 1830s were registered as servants and, unless a specific occupation was mentioned, a man would simply be called a "labourer".

How differently the lists would read in the twenty-first century!'

THE LACE-MAKERS

From the early 1600s, Buckinghamshire was famous for its lace-making. Girls as young as four years old would be taught the skill either at home or in a little lace school which would be situated in a cottage in the village.

The photograph above shows a group of lace-makers posing outside a cottage in Granborough Road in the early 1900s

In the seventeenth and eighteenth centuries most women could make lace, and the lace-bobbins would be handed down from one generation to the next. Aylesbury was a great lace-making town in the 1800s and the wages from lace were much higher than those paid for working in the fields. Women would often sit making lace outside their cottages with a thick pillow (to which the pins and threads are attached) firmly on their knees. Alison Uttley, writing in 1950, said:

"Many countrywomen were all clever-fingered with the bobbins and threads. At North Marston Mr Cheshire told me of his lace-making family. His mother learned to make lace when she was only four years old, but all the family learned and most of the village. Mr Cheshire's mother made black worsted lace for which she got £1 a week, which was a good wage in those days when farm labourers only received 10s....His grandmother made lace by the light of a rush-light and a bowl of water. This round glass bowl was placed between the light and the lace and a soft glow was focused on the work. They used farthing rush-lights in those days, not candles. They made these themselves from the piths of rushes, stripping off the green rind.........They could buy farthing rushlights but it was more economical to make them...using mutton fat for the tallow." (Uttley, 1950)

In the Marriage Records of St Mary's Church for the 1800s there are many lace-makers mentioned (particularly in the 1860s), some marrying as young as seventeen.

By the beginning of the twentieth century, lace-making at home was a dying trade due largely to the introduction of machine-made lace. As early as 1885 Rev James had written in the *Parish Magazine* that *"***Mrs Watkins** *requests us to say that she has given up lace-dealing as it is now not so profitable a trade as it was so we remove her name from our parish directory."*

In the North Marston Census of 1901, a few women were listed as lace-makers: **Ann Foster**, **Ann Ward**, **Betsy Cox** and **Eliza Seaton**. Eliza, who died in 1940 was the mother of Thomas Seaton, the village baker and was the last of the old Bucks lace-makers in North Marston.

Several women in the village listed themselves as *"dressmakers"* in the early years of the twentieth century (**Louisa Garner**, **Ellen Higgins** and **Alice Seaton**), the likelihood being that they were carrying out private work within the village.

THE SHOEMAKERS AND SHOEMENDERS

All villages had their own shoemakers and in North Marston during the early part of the nineteenth century we know of a **Thomas Mayho**, **William Cook**, **Thomas Kibble**, **Joseph Lenney**, **Richard Scott**, **William Butcher** and **William Mayho**.

Before (and after) becoming landlord of The Bell Inn in 1883, **James Garner** (1855-1912) was a prominent shoemaker in the village and was highly regarded by the wealthy parents of boys attending Schorne College (*see Chapter Twelve*) which must have proved quite lucrative. In 1878 Rev James wrote:

"We recommend Garner's boots and shoes. The reason we do that is he makes the best we know of, as half a dozen Schorne parents have voluntarily testified; they are more expensive than ready-made, but they last twice the time."

Mr and Mrs James Garner

Other shoemakers at the time were **James Seaton**, **James Linney**, **George Ward** and **Robert Gurney**. In 1885 the matron at Schorne College decided to send the younger pupils to James Seaton *"as Mr Gurney is not now quite equal to it and has only had occasion to do it for amusement rather than profit"* and she continued to use James Garner for the older pupils.

In 1890 Rev James made the following plea in *The Schornian* magazine:

"George Ward has taken to shoemaking or, rather, shoemending, and parishioners will be doing a kindness in employing him." Could this be the same George Ward who, seven years later, died in Stone Asylum aged forty?

Right through to the middle of the twentieth century it was possible to get one's shoes mended in the village. Many villagers remember in the 1930s and 1940s taking their shoes for repair along Portway to **George "Tanty" Carter** (1877-1954) who worked in a shed in his front garden where the floor was covered with shoe studs. His frequent boast was that he had made his own boots many years earlier and still wore them *every* day! He was also an accomplished musician and played a variety of instruments, including the cornet, on which he would sometimes entertain visitors.

THE CARRIERS

Until the middle of the twentieth century, and before the widespread ownership of the motor car, the village "carrier" (sometimes known as a "carter") would be employed for local deliveries and collections of goods and parcels, being the equivalent of today's van driver.

Henry Linney, **Jeremiah Gregory**, **James** and **Richard Holden**, together with **Mark**, **William**, **Charles** and **John Carter** (aptly named!) were carriers between 1848 and the turn of the century. In the *Kelly's Directory of 1899* are listed **Gaius Carter**, **Josiah ("Joey") Gregory** and **William Ward.**

William Ward 'carried' to and from Winslow on a daily basis and in 1891 he met with an accident:

"William Ward, our useful Marston carrier to and from Winslow, who brings papers, cracks jokes, gives many a kind 'lift', and keeps good time, met recently with an accident. One of his wheels came off, he was pitched into the ditch, and his horse galloped off. It might have been very serious, but providentially Ward took no great harm." (*The Schornian*)

Gaius Carter and Joey Gregory (who both died in the mid 1940s) 'carried' to and from Aylesbury on Wednesdays and Saturdays.

Gaius Carter with a young Clifford Cheshire circa 1936

The carriers also delivered coal around the village and, in order to make things fair, Rev James ruled in 1875: *"Those who live below the Bell must have it of Carter, and those who live above the Bell of Gregory."*

Joey Gregory, who lived in Portway, drove a four-wheeled wagon and appears to have worked as a carrier for at least fifty years as many people can remember him still working in the 1930s:

"Joey Gregory was the carter who collected parcels three times a week from Marston, Oving and Whitchurch, and he'd take them to Aylesbury on his horse and cart. He'd collect medicines for folks on his way back through Whitchurch from the doctor's. Paddy Holden, who lived in Church House next to the school, always had some white medicine each week. If someone was on holiday or something, Joey would still collect their medicine then drink it himself!" (Robin Harwood)

"The carrier was a man called Joe Gregory who lived near the slaughterhouse and had a four-wheeled wagon. I remember him well collecting the trunks to take to Winslow station when my brother and sister went back to school." (Basil Waters)

"My mother used to tell me how she would go in Joe Gregory's cart to Granborough Road Station to pick up a large sack of flour transported from one of the mills by train." (Jennifer Heffer)

The Gregory family's cottage in Portway

THE BARBER

Ted Anstiss (who died in 1962) worked as the village barber from before the First World War through to the 1950s, and tales of him abound! He had his 'salon' in an old shed (some people called it a 'caravan') in his back garden behind what is now Eleanor Cottage near The Wheatsheaf at the bottom of the High Street. The walls were covered with photographs of young local men in their First World War uniforms. As well as cutting hair he also mended clocks and pots.

Many of Ted's customers have clear memories of their visits to him:

"He was a very inventive man who made various toys and puzzles to amuse us boys waiting for the only hair-cut available: short back and sides with a fringe cut one and a half inches above the eyes!" (Tommy Gray)

"He used to cut hair if he felt like it. It wasn't unusual for a lad to come away with half a haircut if he didn't sit still." (Clifford Cheshire)

"I used to dread going there as I'd come out battle-scarred! There were always a few drips of blood!" (David Holden)

However, not everyone was dissatisfied! Ivy Wheeler loved the "Eton Crop" which Ted gave her when she was about fourteen years old in 1924.

Ted Anstiss could evidently be quite an awkward man. As a young boy in the 1930S, Clifford Cheshire accidentally sat on Ted's bowler hat and squashed it flat, with the result that Ted did not speak to Clifford again for years! Ted also owned a 1914 Douglas motor-cycle (*see below*) on which he evidently *"frightened himself to death"*!

Ted Anstiss on his Douglas motor-cycle

THE CHIMNEY SWEEPS

Very little information is available about the village chimney sweeps in the early part of the twentieth century but we do know that **Alfred "Barthie" Walker** (the sweep who lived in the little cottage in the High Street next to the Wheatsheaf) would also be called upon in the 1930s to empty the school privies when they were full! The privy seat would be set above a large bucket in the ground which would be hauled out when full and poured into a hole dug into the ground elsewhere; not a pleasant task for Barthie or, indeed, for any of the householders in the village who would have to have done the same job themselves!

Meyrick Cox who died in 1965 lived in School Hill (in the house now named "The Old Slaughter House") and was the last of the resident chimney sweeps in North Marston (another of his jobs was to light the church coke fires). Meyrick tied his sweeps' brushes to his bicycle to transport them around the village and he was still working in the early 1960s.

All chimneys were swept right to the top with long brushes as there were no vacuums in those days, and both children and adults alike would wait excitedly for the brush to appear out of the top of the chimney! Householders would keep the soot to spread on their gardens as it was thought to be a useful slug repellent.

THE ROADMEN

These days the public areas of the village are maintained by Aylesbury Vale District Council whose workers visit the village on a regular basis to carry out maintenance work. Up to the early 1970s, however, a resident of North Marston was employed full-time as a road-worker, looking after the paths and by-ways of the parish. The road-man would have been responsible for the maintenance of all roads and paths which would have involved such tasks as sweeping, keeping ditches clear, cleaning the gulleys, scything the verges and mending small pot-holes.

In the latter years of the nineteenth century, Rev James alluded to this occupation on several occasions. In 1898 he wrote:

*"Mr **Joseph Tattam** has been promoted from the occupation of road-mender at 15s per week to the office of road inspector at 25s a week; a more efficient and a more honourable man does not exist in the parish of North Marston."*

Around this time **Thomas Ward** (1833-1917) of Brook Cottages, Quainton Road, took over as road-mender (having previously worked as a gardener, groom and agricultural labourer) and we learn that, in 1901, aged sixty-seven and still working, he tumbled off a haystack and was injured so badly he was taken to Aylesbury Hospital (not sustained in the line of duty however!).

After his father's retirement, his son, **Arthur Ward** (1861-1938) of Fulbrook, worked as the village road-man in the years before and after the First World War. He was followed, from the 1930s onwards, by **Harry Heath** who lived in The Bell Cottages, **Teddy Keen** from 11, Quainton Road, **Arthur "Pelly" Pitkin** from Portway and **Felix Gregory** from Schorne

Lane. Felix had been a farm-worker until he took over from Arthur Pitkin in 1956.

When Felix Gregory retired, North Marston no longer had its own resident roadman which was a sad loss.

Back in the 1970s, Ewart Dancer told the following amusing anecdote:

"When I see the mechanical sweeper which, if we are lucky, sweeps the sides of the roads twice during the summer months, my thoughts take me back to another 'sweeper' in the thirties who used a broom. When a cloud of dust was to be seen then he was at his happiest but the spinster ladies who kept the little shop in Quainton Road with its large shining window were not so happy. One sunny day when he was in full swing, out came the elder sister with a large bucket of water; into the air it went, a little of it laying the dust but most of it covering the sweeper. He just carried on with his job but was heard to say, 'Heavy shower of rain all of a sudden'."

Teddy Keen in 1963

Felix and Olive Gregory on their wedding day

THE SLAUGHTERERS AND BUTCHERS

Before and during the nineteenth century, there were no strict regulations about slaughtering animals. In all villages there would have been slaughter-men: most butchers would carry out their own slaughtering of animals (both home-reared and bought in) and then sell the meat, whilst small-holders or families with perhaps just a pig to kill for their own use, might employ a slaughter-man to carry out the deed.

In the early years of the twentieth century, slaughter-men carried a licence. When the Second World War broke out the supply of meat in general was more tightly controlled due to food rationing; this resulted in North Marston's slaughter house in Portway (owned by Franklin's shop) being closed down as Franklin's now had to buy their meat from central suppliers.

There are numerous references to *"Butcher of this Parish"* in the church Marriage and Baptism Records, many of those being fathers and sons. From 1813 to the end of the century no fewer than eight members of the **Buckingham** family, seven of the **Price** family and five of the **Baker** family were butchers.

The "Old Slaughter House" in School Hill

The "Old Slaughter House" at 7 School Hill was a butcher's shop and slaughterhouse until the turn of the twentieth century. Butchers associated with it, either as tenants of the two cottages (3 and 5) next door or as owners or occupiers of number 7, were **Henry Turnham** (1828), **Michael Mayho** (pre 1865), **Joseph Price** (1865) and **Josiah Buckingham** (1873).

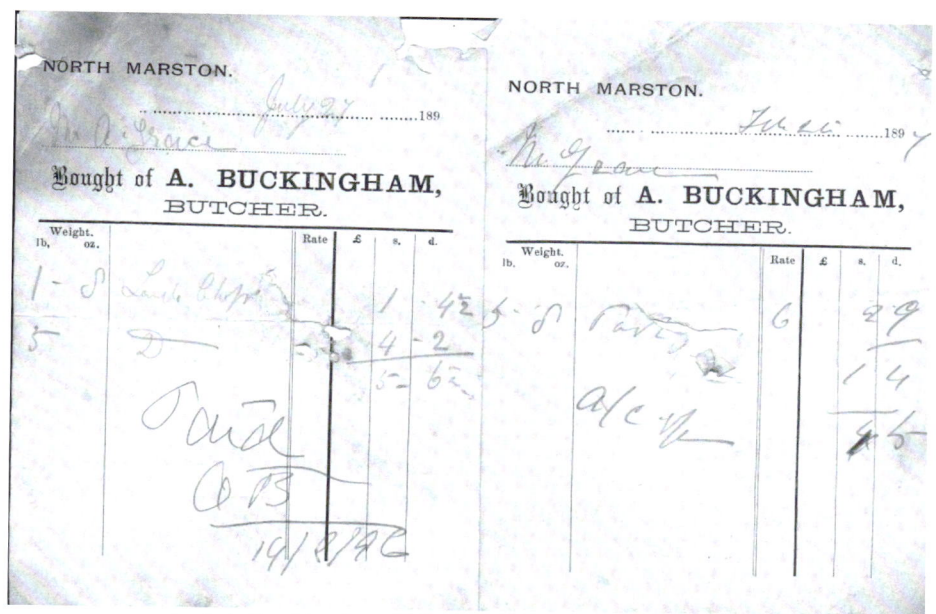

Josiah Buckingham's invoices from 1896 and 1897

Invoices from 1896 and 1897 (*see above*) sent from "A Buckingham" probably relate to Albert Buckingham who, according to the 1901 Census, resided and worked near the entrance to Portway.

In 1881, **Joseph Buckingham**, a butcher in the village, was killed when he was thrown off his mule cart (only a few years after his brother, Matthew, had suffered exactly the same fate). In 1882, we know of **Thomas Price** the butcher buying a prize-winning cow at Winslow market for thirty-nine pounds five shillings.

In the *Kelly's Directory* of 1899 and Census of 1901 there were still six butchers listed: **Denchfield Baker** (also called a calf-dealer) who lived at Home Farm in the High Street and died in 1906 aged thirty-seven, **William Baker** (1836-1912) who traded in Church Street, **Albert Buckingham** who lived near the top of the High Street, **Josiah Baker** who died in 1944 aged forty-one, **James Tattam** and **Thomas Cheshire** (but we also know of Charles Tattam trading as a butcher before this).

The Tattam Family Butchers

Towards the end of the nineteenth century **Charles Tattam** (1833-1900), known as "Charlie", ran a butcher's shop from his family home at 3 Quainton Road (*see picture*).

Tattam's butcher's shop at 3 Quainton Road (note the slats under the eaves)

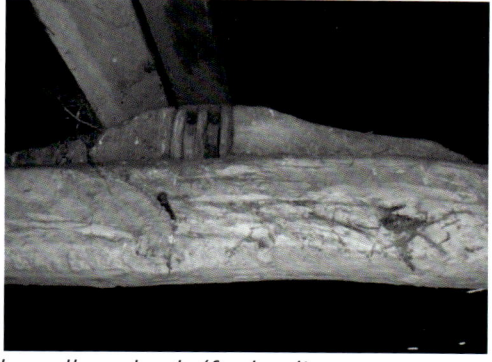

The pulley wheels (for hauling up carcasses) can still be seen on the beam

Charlie Tattam's slaughter-house was situated a little further up the road nearer to The Wheatsheaf.

Charlie's son, **Charles (Jim) Tattam** (1871-1960) who was married to Elizabeth, later sold meat from the backyard of his cottage at 3 High Street where *his* sons, **Fred** and **Sam**, also joined him in the business for a while.

The "Roman Steel Yard" used to weigh meat by Tattam's Butchers

Charles (Jim) Tattam in 1957

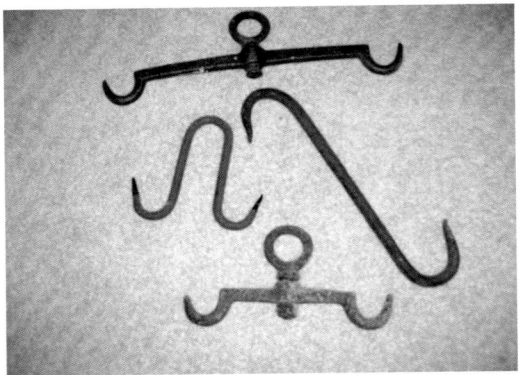

Hooks on which carcasses would be hung

When Charles (Jim) Tattam retired, his sons Fred and Sam continued to make sausages and hog puddings which they sold from the premises. They also had small holdings and milked cows, with Fred running a village milk-round for a time.

David Holden clearly remembers, as a boy, buying sausages every Saturday from **"one of their top sheds"**. Tattams were renowned for their tasty fare and Mona Dumpleton also remembers their **"gorgeous hog pudding and sausages."**

Jim Tattam holding his family's old butcher's scales

Tattam's cottage at 3 High Street

Thomas and Clarence Cheshire

Thomas Cheshire lived for a while at Camden Villas and was only forty-one when he died in 1907, leaving a young son, Clarence. Thomas's grandson, Clifford Cheshire observes:

"People were left in an impoverished state in those days if the breadwinner of the family died."

Thomas Cheshire

Thomas's son, **Clarence Cheshire** (1896-1980) himself became a slaughter-man and butcher, and worked in this capacity for Franklin's Shop (*see Chapter Sixteen*) from the late 1920s until the Second World War. Clarence slaughtered the animals for Mr Franklin in the slaughter-house at the entry to Portway and carried the carcasses, slung over his shoulder, to the shop across the road where they were then hung in the walk-in refrigerator.

When the Second World War broke out new regulations meant that Franklin's Stores could no longer slaughter their own meat but people were allowed to hand in their bacon ration coupons in exchange for keeping their own pig. Clarence was naturally called on to slaughter these animals when needed. His son, Clifford, recalls:

"During the war my dad would kill pigs privately for people. His half-day from the shop was Saturday and he'd often then go out to a farm and kill the animal on a Saturday afternoon, then cut it up on the Sunday morning."

Although, after the war Franklin's slaughter-house was closed down, Clarence would carry on working for Franklin's in a different role until the 1960s.

The slaughterhouse was situated in the yard behind this shed in Portway

Clarence Cheshire

THE BAKERS

Throughout the nineteenth century there were several bakers in North Marston (some with the surname of "Baker"!), one of whom, John Baker, also called himself a *Confectioner*.

We know that in the mid 1800s **George Price** ran a bakery in North Marston and that his son, **Thomas** (born in 1859), also worked in the business. George Price died in 1899 aged sixty-seven and in 1900 Rev James reported:

"Mr Gregory of Oving has removed to North Marston to reside with his son who has succeeded to the prosperous bakery business carried on for so many years by the late Mr George Price."

But where *was* this bakery that had been run for many years by the Price family and which was now being taken over by **Robert Gregory** (whom we know to be twenty-seven years old and a *"Master Baker"* born in Kent)? We might be safe in assuming that it was at 8 School Hill (now called "The Old Bakehouse") near the church, as we know that a bake-house *did* exist there. In the Census of 1901 Robert Gregory's address is given only as *"Top of Village"*.

The baker's oven at 8 School Hill

This beautiful oven (*pictured*) was manufactured by a firm called Thomas Powell in Lisle Street, Leicester Square, London. It is obviously an industrial oven (too big for personal household use) but its date of manufacture is unknown. We do know, however, that Thomas Powell of 49 Lisle Street was listed with the Sun Fire Office as a "smith" in 1828.

In 1912 a Covenant was drawn up on the property of 8 School Hill which stated that bread could no longer be baked on those premises.

James Watkins (1824-1919)

James Watkins ran the Bakery in the High Street from the mid-1800s until the early 1900s. Mr Watkins's bread round, with horse and cart, included at least half a dozen local villages. Neither of his two sons (or daughters) wished to follow their father into the bakery business, it seemed, and it was eventually taken over by one of his workers, Henry Cheshire.

James Watkins

However, James' son, **Charles Edward Watkins**, purchased, in 1888, the old windmill behind Mill House in the High Street (*see Chapter Five*). He demolished the mill but, from these premises, carried on his business as a *"Corn, Cake, Coal and Hay Merchant"*.

The invoices below show Charles Watkins chasing a sum of money owed to him by a Mr Stevens of Lenborough. He added three years' interest to this outstanding debt and, when Charles died in 1908, his brother George took up the case writing in a letter to (we presume) the solicitor: *"I see you have some property up for sale so I suppose this can be settled now"*.

An 1908 invoice from Charles Watkins to Mr Stevens of Lenborough for a sizeable £64 2s 3d

Henry Cheshire (1861-1950)

Henry Cheshire was the son of Reuben and brother of Alfred (*see Chapter Seventeen*). In 1877, aged sixteen, he joined Mr Watkins as a *"journeyman baker"* having spent a few years previous to that with his aunt in Buckingham, working in *her* bake-house.

Henry married Edith Carter in December 1885 and in the early 1900s moved into Winkfield House, Portway. They had twelve children, two of whom, Gilbert and Bernard, were to be killed in the First World War (*see Chapter Fifteen*).

As Mr Watkins became elderly, Henry ran the bakery business for him and when Mr Watkins died in 1919, Henry and his family moved to the High Street and lived on the premises.

In the late 1940s, Henry Cheshire was interviewed by the author, Alison Uttley, for

Henry Cheshire as a young man

her forthcoming book, *Buckinghamshire*, and she wrote:

"I talked to the bright-eyed, ruddy-cheeked man of eighty-five who was up in the apple trees gathering a crop of apples. Never was

such a hale and hearty octogenarian as he is.....He spoke of the baker's oven where pies were baked at 1½d for anything that had meat in it and 1d for other kinds of pies. He was a baker himself. Churchwarden pipes (clay pipes with a long stem) *were brought from the inns to the bakery to be cleaned. Sometimes thirty dirty old pipes would come and they were put in the glowing ashes. They came out as white as when they were new."*

The old bread oven at the bake-house

Village folk would also take their own cakes (especially Christmas cakes) to him to be baked for which he would make a small charge. The only days on which he did not bake were Good Friday and Christmas Day! Henry Cheshire delivered bread around several villages by horse and cart, the horses being stabled behind the bake-house.

The story goes that Henry's horse was so accustomed to visiting the blacksmith that it used to take itself off there (a short trot up the High Street) whenever it felt like it! Henry White, the blacksmith, would tap the horse on its hoof a few times and then send it back home happy! Whenever the family rode out in the horse and cart for an outing it would be a very slow journey as the horse would stop at every house where bread was normally delivered!

Henry Cheshire delivering bread in the early 1900s

When Henry Cheshire finally retired in 1930 he had been baking bread in the village for fifty-three years! He sold the bakery to an employee, Thomas Seaton (whose mother, Eliza, was the last of the old Buckinghamshire lace-makers in North Marston) and he then moved from the Bakery back to Winkfield House.

Henry Cheshire at Winkfield House circa 1930

Henry Cheshire was not only the village baker but also a Governor of the Village School and the School Correspondent from 1930. He was the Chairman of the Trustees of the Clockland and and Poor Allotments, Treasurer to the Organising Committees for Queen Victoria's Silver and Golden Jubilees, and a Special Constable during the Second World War. He was connected with the church all his life as a bell-ringer, Sunday school teacher, sidesman, Vicar's Churchwarden and Secretary to the Parochial Church Council. It was said that, if you could not find him at the bakery, he would be in the church! He was also a very strong supporter of the Temperance Movement.

Thomas Seaton (1901-1963)

Thomas (Tom) Seaton, sometimes called "Sacky" Seaton, had worked as a journeyman baker for Henry Cheshire before taking over the business in 1930 on Henry's retirement.

Tom Seaton's bakery continued to deliver bread daily in a horse and cart (often driven by Cyril Carter) to residents of North Marston, and several times a week to other villages as far as Weedon and the Claydons. Robin Harwood also remembers delivering the bread:

"I used to go round the villages for Tom Seaton, the baker, delivering bread and I'd take the horse down to Archie's field at the end of the day. Ern Seaton, his brother, used to help him too."

In later years the bread was delivered by van.

Tom Seaton at the High Street bakery in 1926

Villagers still took their cakes and Christmas turkey to the bake-house to be cooked, and memories abound of the wonderful bread, dough-cakes and pastries which could be purchased from there and which could be bought even when they were shut:

"He made the loveliest fruit buns and lardy cakes. His hands were always covered in flour." (Valerie Little)

"I can see Mrs Seaton now with her sleeves rolled up kneading the bread dough ready to go in the ovens." (Jennifer Heffer)

"The bread was gorgeous; it had no additives or preservatives and we used to just tear it in half and eat it with no butter or anything." (Graham Ward)

Tom Seaton ran the business until the early 1950s when the village bakery closed for good. What a huge loss to the village that must have been!

Rear view of the old bake-house in the High Street

The old derelict bakery as viewed from the High Street

THE BLACKSMITHS

In the first half of the nineteenth century the main name associated with the blacksmith trade in North Marston was "Ward". Between the years of 1813 and 1857 **John**, **George**, **Robert**, **Charles**, **William** and **Samuel Ward** are each referred to in the church marriage and baptism records as "blacksmith" but we are not sure where their forge was situated.

John White (1844-1923)

John White was the village blacksmith during the last quarter of the nineteenth century and at the start of the twentieth century. He was an industrious and popular man who earned the respect of many in the village, not least the vicar, Dr Samuel James, who wrote about John White in 1891 as being *"an enterprising tradesman….the making of a country parish."*

John White

Born in North Marston in June 1844, John was the son of a bricklayer, George White. In June 1871 John White married Leah Cheshire, the daughter of local farmer William Cheshire and the niece of the Parish Clerk, Reuben Cheshire. Although John was a Methodist he was a generous benefactor to the Parish Church and over the years presented the church with numerous gifts, perhaps the most enduring being the fine pair of wrought iron gates to the churchyard which he gave in July 1887 (*see below*).

The churchyard gates made and donated by John White in 1887

John bought a small house in the High Street, next door to The Bell, which his uncle, the bricklayer William White, extensively enlarged and improved. Dr James wrote in 1885:

"Mr John White has improved his house by handsome iron fencing and, with a new roof and stucco front with small porch it will add to the village street. May we suggest Gordon Cottage as a name?"

Gordon Cottage in 1905

John must have approved of the vicar's proposal because it was named "Gordon Cottage" and to this day bears that name. John and Leah had two sons, Edward and Henry. By 1887 John had established a thriving business and, according to the Village Chronicle, *"Mr John White sends his work….all over England."*

In 1891 he built a new forge at the junction of High Street and Portway. In 1894 he became the first chairman of the newly formed Parish Council and in 1895 was elected a Trustee of the Poors Piece Trust.

John White was one of a small group of Victorian tradesmen who were highly industrious and at the centre of the rapid growth of the village in the last quarter of the nineteenth century.

John White's forge (to the left) at the top of the High Street

He fulfilled a number of functions, contributing as much to the economy as to the welfare of the community in which he lived. As a life-long nonconformist, he also demonstrated an ecumenical outlook that was very progressive at the time. His skill was self-evident in the quality of his work and was passed on, together with the thriving business, to his son and successor, Henry White.

Henry White (1883-1945)

Before the invention of plastic, most household and farming implements were made of metal or wood which could be repaired if broken. Consequently, in the austere years of the early twentieth century, the village blacksmith was kept busy repairing all manner of items, from kettles to engines. This often required the blacksmith to make spare parts from scratch; he was therefore a "jack of all trades" and a key person in keeping the village and its farms running smoothly.

As virtually all transport was horse-drawn until the 1930s, the making and fitting of horse-shoes was a big part of the blacksmith's job. **Henry White**, on inheriting the business from his father as the North Marston blacksmith, went one stage further: his ledger book for 1917 showed that in the spring of that year he supplied a London company with over two thousand horseshoes. Perhaps these were destined for the army fighting in France?

An older Henry White outside the forge (built by his father in 1891)

Henry's customers ranged far and wide. Most of the trade in his earlier years appears to have been in North Marston, Oving and Granborough, but by 1940 he had commercial and domestic customers in Aylesbury, Winslow, Waddesdon and Stewkley. He was also engaged in substantial contract work for Bucks County Council.

All the villagers who knew the forge tell of the unique 'smell' of the place. Valerie

Richardson remembers Henry at work in the forge:

"It was a wonder to me just looking inside the blacksmith's to see him hammer the horse-shoes and make the sparks fly. I was so impressed by him."

Basil Waters remembers:

"Henry White's forge was to me and my brother and sister, as well as to many other children, a source of wonder. Henry himself was a born humorist and no mean craftsman. I believe that some of his handiwork can be seen on the imposing gates to Waddesdon Manor. Many a cart-horse I have watched him shoe and the throaty sound of the bellows rekindling the dying embers of his forge is a sound I vividly recall."

As a blacksmith, Henry was an engineer, a craftsman and an ironmonger. Henry White moved from Camden Villas to Gordon Cottage after his father died (this was the property renovated by his father in the 1880s). By then he had married Elsie Sybilla ("Syb") Cheshire, daughter of village baker Henry Cheshire and they had two children, Nancy and Jean. He died in 1945 aged sixty-two.

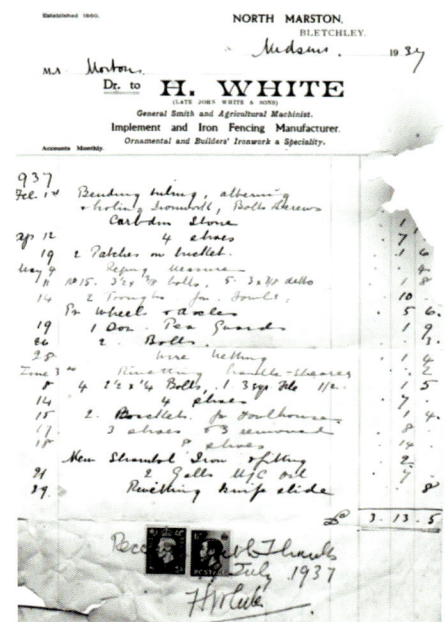

An invoice from Henry White to John Morton dated 1937

THE CARPENTERS, BUILDERS AND UNDERTAKERS

The village carpenter or builder would often double as the village undertaker.

Thomas Ward (born 1841)

We know that from the late 1800s to the early 1900s the undertaker was **Tom Ward**, a carpenter, whose father, Thomas, had also followed the same trade. Tom was married to Mary Anne and he lived at 5 High Street where he had his workshop.

5 High Street in 2012

Tom Ward had the nickname "Tommy Friday" and Jimmy Tattam, his great-grandson tells us why:

"The story goes that he acquired his nickname because his wife was a very religious woman who always had her women friends round on Fridays for prayer meetings at their house. Tom became so fed up with this happening every Friday that one day he nailed up the door and secured the windows to shut them all out!"

The story also goes that, when a young lad called Norman Newman was delivering bread round the back of Tom's house one day, he saw a coffin in the back yard and, as he walked past, Tom Ward rose up out of it from where he'd been having a nap!

The following picture shows a bill which was sent to John Camden Neild (*see Chapter Ten*) from Thomas Ward for mending a gate; this was found in a cupboard at 5 High Street in the 1960s.

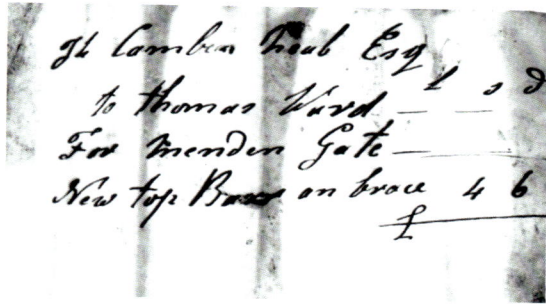

John Price (1830-1899) and Albert Price (born 1864)

Builder **John Price** was able to capitalise on the huge boom in house-building witnessed during the last quarter of the nineteenth century.

John Price's main contribution to village building was Schorne College but he also built his own house Flora Villa (which subsequently became Franklin's Stores), the Parish's Harvest Barn and an extension to the vicarage. Rev James, rector of North Marston, wrote of John Price in 1882:

"Mr John Price...is known as a skilful and energetic tradesman who sticks to his contract and does his work in a workmanlike and efficient manner."

John Price was in the right place at the right time to benefit from the extraordinary boom in house-building in the village from the mid-1870s and for the next two decades.

He was one of four brothers that included Mark Price (the Methodist preacher and parish councillor).

John had a son, **Albert Price** who followed his father into the building trade. Albert had married in 1890 and rented the Red House on the bottom village green.

In 1891, in order to build himself a new dwelling, Albert bought some land, for forty pounds, on the corner of Church Street and Portway and demolished two old cottages and a barn. This new house was then named "Winkfield House" by Rev James (after the village of Winkfield in Berkshire where the vicar had previously lived). That same year Rev James bemoaned the fact that: *"We do not see the name yet on Mr Price's Winkfield Lodge."*

In 1898 Albert raised a second loan on the property and a statement on the mortgage deed reads: *"Albert Price has erected two other houses upon the land and herediment"* which we can safely assume refers to Chapman's Cottages, next door to Winkfield House.

Albert is listed as a *"Carpenter and Builder"* and still living in Winkfield House in 1899 (just after his father's death) but, in 1901, is sadly registered as *"a widower"* and is back living with his mother at Flora Villa with his two young children. He later sold Winkfield House to Henry Cheshire, the baker, for two hundred and twenty pounds.

Flora Villa (now Barnfield Cottage) which was built by John Price

Winkfield House in 1905

Chapman's Cottages (now demolished) on entering Portway from the High Street

Albert Price

Edward Dudley (1875-1950)

Ted Dudley was baptised Edward Laurence Dudley in August 1875 and was the son of Henry and Mary Dudley of 5 Quainton Road.

From a young age Ted appears to have been an all-round participant in village life: in December 1890 he was admitted by the vicar as a bell-ringer; he was very fond of music, having a good tenor voice, and was an instigator and the bandmaster of the village band at the turn of the century; he played an active part in village cricket and football, being a skilled player in his early days; in later years he acted as the village cricket umpire as well as Secretary to the Oving and District Villages Football Association; he was a member of the Parish Council in its early days and helped smooth the way for the provision of the new Memorial Hall; he helped to re-hang the church bells in 1925 and was a very helpful worker in regard to the restoration of the church.

In 1895, when Ted Dudley left the village for London, it drew a comment from the vicar in *The Schornian* magazine:

"Edward Dudley is off to London, and his brass band, and fellow football and belfry friends regret his departure and wish him well. He has kept the club in good order, and acted and spoken independently and pluckily."

The Census of 1901 shows Ted was back living in the village and described him as a *"self-employed carpenter and wheelwright"*. He had also, by this time, met his future wife, Emily Tattam (not a resident of North Marston) and he set about building his new marital home, The Gables, on the High Street.

The Gables

His workshop, however, remained at his family home in Quainton Road where his sister, Lily Young, and her family still lived (this is now the site of Dudley Close). He also had a paddock there where he reared Aylesbury Ducks and kept a big fruit orchard and extensive vegetable garden.

Ted Dudley's workshop (now the site of Dudley Close) clearly visible behind his niece, Eveline Young

Ted Dudley described himself as practising a large number of trades (builder, contractor, undertaker, wheelwright and decorator). He would later add *"Laying on Water Supplies"* , *"Farm Implements"* and *"Tents for Hire"* to his bill headings (he would erect large tents in the Hall Field on special days such as Bank Holidays).

Like his predecessor, John Price, Dudley was responsible for constructing a number of village properties but he also became a specialist in replacing thatch with a tin roof which he also added to his headed paper (*see invoice below*). As his niece, Eveline Parker said: ***"People in those days just didn't want the bother and inconvenience of thatch."***

Memorandum

FROM

E. L. DUDLEY,

Builder and Undertaker.

Old Thatched Roofs covered with iron a Speciality.

Wheelwright. - TENTS FOR HIRE. - Painting & Decorating.

NORTH MARSTON,
Winslow, Bletchley, June. 1947.

To Bucks County Council.

To fitting hot and cold supply to bath, basin etc. and fitting new low-level W.C. suite and connecting up to sewer at Mr. Brazier's, Time.	46	4	6
1 - 30 gall. H.W. tank, 1-40 gall. C.T.tank, 1-2½" cistern head, 1 - 6ft. x 4" smoke-pipe (second-hand).	10	15	10
26ft. 1¼" barrel, 8-1¼"M.& F.bends, 4-1¼"connectors, 8-1¼"sockets, 1-1¼"x ¾"tee, 2-1¼"backnuts, 1-1¼"hex. nipple, 1 - ¾" safety valve.	4	4	6
2-¾"wheel valves, 2-¾"elbows, 1-¾"x ½"bush, 1-¾" plug, 8 - ¾" backnuts, 1 - ½" draining cock.	1	12	0
2-1¼"pipe clips, 1-¾"pipe clip, 1 - 1" bend, 1-½" connector, 6 - 4" pipe nails, 1-1¼" S trap, 1-1¼"cap & lining, 1-1"L.to I.union.		13	10
4-½"unions, 8ft. ¾" lead pipe, 8 bars metal, Oil, Grease, Hemp & yarn.	2	17	0
1 low-level W.C. suite, 3-6'x 4" L.C.C. soil-pipe, 1-4" L.C.C. branch, 1-4" bend, 1-2'x 4" P.W. stack-pipe, 1 - 4" brass thimble.	17	17	3
7ft. ½" lead pipe, 386" of 1¼"lead pipe, 30ft. ½" barrel,	1	6	3
100ft. ¾" barrel, 8ft. 1" barrel, 10ft. 2½" galv. down-pipe,	4	3	0
2 C.I. sq. bends, 1-½" C.P. tap, 1-½" ballvalve,	1	2	6
18-¾" knuckles, 6-¾" tees, 4-¾"x ½"tees, 4-¾"M.& F. bends,	1	1	6
1-¾"x ½" knuckle, 4 - ½" knuckles, 1 - ¾" connector.		3	3
	92	1	5

Ted Dudley's bill heading showing his speciality in tin roofs

Many of Dudley's tin roofs can still be seen to this day both in North Marston and in local villages.

A 'Dudley tin roof' at 3 High Street

Cottages in Quainton Road built by Ted Dudley using reclaimed stone from Schorne College

The bungalow in Marstonfields Road built by Ted Dudley in the 1930s

Ted Dudley in the 1930s

Ted Dudley owned and rented out many cottages around the village. Around 1920 he bought the defunct Schorne College buildings next door to the church and part-demolished them (renting out the remaining part to the Harwood family for five shillings a week) and used some of the reclaimed materials to build a pair of cottages in Quainton Road, one of which was named "Schorne Stones" (*see following picture*). For years afterwards Ted's workshops were full of interesting items such as stained glass windows which he had kept from Schorne College.

Dudley the Undertaker

Not only do people remember Ted Dudley as a builder but equally as the village undertaker. Although it is unclear exactly when Ted started as the village undertaker, we do know that he was doing this in 1919. Robin Harwood recalls in later years:

"If he had to fetch a body from the hospital in Aylesbury in his horse and cart, he'd always come back along Carters Lane and back up to his place via Quainton Road so he didn't have to go through the village. Sometimes he had to take a window out of a house to get a body out."

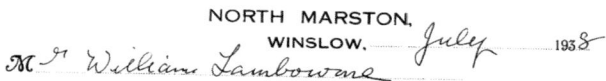

An invoice for Mrs Mary Lambourne's funeral in 1938

Tommy Gray also relates a very funny story:

"Among Ted Dudley's work was the manufacture of coffins. The lads told me that the lean-to shed at the back of the Memorial Hall was used to keep the 'bier'. I had visions of casks and kegs, bottles and crates. I couldn't have been more wrong. It turned out that a 'bier' was a means of conveying the coffins by Mr Dudley to the churchyard."

Prior to their burial, Mrs Evans would 'lay out' the bodies, which would often have remained in the family home until the funeral.

Ted Dudley in later years

Ted Dudley's nephews, Laurence and Raymond Young, continued his business after the war (*see later in the chapter*). On his death in January 1950 his obituary in the local newspaper read:

"An ardent and loyal North Marston man, he was always ready to enter into anything for the good and welfare of his village."

North Marston's old funeral bier, refurbished by Andrew Boyt

In 1994 his old family home and workshop in Quainton Road were demolished to make way for Dudley Close.

Willowdene in 2013

Ted Dudley's family home before its demolition in 1994

William Cumberland (1886-1942)

The Elms in 1994 (before its demolition and re-build)

The house built by Cumberland for Eric Harwood in Marstonfields Road in 1938

William Cumberland was a builder who moved into The Elms in Church Street before The First World War. He and his wife Rhoda had two daughters and two sons. The boys, **Walter ("Cocker")** and **Wilfred ("Son")** both followed him into the building business. They built several houses in the village in the 1930s including Windways and Willowdene (next door to each other along Portway) and 2 Marstonfields Road.

Windways, pictured in January 1962

An invoice from W J Cumberland to Mr F Tattam in 1916

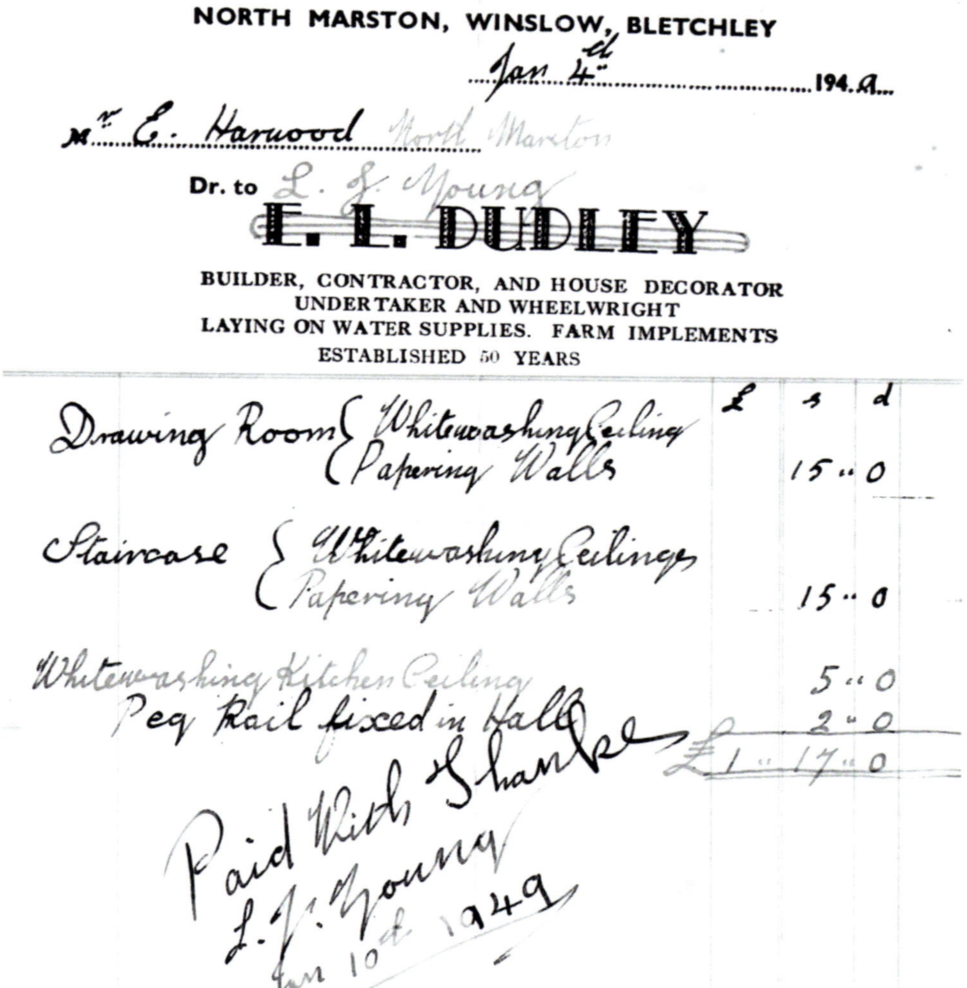

Laurence Young (1907-1983) and Raymond Young (1920-1979)

When Ted Dudley retired around 1945, he left the business to his two nephews **Laurence Young** and **Raymond Young**. Ray, who was a skilled carpenter, joined the business after his return from the Second World War. He married Betty Hogston from Whitchurch and they had a son, Paul, in 1949.

It is amusing to note that, in 1949, Young brothers were still using up some of their Uncle Ted Dudley's old bill heads (*see following picture*).

Church Hill, North Marston, Bucks, May 22nd 1916

Mr F Tattam.

Dr. to W. J. CUMBERLAND,
BUILDER AND DECORATOR.
STOVES, RANGES, & SANITARY WORK.
ESTIMATES FREE. Accounts Rendered Monthly.

		£	s	d
	For repairs & materials at Cottage			
May 16th	Repairs to stairs 8 ft 7 x 1¼ @ 2½		1	8
	5 ft 3 x 2 @ 2d. 10d strip 3d Nails 2d		1	3
	Repairs to floors. 20 ft 6 x 1 @ 2d		3	4
	Alterations to chimney & repairs to ceiling			
	Lias Lime 3/6 sand 1/9 40 bricks 1/9		7	0
	½ Bush plaster 2/-		2	0
	Total Labour. 19½ hrs @ 7d		11	4½
	£	1	6	7½

Received with Thanks
May 27. 1916
W. J. Cumberland

A receipt from W J Cumberland to Eric Harwood 1938

NORTH MARSTON, WINSLOW, BLETCHLEY
Jan 4th 1949

Mr E. Harwood North Marston

Dr. to L. J. Young
~~E. L. DUDLEY~~

BUILDER, CONTRACTOR, AND HOUSE DECORATOR
UNDERTAKER AND WHEELWRIGHT
LAYING ON WATER SUPPLIES. FARM IMPLEMENTS
ESTABLISHED 50 YEARS

	£	s	d
Drawing Room { Whitewashing Ceiling, Papering Walls		15	0
Staircase { Whitewashing Ceilings, Papering Walls		15	0
Whitewashing Kitchen Ceiling		5	0
Peg Rail fixed in Hall		2	0
	£1	17	0

Paid With Thanks
L. J. Young
Jan 10th 1949

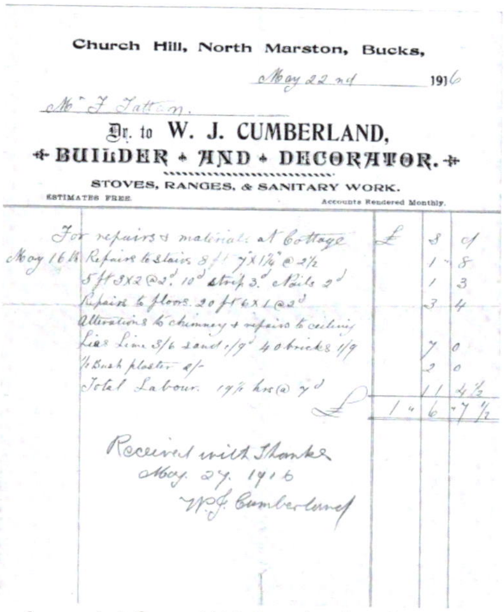

Old invoice showing Dudley heading crossed out and replaced with L J Young (his nephew)

Laurence and Ray Young by their workshop circa 1970

Chris Holden remembers working for them in the 1950s:

"I joined the army on National Service when I was eighteen years old, for two years, and when I came out in 1950 I went to work for Laurence and his brother Ray Young. Laurence built quite a few houses in and around the village.

The bungalow on the junction up to Dancers Farm built for June White and her husband in the 1950s was quite a 'special' build with lots of features. Norman Higgins who worked for him was a very good bricklayer though.

The bungalow in Quainton Road built for Les and June White in the 1950s by Young Bros

Young Brothers also built the bungalows for the council on the left as you go into Granborough and I helped dig those footings out by hand with Leonard Harwood! Ray Young specialised in carpentry and Sid Parker did the painting and decorating.

Laurence bought his first van from Franklin's. He took off the back and made it into a truck. Young Brothers used to do a lot of work around Swanbourne as well. We used to remove thatched roofs and re-tile them. None of us ever wore a mask and some of those thatches were four or five feet thick in places! That probably accounts for my breathing problems!"

The majority of their work involved general building and maintenance jobs in North Marston and surrounding villages. The last house they built in the village was the bungalow for their sister, Eveline Parker, at 2 Church Street where the footings were all dug out by hand six feet deep.

Laurence never married but lived out his latter years in Church Street. He had been a great supporter of village cricket and was the cricket umpire from the 1950s through to the 1970s (*see Chapter Twenty-two*).

Laurence Young circa 1980

Tom Batson (1921-1988)

Tom Batson was born in Whitchurch at the Crown and Thistle pub and, on leaving school, was apprenticed as a bricklayer to Frank Russell Hedges of Station Street, Aylesbury. Having served as a gunner and despatch rider during the Second World War, Tom took up bricklaying again and, in the early days, rode his bike around with his tool kit on the front carrier. He did not pass his driving test until he was thirty-nine and then purchased a green 1947 Austin ten-hundredweight van from the Post Office to use for his business. He and his wife, Dolly, lived in Brook Cottage in Quainton Road for eight years before moving into the house he built himself at 17 Quainton Road, next door to Prune Cottage where Miss Elsie and Miss Lizzie Cox had their little shop.

17 Quainton Road showing old gate leading to the field now the site of Carters Meadow

Tom did a lot of work for Anglian Water Authority, Winslow Council and the Cottesloe Estate in Swanbourne, as well as general building jobs in North Marston. He was multi-skilled and his daughter, Deirdre, remembers:

"Dad always used local building merchants and hardware shops. I remember as a child going with him to Gibbard and Ingram in Winslow and he used Midgleys Hardware there too. He also used Jones and Cox in Aylesbury."

In 1967 he bought, from Alice Carter, a row of old thatched cottages which stood next to his house. They were numbers 19, 21 and 23 Quainton Road, occupied at that time by Bertie and Millie Price, Floss Carter and Jack Price. Over the course of four years he built a bungalow in the field behind them. Tom never charged rent for these cottages but was often rewarded with a bundle of runner beans or such like! When the cottages finally came down the residents moved to the newly-built council bungalows in Portway.

Tom applied for planning permission to redevelop this site together with the old cottage at number 25. However, permission was not granted until November 1988 after Tom had died. When the land was sold, new plans were drawn up for many more houses than Tom had intended, and this area became Carters Meadow.

Tom Batson in the early 1960s (his old van can be seen in the garage)

THE DAIRYMEN

Until the motor-car became a popular means of transport, the milk delivery around the village would have been by horse and cart. An early reference to this comes from 1892 when *"a very serious accident to Mr Chapman's milk-cart from a runaway horse"* was mentioned.

In the 1930s one of the milk-rounds was done by **Arthur Bates** from Crandon Farm (seen here with his horse and cart in Schorne Lane).

Arthur Bates

Jack Gould

In the 1930s the main milk-round was run by **Jack Gould** who was also the landlord at The Sportsman's Arms in Quainton Road and who got his milk from "Son" Brazier at Manor Farm (St John's Manor). Jack wheeled the milk around the village on a barrow and ladled it out of a churn using a jug or measure. Chris Holden can remember helping him out:

"Jack Gould lived at the Sportsman and he went round with milk. I used to meet him at the village hall every morning on my bike and he'd give me a can of milk. Then I'd take it along Marston Fields Road to the bungalow at the first gate to Mr Rogers (who'd moved out of the Mill House) and then I'd take it along Portway to one or two houses along there to save him going along there himself. It was real milk in those days."

Fred Tattam (1904-1991)

In the late 1930s the milk-round was taken over by **Fred Tattam**, whose family had run a butcher's business for many years (*see earlier*); he delivered the milk in churns, again ladling it out as required.

Fred Tattam on his milk cart

When Fred Tattam gave up the milk-round around 1950 he went entirely into farming, and from then on sold the milk from his cows to Nestles. According to his son, Jim :

"My mum always said there was plenty of money in the house when dad had the milk-round."

Harold Carter (1912-1974)

Harold Carter was born in North Marston, the son of Nalder and Florence ("Floss") Carter who lived in Quainton Road. He married Nancy White in 1941 and, on his return to North Marston, having served in Italy for two and a half years during the Second World War, he started up his own milk delivery business in December 1946.

In the early days he, too, can be remembered ladling the milk out of a large churn at each household. Harold lived in Gordon Cottage next to The Bell and Susan Cobbold can remember *"all the crates stacked up outside his house. He was always whistling as he delivered the milk."*

Harold Carter

Tony and Keith Franklin

When Harold died aged sixty-one in 1974 his round was taken over by **Tony** and **Keith Franklin** who farmed at Manor Farm in the High Street. Soon after purchasing the milk-round, they gave up milking cows themselves. The business is still being run by Keith and his son, Jason, today in 2014.

Tony and Keith Franklin

THE VILLAGE POLICEMEN

Before the establishment of the Buckinghamshire Constabulary in 1857, law was enforced in parishes by locally elected Parish Constables and in North Marston this system continued until 1877 (*see Chapter Thirteen*).

An early reference to a crime in the village appears in the *Northmarston Magazine* of 1871 when Mary Ann Linney was charged with stealing a calico petticoat and an apron (valued at one shilling) from her stepmother with whom she was residing. She was arrested by PC Blandy and sentenced to one month's imprisonment and hard labour.

Rev James considered this to be *"richly deserved"* and felt that her step-mother should have *"a little wholesome prison work as well"* for letting her come to the village in the first place! *"Surely"*, he wrote, *"Northmarston* (sic) *is not going to become a refuge for the cast-off profiglates of neighbouring parishes."*

At this time **PC Blandy** and other village constables would have lived in the row of three small cottages named "Policeman's Cottages" which stood behind the church (in the grounds of what is now College House). Around the time that Schorne College was built (*see Chapter Twelve*), these cottages were acquired for the college and renovated, eventually becoming the "Masters' Lodges". This resulted in the village policeman's official residence now moving to Garfield House at the bottom of the High Street. Garfield House, also known as "The Police House", was owned by Ted Anstiss who rented it to the County Constabulary. Jimmy Tattam remembers living opposite the Police House as a child. One day during the war his father wanted to slaughter a pig (which wasn't allowed any more without a licence) and PC Lawrence evidently got to hear about it. Jimmy says:

"PC Lawrence duly turned up asking questions but he was sent off with sausages and a small joint so nothing more came of it!"

Garfield House in the early 1900s before the neighbouring Melba Cottage was built to its right (the Police Constable can be seen standing at the gate)

On his retirement around 1950, PC Lawrence married a village woman, Maggie Walker, a widow, and they then continued to live in Garfield House as a private residence. A new Police House was built at 1 Granborough Road on the site of some old cottages which were demolished to make way for the new building.

After his retirement PC Lawrence obviously kept his old handcuffs hanging on the wall at the back of Garfield House which proved rather too tempting for a young Jimmy Tattam and his friend, Raymond Clarke:

"Actually, PC Lawrence wasn't pleased with us at the best of times! He had some really old cuffs hanging up by his back door on a nail with a big screw-in key and Ray had a real passion about stealing them. He was so determined that one night we crept round there and managed to release the cuffs but Ray then put them on and couldn't get them off again because they were so rusty. It took a lot of oil and wire-brushing to get them off! PC Lawrence never found out who'd nicked those old cuffs!"

The handcuffs in question (*pictured*) were discovered years later in 2012 when Raymond Clarke's old house, The Gables, was being cleared out.

PC Lawrence's handcuffs

After PC Lawrence's retirement a **PC Calloway** arrived, whom David Midwinter remembers very clearly:

"PC Calloway was a good policeman though he put the fear of God into us boys!"

One of his first tasks was to try to persuade the gypsies to move on from Carters Lane. He borrowed Joe Midwinter's tractor, pulled their caravans out onto the road and saw them on their way. He left North Marston after a very short time and he was succeeded by **PC Driver** who was considered to be a very good policeman and a thoroughly nice man; he evidently joined in with everything in the village and got on very well with the youngsters. Some of the lads in the village such as Rod Abbey led him a merry dance, however:

"I can remember being chased by the local Police Constable, Constable Driver, on his pushbike, because I had painted my bike mail-box red and he thought I had stolen it. He never caught us when we went scrumping."

From 1959 until the early 1970s two village policemen, **PC Peter Jacobs** followed by **PC Humble**, lived at the Police House and their children attended the village school. By this time village policing had taken on a different form.

No longer was the constable looking out for his village alone; his job had extended to patrolling a much wider local area and, of course, no longer was he able to give a local miscreant a friendly 'clip round the ear'! After PC Humble left the village, the Police House was sold and North Marston never again had its own resident policeman.

THE VILLAGE GARAGE

Malcolm Holden (1901-1969)

Malcolm Holden was the grand-son of Henry John Holden who founded the tailoring business in the village. When his mother died in 1941, Malcolm moved to her house, The Laurels, at the top of the High Street from where he continued to run the village garage which he had started there in about 1925.

Holden's Garage, Motor and Cycle Engineers offered a wide range of services and their bill heading stated: *"We supply any make Car, Motor Cycle, Radio Sets, Batteries, and all Accessories."*

Malcolm also ran a taxi service and sold bicycles, petrol and paraffin. On comparing two invoices which were sent to John Morton in 1937 and 1945, it is interesting to note that, during this period of eight years, the price of petrol had increased by eight-pence (old money) per gallon.

Malcolm Holden as a young man

Malcolm Holden's garage (left of picture) circa 1940

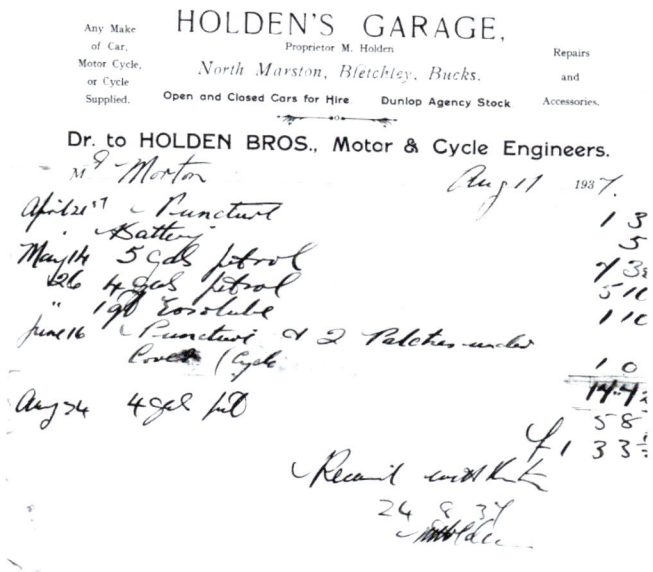

An invoice dated 1937 from Holden's Garage

Holden's Garage in 1963

Holden's garage was not only a place of business, however; it was a social centre of the village! Men of the village would gather there to 'put the world to rights', enjoy a game of cards and dominoes, or place a bet on the horses. As Malcolm was one of the first people in North Marston to have a telephone he could phone bets through to Aylesbury. Pat Brazier, his daughter recalls some of the people who used to frequent the garage:

"Frequent visitors were Harold Chapman, St John Elmer, Son Brazier, Bernard Heritage (Tooley) and many, many more. Dad also ran a taxi service; one of his more pleasant trips was to the 'dogs' at Oxford and to Luton with the young sportsmen of the village."

David Midwinter also says of Holden's Garage:

"That was quite a place, especially on a Saturday morning! There'd be Bertie Price there and Harold Chapman, Ernest Seaton, Leonard Harwood, Eric Harwood and Tom Rickard from Granborough, to name but a few. It was a real institution! Cards and dominoes would be played until 12.00 noon when Malcolm would promptly shut up shop and go in for his dinner! People would call in for their paraffin or petrol and he'd stop the game, serve them and then continue where he left off. During the week he always closed on the dot of 5.00pm; he was a strict timekeeper. Sometimes PC Driver would watch the cards being played and he'd laugh his head off. He'd say, 'I've never seen anything like this before in my life and I know I never will again!'

Although some mild gambling took place this would never happen in front of PC Driver – they just kept the amounts in memory and settled up after he'd gone! In 1963 when it was such a cold winter, Malcolm would look at the outside thermometer and one day he said, 'It`s gone up now, old boy, but this morning she was down to nine degrees'. (That would be Fahrenheit so there were twenty-three degrees of frost)."

Malcolm Holden in 1960

When Malcolm retired in 1967 he decided to knock down the small cottage (Rose Cottage) next door to The Laurels to make a walled garden but, sadly, he died from a heart attack two years later.

Rose Cottage (next door to The Laurels) which was demolished in the late 1960s

THE GENERAL DEALER

Bernard Carter (1901-1963)

Bernard Carter was the son of John and Julia Carter, who lived at 3 School Hill in the early 1900s. His mother had sold home-made wine and sausages to the villagers and had often persuaded her grand-daughter, Ivy, to drive her round the villages in an old Model T Ford to sell her wares! She even ran a tuck-shop from her house for the Schorne College boys; so, general trading was in Bernard's blood! When Ivy was only twelve years old (in 1922) she would go round with her Uncle Bernard, knocking on doors selling fruit. She also used to pick blackberries for him:

"I used to pick a peck a day and he paid three farthings a pound for them. Chivers collected them every fortnight and they'd leave him barrels to fill up. He'd go right out to Brill collecting and selling."

Bernard continued to deal in blackberries right up to the 1960s, and many villagers remember picking them to make a little cash. Tommy Gray recalls selling them to Bernard for three-pence a pound *"which for me meant many hours of work, fingers full of thorns, all for less than a shilling!"*

The berries were then loaded into thirty-six gallon barrels for sending to the jam factory.

Rod Abbey remembers that, in the 1950s he would travel at night to Gerrards (wholesale fruiterers) in London with Bernard's son-in-law, Stan Gurney.

Bernard's grandson, Robert Gurney, recalls:

"Good quality fruit went into punnets and the squashy stuff would be put into drums and taken to London. The good fruit was sold as it was, and the rest used for jam and dye-making."

Villagers talk of the intense smell of the fruit in his sheds.

Something else (used for dyes and eating) which Bernard bought from around the locality were "Blue Stalks" (or "Blue Legs") which grew in fairy rings on pasture land. Bernard even travelled into Oxfordshire to acquire these and they were then transported to Leicester and Nottingham by train from Aylesbury railway station.

In the 1950s Bernard, along with Rod Abbey, Stan Gurney and Simon Carter, would go to London where they would load timber from demolished buildings and bring it back to North Marston to be sawn up, perhaps into kindling wood, which would then be delivered to shops all around. He would buy packing cases from glass factories which he would use to make sides of sheds, and he also carried out furniture removals.

Bernard Carter lived at the top of the High Street next to Holden's Garage with his wife, Alice (who owned the field where Carters Meadow now stands, hence its name). As well as having large storage sheds there (including the old slaughter-house) he also had a very large Dutch barn in Quainton Road (now the site of Shepperds Close) from which he ran another enterprise (which the locals called "Whipsnade") which was open all the time and from where villagers could buy all sorts of goods.

Bernard Carter's shed in Quainton Road (now the site of Shepperds Close)

It was a real "Aladdin's Cave" and Tommy Gray describes it as:

"..an eclectic mix of 'you name it, they had it' items from sewing machines to shirts, trousers to trowels, umbrellas and walking sticks to carpentry and engineering tools, many of which were bought at various railway lost property sales. Outside in a large field were all sorts of agricultural machinery. All was repaired, refurbished and repainted, all ready for sale by auction. Bernard would have a stall where umbrellas and walking sticks were on sale in addition to the mowers, rakes, elevators and pitchforks."

It was evidently 'like a market-place' down in the shed on Sunday mornings (the only day some people got off work); folks came from all around the area.

Bernard Carter is not only remembered for being a good dealer, however. On festive occasions he would bring out his swing-boats and set them up on the village green to raise money for the Royal Bucks Hospital in Aylesbury. He also took a barrel-organ round the villages to raise money (*see photo*). Bernard Carter was a staunch Tory and would gather with his friends in The Bell before going off to Buckingham to get the election results.

```
Phone—North Marston 218
                         NORTH MARSTON, BLETCHLEY
                                                        19......
   M..........................................
   Dr. to  B. L. CARTER
           General Dealer
   New and Second-hand Building Material    .   Log and Firewood Merchant
   Obsolete Salvaged and Bankrupt Stock     .   Farm Implements and Machinery
```

Bernard's bill heading

Bernard Carter's fund-raising float and barrel-organ

Bernard Carter outside the White Hart in Buckingham on Election Day 1955

THE HAY MERCHANT

Lionel Clarke (1910-1995)

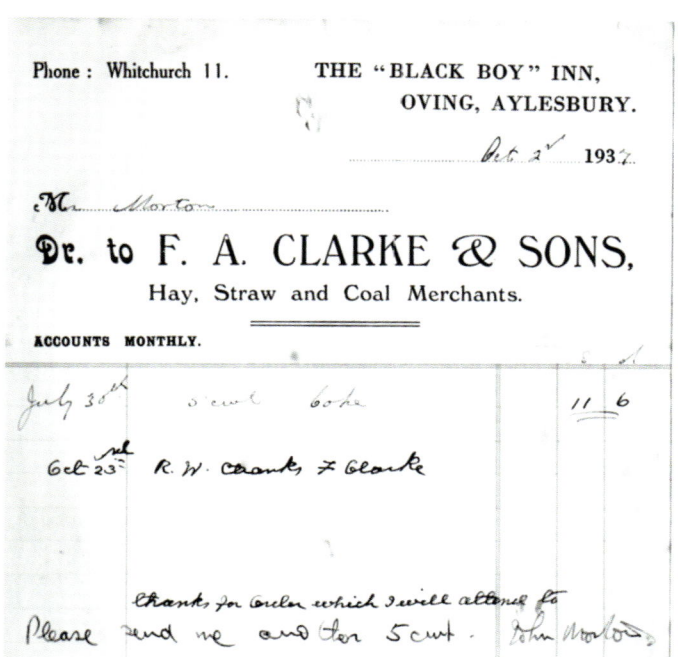

An invoice from F A Clarke & Sons in 1937 before the business moved to North Marston

Lionel Clarke was the son of Frederick "Smoker" Clarke who ran the Black Boy pub in Oving and who was also a Hay and Straw Merchant. Lionel took over this business from his father in the 1940s and ran it from his home at The Gables in the High Street, North Marston. For a while he continued to keep the lorries at Oving but eventually moved them to North Marston, keeping them (together with his bales of hay and straw) in a large barn behind his wife's family home in Quainton Road. He had married Emily Young in 1935 and they had three sons: John, Raymond and Francis.

Lionel Clarke with his family at The Gables circa 1958

The two eldest sons, John and Raymond, worked for the family business driving the lorries, as did several other men from the village at various times. Lionel bought and sold surplus hay and straw, often travelling to places quite far afield such as Hunstanton in Norfolk. The business ran until the mid-1960s.

Raymond Clarke (left) with his friend Jimmy Tattam on a Clarke's hay lorry in the 1950s

THE WINDOW CLEANER (AND VILLAGE HISTORIAN)

Eddie Lambourne (1904-1989)

Eddie Lambourne was a window-cleaner who also had a great interest in village history.

In the 1950s David Holden can remember helping Eddie with his window-cleaning business:

"I used to do odd jobs for Eddie Lambourne when I was about fourteen years old, helping him with his window-cleaning business. He used to go on the bus (Red Rover and United Counties in those days) with his bucket and little ladder to Whitchurch, Winslow and Oving and he'd walk to Pitchcott from there if he had a job to go to."

Robin Harwood also helped Eddie for a while and remembers clearly having to clean the very high windows at Winslow Hall. They only had ordinary ladders but the owner of the large house would not pay them until they had cleaned the tiny round window at the very highest point at the front. Robin can remember climbing very precariously up to this great height and 'flicking' the cloth at the window for effect! They did get paid!

Eddie is also remembered for making wreaths for funerals and at Christmas which he would then sell. He would collect holly from local big houses where he cleaned windows such as Swanbourne House School, Oving House and Nubar Gulbenkian's house at Hoggeston.

Eddie Lambourne

Eddie was an authority on the history of North Marston and collected a huge number of old photographs, documents, deeds, manuscripts, magazines and other memorabilia over the years. On his death he left all this to the Centre for Buckinghamshire Studies in Aylesbury where it can be viewed today. He also wrote a booklet on the Field Names of North Marston.

Eddie was a regular at The Wheatsheaf pub and he, Teddy Keen and other regulars would often sing a song in there called *The Prickly-lie Bush*. In the 1950s a man called Seamus Ennis, who had a radio programme called *As I Roved Out* on the BBC Home Service, was doing research on traditional folk music and Eddie contacted him with the result that Eddie and friends were recorded at The Bell in Winslow in 1952 singing *The Blackberry Grove*. The recording was subsequently played on the radio.

THE 1960S POTTER

Jim Cross

Jim Cross and his wife Violet (Vi) moved into the village in the early 1960s and lived at 3 School Hill. The house at the time needed much renovation and Jim, who at that time was a full-time pottery teacher at Quarrendon School in Aylesbury and also taught evening classes in Aylesbury College, had dreams of setting up a pottery there. Eventually, the large shed on the roadside at the bottom of the hill became Jim's studio as there were large windows looking onto the road.

Jim became interested in building large garden pots and created a range called Delaware which began to sell well. He also made smaller everyday wares, many of which were purchased by village residents.

After a while Jim started to experiment with building a compact robust electric potters' wheel (the only electric models available at the time were very bulky). He had no engineering experience but with the loan of Peter Morton's welding gear, he made a start.

At the time the school-leaving age had just been raised and many of Jim's pupils at Quarrendon became disillusioned so Jim enlisted the help of one of the 'hardest nuts' and together they worked on building the new wheels. The angle-iron used to make the frame was from the sides of old beds and electric motors were taken out of scrap washing machines. So the JX4 Electric Potters' Wheel began its journey in North Marston.

During his time in North Marston Jim was also a bell-ringer and taught at the church Sunday school.

After leaving North Marston Jim went to Morecambe to teach educationally challenged pupils but eventually set up Pilling Pottery in Lancashire which is still thriving after forty-three years.

The pottery workshop at the bottom of School Hill in the early 1960s

Jim Cross

Location of Traders in North Marston

1. Tanty Carter (Shoemender)
2. Clarence Cheshire (Slaughter-man)
3. Malcolm Holden (Garage)
4. John & Henry White (Blacksmiths)
5. Tony & Keith Franklin (Milk)
6. William Cumberland & Sons (Builder)
7. Robert Gregory (Baker)
8. Jim Cross (Potter)
9. John Price (Builder)
10. James Garner (Shoemaker)
11. Harold Carter (Milk)
12. Charles Watkins (Corn Merchant)
13. Thomas Ward (Carpenter, Undertaker)
14. "Jim" & Fred Tattam (Butchers, Milk)
15. James Watkins, Henry Cheshire & Thomas Seaton (Bakers)
16. Lionel Clarke (Hay Merchant)
17. Ted Anstiss (Barber)
18. Police House 1
19. Police House 2
20. Charles Tattam (Butcher)
21. Ted Dudley (Builder, Undertaker), Young Bros (Builders)
22. Tom Batson (Builder)
23. Bernard Carter (General Dealer)
24. Jack Gould (Milk)

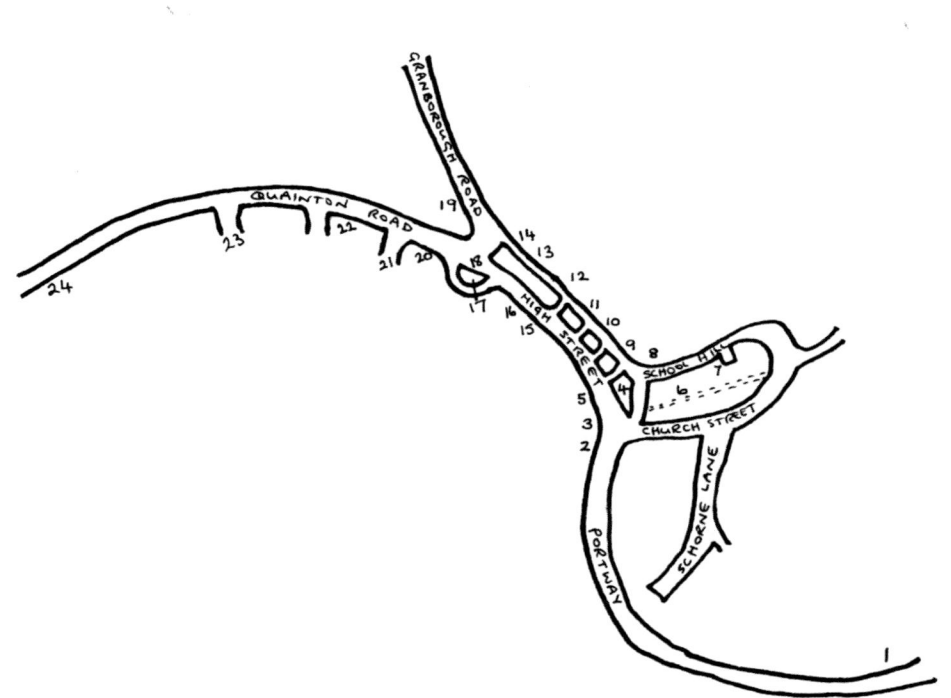

Nineteen

PUBS AND ALE HOUSES

Colin Price

Introduction

In early medieval times, the church controlled the production of ale. After this, its production and sale were relatively unregulated. Beer was an important and much consumed drink; with water unfit to drink unless boiled, beer provided a safe refreshment and was consumed by almost everyone.

With such popularity it is hardly surprising that there were many sources of beer in late medieval times including unregulated inns, alehouses and domestic brewers. But concerns grew, and the first Licensing Act was passed in 1552 requiring alehouse keepers to apply to two Justices of the Peace to receive a licence to sell beer. Subsequent legislation imposed further conditions and time-limits so the licensee periodically had to reapply for a licence. The records of these licence applications tell us that in 1753, North Marston had four licensed victuallers: John Foster (a butcher), George Foster, William Foster and another John Foster. It appears the Fosters had a monopoly but the records do not tell us the names of their establishments.

The records for 1792 are more revealing. These show that, by then, North Marston had only two licensees: Elizabeth Tattam at The Bell (renamed The Pilgrim in 2010) and John Forster at The Wheatsheaf. In the nineteenth century, two more inns were to open in the village: The Armed Yeoman in Church Street and The Sportsman's Arms in Quainton Road.

From 1868 to 1911, North Marston had four inns. This does seem a large number for a small village and the vicar commented in 1903 that there was a public house for every one hundred and thirty-one villagers.

However, it is important to remember that this was before the Village Hall was built and the public houses provided the only meeting rooms other than the vestry for both social and official functions.

Of great importance in the eighteenth century were the many meetings held in The Bell Inn to discuss the implementation of the *North Marston Inclosure Act 1778* (*see Chapter Seven*). Also in this century we understand that The Wheatsheaf was the location for the dispensing of relief to the poor by the vestry.

Inns were the locations for coroners to carry out inquests. We have records of inquests held at The Armed Yeoman on Jane Watson who drowned in the well in 1861 and Henry Tattam who dropped dead in the High Street in 1890. We also know of inquests held at the Sportsman's Arms: Joseph Buckingham who died after being thrown off his mule-cart in 1881 and John Henley who died of natural causes in 1871.

The Bell Inn provided a suitable location for public auctions. For example, this was the meeting place for the auction of the windmill in 1888 (*see Chapter Five*).

Very much as today, pubs provided the ideal location for the discussion of parish politics but they took on much more significance in the days before Parish Councils when they provided the only forums for such debate. We know of forceful meetings at the Armed Yeoman in the 1870s involving individuals described by the vicar as "*a small group of malcontents*".

The public houses also provided meeting rooms for Societies (for example, the meetings of the Royal Antediluvian Order of Buffaloes were held at The Wheatsheaf Inn) and for social functions such as the Patriots' Supper held at The Bell (*see Chapter Twenty-one*).

The Reverend James often used *The Schornian* as a vehicle to censure inappropriate behaviour whenever he encountered anything that displeased him, so it is quite surprising to find him complimentary of many of the landlords. He describes Richard Webb at the Armed Yeoman as *"always anxious to keep his house free from drinking to excess"*. He was also *"quite satisfied that The Bell Inn is most respectably conducted and that Mr Holden allows no disorderly proceedings upon his premises"* and that the other three Inns are *"also very good and respectable inns"*.

We are left with the impression of four well-run and generally respectable inns, providing necessary meeting rooms for many vital functions of the parish.

It is interesting, and possibly surprising, to note the role that female licensees played in the early history of the village inns. The first licensee of The Sportsman's Arms was Catherine Hinton in 1868 and she continued as landlady till 1891. After the death of James Garner at The Bell, the public house remained in the family in the hands of his wife and daughters for another twenty-three years. Similarly, at The Armed Yeoman, Ann Carter was landlady for twelve years following the death of her husband Mark, continuing till the age of seventy-six.

The village could not continue to support four inns long into the twentieth century and in 1911, Aylesbury Brewery Company decided that The Armed Yeoman was no longer viable; it was de-licensed and sold to the landlord, Henry Anstiss.

In 1953, The Sportsman's Arms was the next to be closed by Aylesbury Brewery Company; it was sold to Peter and Delia Ecob.

Only two years later, and despite a petition signed by over two hundred people, The Wheatsheaf Inn was de-licensed by Aylesbury Brewery Company and later sold to Janet and David Long.

Aylesbury Brewery Company's long association with the village came to an end in 1993 when the company (then owned by Allied Lyons) sold The Bell Inn. By 2010, The Bell Inn was in private ownership and was renamed "The Pilgrim".

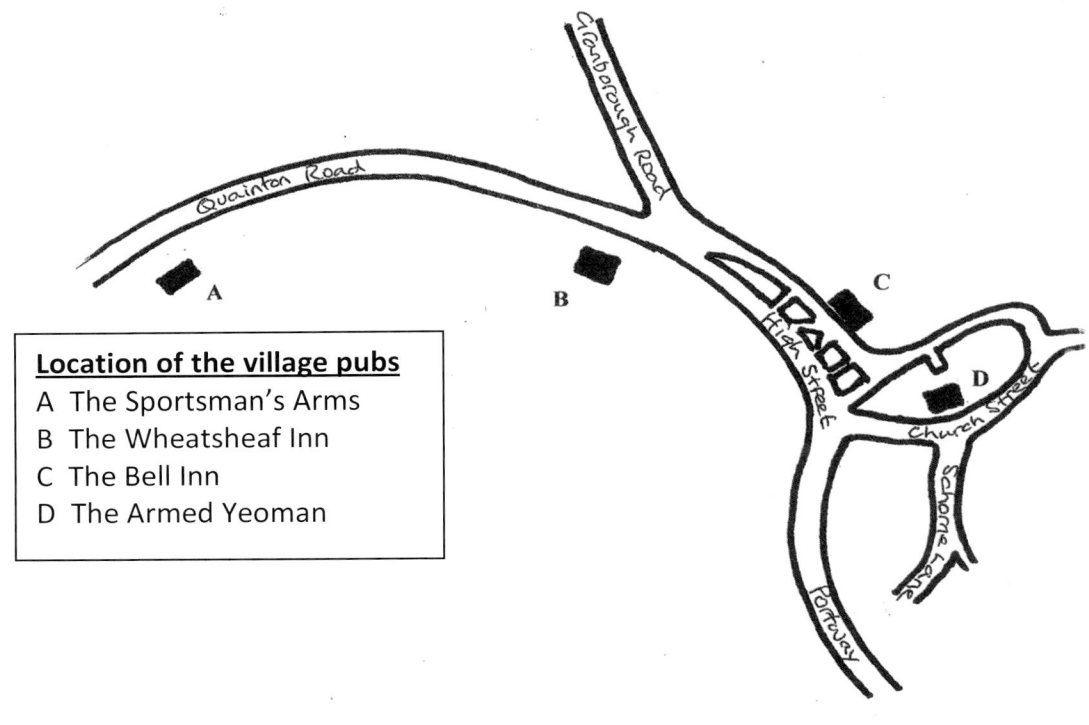

Location of the village pubs
A The Sportsman's Arms
B The Wheatsheaf Inn
C The Bell Inn
D The Armed Yeoman

The Armed Yeoman

The Armed Yeoman viewed from Schorne Lane circa 1900

Throughout its history The Armed Yeoman has also been referred to as "The *Arm'd* Yeoman" and (uniquely in the 1851 census) as "The *Valiant* Yeoman". The original magnificent pub sign is still in existence. It is hand-painted on wood and held together round the edges by wrought-iron. It names the pub *The Armed Yeoman* so that is the name that will be used in this chapter. It was the only public house of that name in Britain.

The Armed Yeoman was built sometime in the early 1600s. We are not certain when it was first licensed but it was referred to as a "Public House" in the 1832 valuation.

Richard Webb was the landlord from approximately 1854 till 1882. The Reverend James refers to him as *"a model innkeeper who never allowed drunkenness on his premises, refused to serve more than was good for his customers and expelled noisy and troublesome visitors."*

It would appear that during Richard Webb's time at The Armed Yeoman it became the meeting place for those members of the village who did not fully support the changes and innovations introduced by the Reverend James. These were the days before Parish Councils and there was no forum for discussion of parish politics. The vicar noted that Richard Webb sympathized with these views but was *"never slanderous or abusive"* and, before his death in 1882, Webb apologized to the vicar for *"some little hostility shown to his improvements and alterations."*

Mark Carter succeeded Richard Webb as landlord in 1882. During his time at The Armed Yeoman there was a successful club run by John Carter. We have a record of an anniversary meeting of the Armed Yeoman's

Club on Whitsun-Tuesday 1887 attended by about twenty members who celebrated *"in a pleasant and satisfactory manner"*.

Mark Carter died in 1887 and his wife, Ann, took over the running of The Armed Yeoman despite being sixty-four years old. Ann Carter held the licence for twelve more years and finally retired in 1899 at the age of seventy-six.

The last landlord of the Armed Yeoman was Henry James Anstiss. He took over as licensee in 1899 and continued until it was de-licensed on 3rd November 1911.

Anstiss himself bought the premises from Aylesbury Brewery Company for two hundred and eighty pounds which was regarded as a bargain at the time

Henry Anstiss is remembered chiefly as the first man in the village to own a car; we are not certain of the date but it was approximately 1914. The manufacturer was Alldays and Onions. Apparently, people would cluster round to watch when he started the motor, warmed her up and drove slowly out of the back yard and down the road. Thirty years later, Jack Gould who was the landlord of The Sportsman's Arms and also the village milkman, was delivering milk to Henry Anstiss when he saw the car under a pile of rubbish in the barn behind The Armed Yeoman.

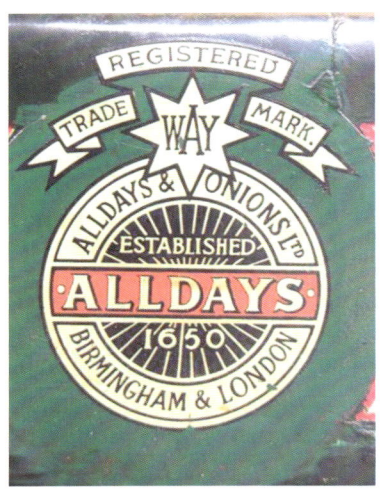

Clifford Cheshire recalls:

"The car was taken down to Jack Gould's at The Sportsman and Harold (Spider) Tattam got it going again; I remember seeing it go up the road on one occasion".

Henry Anstiss on the steps of The Armed Yeoman

The Sportsman's Arms

The earliest records we have for The Sportsman's Arms date back to 1753. It was partly destroyed by fire in June 1837 and the owner at the time, Mr Dell, wasted no time in restoring it. The work was completed by September of the same year and the building we see today dates from that time.

The Sportsman's Arms was first licensed as an "Ale House" by Catherine Hinton in 1868. She kept The Sportsman's Arms right through to November 1891 when she suffered a stroke. There were then briefly two landlords: George Seaton and James Maddams.

Arthur Gregory took over in 1903 and as far as we can tell he remained till the early 1930s. The following photograph is of The Sportsman's Arms taken in the early 1900s. Arthur Gregory's name is on the licensing sign above the door but unfortunately the rest is illegible. Apparently he was known as "Thresher" Gregory and he also sold coal.

Ivy Wheeler recalls: *"He was a real bragger and folks say he decorated his walls with pound notes!"*

The brewery delivered the barrels to the door on the left which led down into the cellar. There was one small room for drinkers behind the window on the left and a small hatch (still present) between the cellar room and the drinking room through which beer was served.

The Sportsman's Arms is remembered as a small quiet Ale House which was at its busiest on Sunday mornings with visitors from surrounding villages. As far as we can tell, The Sportsman's Arms was never licensed as a *Public* House and beer was the only alcoholic drink that it was licensed to sell.

The last landlord was a retired London police sergeant called Jack Gould who came to the village in the early 1930s. By all accounts he was a very popular man in the village. As well as being licensee, he was also one of the village milkmen.

The Sportsman's Arms when Arthur Gregory was licensee

Many have memories of him pushing his milk barrow around the village loaded with its milk churn. As was the norm at that time he had a measuring jug with a handle which hooked into the rim of the churn and was used to fill the customers' jugs at their back doors.

Tommy Gray, a wartime evacuee, recalls with amazement:

"..just put your jug by the back door with a crocheted cover with beads around the edges and the milk is then dispensed from a can by means of a pint measure into the jug and the crochet cover replaced to keep the flies out! Wow!"

Aylesbury Brewery Company decided that The Sportsman's Arms was uneconomical to keep open and it was de-licensed in 1953. Peter and Delia Ecob bought The Sportsman from Aylesbury Brewery Company and moved there in 1956.

The Sportsman in 2010

The Wheatsheaf Inn

The Wheatsheaf in the early 1900s

Mary Stevens and children at The Wheatsheaf circa 1912

The Wheatsheaf Inn has been a public house since the eighteenth century with records going back to 1777 but the building itself is much older. A coin dated 1694 (*pictured*) from the reign of William and Mary was found by Janet and David Long during restoration work; the coin was under a door frame and would have been placed there by a builder to date his work.

Back in the eighteenth century The Wheatsheaf played an important part in village life. The churchwarden's accounts for that period record that *"the Vestry adjourned to the Wheatsheaf"* to dispense relief to the poor of the parish.

The representatives of the church gathered in the snug behind a closed door and the poor met in the tap room. The door separating the two has a small hatch with a sliding door measuring approximately four inches by two inches (*see picture below*).

Tradition states that the Poor Law Relief was passed through the hatch but it was more likely that the hatch was used as a means of identification before admission.

Arthur Leonard Woolf was the licensee at the end of the 1930s and the start of the 1940s

A very rare feature of The Wheatsheaf Inn was the "Twirler" in the ceiling of the tap room. "Twirling" was a very local game unknown outside a five-mile radius of the village. The Twirler in The Wheatsheaf Inn dated back to the eighteenth century. It consisted of a rotating pointer mounted horizontally on an overhead beam. The numbers *1 – 12* were painted in a circle on the ceiling. Everyone in the tap room would spin the Twirler and the unfortunate person with the lowest score would buy the next round! The Twirler was also used to decide who threw first in a game of darts on the basis of a call of "Evens or Odds".

There was a very large meeting room in the building behind The Wheatsheaf Inn. This was the meeting place of the Buffaloes (*see Chapter Twenty-one*). After the Second World War the village cricket team played on a field behind The Wheatsheaf Inn and teas would be served in the meeting room. The outbuilding also housed a skittles alley. Aylesbury Brewery Company bought The Wheatsheaf Inn in 1926.

Lilian and Alf Dymock (pictured in 1960) who were the last landlords of The Wheatsheaf Inn

By 1955, despite its popularity under landlords Lilian and Alf Dymock, the brewery decided to close down The Wheatsheaf because it had become uneconomical.

John Woolley, William Tattam and John Price using the "Twirler"

Wheatsheaf regulars featured in a Bucks Herald article in 1955

A newspaper article reports that at this time the village was divided into the "uptowners" and the "downtowners" and this division has been confirmed by those who were young men in the early 1950s.

The "uptowners" frequented The Bell and the "downtowners" drank in The Sportsman's Arms or The Wheatsheaf Inn. The Sportsman's Arms had closed in 1953 and, when closure of the Wheatsheaf Inn was threatened, the downtowners had no desire to go to The Bell Inn. In fact they threatened that they would go three miles to Winslow in preference!

A petition was drawn up and signed by over two hundred people to try to dissuade the Aylesbury Brewery Company from closing The Wheatsheaf Inn but it was unsuccessful and The Wheatsheaf Inn closed in 1955.

The downtowners responded, not by drinking in Winslow, but by opening their own social club in the side room of the Memorial Hall (*see Chapter Twenty-one*).

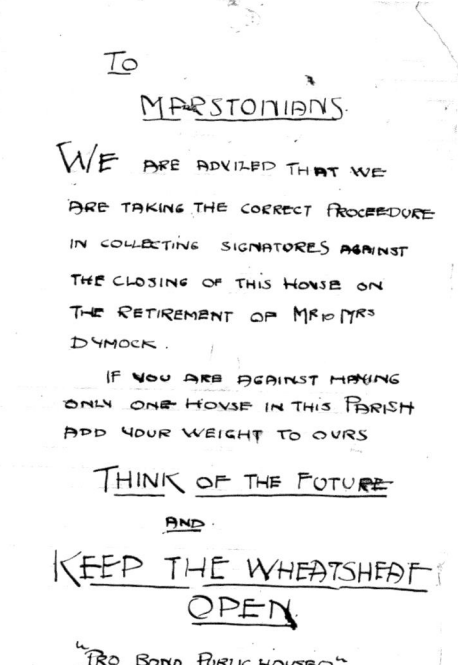

Beer prices at The Wheatsheaf in 1951

The appeal for the Wheatsheaf petition

The Bell Inn (renamed The Pilgrim in 2010)

Jane Garner with two of her daughters, Louisa and Irene Jane, outside The Bell in the early 1900s (note James Garner's shoe maker's cottage next door)

The Bell Inn has stood at the centre of the village for more than three hundred years. We cannot be certain when it first became a public house; our earliest record dates back to 1792 when Elizabeth Tattam was the licensee, but it was probably earlier than this.

The story of The Bell Inn is dominated by the Garner family. James Garner took over the licence from James Holden in 1883 at the age of thirty-eight. He was landlord at the Bell Inn for twenty-eight years until his death in 1912. James' wife Jane took over from her husband for another four years until her death in 1916. Next in line was their daughter Louisa. When Louisa died just four years later, her sister Charlotte took over as landlady right through to her retirement in 1953.

So the Garner family ran The Bell Inn for fifty-two years from 1883 to 1935.

Mr & Mrs James Garner

Jane Garner, standing next to a tailor from Holden's, receiving a delivery from Tompkins, carriers of Granborough, at The Bell in the early 1900s

The Bell Inn circa 1915

During his time as landlord, James Garner was also the village shoe-maker in the cottage next door to the pub. He retired from this role in 1907 at the age of sixty-two. James Seaton is recorded as the next "boot-maker" in the village followed by George Carter and Alfred Cox.

It is interesting to note that Christine Garner became a member of the Band of Hope in 1887. She was one of James and Jane Garner's daughters, brought up in The Bell with parents who were landlords yet she chose to abstain from all intoxicating drinks. The picture on the next page shows her Pledge Card.

After Charlotte Garner retired in 1935 the next landlord was Frank Arnold. Frank and his wife, Gladys, kept The Bell through the Second World War and into the 1960s. From 1955 onwards The Bell was the only remaining pub in the village.

Christine Garner's pledge card dated 1887

As already mentioned, in the early 1950s The Wheatsheaf Inn and The Sportsman's Arms were popular with the "downtowners" and The Bell was the preferred pub of the "uptowners". For some reason Frank Arnold was not popular with many of the "downtowners". After The Sportsman and The Wheatsheaf closed in 1953 and 1955, The Bell had a monopoly apart from the Social Club at the Memorial Hall.

There was a small hatch at the back of The Bell Inn through which Gladys Arnold would serve children. Many of who were young in the 1950s and the 1960s have fond memories of buying Vimto, Hubbly Bubbly and packets of crisps with the salt in a separate blue wrapper. They also recall the men emerging from The Bell after a good drinking session trying to 'pitch pennies' onto the ledge which ran around Holden's shop to see how many they could get to land. This practice is well remembered because there were plenty of pennies for the children to collect on the ground afterwards!

In Frank Arnold's days, the main bar was the public bar straight in front of you on entering through the front door; to the right was a saloon bar that was only opened on special occasions. In the 1970s a very popular landlord called Melvyn Busson converted the two bars into one and incorporated the adjoining cottage into the pub. (This is the cottage which had been James Garner's shoe-maker's shop).

By 2010 the Bell Inn was in private ownership and its name was changed to "The Pilgrim".

The Bell Inn in the 1950s taking a delivery from North and Randalls

Frank and Gladys Arnold 1997

Melvyn Busson (left), Pete Orme, Eileen Busson and Paul Young pictured at Melvyn Busson's leaving party at The Bell

Villagers form a working party in April 2010 to prepare for the opening of The Pilgrim (see Chapter Twenty)

Twenty
EVENTS AND CELEBRATIONS
Sue Chaplin

For hundreds of years the villagers of North Marston have joined together for events and celebrations of all kinds. There have been parties and parades to celebrate coronations, royal weddings, jubilees and victories in war; sales and fetes have raised money for worthy causes; ceremonies have taken place to open a new village facility or building; fairs, feasts, plays, concerts, dances and light-hearted sporting events have provided fun and entertainment.

Over the years these special events, all requiring much organisation and planning by dedicated individuals, have given the people of North Marston the important opportunity to join together as a community. No village is complete without its ongoing mix of events and North Marston has been a hive of activity.

We can go right back to the early twentieth century to read in the school log books of the number of rummage sales, teas and concerts which were held in the old school (which would often close for the afternoon if the premises were needed for a function).

Traditionally, May Day (1st May) was a cause for celebration and in the earlier part of the twentieth century schoolchildren had a day's holiday. Until the 1950s it was the custom for the children to decorate a maypole (usually a stick about two feet in length) with flowers (often begged!) from village gardens or with blossom from the hedgerows. They would then take their maypole round the village, knocking on people's doors, to raise money for a good cause or, in some cases, for themselves! Robin Harwood remembers doing this in the 1930s and admits that, often, the same maypole would turn up at the same door but carried by a different child!

After the Memorial Hall was built in 1924, events such as the Sweet Pea Show in 1926 were held in there instead of in the school. Through the 1930s Ted Dudley, the village builder and undertaker, would erect tents in the village hall field for festivities every August Bank Holiday Monday.

The village has held its fair share of shawl parades, tramps' suppers and Easter bonnet parades (*see Chapter Twenty-one*), comic football matches, quizzes, plant sales, old photograph exhibitions, sports fun days, sponsored cycle trips, balls, dances, Easter egg hunts, Christmas parties and a multitude of fund-raising activities and celebrations. In 2010 an Open Gardens event was also held for the first time.

A jumble sale in the village hall in 1999

Comic football match on the sports field in 1969

A shawl parade behind the Memorial Hall in the 1930s

A shawl parade in the old school playground circa 1950

VILLAGE FEASTS

The tradition of village feast days goes back to early medieval religious festivals celebrating the feast day of the village's patron saint. These would have been almost carnival-like and celebrated with village processions and feasting.

In the earlier part of the twentieth century the Feast Week in North Marston took place near the end of August and the beginning of September after the end of harvest. Village school pupils (who, before 1908 would have been back at school by then) were given a week's holiday.

In the late nineteenth century the "Feast" attracted many people from surrounding villages. By 1870, shows, stalls, booths and tents were set up around the village green with many visitors and stall-holders coming from outside the village. The large number of people descending on the village must have caused problems at times but Rev James wrote (with obvious relief) in the parish magazine that year:

"Walking through the Feast, in the gloaming one night, we saw nothing bad, no improper women, no fighting, no immorality, and heard no swearing, or ribaldry, or indecency......the village of North Marston became quite a busy town for the week....a good many happy children's faces were there."

In 1898 we learn from Rev James of a slight change to the proceedings of Feast Week:

"Feast Week passed off as usual but a new and most pleasant feature was the removal of the 'Shows' from the village street to a field near the Wheatsheaf Inn."

Around 1930 the feast saw the arrival in North Marston of many local gypsies who set up their stalls, selling wares or running sideshows, on both village greens down the High Street. Robin Harwood remembers:

"Alf Cheshire, the village post-master, would tease us boys in the week leading up to the Feast by making us all put our ears to the ground. Then he'd say, 'Can you hear them? Can you hear them? The gypsies are on their way! They're coming!' And, of course, we all did as he suggested!"

By the late 1930s there were no longer stalls run by non-residents, and the entertainment was provided by the villagers themselves. A particular favourite were the swing-boats owned by Bernard Carter, a general trader from the village, who would set them up on the lower village green outside the Red House.

Throughout the 1950s and up until 1963 there was always great excitement in the village by the arrival of Rose's Fair every September. The fairground attractions, including a rifle-range, merry-go-round, dodgem cars and candy floss, were set up in the field behind the Memorial Hall. The most daring ride of all was the "Chair-o'-Plane" consisting of flimsy wooden seats on chains which swung out high, tame by today's standards but considered very dangerous by some parents at the time! Rod Abbey remembers the fair very well:

"The Rose family fun fair used to come to the field behind the village hall every year. There were Mr and Mrs Rose, the twins (Bobby and Joey), their sister Violet, and of course the man the girls all loved, Johnny Eldridge. I also helped out at times. The fair was homed at Whitchurch and it would travel all around Buckinghamshire."

Many years later, however, the idea of holding a "Feast" was resurrected and in 1987 a Marston Feast was held over the course of a week-end in June. The church was beautifully decorated and a five-mile sponsored "fun-run" and a twelve-kilometre road race were held to raise money for the Aylesbury Vale Hospice Appeal. The event also featured a jazz band, clay shoot, mini-Olympics, barbecue, pig roast, craft stands, competition stands and a display by the Haddenham and Stone Folk Dance group.

The Marston Feast was held until 1990.

Feast Day runners in 1989

Rose's funfair still going strong in 2001

CONCERTS AND PLAYS

In the first half of the twentieth century, before the introduction of television and when few families owned a car, do-it-yourself entertainment was the norm and it had an important part to play in binding the village and its traditions together.

The village had a number of home-grown entertainers who would sing, recite a poem, play an instrument or act out a small scene. Most of the concerts after 1924 took place in the new Memorial Hall, as Eveline Parker recalls:

"We made our own entertainment in those days and, after the village hall was built in the 1920s, we would go to village concerts there. They were so entertaining! My sister Dinkie would sing with Mabel Buckingham, and Miss Tattam accompanied everyone on the piano. There was one gentleman always gave a serious rendition of "Come into the Garden, Maud" and we would all fall about laughing at the back! Tom Biggs usually gave a recital and Mr Rogers, who lived at The Mill House, would say poems."

There have been numerous concerts and plays in the years since these early hilarious productions, all performed with gusto, energy and laughter. In the late 1960s the Mothers' Club put on a play called "Puss in Slippers" and since 1977, when MADS (North Marston Amateur Dramatic Society) was formed, the village has been treated to an annual performance in the village hall by a mixed cast of adults and children (*see Chapter Twenty-one*).

Programme from the MADS production of "Sandcastles" February 2010

NATIONAL CELEBRATIONS

North Marston's parish magazines and school log books mention village celebrations for national events as far back as the late 1800s. School children, as well as their parents, were given a holiday of a day or a half-day for royal weddings, anniversaries, births, coronations and funerals and, of course, many of those events, just as today, were a reason for much celebration, dressing-up and frivolity involving the whole village.

Royal Events

Some of our earliest photographs show the 1897 Jubilee Committee, which was formed to plan village celebrations for **Queen Victoria's Diamond Jubilee in 1897**, and the North Marston's village band which would have played at the proceedings.

The 1897 Diamond Jubilee Committee

North Marston's village band

A parade in the High Street, probably in 1902

When Queen Victoria died in 1901 she was succeeded by her son who was crowned as King Edward VII in 1902. The previous photograph dates from about 1902 (scaffolding can be seen on the right of the picture for the erection of The Gables built that year) and shows a procession led by the village band in the High Street opposite The Bell. The parade was probably taking place to celebrate the **Coronation of Edward VII in 1902**.

School children were given a day off school for the **Coronation of King George V in 1911**.

For the **Coronation of King George VI in 1937** Joyce Cumberland was the Coronation Queen and, with her attendants, Iris Rogers, Joan Rawlings and Jean White, was driven round the village by Henry Cheshire on a wagonette loaned by Mr W Young, used normally for the greengrocery round. A party was held outside The Bell and Valerie Richardson (daughter of the village headmistress) recalled: *"We had mugs with pictures of the King's head on them and there were flags everywhere."*

The Coronation Queen and her attendants outside The Bell in 1937

Procession down the High Street celebrating the Coronation of George VI in 1937

In June 1953 the village took to wearing fancy dress for the celebration of the **Coronation of Queen Elizabeth II**. A fete was held in the school grounds and a thanksgiving service led by Rev Martin took place on the village green by The Bell.

Fancy dress parade for the 1953 Coronation celebrations

Coronation service led by Rev Martin outside The Bell in 1953

Eveline Parker, Doris Harwood and Doris Lawrence dressed in Victorian bathing costume on the old school steps in 1953

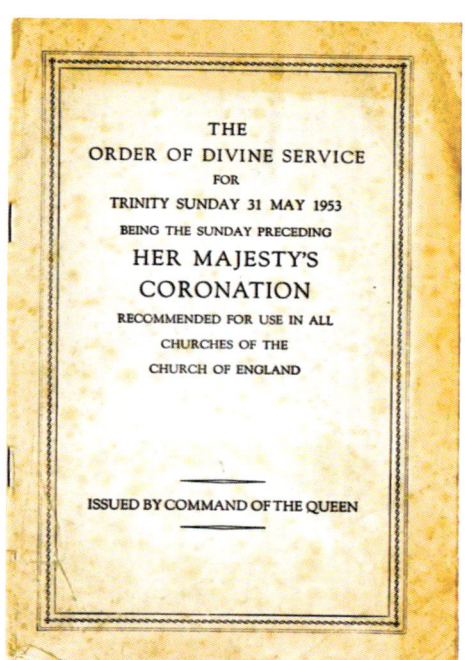
1953 Coronation service pamphlet

Queen Elizabeth's Silver Jubilee in June 1977 saw the village come together for a day-long celebration which included a fancy dress parade, an open-air service on the village green, a picnic lunch, novelty sports (including a comic football match) a sing-song in the village hall and an evening barbecue. Scenes from the day are shown on the next page.

The ladies' football team

Mike and Alison Finnemore in fancy dress

Colin Price judging the Dog Show

Ewart Dancer

Rev Peter Lawrence leads the service outside The Bell for the Queen's Silver Jubilee in June 1977

In June 2002, for **Queen Elizabeth's Golden Jubilee**, a street party took place with chairs and tables set out along the High Street and, as usual, a service was held on the village green. As Her Majesty was unable to be there in person, her place was taken by Gill Warner accompanied by her 'Lady-in-Waiting' (Estelle Heffer), 'Prince Charles' (Tommy Dancer) and the 'Duke of Kent' (David Warner).

The 'Duke of Kent', the 'Lady-in-Waiting', the 'Queen' and 'Prince Charles'

The day's activities were centred around the village greens in the High Street

Wheelbarrow races, tug o' war and fancy dress were part of the fun

The village celebrates the Queen's Golden Jubilee in 2002

In **June 2012 Her Majesty Queen Elizabeth's Diamond Jubilee** celebrated her sixty years on the throne and the village came together once again for festivities. St Mary's Church was beautifully decorated (as always) in red, white and blue for the occasion. Flowers have adorned the interior of the church on *all* special village occasions and the organisers of these wonderful displays, (Jill Dancer and Valerie Price having both taken on this role in recent years), together with the volunteers who give so much of their time doing the flower arrangements, deserve an enormous amount of credit. A special Jubilee Cake was baked by Jean Wright and mugs were given to the children of the village to mark the occasion. The day was full of fun and activity including the children's tea and the performance in the evening from the GranMarstonberries (the home-grown band from North Marston and Granborough). Events finished with the lighting of the beacon in the field behind The Pilgrim, an event taking place simultaneously across the country.

Golden Jubilee service outside The Bell in June 2012

The Jubilee beacon

Flowers in the church were in patriotic colours

The Jubilee saw the village hall and grounds packed all afternoon

The children enjoy their tea

VE Day 1995

The Fiftieth Anniversary of VE Day took place on **8th May 1995**. Victory in Europe had been declared at the end of the Second World War on 8th May 1945 (for which school children and adults at the time were given two days' holiday). The fiftieth anniversary of this event was celebrated across the nation.

A street party was held once again down the length of North Marston High Street and, during the proceedings, two Second World War planes (the Avro Lancaster and a Hurricane of the Battle of Britain Memorial Flight) passed overhead en route to a display elsewhere. A pure stroke of luck!

A celebration cake was cut by two of the oldest village residents, Ewart Dancer and Eveline Parker, who were accompanied by Laurie Foskett and Vince Lilley, both veterans of the Second World War. There was an exhibition of war memorabilia in the Memorial Hall and a service which was led by Rev Kyriacou on the village green.

VE Day street party 1995

The VE Day cake

Cutting the cake

A Second World War motor cycle

A pilot gets a medal

The VE Day service outside The Bell in May 1995 led by Rev Kyriacou
(It is interesting to observe that most services of celebration and remembrance stretching back over many years have been held on the village green outside The Bell)

-- EVENTS SURROUNDING JOHN SCHORNE AND THE WELL --

In the last forty years there has been a resurgence of interest in the story of John Schorne and the Holy Well (*see Chapters Three and Four*) and the village has organised various celebrations. In **1978** a **Pilgrims' Weekend** was held to raise money for St Mary's Church. It was decided to centre the fund-raising round the idea of the by-gone religious travellers and a sponsored walk via Quainton, Whitchurch, Swanbourne and Winslow formed part of the week-end. Ewart Dancer and Peter Morton organised rides round the village in a pony and trap and tractor and trailer, while others followed a "village trail" which included the Holy Well, specially decorated for the occasion.

In **1990** the village celebrated the **700th Anniversary of John Schorne becoming rector here**. There was a weekend of dancing, pilgrim walks, runs, dressing up, drama and fun, including a ceremony at the Holy Well, a procession to church and a service at the Schorne Shrine. Two busloads of villagers visited Windsor for a ceremony where Schorne's remains were buried after their removal from North Marston, some of the villagers walking to Aylesbury to pick up the bus! St George's Chapel also loaned to the village the *Book of Hours* which contains prayers to John Schorne.

A **Service of Blessing and Re-dedication** took place at the well on **21st May 2005** following its complete renovation and rebuilding. In 2006 there was a **Service of Dedication of a new John Schorne panel in the church**. This had been designed by Lauren Isherwood and presented to the church by Alison and Mike Finnemore. It was inserted into the church window above the Lady Chapel altar (*see Chapter Two*). As we write in 2014 the village is preparing to celebrate the 700th Anniversary of John Schorne's death.

The decorated well in 1978

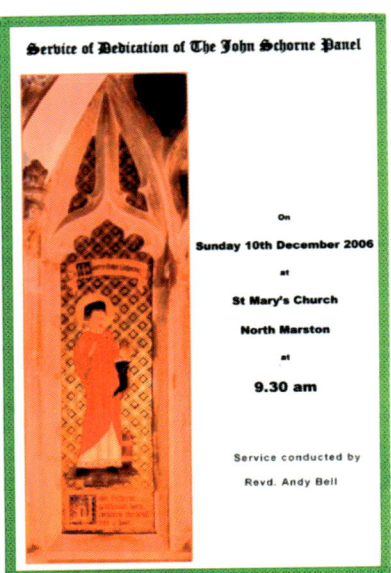
The service sheet for the dedication of the new John Schorne panel in the Lady Chapel window of the church

------- THE OPENING OF NEW VILLAGE AMENITIES -------

The provision of a new building or facility in the village usually calls for an "Opening Ceremony" and a village get-together.

Easter Monday 1924 saw the **Opening of the Memorial Hall** in memory of those who had fought and died in the Great War (*see Chapter Fifteen*) and a horse-chestnut tree was also planted which can still be seen today. In 1937 as part of the coronation celebrations for King George VI, a seat was built to go round the tree. Henry White, the village blacksmith, built the iron frame and Ted Dudley, a village builder, made the oak seat and back.

Planting the tree outside the Memorial Hall gates in 1924

```
                                                North Marston
                                                Winslow
                                                March 18th 1924

Dear Sir or Madam,

     The opening of the North Marston War Memorial Hall
will take place on Easter Monday  ril 21st at 2.p.m.

     The ceremony will be performed by Lord Cottesloe,
Lord Lieutenant of the County.

     The approximate cost of the Building is £1,290,
towards which has been raised £940. It is hoped to
raise a substantial sum on this occasion, when your
presence and help will be greatly esteemed.

                         Yours faithfully

                         W. Tattam, Sec.

A.S. Cheshire (Chairman)      E.L. Dudley,  L. Price
F. Price,  H.J. Cheshire,  S. Gregory,
V. Alderman, Miss Lucy Tattam, A.J. Franklin.
```

Formal invitation to the Opening of the Memorial Hall in 1924

The opening of the North Marston and Granborough Community Sports Field in Granborough Road on 1st July 2009 was a momentous occasion for the village. The field, which had been designated for recreational use in the 1930s, had fallen into disrepair and a re-development project began in late 2006.

A project team eventually raised over £200,000 through grant funding and a variety of fund raising events: plant sales, Race Nights, Boys' Nights, Girls' Nights, Quiz Nights, a London to Cambridge Bike Ride, the Three Peaks' Challenge, a London to Oxford Bike Ride and "GranMarstonbury" in 2011.

Chairman, Karen Parks, headed the Sports Field Committee and between July 2007 (when the first work began) and September 2011 (when the new pavilion opened) the old sports field was drained, levelled and reseeded; a Nature Trail, Trim Trail and Boardwalk were put in place; the old pond and ditch were dredged and a pond-dipping platform installed; hedges were laid and brambles removed; a new pedestrian entrance gate was installed: cricket nets were erected; native species and bulbs were planted; bird and bat boxes were put up and a new pavilion built. The semi-wild nature area and the informal recreational trails were designed to complement the more formal and highly cultivated needs of the playing field.

An early band of volunteers in December 2007

The new sign for the Sports Field

Raising funds at a Race Night in 2009

The new pavilion taking shape in October 2010

Another excellent volunteer turn-out in March 2010

The opening of the new Sports Field in July 2009

The new Community Sports Field was officially opened on 1st July 2009. The first cricket match was played in September 2009 and the first football match in July 2010 (*see Chapter Twenty-two*). On 17th September 2011 the new Sports Pavilion was opened by England cricketer Alastair Cook.

There was a day of celebration which included stalls selling food and drink, various sporting events and ended with an evening gig by the "GranMarstonberries" on an open-air stage.

The GranMarstonberries

Alastair Cook (right) being interviewed by Trevor Lane

The redevelopment of the sports field came about through the hard work and effort of many dedicated volunteers combined with the goodwill of the village people who supported all the fund raising events. It provides a wonderful facility which will serve the village for many years to come.

A huge turn-out of volunteers outside the Pilgrim

In 2010 The Bell public house re-opened as "The Pilgrim" (*see also Chapter Nineteen*) and was an important event for the village. Over a hundred volunteers turned up to help prepare the garden, tidy the green and erect the new sign prior to its opening.

The opening of the Village Community Shop on 9th July 2011 (see *Chapter Sixteen*) by John Bercow MP was a momentous day for the village and was the culmination of incredible effort on the part of the Shop Committee and its Chairman Alison Finnemore. The Shop quickly proved a huge success and much busier than had been expected. As its fame spread it was not long before it started to win awards.

John Bercow cuts the cake

The Bucks Herald photographer takes a group picture of The Shop winning The Bucks Herald's "Community Shop of the Year" Award in February 2012

The old red telephone box on the village green in the High Street used to be an important facility and was used frequently by the many villagers who did not have a telephone at all. Although, perhaps, not a major event, it was, nevertheless, a sad day when the old red box was replaced with a characterless steel and glass structure.

The village pond in Church Street is on the site of the original village green (*see Chapter Seven*). Over the centuries, the area in Church Street had been hedged and become a paddock belonging to The Elms.

At the start of the new Millennium in 2000, the owners of The Elms, Rens and Lucy Dantuma, gave the land back to the village to be used as a pond. The landscaping was finally completed in 2002.

The old red telephone box being removed

The completed pond in Church Street in 2002

---------- MATTHEW'S WAY ----------

Matthew's Way is a six-mile route stretching between North Marston and Quainton but it is no ordinary trail. It was created in memory of Matthew Lane who died of corrective heart surgery a few weeks before his first birthday. His parents, Trevor and Cathy, residents of North Marston, came up with the idea of Matthew's Way as a permanent memorial to their son. As well as County Council approval they had to approach fifteen landowners (over whose land the route would cross) for permission to put up specially designed waymark discs. Cathy and Trevor also planted eleven trees on the trail, one for each month of Matthew's life, and chose mostly oaks because of their longevity.

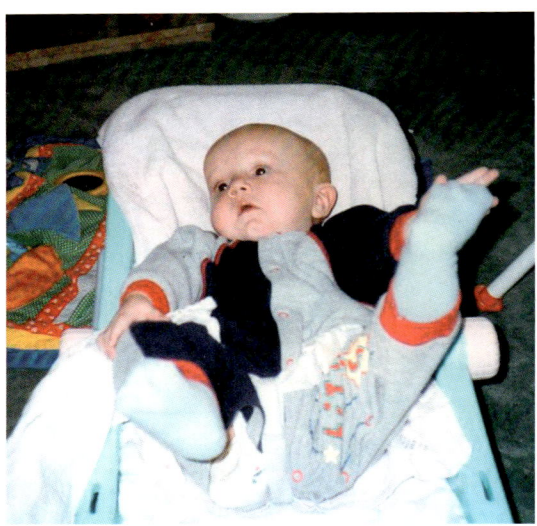
Matthew in 1996

Trevor spent hundreds of hours working on the route. Each tree was fenced off and bulbs planted in the enclosures. The council renewed lots of stiles close to the roads while Trevor worked on the more inaccessible ones.

Matthew's Way opened on 10th May 1997, its route starting near St Mary's Church where Matthew is laid to rest. Many people have walked the trail since then, and booklets describing the route have been sold to raise money for the Special Care Baby Unit at Stoke Mandeville Hospital where Matthew spent part of his early life. Matthew's Way is now shown on the Ordnance Survey mapping, sheet 192 (1:25,000 scale). It is featured as a Recreational Path and it was a very proud moment for Matthew's family when it appeared on the revised map in 2006.

"People will walk the route and wonder why it's called Matthew's Way. They'll ask questions and find out about Matthew. It will keep his memory alive." (Trevor and Cathy Lane)

Trevor, Victoria, Stuart, Andrew and Cathy Lane on Matthew's Way in 2002

Matthew's Way walkers in 2008

Local people gather to start the walk along Matthew's Way in 2012

RAISING FUNDS FOR ST MARY'S CHURCH

For children growing up in the village in the 1950s, 1960s and 1970s there were few events as exciting or as memorable as the Church Summer Fete. Many villagers have fond memories of the experience of the occasion where, each year with comforting continuity, the same people manned the same stalls or games. During the 1950s the fetes were held in the school playground but, from then on, they took place in the vicarage garden. Not surprisingly, the Church Summer Fete was the biggest single event held in the village each year and involved most families in some way or another. Children looked forward to the fancy-dress parade, pony rides, their dance display, races on the lawn, ice creams and the chance to run about in the vicarage garden with their friends.

The church fete in the school grounds circa 1950

Paddy Gurney and June White selling ice-creams in 1962

We are fortunate that cine film, taken by Poppet Brazier and Mary Franklin, of most of the vicarage garden fetes from 1961 to 1980 has survived. Watching these films we are reminded how important these events were to the community. Over the years during which the fetes were filmed fashions changed and individuals got older but the pleasure and enthusiasm for this most traditional of events appears not to have been diminished by time.

There are so many striking and similar accounts of the experience that they suggest the North Marston Summer Fete was very close to the heart of those who lived here because it was a shared celebration of the village community. Johanna Miller (nee Dancer) has vivid memories of the fetes of the 1960s:

"One of the highlights of North Marston village life when I was a child back in the 60s was our annual village fete. It was held at the old vicarage which was the home of Mr and Mrs Charrington, the vicar at the time. Skittles were played on the front lawn surrounded by straw bales, and constant cups of tea and cake were served from Mrs Charrington's kitchen. Lots of ladies from the village had a stall and I remember my granny (Biggs) having one. On one occasion she collected tin waste bins, on which she then stuck different coloured sticky back plastic, and sold them.

Delia and Janet Ecob always did the pony rides and my dad (Ewart Dancer) would tow disused dodgem cars behind his tractor and do a route round the village much to the local lads' delight (it would never be allowed these days!). There was always the fancy dress competition which many a mum would put a lot of thought and hours into, and that was judged by Mrs Charrington.

A week or so later it was always very exciting to go up to the school and watch the cine film of the fete which, in those days, had been filmed by Poppet Brazier."

A group of fete-goers outside the church gates in 1966 surrounding Ewart Dancer's old dodgem car (just visible))

A fancy dress parade at the fete in the school grounds circa 1950

Fancy dress circa 1950 on the old school field

Helen Ward (left) and Suzanne Gratton circa 1972

Pony rides and fancy dress were always very popular events at the Church Summer Fete. Robert Gurney recalls:

"In one fancy dress competition I had to dress up as Mr Cube from Tate and Lyle – it rather sticks in my mind. I was just a big box with arms sticking out. One year my sister Alison was entered for the fancy dress and someone else was dressed as a golliwog which frightened her so much she refused to do it."

Fancy dress at the Summer fete in 1963

Glyn Dancer and John White in fancy dress

Pony rides at the fete circa 1962

Pony rides at the fete circa 1950

During the 1960s the same people ran their stalls at the church fete year after year: Clarence and Clifford Cheshire on the bowling; Fred Gowin and Jack Ayres on the gate; Eveline Parker, Dinkie Clarke and Betty Young on the raffle; Doris Brazier on the bottle stall; Neville and Rosemary Morton on hoop-la; Stella Morton, Doris Harwood and Dolly Holden on cakes; Paddy Gurney and June White on ice-creams; Lizzie Cheshire and Eleanor Cheshire on White Elephant; Betty Linnell, Beryl Gowin, Dorothy Holden and Nancy Carter from the Mothers' Union on teas; and many others.

"The fetes in the 60s were really special occasions. People wore their smart clothes and all the young mums pushed their babies round in those lovely high prams with big wheels. Mrs Doris Brazier always ran the bottle stall and in the week leading up to the fete I had to help her fill up numerous jam jars with bath salts to augment the other bottles on her stall. Nearly everyone left the fete with a jar of bath salts!" (Susan Chaplin nee Parker*)*

The raffle at the fete in 1980

John Morton presents a bouquet at the opening of the fete in June 1968

Villagers of all ages came to the fete
L-R: *Ern Seaton, Willie Ward, Jack Ayres and Harry Price circa 1980*

The church fete eventually moved to the grounds of the Memorial Hall and still raises much-needed funds for St Mary's restoration Fund. Many other fund-raising activities have taken place to raise money for the upkeep and restoration of St Mary's Church, including such events as Regatta Day and Ladies' Day.

Bouncy castle in the village hall field in 2011

"Ladies Day" at Carters Meadow June 2010

"Regatta Day" at Carter's Meadow July 2011

Lining up for the "Boat Race"

THE CHRISTMAS BAZAAR

The Christmas Bazaar has become a regular feature in the village calendar. It is held to raise funds for the Village Hall and always features a visit from Father Christmas who, over the years, has arrived in a variety of modes of transport (*see below*)!

Ewart Dancer's pony and trap in 1981

Neil Tuckett's Model T Ford in 1996

Father Christmas arrives by glider in 1986

The children are carried in a tractor and trailer in 1996

The vintage bus arrives to take the children to see Father Christmas

Stalls at the Christmas Bazaar

THE LIGHTS OF FRIENDSHIP

This chapter has highlighted the warmth, friendship and feeling of togetherness which exist in the village of North Marston. It seems fitting, therefore, to end by mentioning the Lights of Friendship where, each December, everyone has the opportunity to wish their friends "A Merry Christmas and a Happy New Year" as well as to remember those loved ones who have passed away. A Christmas tree adorned with lights stands outside the church door and, for a small donation towards the Church Restoration Fund, the people of North Marston can write a message of goodwill and remembrance to be displayed in the church porch.

Carol Bagni, a North Marston resident, came up with the idea for the first Lights of Friendship in 2002 since when it has been held as an annual event, raising many thousands of pounds for St Mary's Church Restoration Fund over the years. The many messages on display sum up the wonderful community spirit throughout North Marston village.

Father Christmas talks to Dominic Radcliffe at the Lights of Friendship Service in 2009

Twenty-one
CLUBS, SOCIETIES AND CHARITIES
John Spargo & Sue Chaplin

A brief study of North Marston's history tells us that in every generation when a need is identified in the village there is generally an individual with the capacity and commitment to do something about it. In some cases, this is a commercial initiative (like a village builder in a housing boom) but, in many, it is a voluntary effort, and never more so than in the case of village clubs.

Since Victorian times, the notion of a club or society of local people with a common interest (or need) has been commonplace. Often at the centre of their creation have been one or two motivated individuals who were the critical catalysts without whom things would not have happened when they did. *Being in the right place at the right time* is a theme that runs through the involvement of individuals in most village initiatives since time immemorial. Almost without exception, the clubs and societies we look at in this chapter owe their creation to the vision and tenacity of people we can identify.

This chapter is therefore more than a record of village clubs and societies; it is a salute to those people, often volunteers, who made them happen on behalf of their fellow Marstonians. Their community involvement goes right to the heart of the sustainability of a small community like North Marston. This chapter looks at social and welfare clubs. *(If you wish to read about sports' clubs please go to Chapter Twenty-two).*

Why did they start?

In the days before mass communication and a welfare state, rural communities had to be self-reliant and form their own support mechanisms to tide people over illness or unemployment. The vagaries of a village economy that was based substantially on agriculture meant that membership of one of these benevolent or friends' societies was sometimes a life-saver and at the very least prevented families having to be split up and sent to the Union Workhouse in Winslow. Some clubs and societies also acted as village savings banks whereby people could 'put something by' perhaps to cover additional Christmas expenses, clothing or fuel.

Some clubs were part of a national structure; some were associated with the church and chapels; whilst others seem to have been locally unique.

Basically, membership of a club offered an individual or families a form of insurance against hard times. We are fortunate that Dr Samuel James, the vicar from 1870-1909, recorded details of the village clubs in his "Village Chronicles", so we have a snapshot of those that were flourishing in North Marston in late Victorian times.

The Nineteenth Century

The **Clothing Club,** was run by the vicar's daughter, Miss Susan James, from about 1890 until about 1903. It was a local savings club whereby people made regular, weekly subscription payments at Vine Cottage (now The Matronage) and these were distributed at the year's end in time for Christmas. A year's collection typically amounted to a total of thirty to forty pounds across the whole village. Miss James would occasionally entertain the club's forty or so female members to tea at the vicarage.

The **Coal Club** (1870s) appears to have had the same function. The vicar collected subscriptions on Wednesday nights, and membership was limited to one per household. Before central heating or electricity, the coal fire was the only source of heat for warmth, cooking and hot water. That meant that throughout the winter months a family's welfare hinged on an adequate and affordable supply of coal; for many families this presented a real challenge and, for a few households, it proved impossible. Coal Clubs were created to spread the cost of winter fuel throughout the year by enabling households to contribute small amounts of money on a regular basis (childless households paid one penny a week) so that by the time of their greatest need they had accumulated enough investment in the Coal Club to tide them over the coldest months of the year.

Coal Clubs were subsidised by donations of cash or coal from benefactors so that Coal Club investors received coal to twice the value of their savings and some coal was also available to the poorest of households who could not afford to contribute at all. As winter approached, Coal Club members were issued with 'tickets' (vouchers they could exchange with the coal merchant).

As the Coal Club was one of the most important measures to ameliorate the effect of poverty in the village, it was administered by the vicar himself. The donations from wealthier benefactors meant that the recipients of 'charity coal' were informally monitored and any wasteful behaviour noted. In 1874, the vicar wrote somewhat sarcastically, following complaints from begrudging village donors:

"...poor people sat up very late last year burning away their coals! That is very shocking and dreadful, no doubt; and we must have the curfew bell brought into use again. We believe poor people did actually sit up, some of them, till eight 'o clock, and even till nine! What are we coming to?"

The **Primitive Methodist Club** was founded by Joseph Biggs in 1843. The club held an annual celebration dinner when over forty members sat down to a meal in the Primitive Methodist Church (Chapel) in Quainton Road.

The **Armed Yeoman Club** had about twelve members and met at the pub of the same name in Church Street.

The **North Marston United Patriots' Benefit Society** was affiliated to a national organisation, *The United Patriots' Benefits Society* (UPBS), which was an independent Friendly Society founded in 1843 with the aim of providing its members with low cost insurance. It was funded mainly from members' subscriptions and covered such needs as loss by fire, wife's lying-in hospital care, debt imprisonment, militia call-up, old-age relief and funerals. The North Marston Club had twenty members. The local secretary in the 1880s was Mr Reuben Cheshire, the village postmaster, who was later succeeded by Henry Holden. In 1871 the vicar, Rev James, refused to attend a meeting of the UPBS because it was held in The Bell public house!

Reuben Cheshire's enamel brooch from the United Patriots' Benefit Society

The **Parish Lending Library** was formed in 1870 by Dr James, the vicar, and initially relied on books donated by local gentry. The library was based at the Vicarage. The subscription for membership was two shillings a year. The books available covered a wide range of subjects (*see chart on next page*).

By 1880, the village had its own **Reading Room** paid for by membership subscription. Although the exact location is not known, it is likely to have been at Schorne College or attached to the Vicarage. Membership was drawn from a complete cross-section of the village although the list of founding subscribers indicates that it was all-male.

Books on Religious Subjects	Travels	Periodicals
Sunday Afternoons at an Orphanage	The Colonial Empire	Penny Post
Suckling's Sermons		Children's Treasury 1868
Daily Services for the Household	Tales	Monthly Packet 1851-1865
Meditations for Three Weeks	Old Jarvis' Will	Leisure Hour 1854
Spiritual Guide	Poor Little Gaspard's Drum	British Workman
	Scrub the Workhouse Boy	Winkfield Magazine
History & Biography	Kitty Brown Beginning to Think	
My Schools & School Masters	Bessy the Blackberry Gatherer	Miscellaneous
Dark Ages and Crusades	Dermot the Unbaptised	Hymns for the Sick
History of Rome		Health for the Household
History of England	Natural History	Buy your own Goose
	Rambles of a Rat	
	The Ball I Live On	
	Birds' Nests	

A selection of books belonging to the Parish Lending Library in the late 1800s

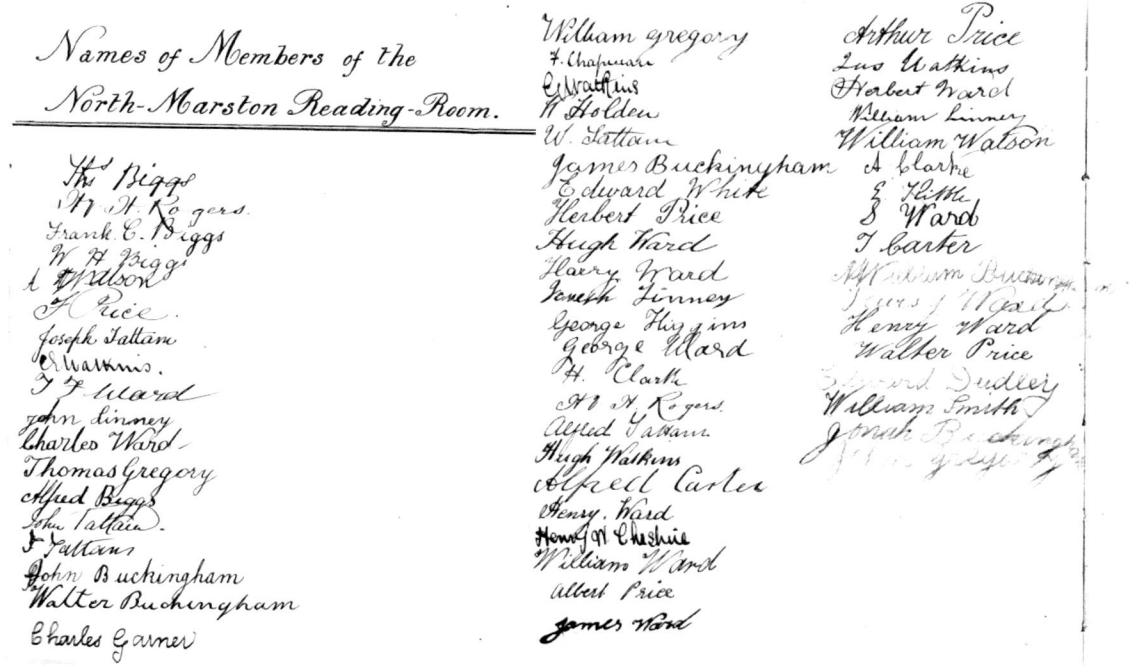

The all-male subscribers to the Reading Room

The **Brass Band Society** was formed in 1894 and soon had eighteen members who paid a half-crown to join. They were largely self-taught musicians but in time were fully equipped with instruments and uniforms, many as a result of donations. They played at all village events and in competitions against other village bands such as the long-established band at Quainton. In fact a slightly inebriated band from Quainton had made themselves most unwelcome in 1879 by disrupting a funeral in this village. The Vicar wrote scathingly about it in *The Schornian*:

"A village band from Quainton turned up and tuned up with drum etc, as the funeral bell was tolling and just before the arrival of the dead body with mourners. Vicar remonstrated

*and warned them that the Rev T Chalk, curate-in-charge of Quainton, should be informed. "Mr Chalk nothin' to do wi' us, nor hus wi' he; we be our own masters, sir." "Glad to hear that, your present conduct would disgrace any clergyman's superintendence." Quainton band will please not repeat their annual petition, never before refused and never again to be granted, of a donation from Northmarston Vicarage, given originally out of respect to the Rev James Pooley, and now discontinued out of disrespect to the band. "Didn't know there was a funeral," said one, in very sound of the bell which kept toll-toll-tolling out the solemn truth. Drowning mourners' tears and funeral bells with badly played noise and trash and clash is not unworthy of the Caffres and Afghans. The band retired, finding (to Northmarston's credit, be it said) no sympathy in our village; and we only hope that when the mothers and fathers, and sisters and brothers, of these rough and certainly **not** teetotal band-folks, are carried out to their burial, no clowns from another village, calling themselves "a band", will trouble the survivors with their coarse and unmusical din and clamour."*

Local villages often requested the North Marston band to play at their functions and, in 1899, they were charging three and a half guineas per day.

North Marston Band at Marston Gate (Stevens Farm) on the day of Queen Victoria's Diamond Jubilee (It is unlikely the Band survived beyond the start of the Great War in 1914)

The Early Twentieth Century

The Band of Hope Trip to Wembley 1937

The **Band of Hope** was a movement opposed to alcohol and was first formed in the autumn of 1847. Its objective was to teach children the importance and principles of sobriety and teetotalism and, in 1855, a national organisation was formed amidst an explosion of Band of Hope work. Meetings were held in churches throughout the UK and included Christian teaching. Towns and villages throughout the country saw the formation of local Bands of Hope, and in December 1899, the vicar wrote in The Schornian :

"Temperance: A Church of England Band of Hope is started with 26 members, in Northmarston, owing to the exertions of Mr Henry Cheshire, chairman of the Parish Council and sidesman of the Parish Church."

The Band of Hope organised many outings one of which was a trip to the "Pavilion Picture House" in Aylesbury. North Marston's Band of Hope was still going strong in the late 1930s as can be seen from the picture above. The **North Marston British Legion** met monthly in the village hall. For many years it was led by Alfred Cheshire (the post master). The British Legion was formed in 1921 as a voice for ex-servicemen after the Great War. It quickly grew with national, regional, county and local branches, some of which also formed social clubs. Eventually, most towns and many villages, like North Marston, had a branch of the British Legion. Although the village branch has now disbanded, the standard of the North Marston British Legion hangs in St Mary's church to this day.

Henry Cheshire and family 1890

The standard of the North Marston British Legion

One of the Legion's Christmas Dinners in the village hall circa 1950

The **Slate Club** was based at The Bell, probably in the 1920s-1930s, but little is known about this club other than it served as a savings club which paid out at Christmas.

The **Chapel Club** a form of savings club into which members paid four shillings and sixpence a month. In the 1950s it was run by Ted Price and offered members a form of sickness insurance if illness prevented them from working.

We know that the members of The **Buffs (Royal Antediluvian Order of Buffaloes)** met monthly in the building to the rear of the Wheatsheaf (which was also the venue for cricket teas). The "Buffs" are a secret organisation based loosely on the Freemasons and, like them, organised into *Lodges*. The RAOB is a fraternal, social organisation founded in London in 1822 by stage-hands and theatre technicians disbarred from an order established by actors. A sliding spy-hole in the door of the building at the back of The Wheatsheaf shows only recognised members would be admitted to a Lodge Meeting (*see picture below*).

The Mid-Twentieth Century

The **Mothers' Union** met at the vicarage. The tall woman in the centre of the following picture is Mrs Charrington, the vicar's wife. When Mrs Charrington left the village, the Mothers' Union appears to have ceased.

The Mothers' Union in the vicarage garden in 1969

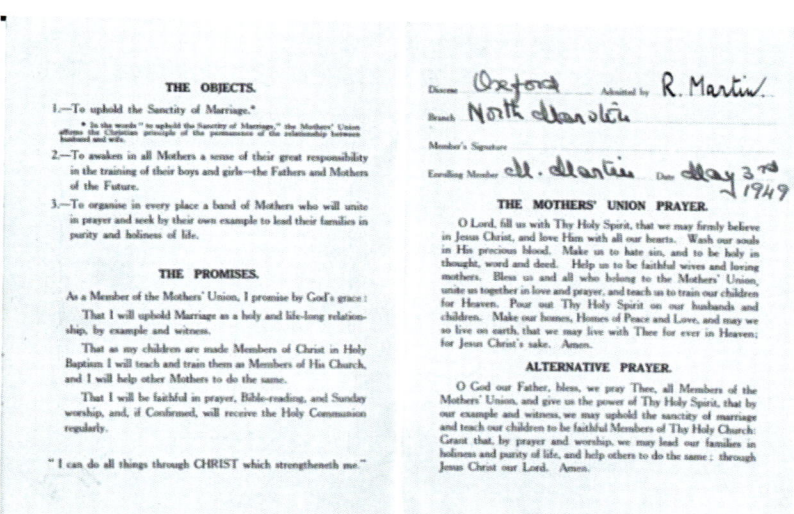

A Mother's Union Membership Card 1949

The Mothers' Union was part of a national network closely associated with the Church of England. The Objects of the Mothers' Union were clearly based on Christian principles: for example *"to uphold the Sanctity of Marriage and to awaken in all mothers a sense of their great responsibility in their training of their boys and girls."*

Although North Marston did not field its own **Women's Institute**, many women from the village attended meetings at Granborough.

A Mother's Union Membership brooch

Women's Institute members in 1957

The Social Club at the Village Hall was formed when The Wheatsheaf stopped trading as a pub in the mid-1950s in order to provide people at the lower end of the village with an alternative to the only remaining pub, The Bell (now called The Pilgrim). The club was founded by Kath Tattam and initially the subscription was five shillings per year. It was (and still is) housed in an annexe of the village hall.

Kath was the organiser of the Social Club's many fund-raising events such as beetle drives, bingo nights, tramp suppers and village dances. She also ran dancing classes for adults in the village hall which were very popular in the 1950s.

The Social Club rules have always been quite strict and prove that it was set up as a respectable, efficient and community-minded organisation.

The North Marston Social Club is based in an annexe to the village hall and has seen many refits and redecorations over the years. This picture was taken in the 1970s and shows Eddie Lambourne and Archie Higgins (seated) whilst Paul Young stands at the bar and Albert Palmer is serving behind the bar.

Kath Tattam

The Social Club Tramps' Supper 1955

The Social Club Easter Bonnet Parade in the 1950s

amongst the Ordinary Members of the Club. Acceptance or rejection of an application for Membership shall be by a majority vote of the Committee.

7. Anybody wishing to become a Temporary Member for not more than six consecutive days may do so on payment of a subscription of 1/-, but such Temporary Members must be introduced by an Ordinary Member and must not reside within a radius of two miles of the Club. No person who is in arrear as an Ordinary Member or who has been suspended or expelled can be admitted as a Temporary Member.

8. Members shall have the privilege of introducing Visitors to the Club, provided the name and address of the Visitor is clearly written in a book provided for the purpose, and that the Member holds himself responsible for the conduct of the Visitor. No Visitor is allowed directly or indirectly to make purchases at the Bar. No person who is in arrear as an Ordinary Member or who has been suspended or expelled can be admitted as a Visitor.

9. Any Member being in arrear will be sent a notice by the Secretary requesting immediate payment, failing which the Member's name be removed from the membership register. Resignation of any Member shall be in writing to the Secretary.

10. The General Committee of the Club shall consist of : Chairman, Hon. Secretary, Hon. Treasurer and not more than ten Members elected by the Club Members. The Committee shall be responsible for the premises, property and accounts of the Club, and shall be responsible for the orderly behaviour of Members whilst on the premises of the Club, and ensure that the bar is open only during the permitted hours, and that a responsible steward is appointed.

11. The Hon. Treasurer shall keep an account book of all purchases and receipts and shall at every Annual General Meeting present a report and financial statement for the preceeding year.

12. The Club shall be opened every week day from 12 to 2 in the daytime and from 6 to in the evening, and on Sundays from 12 to 2 in the daytime and from 7 to 10 in the evening. The General Committee reserve the right to vary these hours when necessary.

13. The Club shall be open for the sale of intoxicating liquor between the hours of 12 noon and 2 p.m. and 6 p.m. and 10.00 p.m. on week days and 12 noon and 2 p.m. and 7 p.m. and 10 p.m. on Sundays, Good Fridays and Christmas Days or any later time which is in operation in the Licensing Division by order of the Licensing Justices.

Two of the pages of the Social Club's original rules

Funds from the Social Club were used to buy bar billiards and table-tennis tables leading to the establishment of a **Youth Club** in the village hall in the 1950s. They had a snooker room (where the present kitchen is situated) and the facility of the table-tennis table led to the eventual formation of a village table-tennis team (*see Chapter Twenty-two*).

Jim Tattam also recalls another Youth Club led by the Rev Stanley Keene which *"was run in the school-room…we wheeled the stuff over from the vicarage along the alley-way on Morton's trolley."*

The Late Twentieth Century

The idea for the **Mothers' Club** began in 1965 when Nurse Monk, the local midwife, suggested that some of the 'new mums' in the village might like to get together.

Initially they held meetings in each other's homes but the first official meeting took place in June 1966 in the Methodist schoolroom when a working committee was formed. Some of the founder members included Daphne Ward, Rosemary Morton and Jennifer Heffer. Others involved at the start were Vi Cross, Cecilia Johnson-Jones and Pat Tompkins. The club became very popular and quickly grew.

Rosemary Morton, Daphne Ward and Vi Cross pictured many years later in 2007

The Mothers' Club was affiliated to a larger organisation, whose rules stated that half of the meetings had to be family-orientated and they had to attend an annual meeting in Aylesbury and give a report. After some years the members realised that there were people who were *not* mothers but who wanted to join, and so in 1986 the name was changed to the Monday Club.

The **Monday Club** had monthly meetings in the Methodist Schoolroom which were extremely varied. There were speakers covering many different subjects; social evenings were held; outings to bowling took place; and outside venues were visited.

In 1978 the club started arranging outings for Senior Citizens in the village, the Clockland's Charity kindly helping with the costs.

A plant sale and coffee morning were held each Spring to raise funds for the club and other events were arranged such as a tramps' supper, quizzes and auctions. Teas were provided for the Feast Day held at that time and regular donations were made to village organisations as well as local and national charities.

At Christmas, members would join with the Methodist Guild and go round the village carol singing complete with tractor and trailer on which Jennifer Heffer played an organ. Father Christmas would go along with sweets for the children and there would be soup afterwards in the Methodist Schoolroom for those who survived the whole evening! The collection was always donated to Cancer Research.

As membership grew, meetings moved to the village hall where the club still meets today and is thriving with thirty-five members.

The **Tuesday Club** was a social club for older residents, run by Gill Warner and Jean Wright from the early 1980s as a subsidiary of the Monday Club.

Gill Warner and Jean Wright making cakes at the Tuesday Club

At first, the Tuesday Club met every other Tuesday at the Methodist Schoolroom, and latterly monthly. Its inception was triggered by one of the founder members, Doris Harwood, who said one day, *"It's alright you young 'uns having a club but what about us old 'uns?"*

The Tuesday Club ran for many years until membership dwindled to six and it became non-viable. Speakers were arranged, and there were social afternoons, competitions and in-house demonstrations. There were also invitations to events such as Cream Teas at the school.

Tuesday Club Christmas Dinner at the village hall during the 1980s

Easter bonnet competition at the Tuesday Club in the 1980s

The mid 1960s saw active **Senior and Junior Methodist Guilds** held in the village.

The Junior Guild met at the chapel schoolroom on Wednesdays from six to seven o'clock in the evenings and ran for about three years, as Sue Chaplin remembers:

"David Heffer ran the Junior Guild at the Methodist Chapel one evening a week and this was incredibly popular with us youngsters in the Sixties. It was a little bit like a youth club and we did all sorts of things such as crafts, quizzes and playing games – just great fun!"

David Heffer in the 1970s

The Senior Guild was also held at the chapel on Wednesday evenings and had slide shows and guest speakers. It continued until 1989.

North Marston Playgroup was set up by a small group of mothers with young children in the village and opened in November 1969 in the village hall. The first supervisor was Mrs Daphne Ward who had a rota of parent helpers. They worked very hard raising funds to buy basic materials and furniture, and opened the playgroup with about a dozen children. There were two morning sessions each week; early in the morning a volunteer had to light the fire in the grate for warmth and the toilets were outside.

During Mrs Spencer's time as Headmistress at the village school she agreed to let the Playgroup have the use of a vacant classroom, so in 1975 the children found themselves on new premises with their own cupboards, toilet area and outside play space. The Playgroup at this time was being run by Jean Wright and Gill Warner.

In 1979 the Playgroup celebrated its tenth anniversary with a bonfire and firework party at Burnaby Farm and in 1989 there was a coffee morning for its twentieth anniversary.

In the Playgroup's early days helpers did not need to be vetted, were not required to attend courses or be subject to Ofsted Inspections; everything was very informal. Many of the original helpers gave their services for many years: in 1984 Jean Wright left after fifteen years' service and in 1989 Rosemary Morton after twenty years!

In April 1989 the Playgroup had to move back to the village hall as the classroom was needed for the school children; by this time the leaders were Jan Quinn and Gill Little who had taken over from Janice Baden.

The Playgroup was later named the **Schorne Nursery** and then the **Schorne Pre-school**. Still based in the village hall (every morning and afternoon of school term-time) and currently under the leadership of Nicky Aiston, it continues to provide a wonderful learning and play environment for the local children.

Some of the Pre-school children help to celebrate the first birthday of "The Shop"

Pre-school pupils Easter 2013

Looking back, it is clear the village was always keen on home-spun entertainment so it was inevitable that sooner or later a local amateur dramatics group would be formed. The early seeds were sown in local productions in the late 1960s but it was not until 1977 that the group adopted the name **Marston Amateur Dramatic Society (MADS)** by which it has been known ever since. David Heffer who tells us how it all happened:

"In 1966 a group of young women met in the Methodist Chapel and formed the Mothers' Club, the idea being to exchange views and organise a programme of events.

A year or so later they decided to put on a show for the Senior Citizens. I was asked to find something suitable and came up with "Puss in Slippers" by Richard Tydeman - a mini drama. It was a great success and inspired us to launch out into concerts which included the children. Audrey Deung was an inspired leader and, with Mrs Win Brazier, a very accomplished pianist, on board together with Vic Russell who played the banjo and generally acted the fool, we put together some very good shows.

The village demanded tickets and what was just designed to provide a Christmas entertainment for older people, became a two or three performance event. We ran these concerts first in the old school, where the playground now is, and then later we performed in the village hall.

The stage consisted of very large heavy pine tables which we roped together. The curtains were pulled by hand and the scenery was sketchy to say the least. Later we updated the curtains and John Wright constructed large scenery panels that actually revolved to make scene changing easier. One year Margaret Carter painted a wonderful village scene on the back wall; we hadn't the heart to cover it up and we incorporated it into other performances.

In 1977 the more ambitious of us decided to attempt a farce and we put on two small plays "The Walrus and the Carpenter" and "Pop! Goes the Patient!"

You would be surprised who made their stage debut that year: Ewart Dancer, Harold Bone, Stella Gurney, Pamela Cheshire, Tracy Swain, Peter Morton, Stan Gurney and others who extended their amateur careers. It was the first time we called ourselves MADS.

Since then we have produced a performance of some sort nearly every year. A number of people have tried their hand at producing: a task that involves much heartache and frustration. Believe it or not, members of the cast do not always learn their lines religiously, nor turn up as regularly as required, thus driving everyone else "MAD"!

When we put on "Hobson's Choice" we made a trap door in the stage through which Willy Mossop (Ewart Dancer) had to clamber every time he made an entrance or exit. Every time we put on a play we have, of course, to pay a fee to the author and this can be expensive so on a number of occasions, we have written our own, amongst them "Under the Holly Bush", "The Wellington in the Cupboard", "Sounds Like Music" and "Once Upon a Time".

In 2002 it was suggested that we might form Junior MADS. This ran for two or three years and involved many of the children of our village some of whom graduated to senior roles. Unfortunately things like Health and Safety made the organisation and the time required a difficult burden to bear, but it was good while it lasted."

Puss in Slippers circa 1969

When MADS first formed, Ann Cheshire designed both the sets and the programmes for over ten years and she too can recall the terribly heavy old tables which were used for staging. Funds raised by MADS purchased the new lighter-weight tables which are used today.

Two of the programmes designed by Ann Cheshire

MADS 2005 production of "Lord Arthur Savile's Crime"

The Cast

John Wilkinson as Lord Arthur Savile.
John plays lead man this year, in his third outing with MADS

Pete Williams as Baines the Butler
Pete's MADS debut, so it was fitting that we gave him a heap of lines to learn !

Helen Shotton as Miss Sybil Merton.
American wife last year, a dippy young English lady this year.

David Heffer as the Dean of Paddington
MADS man of action, acting, directing, producing etc.

Tom Dancer as Lady Clementina
Is Tom now the most famous drag act in North Marston ?

Gill Warner as Lady Windemere
Veteran MADS actress, enjoying her role in high society.

Pat Robinson as Lady Julia Merton
Pat plays the fearsome Lady Julia as if she were born for the role.

Simon Day as Podgers
Simon plays, Podgers who is a cheiromantist… anybody know what that is ?

Bob Webb as Nellie
Nellie is a young parlourmaid. Obvious then that Bob should be chosen for the role.

Paul McSweeney as Winkelkopf
Straight man last year, Paul returns to a 'character' part this year.

Hilary King is our Prompt
Hilary is tucked behind the stage curtains, helping us through those forgetful moments.

The Cast would like to thank David Heffer for his patience in directing Lord Arthur Savile's crime. David puts in a lot of hours to make sure the production happens.

MADS are always interested in new members, so if you are interested, please contact either David Heffer, or Pat Robinson.

Lord Arthur Savile's Crime is a play written by Constance Cox, based on a Oscar Wilde story. It is about to go on a national tour with Bill Kenwright's company

The cast of the 2005 production

Twenty-two
VILLAGE SPORT
Sue Chaplin

Sporting activities have always played an important part in the life of any village, helping to bind a community together and providing entertainment, camaraderie and the opportunities for individual sporting prowess to shine. Participation, whether as a player, spectator, scorer, umpire, referee or tea-lady has, through the years, left an indelible imprint on many villagers' lives.

FOOTBALL

THE 1870s AND 1880s

The earliest reference to village football is to be found in January 1876 when it was reported in the Parish Magazine that, following the example of the boys at the newly-built Schorne College (*see Chapter Twelve*), the villagers had started a football club and had already played several matches. As always, the ubiquitous Rev James, rector of the parish, had something to say on the matter:

"That is the kind of manly thing to do, far better than loafing about streets, or idling away young lives in inactivity. Prosperity to Marston Football Club!"

The Football Club continued to prosper through the 1880s and in 1883 was considered by Rev James to be the strongest in the area. Naturally, the matches were played locally (and many were played against Schorne College itself). In 1883, when North Marston beat Aylesbury, the players in that match were: E Price, J Anstiss, H Anstiss, H Cheshire, C Watkins, J Tattam, T Newman, W Ward, A Clark, J Evans and T Anstiss.

It is possible that the following photograph of Henry Cheshire shows him wearing his football kit.

Henry Cheshire circa 1880

It appears that no piece of land was permanently designated for use as a football pitch and the team relied on the goodwill of local farmers, such as Mr Chapman of Manor Farm in the High Street, Mr Kibble of Glebe Farm by the church and Mr Biggs of Marston Gate Farm (also known as Stevens Farm) to provide them with a field on which to play. Sometimes the fields were a considerable distance from the village.

The Oving Villages Cup 1889

The Oving Villages Cup Competition (which still exists today) was formed in 1889 by the Reverend Hill, rector of Oving at the time, and is today believed to be the second oldest competition of this kind in the country. Villages within a twelve mile radius of Oving were allowed to subscribe to it and the founder members were Waddesdon, Oving, Granborough, Quainton, Long Crendon and North Marston.

Considerable interest was generated in this new "Villages Cup" (or "Rural Cup" as it was sometimes referred to) and the first season of

1889-1890 saw Oving themselves as the victors.

1891 TO 1900

North Marston's Champion Side

During the next ten seasons of the Oving Villages Cup, North Marston became champions six times (1890-1, 1891-2, 1892-3, 1894-5, 1896-7, 1899-1900) and runners-up twice (1893-4, 1897-8) which was a considerable achievement! If a match was drawn, it was replayed at a later date; there was no extra time allowed in those days!

Ted Dudley's Oving Cup medals

The medals pictured above were won by a young Ted Dudley who joined the team aged sixteen in 1892. (Many years later, in the 1920s, he became the Honorary Secretary of the Oving Village Cup).

Such was the enthusiasm for the newly-formed Villages Cup that Mr Ralph Chapman of Manor Farm (High Street) offered to provide the kit:

"Mr Ralph Chapman's uniform will be seen among us this season, up and down the field with, we are sure, its usual rapidity." (Rev James)

Mr Chapman, Mr Gregory, Mr Kibble and other farmers continued to allow village (and Schorne College) matches to be played on their fields, with Rev James commenting in 1896:

"We do not quite know what college and village football would have done this season without Mr Kibble's fields."

During the 1890s North Marston also won the Aylesbury & District Football Association Cup in the 1893-4 season.

Throughout the 1890s there were frequent comments in the Parish Magazine about football. In 1891 the introduction of "gate-money" at North Marston of two-pence per person caused a stir at the match between North Marston and Aylesbury Printers, especially as ladies went free! Rev James commented thus: *"Why ladies free? They can afford to pay just as well as gentlemen can."* The takings that day amounted to eighteen shillings and four-pence for North Marston Club funds (which at two-pence per head amounted to one hundred and ten spectators).

In 1892 a second and third eleven were mentioned in the Parish Magazine such was the popularity of the game.

The referee's decisions were often criticised, as in the match against a *"rough Waddesdon team"* in 1896 whose player kicked Ted Anstiss in the face and got away with it.

One particularly accident-prone player appears to be Arthur Price who was the only one ever to get mentioned in this context in the Parish Magazine. In 1892 it was written:

"Arthur Price should be glad the football season is over that he may not be tempted to play again just yet" and in 1896: *"We are glad that Arthur Price has been cured of his football wound."*

Rev James (who considered himself an expert on all things) commented most months on the ability of the players:

"The most improving man in the club is Garner; not the best man but the most promising if he played less roughly; Dudley and Garner are about the two best footballers the village club ever had.....and play splendidly

for the Aylesbury United." (Does this suggest that they were loaned out?)

By the mid-1890s the North Marston first team comprised F Anstiss, W Anstiss, A Anstiss, Warr, Garner, Brickhill, Mercer, Gowin, Dudley, Edwin Lambourne, Price and Carter.

North Marston Football Club in the late 1890s

It is interesting to note that the practice of collecting money at the gate continued through the 1890s (though whether ladies *were* ever asked to pay is not recorded!) and the following extract from the April 1898 Parish Magazine reflects just how popular football, and particularly the North Marston Club, had become during this decade:

"Our Village Football Club has earned the respect and sympathy of all the countryside, and in its last match, contending for the Buckingham League Cup, it took £3 15s as gate money in simple three-penny admissions." (That amounts to a crowd of three hundred people!)

North Marston Football Club circa 1900

Fred Anstiss was so proud of his cup medals that he had the following photograph taken wearing them:

Fred Anstiss wearing his Oving Cup medals

The Schorne College Football Team

It must not be forgotten that Schorne College, the prestigious school set up by Rev James next to the church (*see Chapter Twelve*), had its own football team and in 1889 a team comprising old and current students played in the Association Challenge Cup (FA Cup) winning their first round match against Millwall Dockers but losing to Watford Rovers in the second round.

1900 TO 1930

After 1900 there is little on record about the fortunes of the North Marston Football team; they certainly never again won the Oving Villages Cup. However, we do know (from the following photo) that a team existed in the 1920s.

North Marston football team circa 1926

THE 1930s

In the 1930s North Marston's football team was once again showing a winning streak. Matches were played on the field known as "The Green" which lies opposite Gibbings Close between the Granborough and Quainton Roads.

In the 1934-5 season the team won the Aylesbury District League Second Division Cup, beating Wendover in the final. The photograph below was taken on the old Vale Ground in Aylesbury.

North Marston football team 1934-5
L-R Back: *McLaren, L Warner, A Janes, E Harwood , W J Woodford, L Harwood*
L-R Front: *H Harwood, R G Woodford, B Heritage, C Harwood, W Walker*

North Marston's team (some of whom are pictured below) was again successful in the 1936-7 season of the Aylesbury and District League.

Back L-R: *R Woodford, B Heritage, H Cranwell, F Tattam, S Parker* **Front L-R:** *R Young, H Cheshire*

1956 TO 1966

Records show that in 1956 North Marston had a football team which played in Division Two of the Aylesbury and District League. Other teams in this division at the time included Whitchurch, Ellesborough, Kimble, Tring Corinthians, Negretti's and Hazell's. At the end of the 1956/7 season the team finished half-way down Division Two but by the middle of the 1960s it had unfortunately been demoted to Division Three.

Although they experienced many defeats, there was a great sense of camaraderie, enthusiasm and fun with Peter Morton travelling round the villages picking up players before each match. George Barrett, wearing his full football kit, travelled to matches from Granborough on the double-decker bus but, on the way home covered in mud (there were no showers in those days), was not allowed inside the bus and had to stand on the platform at the back!

North Marston men in the team in the 1960s included Mick Swain, Peter Morton, Cyril Carter, Brian Carter, Roy Randles, Roger Lambourne, Pete Coneron and David Holden; many players came from Granborough and several from the Claydons, Padbury, Oving and Winslow. The team managed to hold on to their place in Division Three until the club came to an end in 1966.

1972 TO 1995

Between 1966 and 1972 North Marston did not have a football team but the idea of starting one up again began in 1971 over a darts match at The Bell (now The Pilgrim).

The North Marston darts team, so fed up with losing to The White Hart at Preston Bissett, challenged them to a football match (two legs, home and away). Both landlords agreed to pay for the cup. North Marston lost the first leg 7-4, not helped by the fact that half the team did not turn up until half-time and spectators, some getting on in years, were roped in to play!

Fortunately, the rest of the team eventually appeared including Mick Swain, the "goalie".

Other players for The Bell that day included Ken Grant, David Smith, David Holden, Bill Daubney, Robert and Richard Ayres, Barry Kent and Harold ("H") Bone. After the second leg, having won the tournament on aggregate, North Marston's players were spurred on to create a *regular* football side (whilst the 'friendly' tournament against Preston Bissett continued as a yearly fixture for four years).

Melvyn Busson (left) with Eric Tomlinson celebrating in The Bell following a North Marston victory

So in the 1972/73 season North Marston started their twenty-three year campaign in the Aylesbury Sunday Football Combination League. The balance sheet from 1966 had left them with just over thirty-four pounds in the kitty. The first manager, treasurer (and pitch-marker) was Eddie O'Keeffe with key helpers, Bill Daubney, Pete Orme, Terry Holden and Ken Grant.

The club prospered throughout the 1970s though its pitch was in a sorry state at times! One year all the home games had to be played away due to the water and mud on the pitch but, determined to play the last two games at home, Eddie O'Keeffe and Bill McWhirter marked the pitch out by hand with paint brushes (the line machine just sank into the mud) and the task took them four hours!

A monthly report of the football club's fortunes and general news was posted in the village magazine, and fund-raising activities often took place to raise money for the club. In 1976 it was reported that two hundred and fifty pounds were needed to run the club for the next season. Discos and a "100 Club" were popular fund-raisers and a sponsored walk was held through Granborough and Swanbourne.

North Marston football team 1973-74
L-R (back row): Eddie O'Keeffe, Philip Brazier, Richard Parrot, Jim Walker, Mark Gurney, Dave Lambourne, Nigel Smith, Ken Grant, Pete Orme, **L-R (Front row)**: Ralph Spinks, 'H' Bone, Pete Lawes, Bill McWhirter, John Daubney **Young boys**: Gary Grant & Keith McWhirter

At the end of the 1975-6 season (with Bill McWhirter as Manager by now) the team's excellent performance resulted in a promotion to Division One (they had finished equal on highest points but came second on goal difference).

DIVISION TWO

Nth. Marston	17	15	0	2	81	25	30
Saracens Hd.	14	12	0	2	59	16	24
Bucks Nalgo.	17	10	2	5	54	35	22
New Zealand	15	9	3	3	52	29	21
Kl. Moeller	14	6	2	6	31	31	14
Claydon Rang	17	5	0	12	34	68	10
Black Horse	18	4	2	12	22	53	10
British Rail	12	5	0	7	27	35	10
Waddesdon V.	15	4	0	10	32	47	9
Tesco Utd	17	3	2	12	17	60	8

Aylesbury Sunday League Division Two Table showing North Marston at the top in February 1976

A Presentation Evening in the Village Hall on 28th May 1976 saw the attendance of seventy players, wives and girlfriends, and Harold Bone received the League Runners-Up Trophy on behalf of the North Marston team. Bill McWhirter (Manager) and Eddie O'Keeffe (Secretary) received special awards for their sterling work throughout the season and, of course, the ladies who had the unenviable task of washing the kit (Jean O'Keeffe and Daphne McWhirter) were not forgotten! Not all players resided in the village; many were recruited from the local area.

Success in the Berks and Bucks Junior Cup came their way during the 1976-7 season: David Rowe not only received the Top Goalscorer Award that year but also received the Player of the Year Shield and Silver Goblet.

During one Berks and Bucks Cup qualifying match, the referee announced that he was abandoning the game due to the bad language coming from the North Marston supporters (and some of the players!) but disaster was averted by the 'culprits' apologising to the referee and agreeing to buy him a drink in the pub afterwards! (If the match *had* been abandoned, North Marston would have been thrown out of the League).

In Division One North Marston faced some of the best teams in Aylesbury and the surrounding area. Some excellent results in the Challenge Cup in the 1978/9 season saw them reaching the final versus Cosmos, a great achievement though they eventually lost 3-1 after a hard-fought game.

This was a highly successful period for the North Marston team, the players continuing to play well in Division One and finishing third in the League in two consecutive years 1979/80 and 1980/81. They also reached the semi-finals of both the Vale Cup and the Challenge Cup in the 1980/81 season.

Sadly, despite having come third in the League at the end of the 1981/82 season, the North Marston team was demoted to Division Two for the forthcoming season due to its changing rooms not having showers or toilets. All they had in the pavilion at the time was a tin bath to wash in!

Between the 1977 and 1983 seasons David Rowe had been awarded the Leading Goal Scorer Award on six occasions with Paul Young, Phil Ginger and Eddie O'Keeffe picking up Clubman of the Year Award several times. Will Walker, "H" Bone, Ralph Spinks and Russell Clarke were recipients of the Player of the Year Award.

During the 1980s the team began to lose players due to retirement or moving out of the area but they continued to play in Division Two (reaching the final of the Chris Payne Trophy in 1988). The team played its last game in May 1995 when the club folded.

Throughout the years North Marston players had included David Bone, "H" Bone, Terry Holden, Ralph Spinks, Bill Daubney, John Daubney, Ken Grant, Nigel Smith, David Smith, Stewart Craggs, Tony Bevan, Kevin O'Donoghue and Roy Randles. Thirty-two players from local villages had also played in the squad.

Long-standing stalwarts of the club who, throughout the years, took on one (or more) of the roles of Chairman, Manager, Secretary, Treasurer, Linesman and Pitch Marker included Eddie O'Keeffe, Pete Orme, Bill McWhirter, Paul Young, Phil Ginger, Terry Holden and Bill Daubney. Christine Lambourne acted as "kit washer" for years, having taken over the role from Jean O'Keeffe and Daphne McWhirter.

Philip Ginger and Eddie O'Keeffe

"H" Bone played football for North Marston for twenty-two years and was still playing for Oving in 2013!

"H" Bone in the early 1970s

AFTER 1990

Junior Football

In 1991 an "Under 11" Club, run by Peter Hemus, was established in North Marston with twenty members. Matches were played in the Westcott Friendly League and the youngsters finished fifth in the League at the end of their first season.

Junior football returned to North Marston on Sunday 18th October 1998, set up by four 'dads' who wished to get their sons away from the television and into the fresh air! The dads also had to double up as the coaches: Kevin Hooker, Trevor Lane, Jeff Scott and Graham Tomlins gained FA Junior Managers' Certificates and the new football club was born.

During the next few years enthusiastic youngsters ranging in age from six to eleven years turned out, whatever the weather, on Sunday afternoons from October to April. Training sessions were held on their 'home' pitch at North Marston C of E School.

A fee of fifty pence per training session was requested and during their first couple of seasons the money raised bought all the necessary items for the club. Attendances of fifteen or more children were a regular occurrence and the club's membership stood at up to thirty boys and girls at any one time.

North Marston's junior football team circa 2000/2001

In September 2000 the Club became affiliated to the Football Association which resulted in additional avenues of funding. It was not long, therefore, before the Club was able to buy kit for two teams and the school benefited from new goalposts through the football club.

Their first competitive fixture was at home to Marsh Gibbon on Sunday 19th November 2000 which North Marston won 4:2. Further fixtures followed during that season and the team enjoyed success in many of their games.

By 2004, Des Ewing and Tony Bennion had replaced Jeff, Kevin and Graham as team coaches.

Between 2000 and 2008 the Juniors attended regular mini-soccer tournaments and non-league fixtures against local villages including the 'mighty' Moretonville (Maids Moreton) who, despite having a large pool of players from which to choose, found the North Marston side too good for them!

The junior football team in May 2004

In 2007 Neil Mobsby and Ian Mordue joined Trevor, Tony and Des on the coaching team and then jointly took over the reins in 2008, continuing with the coaching before taking the team into the Milton Keynes Development League in 2010.

AFTER 2006

North Marston and Granborough Football Club was created in February 2006 and began with a five-a-side training session once a week. A few friendly eleven-a-side matches were then played a few times a year. It was born out of a desire to improve fitness and to help build a community spirit within and between the villages. The first fixture was the revival of the old "Village Cup" and took place on a very hot day in June 2007 at Oving Football Club, with good support from both villages. North Marston eventually won 4-2 after a penalty shoot-out and the North Marston goal-keeper Gordon Bowden was voted Man of the Match for his heroic saves!

The winning North Marston side in June 2007

The problem of pitch availability was solved with the opening of the new North Marston and Granborough Community Sports Field in 2009 (*see Chapter Twenty*) with the first football match being played there on 17th July 2010.

This first game was an intra-club affair with players turning out in the elegant black and white strip (home) and all-white strip (away). The team captains were Trevor Callender and Roger Hall, both of whom were soon to emigrate.

This was a very proud moment for all those involved in the club and the match was to become an annual fixture dedicated to the memory of Dean Easterbrook, a keen footballer, who had been an inspiration to them all, and who had sadly died of cancer.

North Marston and Granborough football teams on 17th July 2010

Today in 2014 there is no regular eleven-a-side football team playing either friendlies or in a league. However, the club members meet every Wednesday at the Winslow Centre and some of the young sons from yesteryear have now turned sixteen and have joined their fathers on the pitch!

CRICKET

1870 TO 1900

In the early 1870s North Marston's cricket team played against local sides such as Brill, Quainton, Oving, Wingrave and Aylesbury and the matches were reported (and scrutinised) in great detail every month in the *Parish Chronicle*. They had a large following of supporters but, it seems, no permanent cricket ground:

"Considerable enthusiasm was manifested by the North Marston folk who mustered in great force on the cricket field, on the 'tented field' we may say and who cheered the good hits lustily......The dinner at the Bell was excellent, we are told...North Marston ought to hurdle-in a piece of ground somewhere (it could be hired for a small sum), roll it, mow it, keep it and take pride in it. But that would cost money and need a little pluck and perseverance, and besides – Rome wasn't built in a day." (Parish Chronicle, August 1870)

Without a well-kept wicket one can only imagine how precarious it must have been to be on the receiving end of the bowling! Mr Kibble from Glebe Farm next to the church allowed cricket matches to be played on Fallow Close (behind the vicarage), and The Wheatsheaf pub allowed the team to use their field at the back.

The cricket matches appeared to be well supported by enthusiastic crowds with beer and ginger beer in plenty! On one hot August day in 1871 the following report appeared:

"The tents and eatables for sale, also the visitors and general cheerfulness, were pleasant to see. There was a Northmarston (sic) barrel organ which struck out every time that a new fresh Brill player went in, an act of politeness towards the new player which cannot be sufficiently commended. Good manners, even at cricket matches, are not bad things."

It is interesting to note that, after this match, some of the Brill players stayed overnight at The Wheatsheaf.

North Marston cricketers we know of in the 1870s were: L Chapman, H Baker, R Holden, N Baker, E Watkins, R Price, J Price, T Ward, E Holden, G Price, W Kibble, W White, J Julian James, J Keen and J Gurney.

In June 1880 North Marston Cricket Club re-formed and consisted largely of the members of the village football club. However, little is recorded about these years and it appears that, by the early 1890s, no team existed in the village. In 1891 Rev James exasperatedly wrote:

"Surely a village which holds the football cup should be able to manage a cricket club."

We do know that, in 1892, interestingly enough, a cricket match took place between eleven North Marston *ladies* (captained by Miss Lucy Tattam) and eleven gentlemen. One can imagine the scene with the ladies in their long sweeping skirts! The gentlemen were handicapped by having to bat with broomsticks and field left-handed, the result being that the ladies won by forty-three runs!

By the late 1890s, however, North Marston once again had a worthy cricket team and matches often consisted of two innings, with North Marston running up high scores at times: they were very proud to beat Granborough by one hundred and one runs *and* an innings in 1900!

Granborough, Quainton, Oving, Waddesdon and Addington were just some of North Marston's opponents during these years, though it is interesting to note that they sometimes only played about half a dozen matches in total during the season (several of them in Feast Week) which is possibly why each match attracted many spectators and became such a festive occasion.

Great fun was always had on the cricket field during Feast Week every year (*see Chapter Twenty*) during which the cricket team played several matches (some people suggesting that it should be called "Cricket Week"). Schorne College obligingly lent their 'tent' for the occasions and many spectators would turn up to watch the cricket, refreshments being provided by Henry Anstiss at The Armed Yeoman pub in Church Street.

During the 1898 Feast, there was quite a skirmish after the match against Hoggeston during which Watkins had been given out "leg before wicket". It was reported in the village magazine that:

"..really the ball would have gone over the wickets. The Hogston (sic) umpire who gave Watkins out is a fair man enough in intention but evidently unskilled or unobservant. Watkins would have won the match for his side no doubt but the scene that followed was most distressing....However we are glad to hear that the teams parted in a friendly way."

At the Cricket Club's Committee Meeting in 1899 it was reported that, of the *five* matches played, two were won and three were lost. The Cricket Club's balance sheet for 1899 stood at four pounds six shillings and twopence 'ha'penny'; players' subscriptions were half a crown and the expenditure for a horse, trap and umpire amounted to ten shillings and a penny 'ha'penny'.

North Marston cricket team circa 1896

There still appeared to be no established cricket ground for the North Marston village team as Mr Anstiss of Hill Farm lent out one of his fields for cricket during Feast Week. We do know that, by 1900, Schorne College was allowing the village team to share *their* ground (belonging to Mr Kibble of Glebe Farm) so there is the possibility that at least *this* field and wicket were being kept in reasonable shape!

The following photograph shows a pair of "horse slippers" (believed to have been used on the Schorne College cricket field) which were attached to the hoofs of the horse to protect the pitch when it was pulling the mower or roller over the grass. These "slippers" belonged to Ted Dudley (the village builder) who, it is thought, found them in the old Schorne College building when he was demolishing it in the late 1920s (*see Chapter Twelve*).

Horse slippers worn by the horse when working on the Schorne College cricket pitch

In March 1900 a meeting of North Marston Cricket Club was held and the suggestion was *again* made (having first been put forward thirty years earlier!) that a reserve fund should be started towards hiring a *permanent* ground for the club and that the cricket and football clubs should be amalgamated.

North Marston cricket team circa 1900 Ted Dudley (3rd left at back) Tom Biggs (1st on left at front) William Harwood (far right) Fred Holden (middle front)

THE 1930s AND EARLY 1940s

During the 1930s the cricket team, as in years gone before, still played on various fields around the village.

One was "Andrew's Oaks" (known as "Anders Oaks") behind The Wheatsheaf pub. Laurence Young, whose family building business was nearby at the top of Quainton Road, started off the cricket there and would store all the kit and equipment needed for looking after the pitch.

The team also used the field which today is called the new North Marston and Granborough Community Sports Field but, with the onset of the Second World War, this field was ploughed up and subsequent matches were played on Home Close (along Portway) and The Green (the field opposite Gibbings Close which lies between the Granborough and Quainton Roads).

The following photograph (probably taken behind The Wheatsheaf in Anders Oaks) shows the North Marston cricket side on 4th September 1936.

North Marston cricket team 4th September 1936
L-R (Back): Unknown, Arthur Lambourne, PC William Lawrence, Will Woodford, Dick Harwood, Ezra Rawlings (Umpire), Eric Harwood, Dick Curtis, Ted Dudley (umpire)
L-R (Front): Clarence Cheshire, Walter Carter, Laurence Young, Walter Walker, Chib Harwood

The village team did not belong to a Cricket League during these years; just 'friendly' matches were played. During one particular match the village policeman, PC Lawrence, was bowling for North Marston and the story goes that, every time he appealed for a wicket, the North Marston umpire Ted Dudley called "Out" (even if it clearly wasn't) as he was rather in awe of the policeman and did not wish to offend him! After the match the opposing team (who had lost) picked up Ted and threw him in the pond at the bottom of the field! Whether this was done light-heartedly we shall never know!

A cricket cap badge from the 1930s

THE LATE 1940s AND 1950s: NORTH MARSTON'S GOLDEN YEARS OF CRICKET

This was an outstanding period in North Marston's cricketing history. In 1947 the Buckingham and District Cricket League was started up again and, during the next seven years, North Marston totally dominated it, winning the League Championship six times (in 1947, 1948, 1950, 1951, 1952 and 1953)! The President of the League was Tom Biggs, a North Marston resident. The village team also won the Buckingham Challenge Shield in 1952 and the Holton Festival Cup in 1954.

North Marston Cricket Club still had no permanent ground for their matches and many home games were still being played in the field opposite Gibbings Close. Laurence Young was the regular umpire who also continued to look after the pitch and the kit, and Eveline Parker travelled round with the team as the scorer.

At the celebration dinner following their 1947 League Championship victory, the captain, Ray Young, expressed the hope that the next season they would be able to play their matches and practise on the pitch being prepared in the Recreation Field (in Granborough Road). In 1953 a new pavilion was erected on this field.

The Teams and the Finals

In 1947 North Marston started off their championship run in the Buckingham and District League by beating Twyford in the final. Members of the winning team were awarded medals which, in those days, were made of real silver inlaid with gold.

Bourton Road Ground in Buckingham, scoring only twenty-six runs to North Marston's one hundred and thirty-nine! In fact, that season, North Marston topped the century mark on seven occasions in the run-up to the final.

In 1950, North Marston continued to show their superiority by beating Hillesden by one hundred and one runs.

North Marston's 1947 league-winning cricket team (Captain: Ray Young)

In 1948, Gawcott were the unfortunate side to meet North Marston in the League Championship Final which took place on the

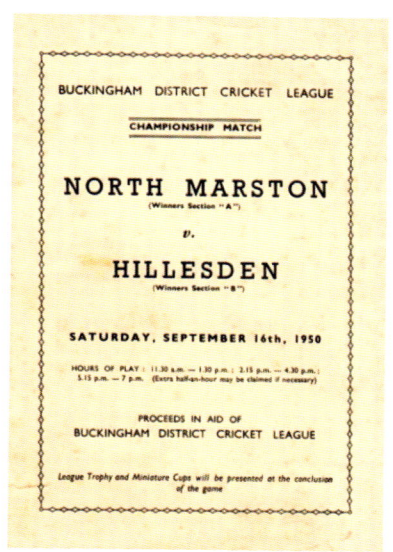

North Marston cricket team with their opponents, Gawcott, and league officials at the final in 1948

North Marston Cricket League Champions 1950
L-R (Back): Walter Carter, Dennis Higgins, Howard Cheshire, Jim Smith, Cyril Gawthrope, Norman Higgins **L-R (Front):** Sid Parker, Gordon Alderman, Robin Harwood (Capt), Chib Harwood, Eric Harwood

In 1951, with Jim Smith now as captain, North Marston beat Buckingham CESC by just seven runs and, in 1952, after gaining victory against Hillesden (by seven wickets), the Buckingham Advertiser reported:

"North Marston have now, without a doubt, proved themselves one of the outstanding village sides in post-war cricket".

The 1951 winning side
L-R (Back): G Alderman, R Harwood, N Higgins, G Laishley, A Hall
L-R (Front): C Gawthrope, S Parker, J Smith, D Higgins, C Harwood, E Harwood

That same year North Marston also won the Buckingham Challenge Shield and, in 1953 after beating Finmere in the final, they equalled Steeple Claydon's record of four successive wins in the Buckingham & District League which was a considerable achievement. In 1954, North Marston, although not regaining the League title, were victors in the Holton Festival Cup.

The following photograph was taken after the match. In one season Robin was voted Best Bowler and Best Batsman throughout the Buckingham League.

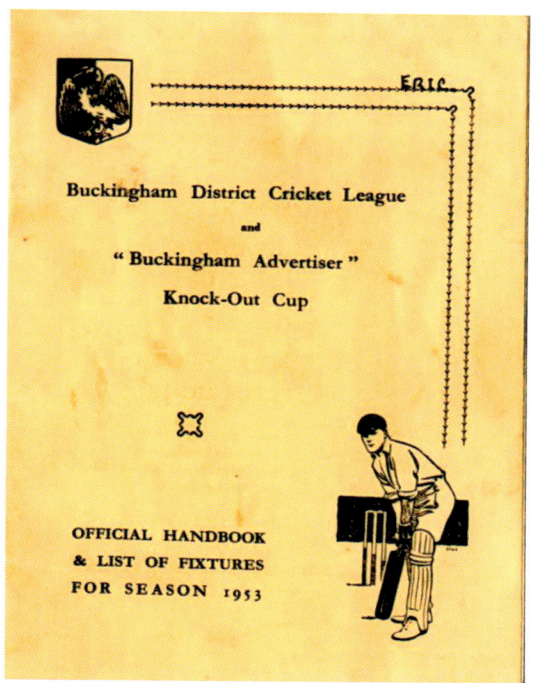

The 1953 Buckingham & District League Fixture List

Robin Harwood after his memorable League Final

The Players

Every member of North Marston's cricket team during those "Glorious Years" played a part in its success, whether as a batsman, wicket-keeper, bowler or sprightly out-fielder. In 1948, the Buckingham Advertiser (in its run-up to the forthcoming League Final between North Marston and Gawcott) reported: *"The Marston attack centres around the Harwoods."*

The "Harwoods" referred to were the Harwood brothers (Eric, Chib and Robin).

Robin Harwood was an extremely talented batsman and bowler and in one memorable League Final against Buckingham he scored ninety out of North Marston's one hundred and twenty runs! (He also took two wickets and bowled thirteen 'maiden overs' that day).

Eric Harwood and Chib Harwood had been playing cricket for North Marston since the 1930s; Eric was still a formidable batsman and bowler, in one cup match taking seven wickets for thirteen runs, whilst Chib's strength was with the bat. Graham Ward remembers:

"After the war village cricket got going again and North Marston was well blessed with a plethora of talent and, as I was playing school cricket, I took great interest. North Marston were usually dominant and, if batting last, they would knock off the runs for the loss of four or five wickets. Robin and Eric Harwood opened the batting and they were very contrasting in style; Eric was a reliable stone-waller who blocked everything so it was really hard to get him out, and Robin swung the bat and blasted anything loose."

Ray Young was another talented batsman who, according to Robin, *"could really cut the* *ball*". He captained the village side in their victories in 1947 and 1948 but then became ill and in 1949 a Benefit Match was played for him. The Buckingham Advertiser reported:

"(Ray Young) is one of the best batting members of the team. Unfortunately due to illness, the after-effects of Army service abroad, he has not been able to play this season and has been greatly missed."

In the mid-50s Ray returned to village cricket and was scoring high numbers of runs again.

Norman and Dennis Higgins were also mainstays of the team, both fine batsmen, and Norman a good bowler too. **Gordon Alderman** was indispensable as wicket-keeper, **Arthur Hall's** accurate bowling helped North Marston to victory on many occasions and Graham Ward's summary paints a good picture:

"The pitch at the present site was lethal and batsmen needed to duck and dodge to avoid being hit by Robin Harwood, Eric Harwood, Norman Higgins and Arthur Hall who were a formidable quartet producing basically hostile bowling. Ray Young and Dennis Higgins were very stylish at three and four; Ray was a class player."

All-in-all, the North Marston "First Eleven" of the 1950s, was an incredibly talented side. It must not be forgotten, however, that in the early 1950s, such was the keen interest in cricket, that the village also fielded a 'Second Eleven'.

Robin Harwood recalls:

"The local village games were always needle matches and none more so than those against Granborough. Everyone wanted to play in these and one evening we arrived for an away game and were just about to start when the farmer who owned the field rushed across and stopped the game because he hadn't been picked to play!

In another game against Mursley, the opposing wicket-keeper stood with his foot near the wickets and, as the ball passed, he tapped them with his foot, the bails fell off and the batsman was given out. In the pub afterwards he laughed with the batsman and admitted what he'd done.

The umpiring was a bit suspect sometimes – it wasn't unusual to hear from a bowler whose father was umpire, 'How's that, dad?' and the answer would come back, 'Out! Well bowled, son!'"

Robin Harwood with the League Cup in 1951 on the steps of The Bell

Church Thanksgiving

Every year in November the North Marston Cricket team attended an Evensong service in St Mary's Church as a thanksgiving for the past cricket season with two of the players reading the lessons.

The Cricket Dinners

The photographs on this page illustrate the popularity and importance of village cricket in the late 1940s and early 1950s. The photographs immediately above and below show the team and members of the Committee with the League Trophy. *(Below can be seen **L-R Back**: Gordon Alderman, Arthur Hall, Laurence Young (Umpire), Doug Bevan, Harold Chapman, Harold Carter, Jim Smith, Archie Higgins, Sid Parker, **L-R Front**: Robin Harwood, Tom Biggs, William Hall, Cyril Gawthrope, Clarence Cheshire).*

THE 1960s AND 1970s

Cricket matches continued to be played in the Buckingham and District Cricket League until the end of the 1950s when the team was disbanded but, in 1966 it reformed with David Heffer as captain. The team played friendly matches and also took part in the Coronation Cup competition.

It did not take long to get together a keen and enthusiastic team who played matches every Saturday and sometimes on evenings during the week. In 1967 there were fourteen subscription members, a few players from Granborough joining the team. David Holden recalls:

"I remember watching the old cricket team of the 1950s playing and I can recall them finishing. There were quite a few years before we had a proper team in the village again – probably late sixties. Our first match was over at Mursley. Laurence Young was the umpire. He used to fetch the gang-mowers from Addington to do the outfield. He did a lot for the team; he was a great cricket fan and had done a lot for the 1950s team too."

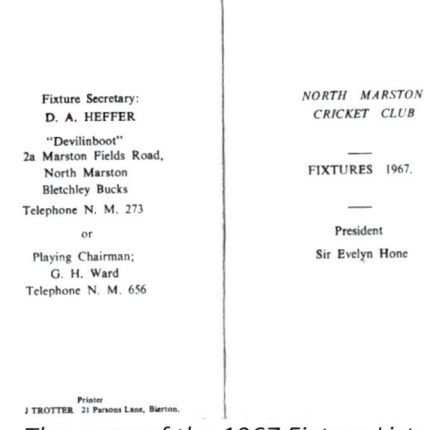

The cover of the 1967 Fixture List

It is interesting to note that Laurence Young, as umpire, and Eric Harwood, Dennis Higgins and Sid Parker, as players, were still involved in village cricket, having first turned out for the team in the 1930s.

In 1967 David Heffer wrote:

"We would like to congratulate Mr Dennis Higgins who returned to cricket last week and cracked fifty-eight runs against the Aylesbury GPO. North Marston are indeed fortunate that, after nine years absence from the game, his skill has not deserted him."

The 1967 Fixture List

North Marston's cricket team after a friendly match against GPO at Alfred Rose Park in Aylesbury in the 1970s
L-R Back: Laurence Young (Umpire), Eric Harwood, Bligh Barnes, Peter Morton, David Smith, Graham Ward, David Holden, David Heffer **L-R Front:** Dennis Higgins, Sid Parker, Roger Lambourne, Bill Daubney, Hugh Bevan

In the Parish Magazine early in the season of 1967, David Heffer (referring to the 1950s team) wrote:

"Recent defeats have not dampened the spirits of the North Marston Club members, and we shall continue to brandish our bats optimistically. We hope eventually to prove to the "tribal elders" that good cricket did not vanish for ever when they hung their bats up

over the mantel- piece, and their boots in the back shed."

In August that year the "old 1950s players" had obviously agreed to a match against the new village side:

"On Wednesday July 12th the 'tribal elders' could bear it no longer! After a search in the attic and amongst the moth balls, they sallied forth to show us a thing or two! It wasn't long before the old cunning began to show and the youngsters were returned to the pavilion for a modest fifty-five runs...The elders scampered to their fifty-fifth run on the last ball of the game. This game will be talked about for a long time."

Although the North Marston team of the 1960s had mixed fortunes, it had a keen following and in 1968 proposals were made outlining improvements such as the purchase of gang mowers. In 1968, an Under-16 team, organised by Bligh Barnes, played a young side from Whitchurch and this Youth Team (North Marston Colts) did very well during the next few years.

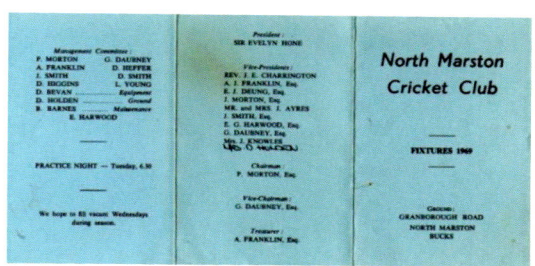

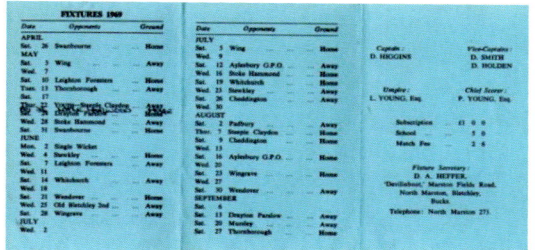

At the Annual General meeting each November, presentations were made, including the Knowles Cup (*pictured*) which was given each year to someone (not always a player) who had done a lot for the club during the season.

As the Seventies wore on the Cricket Club persevered and entered several competitions such as The Picton Cup, The Coronation Cup and The Presidents' Cup. They were also playing in the Aylesbury and District Mid-week League Second Division and came very near to promotion in 1976.

The yearly awards for batting and bowling continued to be given out. In 1974 Rob Symonds received the Knowles Cup; Paul Barnes was top of the batting averages and David Holden top of the bowling averages; both David Smith and David Holden had taken fifty wickets during the season and Bligh Barnes and Rob Symonds had both taken eleven catches each.

In the late 1970s North Marston Cricket Club ceased.

AFTER 2009

In 2009 the new North Marston and Granborough Cricket Club was formed and played its first match on the new North Marston and Granborough Community Sports Field on 20th September 2009 (*see Chapter Twenty*). Twenty-two villagers from North Marston and Granborough made up two teams (the 'Full Tossers' and the 'Golden Duckers'). Cheered on by families, friends and fellow villagers who had prepared picnics and barbeques, the match turned out to be a truly remarkable occasion and resulted in a tie with both teams all out for eighty-five runs.

On 17th September 2011 a new pavilion was opened by the England cricket captain, Alastair Cook (*see Chapter Twenty*).

The first home cricket match on the new sports field in September 2009 (left) and the fixture list for 2012 (right)

North Marston and Granborough Cricket Club today play senior friendly fixtures on Sunday afternoons as well as holding evening net sessions throughout the summer. There are also junior teams (Under 9s, Under 11s and Under 13s) who play many fixtures, both home and away, throughout the season on various weekdays, with coaching sessions on Saturday mornings.

TABLE TENNIS

The Table Tennis Club in North Marston began in the mid-1950s after The Sportsman and The Wheatsheaf pubs had closed down and Kath Tattam had applied to open a Social Club on the premises of the village hall (*see Chapter Twenty-one*). Once a month there was a village dance in the hall which attracted youngsters from Oving and Granborough, and it was at one of these dances that Dennis Higgins suggested getting a table-tennis team together and entering it in the Aylesbury and District League. So, Dennis, together with David Midwinter and Tony Ball (from Oving) and Rupert Stonnell (from Granborough), started up the North Marston Table Tennis Club. They met on Tuesday and Thursday evenings and the club evolved as gradually more people joined in.

On Tuesday evenings the team played in the Buckingham Cup. The first season 1956-7 saw them win the Third Division League (*see photograph below*). The following year the team (with the same four players) again came top of their division resulting in their promotion to Division One for the 1958-9 season.

The North Marston table tennis team after winning promotion from the Third to the Second Division of the Aylesbury and District League in April 1957
L-R: David Midwinter, Rupert Stonnell, Dennis Higgins (Capt) and Tony Ball

The Table Tennis Club became very popular and successful. One member, Pete Coneron, encouraged many of his friends from the New Holland Works in Aylesbury to travel over to North Marston to play. Other teams were formed including Dennis Brazier, John Turner and Den Carter (from Granborough) and Tony Franklin, Keith Franklin and Graham Ward (from North Marston). At one time there were at least six teams playing in the League. Two or three nights a week would be taken up with table tennis and the village hall was in constant use hosting the home matches. The teams often won their league and gained promotion; Tony Franklin himself remembers doing so in 1964 and 1967. The club continued right up to the early 1970s when it was run by Den Carter from Granborough who wrote the following report in the Parish Magazine in 1970:

"Although the 1969/70 season is coming to a close, thoughts are already on the 1970/71 season which commences in October.

Unfortunately, we shall be losing the nucleus of our 'A' team which this season competed in Division Two. We shall be more than sorry to lose the services of Dennis Higgins, a founder member of the club. Our 'B' team is made up of Keith Franklin, Tony Franklin and Steven Upton, and this season they were successful in reaching the quarter-finals of the local Handicap Tournament. This was a fine achievement on their part.

We would be pleased to welcome new members to our club especially the younger element, boys or girls. The Aylesbury and District League is one of the most successful in the country and consists of over ninety teams playing in seven divisions. Recent alterations and decorations to the Village Hall have been appreciated by us, and visiting teams have also been appreciative of the new surroundings."

TENNIS

In the 1930s new tennis courts were laid behind the Memorial Hall. These proved very popular and were used quite frequently, with matches being played against local villages such as Oving. Fred and Sam Tattam were two of the villagers who helped to lay the courts.

A tennis match circa 1930
L-R Front: *Stella Cheshire, Emily Young, Mabel Buckingham*

DARTS

Over the years, both 'friendly' and League matches have been played at The Bell against other local pub teams.

In the 1980s a darts team from The Bell joined the Winslow and District Darts League and, later, the Wing and District Darts League. The landlord at this time was Vic Hinde whose second-hand minibus was often used to transport the team to away matches.

Vic himself was a member of the team. The captain was Paul Young and there were many team members some of whom included Stephen Wright, "H" and David Bone, Richard and James Tattam, Jason and Andrew Franklin and Dean Bunyan. Both doubles and singles matches were played.

In both the 1984-85 and 1987-88 seasons North Marston won Division Two of the Winslow League. The 'big match' of the season was the local derby against The Crown at Granborough (as both teams were in the same league).

It is interesting to note that, today, many of the pubs whose darts teams played against North Marston in the 1980s are no more: The White Horse and The Crown and Thistle in Whitchurch; The Devil in the Boot, The Crooked Billet and The Windmill in Winslow (to name just a few).

Twenty-three
THE VILLAGE AT WAR
THE SECOND WORLD WAR 1939-1945

John Spargo

During the Great War the day-to-day lives of the village people (with the exception of the blacksmith who had secured a huge contract to supply the army with horse-shoes) appear to have been largely unaffected by the Great War being fought "far away in some foreign field"; but from the outset, the Second World War was to have a more profound effect on the village population. Probably one of the first indications was the arrival of London school children evacuated to North Marston.

The Arrival of Evacuees

After the announcement that Britain was at war with Germany on 3rd September 1939 the capital braced itself for anticipated air-raids. Immediately, plans were implemented that had already been drawn up for a massive programme of evacuation of London children to foster homes all over the country. The sheer scale of the administration was mind-boggling, and every 'host' community appointed a Billeting Officer responsible for pairing the children with host families. North Marston's Billeting Officer was Alfred Cheshire the village Post Master and ARP Warden.

Alfred Cheshire, the Billeting Officer, pictured wearing his British Empire Medal in 1954

We have only to look at the School Admissions Register to appreciate the impact this must have had on the village: when the school broke up for the summer in 1939 there were forty children on the roll; when it re-opened on 12th September, *a mere nine days after war was declared*, there were ninety on the school roll, including fifty London evacuees! New arrivals would report to the Village Hall (which was called the Rest Centre) whilst awaiting allocation. For some, this appears to have taken longer and so the Rest Centre became their temporary home whilst a longer-term address was identified.

Young children at the start of their evacuation

However, the anticipated bombing raids over the capital failed to materialise, and within a couple of weeks forty-eight of the children had returned to their London homes during a period described as "The Phoney War".

When the London air raids finally started in August 1940 the children began to return to North Marston. With its proximity to London and good rail links, Buckinghamshire had a disproportionate share of wartime evacuees; it was estimated that in March 1941 the total population of the county had increased by thirty-five percent, *the largest percentage increase of any county in the country.*

The effect on the village must have been astonishing. By the end of the war North Marston had housed, in total, one hundred and twenty-seven children and provided education for an additional twenty-one children who were billeted in Granborough. Such were the numbers involved that, in 1942, the school buildings were opened during the summer holidays for children to attend for recreational work.

We are fortunate that we have a first-hand account of what it was like to be an evacuee child in North Marston. Tommy Gray arrived here in 1941 and has remained in the area ever since. Here he tells us what it was like:

"In 1941, and after many months of The Blitz, my father decided that Hitler would celebrate his birthday by bombing London with even more ferocity (though his fear was misplaced). So, on the morning of 20th April my mother Maud, brother Laurie, sister Jean and I were despatched to our aunt, Mrs Geall, in North Marston. Our father stayed in London to run our corner sweet shop. We lived very close to the Victoria and Albert Docks and the India Docks as well as Woolwich Arsenal so it was in a prime bombing target area.

The cottage was not big enough to sleep us all so my mother and I were billeted further down the road towards the Memorial Hall near Fred Tattam's dairy. It was, for me, a traumatic experience moving from London, where we hardly knew any neighbours, to a place where, horror of horrors, not only did everyone know everyone else but high proportions were related to each other!

Life became a big learning curve. In London milk used to be delivered by United Dairies in bottles left on the door step. Not now! Milk is delivered by Fred Tattam – just put your jug by the back door with a crocheted cover with beads around the edge and the milk is then dispensed from a can by means of a pint measure into the jug, and the crocheted cover replaced to keep the flies out!

For an evacuee in a small village it was very much a 'them and us' affair.

However, luckily a local lad of about my age, Chris Holden, decided we should become friends and we have remained so for seventy years. We formed a trio with another evacuee, Arthur Bevan, who was billeted with Mr and Mrs Joe Wilkins in the end cottage next to Franklin's shop.

It was a shop that sold everything, being a butcher's and owner of the slaughterhouse run by Clarence Cheshire. Another first was to see him wield his 'humane' killer and dispatch a pig or cow, hoist it with block and tackle, gut it, bleed it, scrub it and finally joint it. Quite an achievement for Clarence who was not the biggest of men! He also drove the delivery van serving the surrounding villages.

It was becoming obvious that I had landed in a very self-sufficient society in North Marston."

Tommy Gray and Chris Holden outside Bell Cottages

Laurie Gray, Mrs Geall and Maud Gray

Tommy's parents, Tom and Maud

However, not all evacuees settled into the village quite as well, as Eveline Parker remembers:

"We had an evacuee living with us in the war and one day he stole my brother's bike and disappeared. PC Lawrence found him half-way up Oving Hill; he said he was cycling back to London as he was home-sick! The mother of another evacuee who lived with us was visiting him the night the bomb exploded down Granborough Road, and she took him back to London the next day as she thought it was safer there than in North Marston!"

The Bomb that Exploded along Granborough Road

The bomb referred to as "down Granborough Road" was a parachute bomb or a land-mine, a huge explosive designed to detonate as it approached the ground so the shock waves caused extensive damage to property. Several cottages in the village were badly damaged by this explosion and they still bear the evidence to this day. It was the nearest the village came to suffering fatalities due to an enemy bomb. Robin Harwood remembers:

"Two bombs were dropped in North Marston; one exploded down Granborough Road and the other landed in the field opposite but didn't go off. Police Constable Lawrence stopped people from going anywhere near, so we boys went up Anstiss's field and looked down from there. The bomb that exploded cracked the Shell sign on Malcolm Holden's garage and it fell off the wall."

Chris Holden also went for a look:

"One exploded just about fifty yards further on from the present sports field on the opposite side of the road and for years nothing grew there where it had landed – there was always a gap in the hedge. I could take you to that exact spot now. It went off with a terrific shudder and a bang; everything shook.

A German plane had off-loaded it and they always carried two to balance things up so another was dropped, but that landed in the field next to where the sports field is now and didn't go off. It was in Ern Seaton's field about half-way between the cow-house and the road. The bombs looked like forty gallon oil drums, all packed with explosives. The road had to be closed.

We boys walked up the fields and looked down and saw it lying on top of the ground (it didn't go into the ground at all). If it had landed in the middle of the village it would have killed lots of people. One house that took a good shaking from the explosion was the bungalow along Marston Fields Road at the first gate. Mr Rogers lived there and the bomb's explosion cracked the corner of it.

The bomb that didn't go off was defused by Bomb Disposal people and taken away."

Alarmingly, it seems the unexploded bomb wasn't noticed at first. Cliff Cheshire recounts:

"It wasn't until the clear light of day that it was realised there was another bomb sticking out of the ground in the field opposite that hadn't gone off! The funny thing was that Granborough Road was cleared that night to let the late bus through and the next day, when they discovered the unexploded bomb, nothing metallic was allowed anywhere near!

We were told these land mines were carried under the wings of the plane and they had to drop two for balance. I've heard it said that we were on the flight path to Coventry. Whether the German plane was in trouble and had to shed its load, I don't know. People said they heard the plane making a funny noise. Our house down Quainton Road opposite the threshing barn has tie rods in it because the blast blew out our fireplace and front window but hardly did any damage to Jack Ayres' adjoining house!"

The Bomber Crash in North Marston

During a war there are thousands of tragedies, but one in particular during the Second World War left a permanent mark on the memories of many villagers. This was the crash of a Wellington Bomber from Westcott in a field alongside Stone Hill (at the end of Quainton Road) on the evening of 4th January 1945.

A WW2 Wellington Bomber

Buckinghamshire was a strategically important county for the RAF in the Second World War with Operational Training Units (OTUs) at Wing and Westcott. The HQ for "No. 92 Group Bomber Command" was at Winslow Hall.

The airfield at Westcott, about six miles from North Marston on the road between Aylesbury and Bicester, was the home to "No. 11 OTU" where young pilots and their aircrew were trained to fly bombers in planes like the Vickers Wellington.

At its height the airfield at Westcott, together with its satellite at Oakley, held around two thousand officers, airmen and airwomen. There were also satellite OTUs at Little Horwood and Finmere. The trainees, some of them young men from Australia and New Zealand, were urgently needed to replace men killed in action.

The bombers would take off from Westcott and fly on cross-country navigation exercises or practise bombing at targets in the fields between Granborough and North Marston. This latter area was known locally as "The Bombing Ground".

Training flights were not without hazard and indeed the worst World War Two bomber crash in Buckinghamshire happened when a bomber on a training flight from Wing crashed into cottages in Winslow in 1942, killing seventeen people, ironically including a family of four evacuated from London.

The devastation in Winslow High Street after the bomber crashed

For people in North Marston, however, the nearest the village came to a repeat of the Winslow disaster was the Wellington Bomber crash. It happened just outside the village a few years later on the evening of 4th January 1945. Many local people, such as Clifford Cheshire, still remember the incident clearly:

"In the Second World War a Wellington bomber crashed up Stone Hill in the field which I think was called Langlands. It was on 4th January 1945 at about 7.30pm and I know this as I recorded it in my diary at the time.

I was only a schoolboy then and I was out making deliveries for Franklin's shop with my dad in a van. I often used to go with him when he went delivering late in the day. We were down Hogshaw on this particular evening and we had stopped to open one of the gates on the road when we heard a plane coming over Quainton Hills. I was just getting back into the van when I heard a terrible crash over the village; it looked as if the village was on fire from where we were. We came rushing back along the road from Hogshaw, round the bend and towards Stone Hill and the road in front of us was on fire. The plane had crashed in the field at the bottom of the hill."

Whether or not this particular aircraft (HE470) piloted by twenty-one year-old New Zealander Michael Reece had been taking part in one of these practice bombing runs, or was on a navigation exercise, is not known. However, the plane got into trouble, and it was heard flying very low by people in the village. Eveline Parker retells her experience of that night:

"I remember the Wellington bombers always coming over the village, often on their way to and from Horwood air-field, but I shall never forget that terrible night when the plane crashed up Stone Hill. I was in the outside privy at home in Quainton Road and the plane was on fire as it came over the house. I'm sure I heard those poor men screaming."

The impact of the crash must have been heard by everyone and Chris Holden recalls the aftermath:

"When the Wellington bomber crashed up Stone Hill I went down there to have a look the next morning with Tommy Gray and Arthur Bevan. There were men with wicker baskets picking up body parts. I often think it would have been nice to have had a memorial in the church for them".

The pilot and crew were all killed instantly. The six men who died were:

Function	Name	Age	Home
Pilot	Flight Sgt Michael Reece	Aged 21	Otago, New Zealand
Navigator	Ian Smith	Aged 22	Beckenham, Kent
Air Bomber	Flight Sgt Alexander Bolder	Aged 23	Otago, New Zealand
Air Gunner	Sgt Reginald Price	Aged 19	Brighton, Sussex
Air Gunner	Sgt S.W Wenham	N/K	N/K
Wireless Operator	Flight Sgt D.W. McLellan	N/K	New Zealand

Although we know about the plane and its crew, the cause of the tragedy remains a mystery.

It is a sobering thought that an incident that in peace-time would make front page national news was treated as a sad but minor hazard of war.

Thirty-four years after the crash, local man Rowland Linnell gained permission from the Ministry of Defence to recover the aircraft from the ground where it had been buried since 1945. However, it seems he never pursued the recovery of the wreckage, so it remains to this day buried in the ground: an invisible memorial to the six young men who lost their lives so suddenly and dramatically.

Bombers Collide in Mid-Air

Another incident occurred near the Bombing Ground when two bombers flying between North Marston and Granborough collided in mid-air. Chris Holden remembers:

"I was standing on Tommy's doorstep by the Bell when the two planes collided over the Bombing Ground along near Granborough. It is a very vivid memory and it almost seemed as if they'd hit each other much nearer over the village. There were flames and sparks everywhere. We heard the bang and I think it was about nine o'clock in the evening. I heard it said that one was on a bombing mission and that the other one was just practising. You could see the two main parts of the planes falling out of the sky and the wind carried a lot of the debris towards the village. I often think about that crash and that eight or ten men lost their lives at that moment. At the time, being children, it didn't sink in – it was just a 'plane crash' and the deaths didn`t enter our heads."

Secret War Work in Whitchurch

The Firs, a mock-Tudor country house in Whitchurch, was acquired by the War Office during the Second World War and became a top secret weapons development centre known as Military Intelligence (Research). It was directly accountable to the Prime Minister and was quickly dubbed "Churchill's Toy Shop".

Wartime buildings at The Firs photographed after the war

In the course of a few years, the team at The Firs successfully developed a range of weaponry that found its way into operational use. They ranged from small booby traps to heavy artillery, aircraft bombs and naval mines. These included the famous limpet mines used to devastating effect by *The Cockleshell Heroes* in the sinking of numerous German vessels in a daring commando raid behind enemy lines in December 1942, an exploit subsequently made into a feature film.

The development and testing of these weapons called for great secrecy and a large team of people working round the clock. Consequently, The Firs became a major employer of local people, many of them women, and developed a strong *esprit de corps* so typical of intense, clandestine operations. About two hundred and twenty people were billeted on the site supported by a group of non-resident workers from neighbouring villages like North Marston. One of these women was Eveline Parker:

"During the war I worked at The Firs at Whitchurch where I made detonator parts for bombs. Mona Holden worked there too. I was paid seven pounds a week. I made friendships there which have lasted through my life. There was a wonderful camaraderie."

The women from the village were very well paid by contemporary standards but worked unbelievably long hours as Mona Dumpleton (Holden) recalls:

"When the War came I went to The Firs at Whitchurch where we worked on munitions. A few other girls from the village worked there as well: Eveline Parker, Jean White, Joan Rawlings and Lucy Bates. We worked there from 8.00am to 9.00pm Monday to Friday, and 8.00am to 5.00pm on Saturdays and Sundays. During the war we only had Christmas Day off. We cycled up to Whitchurch or sometimes took the bus. Lucy Bates lived at Crandon Farm and there was no road from there to the village in those days so she had to walk across the fields."

Oddly, despite being a secret establishment, The Firs held an Open Day during the war to which young Chris Holden and his pal Tommy Gray went and watched a weapons' testing demonstration in the field below the house. Chris recalls that he and Tommy collected souvenir rockets which they concealed in their trousers and took home!

Civilian women at The Firs during the Second World War

Stuart Macrae was the man responsible for the day-to-day running of The Firs for the duration of the war. One of Macrae's first tasks was to assemble a team of military personnel with the skills and aptitudes needed for the job. These were no ordinary military types, however: they were basically inventors in uniforms. The common factor was their ability to innovate and solve problems through lateral thinking and pure inventiveness. This meant the military aspect of The Firs was informal and the usual protocols of rank and authority went largely unobserved.

The social needs of this closed community, however, were well addressed and it seems that dances at The Firs were regular, celebrated events.

Death of Sergeant George Tattam

In contrast to the Great War (when twenty-two young men from the village lost their lives) the Second World War claimed only one North Marston serviceman. Sergeant George Thomas Tattam, an air-gunner in the RAF 487 Squadron, died in a Lockheed Ventura bomber on 3rd May 1943 in a low-level attack on the Amsterdam power station in occupied Holland. Of the ten planes in his squadron which took part that day, every one was lost. He had been a regular bell-ringer at St Mary's church.

George Tattam

An appeal was made to raise funds to create a memorial. As a result of the appeal, a plaque to his memory was commissioned. It was unveiled in 1947 and can be seen at the back of the church.

A memorial to Sergeant George Tattam was also erected in Holland

Sergt. George Thomas Tattam.
MEMORIAL TABLET.

In the world war 1914-1918 twenty-seven personnel of North Marston on active service gave their lives for the cause of freedom. In world war 1939-1945 Sergt. George Thomas Tattam alone made the supreme sacrifice serving with the Royal Air Force, of whom it has been said "Never before had so many been saved by so few."

The Diocesan Authority having accepted the petition of the Parochial Church Council to erect an approved Tablet in the Parish Church have forwarded the required faculty, and the work is being carried out by Mr. Heritage, Winslow, and is nearing completion.

The Tablet bearing his name commemorates his honoured memory and the services of all the boys and girls of the Parish as a Thanksgiving to God for the preservation of our homes.

Any of the undersigned will be glad to receive donations towards the fund to assist in the cost of erection.

BERNARD CARTER.
FRANK BRAZIER.
THOMAS BIGGS.

The memorial to George Tattam in North Marston Church

Search-light Battery

The nearest operational military unit to the village was the search-light battery situated at the foot of Oving Hill. This unit was responsible for manning a mobile search-light used to detect enemy aircraft at night.

A typical World War Two mobile search-light

Semi-permanent tents adjacent to the battery housed the soldiers who operated the search-light and who were armed with a Lewis Gun to fire at enemy aircraft within range.

It is unlikely the gun was ever fired with hostility and the reason for the location of a search-light at the foot of a hill on the edge of a village in North Bucks is unknown; perhaps low-level enemy aircraft attacks on local airfields or The Firs in Whitchurch were feared.

Rationing

Throughout much of the war, Britain relied heavily on imported goods from Canada and America and these could only be brought to the country in convoys of ships that often came under attack. Since British manufacturers were largely engaged in war work, household commodities, clothing, food and confectionery were strictly rationed. Families received books of coupons (ration books) which were used in exchange for the limited supplies. Although rural communities fared better for food during the war, as most families grew their own vegetables, some staple foods such as sugar, fats, eggs and meats came under general ration.

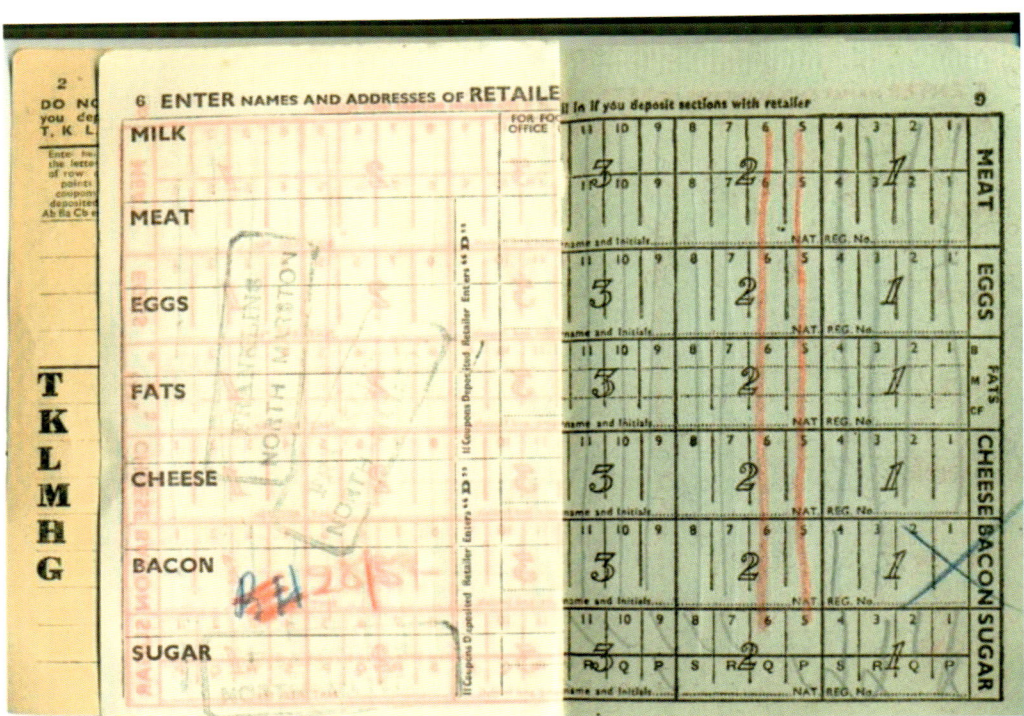

A food ration book, used in Franklin's Stores, North Marston

Whilst many families re-cycled clothing to reduce the need to buy clothes (the watchwords being "Make Do and Mend") families with growing children needed to buy clothes for the oldest child from time to time which then became a 'hand-me-down' for younger members of the family. Accordingly, families were issued with books of tokens for children's clothing along with their food ration books.

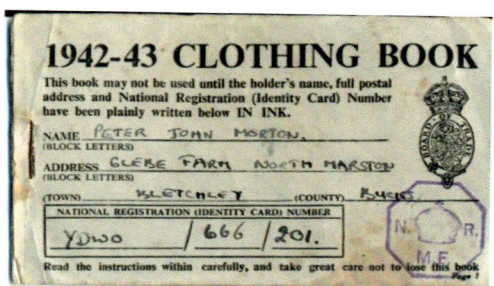

Peter Morton's clothing (ration) book for the mid-war years

Farming in Wartime

In North Marston, in common with most of the agricultural land in the northern half of the county, the land was principally pastoral and used for sheep and cattle. In the Chilterns and southern half there was more arable land used for growing crops, but across the whole county farms were poor and had little money or incentive to make improvements.

Once war broke out, a County War Agricultural Executive Committee (CWAEC) was set up in Buckinghamshire under Lord Addison, a local man who had been Minister for Agriculture in the 1929 Labour government. Its challenge was to maintain milk production while greatly expanding the crop production and to do this it had to improve the land and enable the farmers to get as much out of it as possible.

One of the first acts of the County War Agricultural Executive Committee was to conduct a survey of all farms, grading them and making recommendations for improvement. If farmers refused to comply, the committee had authority to take over the farm.

At the beginning of the war many farms were still using horses and hand machinery, although tractors were beginning to be used instead. The CWAEC set up depots of tractors and modern farm machinery which could be borrowed by farmers. The nearest depot to North Marston was at Winslow.

The County War Agricultural Executive Committee depot at Winslow

A deal struck with the American forces when they came into the war (called "Lease-Lend") meant that the Americans sent over new tractors and combine harvesters which were rarely seen before in this country. A scheme called the Goods and Services Scheme enabled even quite poor farmers to buy these over a period of years. One of the conditions of buying through these schemes was that the machinery could be used on other farms in the area too.

Farming was made even more difficult during the war years by the shortage of labour. Young women were recruited to join the Women's Land Army as "Land Girls" to help out but not every farmer was to benefit, as David Midwinter recalls:

"Many of the young men of working age left the land to go in the army. Older men and those not fit to fight stayed behind, although the farm owners themselves got dispensation and those with very large farms needed some of their workers to stay as well. Not every farmer had the benefit of being able to employ a Land Girl; a group of larger farmers ran the Agricultural Committee and they had first call on them!"

Land Girl, Enid Payne

Local girl, Enid Payne, joined the Land Army and worked on a number of farms in the area. She later married Geoff Ayres, the son of the Infants' teacher at North Marston School.

The Women's Land Army recruited girls from all over the country to help work on the farms. Much milking was still done by hand and the need for fresh milk, combined with the shortage of men who had been called up for military service, meant the Land Girls were in great demand.

They often worked in teams and lived in local hostels, the nearest of these being in Winslow though several Land Girls were billeted with village families. Many had no experience of farming whatever. By October 1943 there were nearly two thousand Land Girls in Bucks, and some (like Enid Payne) married local men and settled here.

With circumstances being what they were, co-operation between farmers was the only way to get by. David Midwinter explains:

"During the Second World War there was a large amount of co-operation between farmers. At farm sales during the war any machinery would be auctioned normally but if a tractor came up for sale it would be valued at what was considered to be a good fair price and then anyone who wanted to buy it had to buy a raffle ticket for a pound. If their name was drawn out then they could buy the tractor at the asking price. At a local sale my father, who already had a tractor, let the Tattams have his ticket so that they had an extra chance of getting it but unfortunately their name wasn't drawn out!

Tractors in World War Two were not terribly common and mostly they were Fordsons. People like Victor Alderman who was a licensed threshing contractor had a W9 International tractor which he had ordered from the USA".

Victor Alderman and his thresher

For farmers (excused military service because of the vital work they were doing) life was far from easy, especially at harvest-time. David Midwinter explains:

"During the war there was 'double summertime' and this was to enable the farmers to work later than normal when bringing in the harvest. The men used to work until about eleven o'clock at night; they all worked so hard. I can well remember the 10.50pm bus going past my window in daylight."

Prisoners of War

North Buckinghamshire had a number of prisoner of war camps such as Shalstone near Buckingham, Quainton and Hartwell Dog Track at Stone. Not surprisingly, given the lack of able-bodied local men, work on farms was often augmented by prisoners from the local POW camps transported to farms as day-labourers. These were mostly Italians but there were a few Germans. Many of the Italian and German families who still live in the Aylesbury area are descendants of POWs who decided to stay in Britain after the war.

The Home Guard

In the War, it was common for people to have multiple responsibilities, doing one job during the day and another at night: Alf Cheshire, in addition to being the village postmaster, was the Billeting Officer for evacuees *and* the village's ARP (Air Raid Patrol) Warden at night; Bill Ward, from Franklin's shop, was also a warden with the ARP; Henry Cheshire, the village baker, was the official Salvage Steward (authorised to collect or organise salvage from war damage) and was also a Special Constable, as was Joe Holden.

Henry Cheshire's Salvage Steward badge

Similarly, a lot of men too young or too old to join the armed services, or who were needed in essential occupations like farming, became volunteer members of the Home Guard, immortalised in the TV series *Dad's Army*. Here in North Marston there was an active Home Guard Unit; Jack Gould from The Sportsman pub in Quainton Road was in charge. One of the members of the platoon was farmer John Morton.

Peter Morton in his father's Home Guard uniform

After the war he and his fellow volunteers were presented with a certificate of recognition from a grateful monarch.

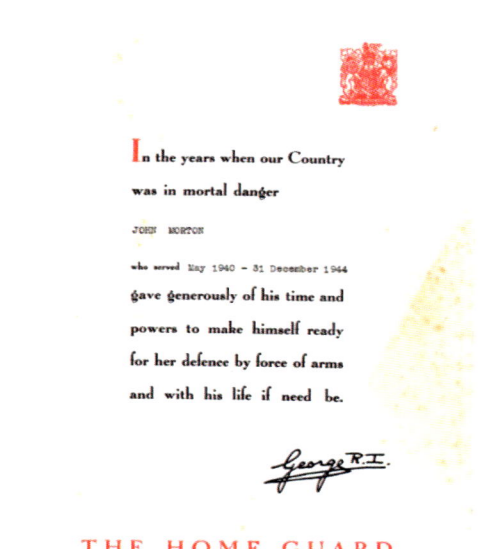

John Morton's certificate of thanks for his service in the Home Guard

George Harry Heath

Although not strictly in World War Two, the village was to lose another local man to armed conflict a few years later. George Heath, a regular soldier with the Royal West Kent Regiment, had fought in the Far East during the Second World War. Captured by the Japanese in Singapore, he was held as a POW. After the war, he was back in service in the Malayan Emergency that was to claim the lives of over five hundred British personnel between 1948 and 1960. Ambushed in the jungle in October 1951, George Heath (aged thirty-two) and ten others were killed.

Post-War North Marston

With the end of hostilities, things gradually returned to normal. The evacuees and Land Girls went home. Most of the men returning from war went back to their old jobs and the rhythm of village life took on a semblance of pre-war years. However, expectations were high that life would be different. The war had made the world a smaller place, many young women had found financial independence and war-time advances in technology were anticipated to filter down to everyday life. Yet, economically, the country was almost bankrupt and so rationing was to continue for several years longer through a period of austerity: petrol was rationed until May 1950, tea until October 1952, sweets until February 1953, sugar until September 1953 and meat until July 1954.

Slowly things improved, however, and by the late 1950s more and more families were able to buy a television, refrigerator, twin-tub washing machine and, some, a car. Gradually, as the decade of the 1950s came to an end, the harsh austerity of the immediate post-war years in North Marston began to fade into a memory.

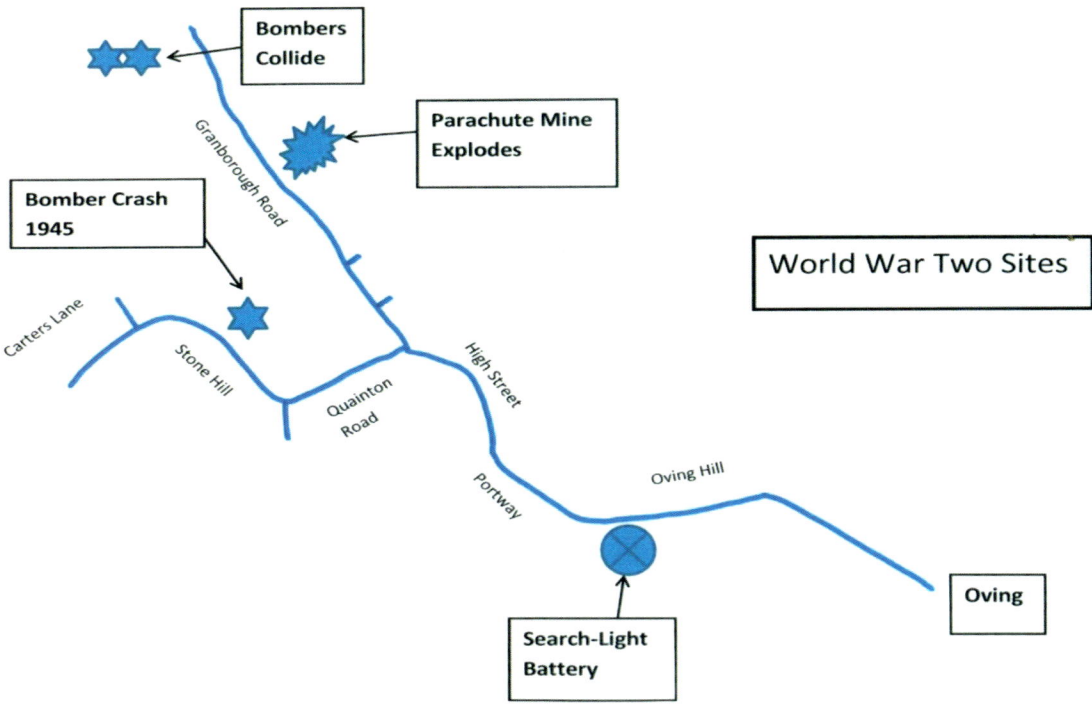

Twenty-four
FARMING
PART ONE: THE HISTORY OF FARMING FROM 1778
Colin Price

For centuries, farming was the mainstay of North Marston's economy and, right through to the start of the twentieth century, the majority of men in the village were farmers or farm labourers and many more were employed in trades dependent on farming. Being such a key factor in its welfare, the success or failure of local farming was always a matter of great importance.

The dramatic changes to the village that followed the implementation of the *North Marston Inclosure Act 1778* have already been explained in Chapter Seven. The open spaces that had been laid down to "ridge and furrow" for centuries were divided into enclosed fields. It is remarkable that the pattern of fields created in 1778/9 is virtually unchanged today. Some fields have been divided further by new hedgerows but very few hedges have been removed. This is in marked contrast to so many areas of the country where the wholesale grubbing out of hedges has produced enormous fields for cereal production. North Marston's heavy clay soil is not the preferred soil for cereal growth but is ideal for permanent grassland. It provides excellent grazing for sheep and cattle and rarely needs to be ploughed and re-seeded.

1778-1850

The marked decline in arable farming at the end of the eighteenth century set in train enormous problems for the agricultural community in North Marston. Land used for the cultivation of wheat, oats and beans was replaced by grazing for cattle and sheep. By 1810, of the one thousand six hundred acres of farm land in North Marston only one hundred acres were arable. Furthermore, grain production was labour-intensive, pastoral farming was not, and, to add to the problem, labour-saving machinery was being introduced as early as 1809.

By 1831 there were approximately eighty labourers unemployed in North Marston and the high levels of unemployment and poverty triggered a vast increase in the Poor Rate. This was a local tax levied on property owners and occupiers of the parish. It was collected by local parish officers known as Overseers of the Poor and distributed for a time (as we saw in Chapter Nineteen) in the Wheatsheaf Inn.

The swingeing increase in the Poor Rate brought its own problems for farming. Landowners were unable to find tenants for their farms because the tenants would not only have to pay rent but also the unaffordable Poor Rate. Tenancies were being abandoned and landowners were unable to find new tenants prepared to meet the costs. We know of a good farm in North Marston of two hundred and seventy acres unable to find a tenant in 1830 because the Poor Rate in just one quarter was forty pounds (Morley, 2007). By October 1831, another two farms, totalling between three hundred and four hundred acres, were unoccupied. We know (from *The Northampton Mercury* of 29th October 1831) that one of these was owned by John Camden Neild but the owner of the other is unknown. John Camden Neild's refusal to pay the Poor Rate came to a head the following year when he was served with a court summons. He held out till the last moment, paying the one hundred and ten pounds due on the morning he was to answer to the magistrates in Quainton.

It became increasingly difficult for the Overseers to collect sufficient rates and people said "the poor law has eaten all the farmers up".

In order to decrease the burden on landowners and occupiers, the Poor Law

Amendment Act was passed in 1834. This Act reduced the parish poor rates by reducing the relief paid to the poor and by forcing the unemployed and their families into workhouses. The local workhouse for North Marston was in Winslow where conditions were appalling: husbands, wives and children were split up, labour was hard and food minimal.

Winslow Workhouse

This Act was the final straw, and labourers returned to their last resort: civil unrest. The *Morning Chronicle* of February 1st 1830 reported that:

"On Wednesday last the village of North Marston was thrown into a state of great agitation in consequence of a disturbance amongst the labouring poor arising, it is said, out of the following circumstance: one of the Overseers was paying the poor at his house when a young lad called for his allowance – amounting to three shillings. The Overseer refused to pay him more than two shillings and three pence. The pauper, however, refused to leave the house unless he was paid the remainder. An attempt was then made to turn him out when some of the men interfered, and the constable, being present, eventually took four of them into custody. This proceeding roused the indignation of the poor of the village, who, being joined by a number of the poor from the adjoining village of Oving declared that the men in custody should not be taken to prison unless they were all taken there. Such was the threatening aspect of affairs that the other Overseer, Mr Kingham, fled for safety, under the apprehension of his life being in danger. Fifty of them, armed with sticks, proceeded to the house of a Magistrate in the neighbourhood, the Rev Mr Archer of Whitchurch. Lord Nugent (who is highly respected by the poor of the neighbourhood) being at his seat at Lilies, about two miles distant, proceeded to Whitchurch, accompanied by his brother-in-law, Captain Poulett, who, in conjunction with Mr Archer investigated the case and, after hearing the different statements, they discharged the men, considering that both parties were to blame. They further conciliated the poor, by assuring them that justice should be done in attending to their complaints, and advised them to return peaceably to their homes, which advice was instantly complied with. The prudent step taken by the worthy magistrates, it is believed, was the means of preventing much evil, as, from the excited state of feeling which prevailed among the assembled poor, had a different line of conduct been pursued towards them, it is more than probable that consequences of the most serious nature would have ensued."

Jackson's Oxford Journal of December 19th 1829 reported:

"An inflammatory and diabolical letter has been sent to Mr Kingham, the overseer of North Marston, Bucks, threatening to murder him for stopping money for the poor, adding that, sooner than starve, they will be up to their knees in blood, and burn him in his house, if they cannot do for him in other ways. Mr Kingham has offered £10 reward to discover the writer."

The *London Examiner* of July 5th 1835 reported on a case tried in Aylesbury involving seven men from North Marston who were charged with creating a riot and assaulting a man named Grace. Grace had been employed by the authorities of North Marston to superintend the surplus labourers of the parish and we learn from other sources that the men *"had put him in the parish pond"*. It is reported that the court was crowded to excess at a very early hour, such was the interest in the case. The men were named as Young, father and son, Christopher and John Price, Cook, Buckingham and Stonhill. The men said that they were willing to work if Grace had offered them a fair price for their labour. They were all found guilty; Price and Stonhill were sentenced to two months' imprisonment and the other prisoners to four months'.

It is clear that the first half of the nineteenth century was a very difficult time for the village but, despite that, farming was still the mainstay of North Marston life. The census of 1851 showed that, of two hundred and two males in the village over the age of sixteen, one hundred and thirty-six (sixty-seven per cent) were either farmers or farm labourers, and a sizeable proportion of the remainder were in occupations supporting farming. Unfortunately, agriculture would come under even greater pressure in the second half of the nineteenth century.

1850-1900

The Great Depression of 1873-1879 was a world-wide economic recession which had a profound effect on UK agriculture. The farming industry recovered far more slowly than others and is regarded as having been in recession right through to 1896. North Marston was affected in the same way as all farming communities, creating a sharp decline in the number of agricultural workers throughout this period; there was simply not enough work in the village and many had to leave and seek work elsewhere.

Fortunately, for the first time in history, alternative means of support were available. In the second half of the nineteenth century, it was possible to escape poverty and the workhouse by finding employment outside the village, and many did. The population of Aylesbury trebled during the nineteenth century and in Newport Pagnell it doubled; but the most spectacular increase was in Wolverton and Bletchley due directly to the coming of the railway.

By the 1860s Agricultural Labourers' Unions were emerging to assist the movement of labourers to other parts of the country to increase their wages, and even to emigrate. The Union's activity did force an increase in farm wages in some areas due to the scarcity of labour. *The Pall Mall Gazette* of May 6th 1867 reported that *"the farmers of Bierton, Aston Abbotts, North Marston and other villages in the district have been compelled to raise the wages of their farm servants one shilling per week."*

In North Marston the number of males above the age of sixteen fell from two hundred and two in 1851 to one hundred and fifty-one in 1901. This was despite an influx of tailors attracted by Holden's shop and teachers (and others) employed by Schorne College. The total number of farmers and farm labourers fell from one hundred and thirty-six to eighty-six during this period.

Thomas Biggs and William Kibble

During the closing decades of the nineteenth century, two farmers played prominent parts in the village history: Thomas Biggs at Marston Fields Farm (later known as Marstonfields Farm) and William Kibble at Glebe Farm. Both men were churchwardens; William Kibble was the vicar's warden and Thomas Biggs was the parish warden. As befits these roles, William Kibble supported the vicar and Thomas Biggs spoke for the parish and was a frequent irritation to the vicar. William Kibble and his son Edwin were very active in the village during the late years of Victoria's reign when the village saw so much progress. We know particularly of Edwin Kibble's chairmanship of the School Board from 1892-1902 when he oversaw the enlargement of the school and the purchase of the playground.

Thomas Biggs

Thomas Biggs was chairman of the Parish Council, Justice of the Peace, a District Councillor as well as a trustee of both The Clocklands Charity and Poors Piece Charity. He was also Overseer of the Poor (a role that had put his predecessor in such great danger half a century earlier!) and in that role he would entertain at Marston Fields Farm a number of people from the workhouse. Prior to the arrival of the Reverend James, Thomas Biggs had been taking a leading role in the Vestry Committee meetings, (the fore-runner to the Parish Council) effectively becoming the "mayor" of the village.

When the vicar asserted his rightful position as chairman of the Vestry Committee, conflict was inevitable. It came to a head in 1876 when (in the vicar's view) Thomas Biggs became *"somewhat excited"* during the Easter Vestry requiring the vicar's intervention to save him *"from any unnecessary humiliation"* as Biggs had failed to be re-voted as the parish warden. The Reverend James alluded somewhat darkly to Biggs representing *"former days and former doings"* prior to the vicar's arrival to sort things out.

The two had multiple confrontations over the years which the vicar recorded in the parish magazine often in scathing language. The conflict culminated in Biggs suing the Reverend James for the defamatory remarks he had written about him. Thomas Biggs won the case but was awarded only forty shillings, a paltry sum compared with the two thousand pounds that he had claimed.

The animosity remained scarcely hidden and open hostility surfaced again in 1900 when Biggs tried (unsuccessfully) to prosecute two Schornian boys for trespass on his land, clearly an attempt to antagonize the vicar again! The vicar took great delight in publishing in full the Magistrate's dismissive comments about Biggs.

While attending a lively and noisy meeting in Oving in 1910, Thomas Biggs collapsed and died. It was in the middle of winter and he was taken back to Marston Fields Farm on a horse and cart. He was aged seventy five.

The Threshing Barn

The Threshing Barn is also referred to as the "Harvest Barn", the "Labourers' Barn" and the "Parish Barn". It is in Quainton Road more or less opposite the entrance to Shepperds Close.

The Parish Barn or Threshing Barn in Quainton Road, pictured in 2013

It was built in 1888 for farm labourers to thresh their own harvest. Labourers grew a small crop of cereals to feed their chickens for egg production. Up to that time, one or more farmers had allowed labourers to use their barns to thresh the corn but over the years less space was available.

When, in October 1888, Mr Kibble told the labourers that the barns at Glebe Farm were too full that year for him to be able to let the men thresh there, an emergency meeting was called. A large number met in the Parish Schoolroom on October 5th and the plan to build an independent barn for the use of farm labourers of the village was conceived. A committee was elected with Alfred Carter as chairman.

Fund raising events were held but the barn was primarily financed by donations from individuals from within and outside the village. A remarkably large number of people donated; it seemed that everyone gave what they could afford albeit small amounts in many cases.

The barn was formally opened on 29th December 1888, less than three months after the first meeting. A celebratory "Barn Tea" was attended by one hundred and thirty people. There was a long list of self-congratulatory speeches and the vicar cheerfully accepted compliments for his role in the venture. There was much praise for the concept of *"helping those who helped themselves"* and an expression of hope that the barn would not be used for political or religious meetings!

The barn was built by John Price at a cost of twenty six pounds. The total cost including all expenses amounted to thirty two pounds and five shillings. Some of those who promised donations initially in order to get the project started were very slow to come up with the money and were named in the North Marston chronicle as G Carter, F Smith, T Walker, N Young, F Gowin and F Price. Nearly two years later, a Social Tea on behalf of the Barn was held in October 1890 and finally raised sufficient money to pay John Price in full.

1900 TO THE SECOND WORLD WAR

The Smallholdings and Allotments Act 1908 empowered county councils to purchase agricultural land to lease as farms and small holdings. Three farms were purchased by Buckinghamshire County Council in North Marston. In 1913, the two hundred and twenty acre Manor Farm (St John's Manor) was purchased which was sufficient for four holdings. In 1920, two small plots of land known as Hagditch and The Slad were sufficient for one smallholding and in 1923 one hundred and thirty-seven acres of Brook Farm were purchased and were, subsequently, sufficient for one farm and three small holdings. We will encounter these farms and smallholdings again when we look closely at the village after the Second World War.

Between the wars most farmers took their milk by horse and cart to Granborough Road Station. From there it was taken to Brazier's Dairy in Kenton in north London. The dairy had been set up many years earlier by members of the Brazier family from Granborough.

Most of the farmers travelled along Carters Lane and down what is known as Deadman's Lane to Granborough Road station; but those who farmed land behind Brook Farm would just have cut across the fields. Some of the milk, such as that from John (known as "Son") Brazier's herd, was sold in the village and delivered by the milkman, Jack Gould, landlord of The Sportsman's Arms. These were very hard times for farmers as David Midwinter explains:

"Early in the 1920s there was a recession and the farmers just couldn't sell their milk. Many milk buyers reneged on their contracts (though I don't know if Braziers did, as they had so many family connections). Many farmers were feeding their milk to their hens and several gave up milking altogether.

My father and his brother went to the Dominion Dairy Company in Bicester Road in Aylesbury (this later became Cow & Gate) and they eventually agreed a deal to pay my father 1/6d a gallon for his milk to be made into butter. In 1929 several working men in the area stopped working on the land because they could claim 29/- a week unemployment benefit and were better off! They called these men the 'Twenty-Ninth Brigade'.

During the 1930s there was another terrible Depression when people farming land made no money at all – they just survived off the land really. My father and Horace Elmer went to Buckingham Sheep Fair at that time and bought ewe lambs for 19/- each and then walked them home past the Folly at Adstock where they stopped for refreshment (penning the sheep up along the side of the pub for a while). The next year they went back to Buckingham to sell the sheep and got 9/6d each for them! So they'd lost ten shillings per animal during that year.

Many farmers went broke in the 1930s and that's when Bill Pipkin gave up farming. Some smallholders like the Tattams managed to carry on but it was a period of very tough times for everyone."

Joe Midwinter in the 1920s

DURING THE SECOND WORLD WAR

Things picked up in the late 1930s as war approached and food was needed. Farming nationally was overseen by the War Agricultural Executive. This body had enormous power to maximise food production. Their decisions were not always popular with local farmers but their authority was absolute. The Executive even had the power to remove bad farmers from their land. In North Marston, the Executive insisted that many fields of grazing were ploughed and turned over to cereal production. It seems very strange to us now, but the Executive insisted on cereal growth on the Quainton hills.

Interestingly, two fields, Big Grove and Brickhill Piece, which were in the very south of the village close to Pitchcott, were turned over to market gardening. A sizeable gypsy community lived in caravans along the side of Carters Lane at that time and they were compelled to work on this land cultivating vegetables.

During the war years many of the younger men left the land and joined the military services, leaving a shortage of agricultural labour, but farmers themselves were given a dispensation from 'joining-up' and those with very large farms were allowed to keep some of their workers as well. Several farmers, for example John Morton from Glebe Farm, joined the Home Guard (*see Chapter Twenty-three*).

Land girls were sent to country areas to help out on the farms. Quite a few land girls were billeted at Pitchcott and at a Land Girl Hostel in Winslow, and several of them worked on the market garden. One of them, Enid Payne (*see Chapter Twenty-three*) married Geoff Ayres from North Marston. Another land girl called Rosie worked on Jersey Farm. David Midwinter recalls: ***"not every farmer had the benefit of being able to employ a land girl; a group of larger farmers ran the Agricultural Committee and they had first call on them!"***

Towards the end of the war, several German and Italian prisoners-of-war worked on farms in the village. One Italian worked at Manor Farm (in the High Street) till the late 1940s. Jim Tattam also remembers his father, Fred, having German and Italian prisoners-of-war helping him with the threshing.

Imported tractors at the War Agricultural Executive's Depot at Winslow

Tractors were limited during the war and when a tractor came up for sale at an auction it was sold by lottery. It would be valued and then anyone who wanted to buy it would buy a raffle ticket for a pound. The lucky winner could buy the tractor at the agreed price. Victor Alderman at Stonehill Farm was a leading agricultural contractor in the area. He had a W9 International Tractor. This was one of a consignment of four tractors sent from the USA on two separate ships. The other three were on the ship which was sunk by a U-boat. Victor's tractor was the only one to cross the Atlantic safely. He also had two threshing machines which were widely used locally.

During the war there was a large amount of co-operation between farmers, all helping each other out where possible. David Midwinter can still remember the "Double Summertime" which was introduced throughout the war years to help out the farmers:

"During the war there was 'double summertime' and this was to enable the farmers to work later than normal in bringing in the harvest. The men used to work until about 11 o'clock at night and they all worked so hard. I can well remember the 10.50pm bus going past my window in daylight."

HORSES, HARVEST AND HAYMAKING

Before the introduction of tractors and modern machinery, the cart-horse was indispensable to the farmer. It was used for a multitude of tasks on the farm: working machinery such as elevators; pulling ploughs, harrows, rollers, binders and mowers; and hauling heavy carts. Hay was cut with a mower and, before the invention of the baling machine, was allowed to dry in the field before being tossed loose onto a horse-drawn cart for transportation to the rick. Following both the hay and corn harvests, farmers would have built large ricks; hay was stacked up loose whilst straw was piled up in sheaves (with the heads of corn pointing inwards) until such time as it needed to be threshed. Both ricks would then be thatched for protection from the weather and, in the late 1800s, Rev James made the following comment in the village magazine in July 1886: *"Hayricks mostly thatched or begun to be thatched by this date. We notice that Mr W Cheshire's ricks are some of the first thatched and best thatched in the parish."*

Basil Waters can remember very early days before the introduction of the horse-drawn mowing machine:

"Hay making in those days still meant making hay, tossing and turning it before making it into ricks. Later these would be thatched and the hay cut with vicious hay knives into trusses on cold winter mornings for the cattle. The few hay elevators that there were, were driven by a horse that would walk in endless circles to provide the power to drive the mechanism. There were few haycutters and most of the fields were still mown by scythe and the hay loaded on carts and ricked by pitchfork."

Crandon Farm in 1913

A loaded hay cart on the Alderman's farm in the 1930s

Crandon Farm in 1936

Gerald, Philip & Arthur Bates, Thomas Philips and William Harwood with a horse-powered hay elevator at Crandon Farm in 1929

The introduction of the horse-drawn elevator made it easier to build the ricks and Graham Ward remembers:

"During hay-making the elevator which took the hay up onto the rick was driven by a horse walking round in circles. There were huge sheets on poles over the ricks to keep them dry and we boys used to play under there; it was really hot! A very early memory of mine is of Uncle Albert mowing with two shire horses, Flower and Dolly, who were grey and bay."

Jim Tattam also has very personal memories of that time:

"When I was only about eight years old I would ask to sit on the old horse which drove the hay elevator. It would walk round and round in circles, stepping over the drive shaft each time, and its only rest would be between loads of hay; the only trouble was that I used to fall asleep!"

Harvesting the corn was a very laborious time. The corn was cut with a binder (pulled by a horse in the early days and later by a tractor) which also tied it into sheaves. The farm workers would then put the sheaves into "stooks" or "shocks" in the field (each comprising perhaps six or eight sheaves) and these would be transported by horse and cart (or tractor and trailer) to the rick.

Jim Tattam rides round in circles on the horse powering the hay elevator watching a rat-catching terrier do his job in the early 1950s

Stooks in a field after harvesting and before the ricks are prepared

During the 1940s the Braziers at Marston Fields had three carthorses of which two were called Franklin and Busby. Chris Holden recalls:

"One day, one of the carthorses needed shoeing and Mrs Brazier made me ride it bare-back all through the back fields, past Christmas Gorse, to the blacksmith in Vicarage Road in Winslow (Henry White had retired by this time and there was no blacksmith in the village)***. Then I had to ride it back again. I ached for days. I'd never been on a horse before and it put me off ever going on one again! I used to love going down there to Marston Fields. The only tractor that came there had a binder on the back to cut the corn and I used to go in the fields 'shocking' up the corn (some call it 'stooking')."***

Around this time, Albert Franklin at Manor Farm in the High Street had four horses; Dolly, Duke and Flower did the heavy work, such as mowing, and Punch worked the elevator. The four shoes for each horse cost fifteen shillings a time!

When Victor Alderman's threshing machine came to a farm all available men (and some women) turned up to help. At this time Vic Alderman had two threshing machines; the younger one was quite efficient but the older, steam driven, one was very labour-intensive needing eight to ten men to work it.

"Vic Alderman had a steam-powered threshing machine which he took round to the local farms when they needed their threshing doing, but those villagers who grew a bit of corn on their allotment in Granborough Road would take that to the threshing barn down Quainton Road and do it themselves. Cyril Carter once cut off the top of his finger using that machine." (Robin Harwood)

The harvest would have been cut in late summer, dried and stored in a rick until a thresher was available. Victor Alderman serviced a large area so it might be as late as the following May before a machine was free. Once it was on the farm everyone available would come to help. The thresher separated the grain from the straw and chaff.

It was a very noisy, dusty process and one thing that everyone remembers was the large number of mice and rats that emerged from the rick as it became lower and lower. It was common practice to enclose the base of the rick in wire mesh so that the rats couldn't escape and then when the rick was low enough the terriers would be sent in to deal with them. Amusingly, Chris Holden remembers one rick that contained just one, very well fed, weasel!

"Aldermans had two threshing machines and the early machine was run on steam. I rode on the steam engine the last time that machine was used (this would have been about 1952) and we took the machine from North Marston to Waddesdon Manor and, after that, they just used the one machine and something called a 'blower'. This was an American invention, driven by the tractor, but it wasn't as effective because it didn't separate the corn and the straw as well as the other one; it wasn't as sophisticated. Its advantage was, however, that it only needed three to four men to work it whereas the old steam thresher had needed eight to ten men." (David Midwinter)

Vic Alderman's tractor-driven threshing box probably in the 1930s

Victor Alderman drives his steam traction engine at Banbury Steam Rally in 1972 after it had been sold and fully restored

Some farmers, such as the Mortons, had a motorized elevator which is seen here being used to build a rick at Glebe Farm in the 1940s

Ted Price forking stooks onto the elevator to create the rick

This was a time when everyone who could would help out with hay-making and harvesting. June Swain remembers the 1950s:

"The friendship was wonderful in the village; when hay-making, everyone came to help, even the policeman. If rain threatened, the men came straight from their jobs without going home in order to get the hay picked up and into the rick, and safe for winter feed for the animals."

"Granny Tattam" in her Kleino car in which she took refreshments to the workers in the fields during harvest

Many people from the village can still remember those days and look back with fondness on this by-gone era:

"My grandfather worked with horses and, as a child, I remember he always had sugar lumps in his smock pocket for me to give to the horses. I would ride on them bare-back when they had finished work for the day, also on top of the hay-cart, and I remember the binder coming in to cut the corn. I would help stook up the sheaves in sixes to dry then, later, we would carry them in the cart to the rickyard and make them into a rick. My father, who helped Grampa, would thatch the rick to protect the corn through to winter until the threshing machine came (Vic Alderman's). I would watch as the rats and mice ran from the rick as the sheaves were moved to the hopper on the threshing machine and be amazed to see the sacks of grain fill up at the back of the machine and all the chaff and dust – a hot, dirty job."
(Jennifer Heffer)

THE VILLAGE IN 1950

After the Second World War, much of the land ploughed for cereal and vegetable production as part of the war effort was allowed to revert gradually to permanent grazing but some remained in cultivation. North Marston continued to be a predominantly agricultural community and dairy farming was the mainstay of the parish's economy.

At this time, there were twenty farms and small-holdings. The majority of cows were Dairy Shorthorns and Dairy Shorthorn crosses but Ewart Dancer had a large herd of Ayrshire cattle; the first black and white Friesians were just appearing in the 1940s and would soon predominate.

Around this time, the number of tractors in the village increased and there was a gradual change from horse power to tractor power although a few smallholders relied on their horses right through to their retirement from farming.

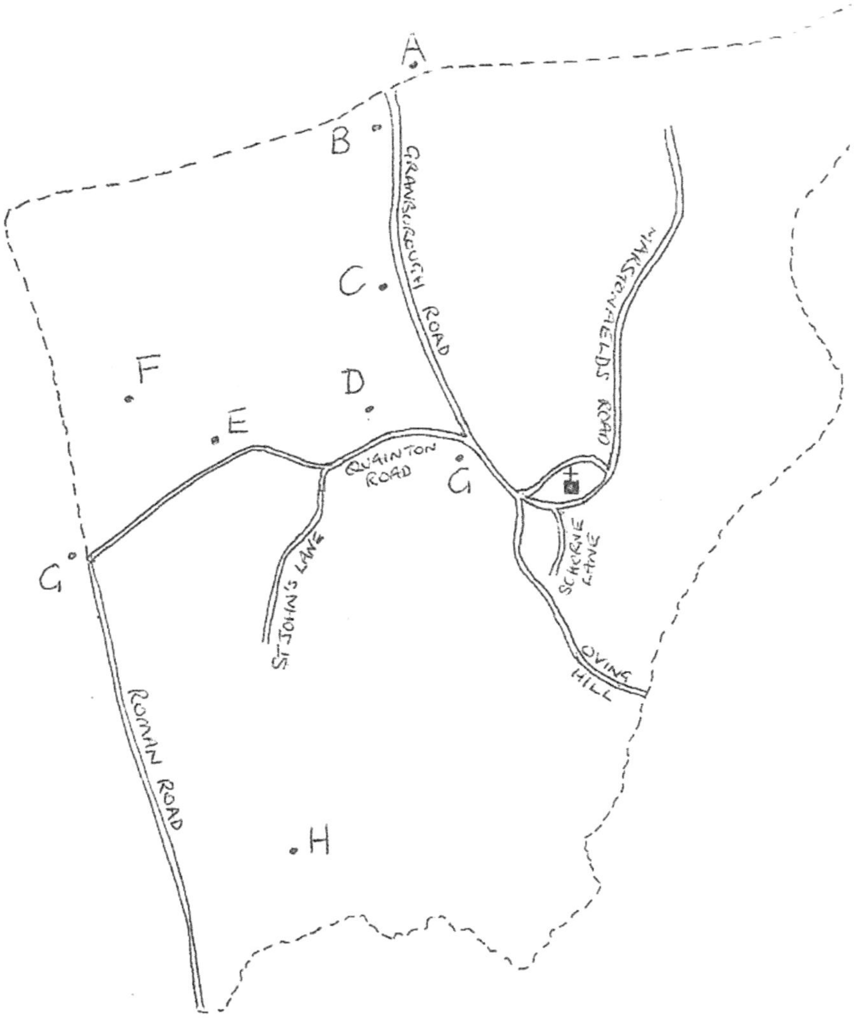

Map 1
Smallholders in the 1950s
A Eric Harwood
B Tom Cox
C Archie Higgins
D Leonard Harwood
E Ern Seaton
F The Price brothers
G Fred Tattam
H Joe Midwinter

(ROMAN ROAD = CARTERS LANE)

It was generally considered that between ten and twelve cows were as many as a single small holder could manage successfully and there were six herds of this size. All of these small herds were milked by hand.

Those with fields close to the road would transport the churns on a churn trolley or by pony and trap to the churn-stand. The churns were collected by the milk lorry and taken to Nestle's factory in Aylesbury.

Milk churns being collected by a lorry

Those like the Price brothers, whose fields were a distance from the nearest road, would carry their milk in buckets on yokes across their shoulders to a churn at the roadside.

All the small holders lived some distance from their holdings and every day would travel to and from their fields. Along the Granborough Road, Eric Harwood, Archie Higgins and Tom Cox would cycle to their smallholdings, Archie with his dog running alongside him and Tom with his little dog tucked under his arm.

Eric Harwood

Archie Higgins in 1952

Eric Harwood and Archie Higgins both milked between ten and twelve cows each. They also kept a few sheep and chickens. Tom Cox on the other hand kept only chickens but in large numbers – many hundreds.

Travelling along the Quainton Road to their fields were Ern Seaton, the Price brothers, Leonard Harwood, Fred Tattam and Joe Midwinter. Leonard Harwood had the least distance to travel as his land (rented from Bucks County Council since the early 1940s) was opposite the Primitive Methodist Chapel. He had a yard and milked cows by hand in a small wooden milking shed. He also had sheep and two hundred chickens. He had a horse and cart at this time and never used a tractor. His land extended through to the Granborough Road and he also farmed a small field near Deadman's Lane.

Leonard Harwood

Ern Seaton and the Price brothers (Harry, Bertie and Arthur) farmed land that is now part of Brook Farm and all cycled from their homes to their fields. Rod Abbey remembers riding to the Prices' smallholding on the cross bar of Bert's bike:

"Bert had sheep but no sheep dog and no motorized vehicle, so I was the 'sheep dog' and, once we had them in the yard, Bert would shear them while I turned the handle on the shearing lead to the shears. None of these are used today and I don't think anyone would stand there turning the handle for a full day."

The Price brothers also hand milked a small herd of cows in sheds without electricity. Ern Seaton was still using horse power at this time but he did eventually buy a tractor.

there, and kept sheep and beef cattle. He also milked at Leycroft (reached from the old lane opposite Dancers Farm) near his two other fields, Cats Brains and Lower Shotshill.

At this time he also had land behind the Wheatsheaf Inn where he kept pigs, chickens and Aylesbury ducks (one of the last in the village to have ducks). He bought New Forest ponies to break in which he kept in a shed beside the Wheatsheaf Inn. Fred had bought the milk-round from Jack Gould, landlord of the Sportsman's Arms and sold milk from his own cows door to door, ladled from a churn with a measuring jug. He gave up the milk round in 1950.

Arthur Price

Ern Seaton (left) and Harry Price (right)

Fred Tattam with his son, Jim, in the 1960s

Joe Midwinter had by far the longest journey to his smallholding as he lived in Oving and needed a car to get to his fields off Carters Lane. His route along Quainton Road and Carters Lane was still gated and he had to open and close three sets of gates on each journey! When he finally made it to his fields he kept beef cattle and sheep.

Travelling in the opposite direction in earlier years would have been Jim Buckingham who farmed thirty-three acres off Portway and milked cows with the help of Felix Gregory. His old sheds can still be seen across the field on the right as you leave the village.

Fred Tattam had land in Steart Lane (the gated road leading from Carters Lane to Hogshaw) which was just outside the parish. He milked between ten and twelve cows

Jennifer Heffer remembers the smallholding belonging to her father and grandfather along the Granborough Road:

"My grandfather was a farmer and would walk to Jersey Farm, Granborough, twice a day to milk his cows. Daddy also milked cows. I was allowed to sit on the three-legged stool and milk one of the quieter cows. Of course all the cows were milked by hand in the early days until my father got a milking machine which made it much easier. After cooling the milk we would put it in churns and then onto the milk stand by the gate to be collected by the milk lorry."

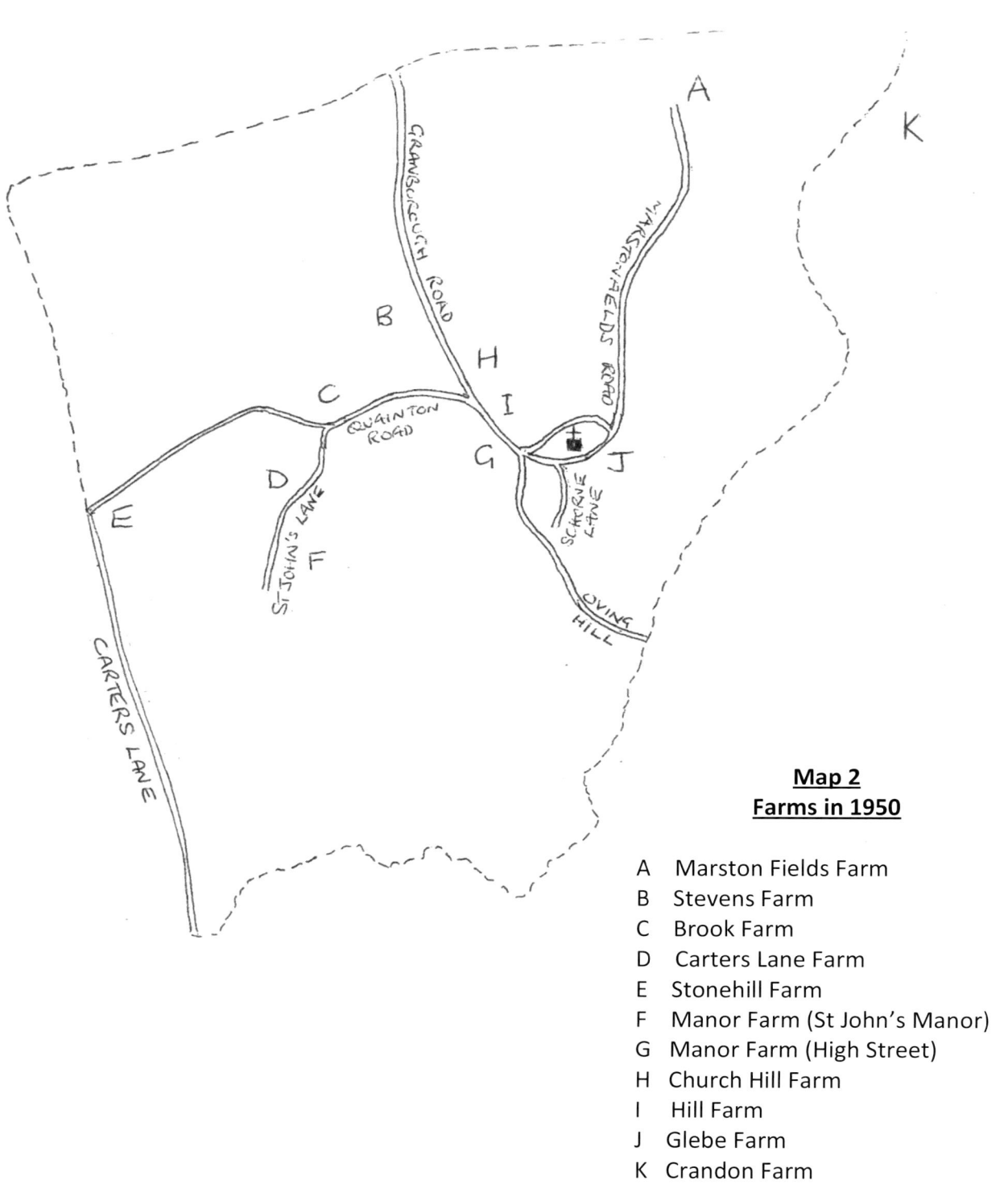

Map 2
Farms in 1950

A Marston Fields Farm
B Stevens Farm
C Brook Farm
D Carters Lane Farm
E Stonehill Farm
F Manor Farm (St John's Manor)
G Manor Farm (High Street)
H Church Hill Farm
I Hill Farm
J Glebe Farm
K Crandon Farm

In 1950 there were eleven farms in the village with milking cows.

Albert Franklin farmed Manor Farm in the heart of the village and had mainly dairy and sheep with some arable. Before the 1950s he had travelled by pony and trap to hand-milk two small herds (one of eight cows and the other of about ten cows) in fields away from the farm and the milk had then been brought down by pony and trap to the farm to be cooled ready for transporting to Winslow Station. At Manor Farm in 1950 he milked, by hand, a herd of approximately a dozen cows.

At this time there were three members of the Brazier family farming in North Marston: Charles at Marston Fields Farm (later known as Marstonfields Farm), Frank at Brook (Potters) Farm and John ("Son") at St John's Manor. Charles and Frank were brothers, and "Son" was their cousin.

Before they moved to Marston Fields in the mid-1940s, Charlie and Doris Brazier had lived in a small wattle and daub cottage opposite the entrance to Brook Farm (where Charlie's father Ashley farmed). They had a milking herd at Marston Fields and kept sheep and beef cattle.

Next to Marston Fields stands Crandon Farm. Before the war this had been farmed by the Bates family, followed by Ian Whyte, but in the early 1950s it was taken over by Doug Percy who milked a small herd of Ayrshires. He later changed to Friesians. He would transport his churns up to the village where he left them to be collected with those of the Mortons at Glebe Farm.

Frank Brazier at Brook Farm is remembered as a very good farmer with a milking herd, sheep and beef cattle. He had taken over the farm when his father, Ashley, retired.

"Son" Brazier at St John's Manor milked a small herd of cows, had a few sheep and grew a little corn and beans.

Victor Alderman farmed Stonehill Farm with his brother Lewis. They hand milked a small herd of cows but, as mentioned above, Victor's main role in the community and beyond was as an agricultural contractor.

St John Elmer lived at Home Farm but he had very little land there and actually farmed on the other side of the road at Hill Farm (rented from the Anstiss family) and where he hand-milked a few cows. The Anstisses had retired from farming it themselves by this time (and Hill Farmhouse from then on has remained a private residence).

In Granborough Road were Stevens Farm and Churchill Farm. Both had been owned by Albert Line but in 1948 Stevens Farm had been sold to Gladys and William Hall who moved to the village from Hogshaw (Fulbrook) with a herd of Friesian cows that was to play a major part in the village's agricultural future.

The two major farms that have not yet been mentioned are Carters Lane Farm and Glebe Farm.

Both farms had large herds of milking cows; they were well-equipped farms with milking machines and tractors. They also had small flocks of sheep and fields of cereal which they had kept going after the war.

At Carters Lane Farm (Dancers Farm), Ewart Dancer was milking a herd of Ayrshire cows whereas at Glebe Farm, John Morton had one of the earliest herds of Friesian cows in the village.

Most villagers at this time grew their own vegetables as did the farmers and small holders. "Son" Brazier at Manor Farm (St John's Manor) was typical; he had a huge vegetable garden tended by Jack Price which supplied all his family's needs. Poppet Brazier remembers that it was self-sufficient: *"...the treat being to drive to Winslow in the pony and cart to buy a kipper once a fortnight."*

Jim Tattam recalls his father and uncles having huge allotments along the Granborough Road where they grew hundred-weights of potatoes and swedes among other things.

North Marston is remembered at this time to be such a peaceful place to live. There was always time to stop and talk. It was a very different way of life from today and some farmers seldom left their farms:

"My mother, Mabel Harwood (nee Buckingham) was born in North Marston in 1908, and lived here all her life until her death at the age of ninety-three. The only time she ever slept out of the village was

when she went into Stoke Mandeville Hospital. Being farmers they did not have holidays as their work was a way of life, hard at times, but they were content and happy."
(Jennifer Heffer)

"During the 1950s when I drove with my dad through the village it was such a peaceful place to be. We would slow down and talk to people down Quainton Road: Leonard Harwood would come past on his bike and Laurence Young would be out in the road doing something. Life was like that. It was only when we were busy with hay-making or harvest that we didn't have time to stop to talk and had to get on with our work. It was a different way of life." (David Midwinter)

It was still a community centred on agriculture and many earned their living from farming. Few at the time would have realised that this was the end of an era, and that life in North Marston would change dramatically over the next half century.

DAIRY FARMING THROUGHOUT THE SECOND HALF OF THE TWENTIETH CENTURY

Throughout the second half of the twentieth century, eight dairy herds were predominant in the village. These were at Glebe Farm, Carters Lane Farm, Manor Farm (in the High Street), Stevens Farm, Church Hill Farm, Hill Farm, Marston Fields Farm together with Geoff Cheshire's farm which was created in 1976 and also known as Manor Farm (*see Map 2*).

By the end of the 1950s, although most small-holders still mainly milked by hand, some farmers, especially those with larger herds, would have installed a milking machine, a mechanized system which was usually powered by electricity (though it could be run off the tractor). Milk would still be put into churns and collected by a lorry.

Charlie Brazier with his milking equipment outside the dairy at Marston Fields

"When I was very little Mr Brazier at Marston Fields used to let me sit on Mabel the cow in the milking shed. All the cows knew their own place in the shed and automatically walked into it each milking time." (Sue Chaplin)

"When I started milking on my own I was quite inexperienced so I learned as I went along. There was originally a cowshed and the cows were milked by a vacuum pump; the milk went into buckets which you then tipped out over a galvanised cooler. Later we used in-churn coolers. I had a milk stand (made of old wooden sleepers) at the entrance to the farm out in the road near Jimmy Tattam's and I would put the full churns of milk out there to be collected by the milk lorry. My old milking shed was replaced by a modern 'abreast parlour' and a new covered collecting yard before I moved to Padbury in 1974, by which time I milked about twenty cows." (Graham Ward)

At Manor Farm, in the heart of the village, Albert Franklin and his sons, Tony and Keith, moved on rapidly and, between 1968-70, installed a milking parlour and bulk tank; at their peak, they were milking eighty cows.

Albert Franklin at Manor Farm, High Street in 1968

Similarly, John Morton at Glebe Farm and his sons, Peter and Michael, installed a contemporary milking parlour and bulk tank and developed a herd of eighty Friesian cows.

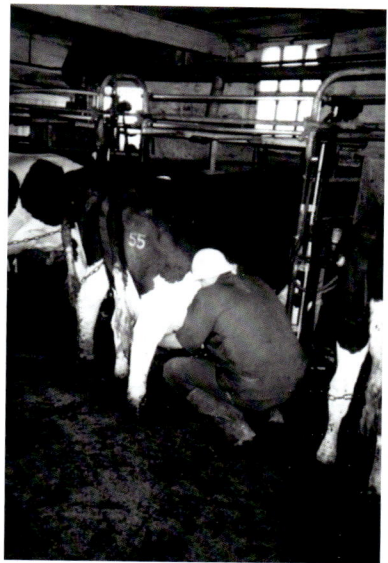

Peter Morton milking at Glebe Farm

Ewart Dancer at Carters Lane Farm began this period with a large herd of Ayrshire cows; he subsequently changed to the smaller Jersey breed. The milk of Jersey cows is very creamy and this was at one time considered desirable but as the health dangers of high fat content were appreciated, Jersey milk became very unpopular. So Friesian cows were introduced to the herd to reduce the overall fat content of the milk. Subsequently, the farm was renamed Dancers Farm, and Carters Lane was renamed St John's Lane.

Tommy Dancer milking the Jersey cows in 1979

After the death of Charlie Brazier in 1967, his son, Michael, ran Marston Fields Farm. As well as having a considerable number of sheep there was a milking herd of about twenty-five cows which were mainly Friesians.

Michael Brazier in the milking shed at Marston Fields Farm in the 1960s

Jack Selmes at Church Hill Farm milked a dairy herd of approximately fifty cows from 1968 till 1983. Initially they were Ayrshire cows but in 1975 Jack changed to more productive Friesians.

Jack Selmes with the first calf born at Church Hill Farm in 1968

Gladys and William Hall had moved the Horwood Herd of Friesians from Fulbrook Farm in Hogshaw to Stevens Farm in 1949.

Over the next fifty years this pedigree herd would win prizes at local, county and national levels. Its cows were exported to Japan, Colombia and Jamaica and thousands of visitors from all over the world came to Stevens Farm to view the herd (*see Part Two of this chapter*).

Bill Hall in his milking shed at Stevens Farm

Graham Ward ran Hill Farm from 1962 to 1975. Graham built up the "Northmarston Herd" of British Friesians which became very well known nationally. He recalls:

"I started with a few non-pedigree cows and then William Hall from Stevens Farm really got me going in the Friesian business by persuading me to buy some pedigree animals. Two of my early calves were Pewsey Bluebell who went on to produce a hundred tonnes of milk in her lifetime, and Thamesland Afie15 whose descendant, Northmarston Afie, won a first at the Royal Show in 1974."

In 1975 Graham moved his pedigree Friesian herd from North Marston to Padbury where it continued to win national prizes.

Graham Ward showing his cows

When Geoff Cheshire took on the re-amalgamated land of Manor Farm (*see Part 2 of this chapter*) it was just green fields with a few derelict old cowsheds scattered amongst them. It took one year to build a house and farm buildings and in Autumn 1975 Geoff Cheshire moved his ninety-six British Friesian cattle from Hogshaw Farm along the gated road to Manor Farm. Esme drove in front in the Landrover and Geoff drove from behind on his horse with two dogs.

Geoff Cheshire's "Shipptonlea" herd of British Friesian cattle won the Bucks Herd Championship five years on the trot as well as Supreme Champion at the Bucks County Show.

Geoff Cheshire's cows (left) being shown at the South Beds Show in 1986

An aerial view taken in the 1980s of the new buildings at Manor Farm

Whilst these eight herds were developing and expanding, the smallholders in the village were disappearing one by one. The change in practice which led to the demise of the small herds was the introduction of the bulk tank for the collection, refrigeration and storage of milk.

As explained earlier, up to this time milk had been stored and collected in milk churns. Full churns were very heavy and the process was labour intensive. Bulk tanks, on the other hand, allowed milk to be transferred by hose directly from the tank to the tanker lorry greatly increasing efficiency. Bulk tanks were phased in during the late 1960s and purchased by those with large herds but they were completely uneconomical for the smallholder with less than a dozen cattle. When the Milk Marketing Board stopped collecting churns, the smallholders gave up milking and instead used their land for grazing sheep and beef cattle.

In the same way that the small dairy herds had disappeared one by one through the 1960s, the larger herds gave up milking through the latter years of the twentieth century. The reason for the decline was the unprofitable nature of dairy farming; it was very difficult to make a living and one by one they sold their herds.

The first to be sold were the Franklins' herd at Manor Farm in the High Street and the Braziers' herd at Marston Fields (*see following poster*) both in 1975.

Then, in 1983, Jack Selmes sold his herd at Church Hill Farm and moved to Brook Farm. The land at Brook Farm was owned by Buckinghamshire County Council and the farm was formed by merging land formerly farmed by Archie Higgins, Leonard Harwood, Frank Brazier, Ern Seaton and William Hall. The development costs were supported by an EEC grant.

**MARSTON FIELDS FARM,
NORTH MARSTON, BUCKS.**

(3 miles from Winslow and 6 miles from Buckingham)

SALE OF LIVE AND DEAD FARMING STOCK

123 ACCREDITED CATTLE

Viz.: 32 Friesian Cows and Heifers in Calf or in Milk, Accredited milk recorded and home bred. 3 Friesian Heifers by Whitgrove Marksman, all in calf to Angus Bull. 12 Friesian Bulling Heifers mainly by Linmack. Friesian Suckler Cow with 3 Calves. Friesian Suckler Cow in calf. Friesian Barren Heifer. 14 Friesian Steers (15-20 months). 4 Hereford Cross Steers and Heifers (20 months). 1 Charolais Cross Heifer (2 years). 5 Charolais Cross Steers and Heifers (18 months). 7 Angus Cross Steers and Heifers (18 months). 7 Angus Cross Steers and Heifers (10 months). 6 Hereford Cross Steers and Heifers (10 months). 10 Friesian Heifers, 12 months (mostly by Oakridge Reflection). 9 Friesian Steers (12 months). 1 Charolais Cross Heifer (8 months). 6 Friesian Steers and Heifers (7 months).

141 SHEEP

20 Suffolk Cross Double Theaves. 47 Scotch half bred Ewes (FM and BM). 4 Cross bred Ewes (FM). 70 Suffolk Cross Lambs.

FARM MACHINERY

1959 Fordson Power Major Tractor with Horndraulic fore loader. 1957 Nuffield Diesel Tractor. 1948 Fordson Major TVO or Petrol Tractor. Lister Bale Elevator with reconditioned engine. Vicon Lely Acrobat. Haytor Mower. Perry Bale Loader. M.F. Finger Mower. 3 Covered Sheep Racks. Single row Hay Tedder. 18 Wooden Sheep Troughs. Two Ladders. Two Fuel Tanks. Ransome Transport Box. Cross Spreader Fertiliser Distributor. Wolseley Shearing Machine. Massey Wheel Weights. Sack Lift. Tractor Saw Bench. Sack Weigher. Garden Roll. Sundry Small Tools and 20 Laying Hens.

Will be Sold by Auction, by

MIDLAND MARTS

LIMITED

on MONDAY, 15th SEPTEMBER, 1975

By direction of Mrs. D. M. Brazier who has retired from farming.
Sale to commence with Machinery at 1.30 p.m. and Cattle will be sold at 2.30 p.m.
Licensed Refreshments have been applied for.
NO CATALOGUES.
AUCTION OFFICES, 30 High Street, BANBURY.
Tel.: Banbury 50501.

Bicesterprint Ltd., Market Square, Bicester.

The poster advertising the sale of Marston Fields Farm in 1975

The next to disappear was the Morton's milking herd at Glebe Farm in 1988. Quite a few of the cows were retained as sucklers to young calves but the rest of the herd was sold.

By the very end of the twentieth century, the financial return on milk had crashed and farmers throughout the country were getting out of milk and selling their cattle. In 1999, both Cynthia Hall and Ewart Dancer sold their herds. Ewart retired in the same year and his son Tommy took over the farm which now grazes sheep and beef cattle.

Cynthia Hall with her Horwood herd

This left Geoff Cheshire with the only milking cows in the village. He carried on for one year more and sold his herd of ninety cows in 2000.

FARM BUILDINGS

The demise of dairy farming has resulted in considerable residential building in the village. The barns and milking parlours became redundant as soon as the cows left and the farmyards became the sites of residential housing. This happened at Stevens Farm, Marston Fields Farm, Glebe Farm, Church Hill Farm, Hill Farm and the Manor Farm (in the High Street). In fact, Dancers Farm and Geoff Cheshire's Manor Farm are the only former dairy farms that have not demolished or redeveloped their farm buildings. It seems unlikely that we will ever see milking cows in the village again.

A view from the church tower of Glebe Farm at the start of the conversion from a working farm to residential housing in the late 1980s

Glebe Farm in the 1940s and the same scene in 2013

Glebe Farm roadside hovel in the 1970s and the same scene in 2013

The new houses built on the site of the old Hill Farm

Additionally, most of the old farmhouses in the village are now private residential property: Stevens Farm, Church Hill Farm, Hill Farm, Home Farm, Manor Farm (High Street), Stonehill Farm, Crandon Farm, (St John's) Manor Farm, Marstonfields Farm, Burnaby Farm and Brook (Potters) Farm).

At the last four farms, a new house has been built for the farm owner. It is interesting to note that at Brook Farm, Ern Seaton's barn has been incorporated into the new house. The old Brook Farmhouse is now called Potters Farm.

Stevens Farm in 1999 (above) and in 2001 after conversion of the farm buildings (below)

Ern Seaton's former sheds which are now part of the house at Brook Farm

FARMING TODAY

Following the disappearance of milking cows, the only livestock to be seen now in the fields of the village are sheep, and cattle reared for beef. At the time of writing the only farming families still actively farming in the village are Geoff Cheshire's family at Manor Farm (St John's Manor), Tommy Dancer at Dancers Farm, Jack Selmes at Brook Farm and Mary and Neil Tuckett at Marstonfields Farm. There is still some arable farming and, in a recent development, stable yards have been built at various sites throughout the village. Horses are now grazing where farmers used to farm.

Although the acreage of farmland in the village has diminished little in the last two centuries, farming only employs a handful of people today, in marked contrast to the days only a few decades ago, when large numbers were employed full time and many more on a casual basis for hay making and harvesting. Farming is no longer the mainstay of North Marston's economy and the success or failure of local farming is of little financial significance to the community as a whole.

At the same time, it is important not to overlook the vital part that farming plays in maintaining the environment in which we live. It is remarkable that such a small number of people contribute so much to the quality of life for all who live in the village with efficient livestock management and agricultural practices which conserve our landscape and our wildlife.

Twenty-four
FARMING
PART TWO: FARMS AND FARMING FAMILIES
Sue Chaplin & Rosemary Morton

Part One of this chapter outlined some of the important changes, developments and events in North Marston's farming history from the eighteenth century to the present day. As such, it sketched a broad picture of how farmers and agricultural workers responded to the pressures and opportunities at the time.

This chapter follows the stories of the *individual* farms in North Marston through the twentieth century: the people who farmed them, the villagers who worked there and the ways in which farmers and small-holders went about their daily business. It shows how some farms changed hands whilst others remained in the same family for several generations.

NB The field maps show the location of each farm in the village. Fields have changed hands over the years and the maps shown vary in date. They do, however, give the reader an idea of the size of the farm in question.

---------------- BURNABY FARM ----------------

An aerial view of Burnaby Farmhouse and buildings in Church Street in 1959
(in the centre of the picture can be seen Chapman's field on which the Portway houses were later to be built)

Burnaby Farmhouse in the mid-1900s

The original Burnaby Farmhouse today

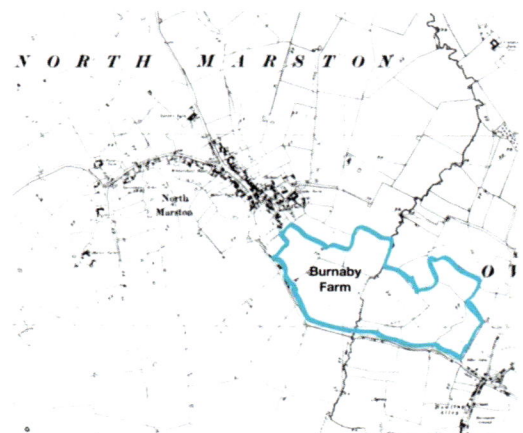
Burnaby Farm field map

The new Burnaby Farmhouse

Burnaby Farm today covers an area of one hundred and eight acres, many of which lie alongside the North Marston to Oving Road. Much of the land is situated in Oving Parish. In the mid 1970s a new house and farm buildings were built in Well Leys Field (accessed from Schorne Lane). However, the original farmhouse (now a private dwelling) stands in Church Street. Today, most of the fields are grass and rented to local farmers for sheep and suckling herds (two are still used for corn production). Due to many of the fields being ridge and furrow, they are unsuitable for ploughing nowadays.

We know from the 1901 Census that **Ralph Tattam** owned Burnaby Farm but, after him, the ownership of Burnaby Farm stood firmly with the **Holden family**, tailors of this village (*see Chapter Fourteen*).

Tractor work in Mill Piece, Burnaby Farm, in the 1940s

John Morton farmed this land as a tenant with his sons, Peter and Michael Morton, until 1973 when he purchased the land (but not the house). He had sheep, beef cattle and arable crops on this land.

John and Stella Morton 1962

Michael Morton in 1974

When **John Morton** took on the tenancy of Burnaby Farm in 1937 it comprised the farmhouse in Church Street together with "one hundred and eight acres, three roods and thirty perches". The rent was two hundred and twenty-eight pounds ten shillings per annum. There was a small paddock behind the house and calves were kept in the buildings around the farmyard.

The farmhouse in Church Street was sold as a private residence in 1976 and the adjoining paddock and vegetable garden later became Morton Close. The new farm buildings for Burnaby Farm were completed in 1974, and Peter and Rosemary Morton moved into the new house in Well Leys field in 1975.

Harvesting and binding at Burnaby Farm in the 1940s

Peter and Rosemary Morton in 2010

CHURCH HILL FARM

Church Hill Farmhouse today

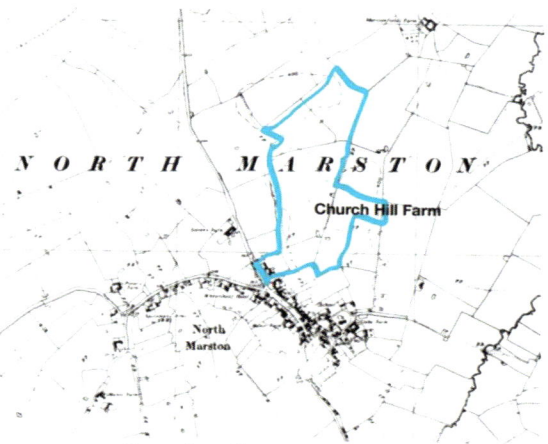
Church Hill Farm field map

An aerial view of Church Hill Farm in the 1950s

The fields of Church Hill Farm comprised fifty-four acres. The old farmhouse was sold as a private residence in the early 1980s whilst the farm buildings were demolished and the site sold for development, becoming Elmers Meadow in the 1990s.

Albert (Bert) Line bought Church Hill Farm in 1948 and farmed there with his wife, **Martha (known as "Tilley")**, having sold his previous farm (Stevens Farm) to Gladys and William Hall.

Bert and Martha LIne

Jack Selmes started farming at Church Hill Farm in 1967, after Bert Line died, and he farmed it whilst living in Granborough, as Martha still lived in the farmhouse. In 1968, Jack modernised the buildings with the help of Ken Grant, who did the brickwork, inserting a bulk tank for his milking herd of about fifty cows (initially Ayrshires but later Friesians).

The site of the old farm buildings was sold in 1992 and developed as Elmers Meadow. The rest of the land was then sold to Tommy Dancer.

Inside the new milking parlour in 1968

Jack's Ayrshire cows behind Gibbings Close

Martha died in 1978 after which Jack moved to Church Hill for a few years. He continued milking there before he gave up the dairy herd in 1983 and moved to the newly amalgamated Brook Farm in Quainton Road. Church Hill Farmhouse was sold as a private residence in the 1980s.

Jack and daughter, Gemma, in 1979

---------------- CRANDON FARM ----------------

Crandon Farmhouse in the 1930s

Crandon Farmhouse in 2008

Crandon Farm field map

Crandon Farmhouse in the 1920s

Crandon Farm comprises one hundred and seventeen acres and lies within the parish of Oving. However, for over a hundred years, it has been considered a "North Marston Farm" as it is accessed from the Marstonfields Road (though this has not always been the case) and the residents of the farm have always taken part in North Marston activities.

Crandon Farmhouse has been a private residence since 1980 (together with twelve acres) but the fields formerly attached to it now belong to the Morton family and are today used mainly for arable production. The farmhouse was built in the late 1880s after the original house burnt down. A survey map of 1898 shows the house in its current position but an earlier map of 1879 shows the original house a few fields away.

In 1868 **Philip Bates** (1817-1886) became the tenant farmer of Crandon farm and lived there with his wife, **Fanny**, and eight children. The prospect was daunting: Crandon was an isolated farm, set in fields which had to be crossed to reach a surfaced road. The farmhouse was old and decayed and the farm buildings were even worse. It took Philip many years to persuade the landlord to build a new house with its planned set of buildings, but the construction was finally completed in the mid 1870s.

Philip's son, William, settled in North Marston after his marriage and worked on the farm but, in 1886, Philip died and **Fanny Bates** took over the tenancy of the farm. Her son, Harry helped her run it for a while until he married and moved away, by which time her younger son, Arthur, was old enough to help her.

A very early picture of the Bates family

Arthur married Julia Philips in 1902 and lived in the cottage next door to the church in School Hill.

Fanny Bates with her daughter-in-law Julia (right) and her grandchildren Gerald & Fanny in the early 1900s

Julia Bates with her children, Gerald & Fanny outside their cottage in School Hill

After managing Crandon Farm for twenty-five years, often living alone with her dogs as company, Fanny retired in 1911 and moved in with her daughter, Belinda, and her husband, Samuel Hodges, who was the tenant farmer at Brook Farm. The tenancy of Crandon was transferred to her son, **Arthur Bates,** who then moved there with his family.

Arthur Bates and his wife Julia with their children (circa 1914)

In 1920 Arthur bought the farm for four thousand two hundred and fifty pounds and he farmed it until 1944 when he sold it (for four thousand pounds) and retired, bringing to an end seventy-five years of the Bates family connection with Crandon Farm.

Julia Bates with son Philip, daughter Fanny and grandson Tom Gregory (circa 1920s)

In the harvest field at Crandon in 1931

Philip and Gerald Bates shearing sheep in 1931

Philip Bates hedge-laying in 1935

Crandon Farm sale catalogue in 1944

The next owner of Crandon was **Iain Whyte** who was related to the Whyte & Mackay whisky dynasty. Robin Harwood can remember helping to pluck chickens there after the war and another of the workers there was Chib Harwood.

During his time there Mr Whyte fought to get a "right of way" legally established to Crandon Farm from the Marstonfields Road (Marston Fields farm then being in the ownership of the Biggs family). Arthur Bates testified to the fact that this route had been used to access Crandon Farm throughout his (and his mother's) time there and in 1947 an agreement was finally reached giving "right of way" to Crandon from the Marstonfields Road across another field owned by Glebe Farm for a yearly rent of sixty shillings (three pounds). Various deeds and agreements have been drawn up regularly since then regarding this right of way, with the yearly rental increasing gradually each time.

In 1950 Iain Whyte sold Crandon farm to **Owen Bailey** for ten thousand pounds but a year later it was sold again to **Joseph Percy** for eleven thousand two hundred and fifty pounds. Nine years later, Joseph sold the farm to his son **Douglas Percy** for eight thousand nine hundred and eighty pounds.

Douglas lived there with his wife, Chloe, and their children for nearly twenty years. In the beginning, he milked Ayrshire cows but later

Douglas and Chloe Percy in 1962

changed to Friesians. He would take his milk churns to a milk-stand outside Glebe Farm (by the church) to be collected by the milk lorry.

When he stopped milking he continued to keep calves and turkeys. In the 1960s he diversified to building trailers for boats out of old railway wagons which were used to transport expensive yachts all over the world.

In 1978 the farm was sold to **John Morton and Sons** who, two years later, sold the farmhouse and twelve acres to **David and Janet Bayl**y. The house has remained in private ownership ever since but the Morton family still own the land which is rented out to a local farmer. John Morton, son of Peter, has a field of "cricket bat willows", planted by Gray Nicholls, the cricket bat manufacturers, in 2001. (There are about two hundred of these sites across the country).These willows reach maturity around eighteen to twenty years of age when a number of cricket bats will be made from each tree.

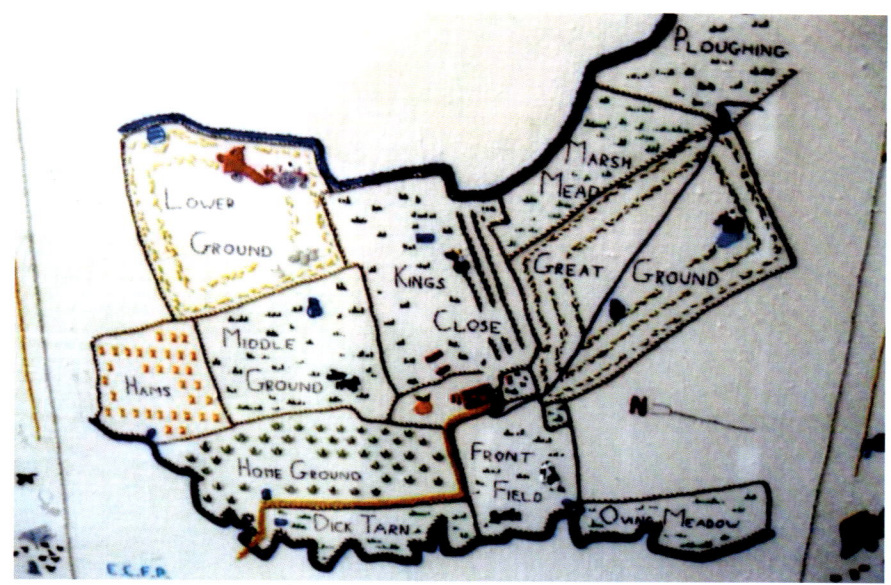

A tapestry of Crandon Farm (worked by Chloe Percy)

DANCERS (CARTERS LANE) FARM

Dancers (formerly Carters Lane) Farm today

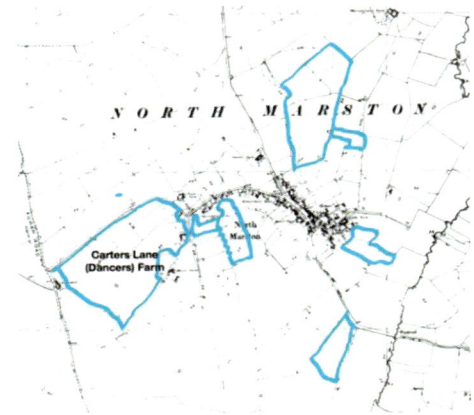
Dancers Farm field map

Dancers Farmhouse stands in St John's Lane (formerly called Carters lane) which leads off the bottom of the Quainton Road. Dancers Farm was, until 2008, called Carters Lane Farm. The name was changed after the lane in which it stands was re-named. Most people locally knew the farm as "Dancers Farm" and so the change was made. It is an operational farm today and is owned and farmed by Tommy Dancer who rears beef cattle and sheep. The fields belonging to the farm today are scattered around the village and comprise about one hundred and seventy-seven acres (though the farm was not always that large).

In the early 1900s **William George Harwood** and his family lived at Carters Lane Farm (as William was employed there) but around 1917 they had to move out and they lived for several years at Schorne College. (By then the college had closed to pupils and had been bought by Ted Dudley, the local builder, who was slowly demolishing it). The Harwood family lived there until the early 1930s.

We know (from the school records) that a William Lambourne then lived at Carters Lane Farm until **Alfred Dancer** took on the farm in the 1920s. Alfred had married Emily (Rebecca) Cheshire in the 1920s. Rebecca's father, George Cheshire, was friends with Mr Watkins who lived in Mill House and was the owner of Carters Lane Farm (plus a field called Turners Piece). When George Cheshire asked him if his son-in-law could go to live at Carters Lane Farm as a tenant, Mr Watkins said he would agree if George Cheshire bought Turners Piece from him - which he did. Alfred and Rebecca had three sons, George, Ewart and Peter.

Alfred Dancer in 1914

George and Ewart Dancer

When, in 1951, Alfred's son, **Ewart Dancer** married Angela Biggs (daughter of Thomas Biggs who had previously farmed Stevens Farm) he took over the tenancy at Carters Lane Farm and Alfred and Rebecca went to live in Granborough. In the 1960s the Watkins family (by now living in France) offered to sell the farm to Ewart and he accepted, purchasing the farmhouse, buildings and approximately fifty acres.

Ewart on horseback at Hagditch in 1975

The wedding of Ewart and Jill Dancer in 1951

In 1989 Ewart's son, **Tommy Dancer**, moved with his wife, Jayne, and sons George, John, Archie and Reuben to Carters Lane Farm. Today Tommy no longer milks cows but rears beef cattle and sheep.

Jim Tattam remembers working for Ewart: ***"When I left school I did stuff such as hedge-laying for Ewart Dancer where I earned five pounds per chain (twenty-two yards)"*** and Rod Abbey remembers that the house cow was called "Favourite". Ewart initially milked an Ayrshire herd but, as the higher fat content of Jersey cows became unpopular, Friesians were introduced to the herd. Ewart also had sheep.

Ewart and his wife, Jill, were stalwarts of the village and Ewart would often use his horse and cart, or tractor and trailer, for village events. For numerous years, Ewart was churchwarden at St Mary's, North Marston.

Tommy and Jayne Dancer with their grandson, Fergus, at lambing time

Ewart Dancer with village children in his horse and cart

Tommy and his parents with a new tractor in 2001

GLEBE FARM

Glebe Farmhouse in the 1940s

Glebe Farmhouse today

An aerial picture of Glebe Farm in 1959 when a working farm

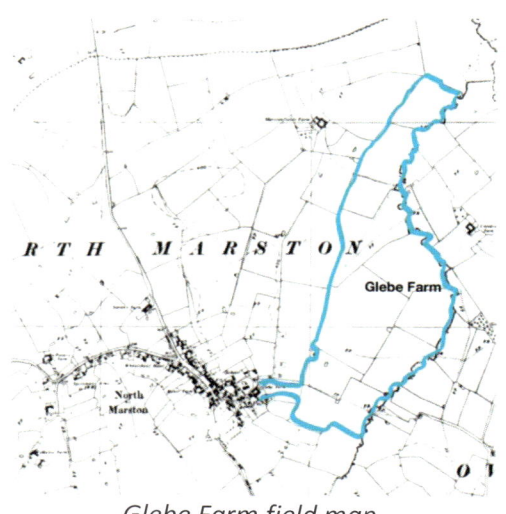
Glebe Farm field map

Glebe Farm comprises one hundred and seventy-three acres. The buildings were converted to residential dwellings in the late 1980s but the land today remains in the ownership of Peter and Michael Morton, with Michael still residing in Glebe Farmhouse. The fields, all grass, are rented out to local farmers for suckler herds, beef cattle and sheep.

The word *Glebe* means "belonging to the church" and tells us that Glebe Farm occupies land that was once set aside for the maintenance of the parish priest. The land that comprises Glebe Farm was owned by the Dean and Canons of Windsor who had appropriated the church and its land-holdings in 1501. Lessee landlords of the Dean and Canons of Windsor (who in turn let the land out to tenant farmers) included the wealthy, eccentric **John Camden Neild**.

He inherited the lease of the estate in 1814 from his father, James Camden Neild, a prosperous London goldsmith and pioneer of prison reform. It was at Glebe Farm (also known then as Rectory Farm) that in 1828 John Camden Neild tried to commit suicide and was prevented from doing so by Martha Neal, the tenant's wife (*see Chapter Ten*).

An early reference to Glebe Farm can be found in *The Schornian* of September 1895 where Rev James noted:

"The Glebe Farmhouse is 'down to the ground' and a new one is building. A Wantage builder is, we believe, employed by the Ecclesiastical Commissioners. He politely called at the Vicarage to express a hope that we should not be put to any inconvenience and he employs a good staff of workmen who get over their work swiftly and quietly and clear away any debris as soon as it falls on Vicarage premises."

In May 1896 he wrote:

"The new Glebe Farmhouse is...like our new organ, a handsome structure in the wrong place; but we trust that our friends will spend many happy and prosperous years within its well-built walls. It is, with the exception perhaps of the Vicarage, the roomiest house in the parish we fancy, and would have looked, placed further back, quite a striking residence."

Rev James refers above to the fact that Glebe Farmhouse was built right up close to the road which passes alongside the church.

William Kibble, the tenant farmer at Glebe, had died in 1892, the new tenant being his son, **Edwin Kibble**, who was a very prominent man in the village. He was a close friend of the vicar, Dr Samuel James, and was what would have been described as a "gentleman farmer". He held various posts in the village such as Churchwarden and School Superintendent and happily allowed Schorne College boys to use one of his fields as a football pitch and to use his land for cross-country running.

Edwin Kibble (1847-1932)

A young village lad, Eric Harwood worked for Mr Kibble after leaving school aged twelve and learned how to drive four horses in a plough team. He left Glebe Farm in 1924 aged fifteen.

In 1920, Edwin Kibble bought Glebe Farm from the Ecclesiastical Commissioners for six thousand five hundred pounds. After his death (in 1932) the farm was bought in 1935 by **Helen**, **Florence**, **Constance and Alice Biggs**, who resided in Cublington and, in 1936, **John Morton** became the tenant farmer. (John Morton was also to take on the tenancy of Burnaby Farm a year later). It remained in the hands of the Biggs family until 1990 when it was sold to **Peter and Michael Morton**. During the war years the Mortons' farm was one of the first in the village to have a tractor:

an International. They had a milking herd, sheep and arable land.

John Morton carrying a sheep on his shoulders in the 1940s

John Morton and his wife, Stella, had three sons: Peter, Michael and Neville. Neville eventually left to pursue a career in accountancy but Peter and Michael remained in the village and worked on the farm.

Stella Morton outside Glebe Farm with her sons (L-R) Neville, Michael & Peter in the 1940s

Peter and Michael Morton shearing at Glebe Farm in 1963

Villagers also have memories of time spent at Glebe Farm in their youth. Rod Abbey recalls the 1950s:

"My memories go back to the dairies in the village, where I would go and help with the milking, learning the ways of life, seeing the bull doing his job, the cows having their calves, the new born lambs. One I can remember was at the Mortons' farm. If there was heavy snow, the dog would go out and bring back new lambs that were in trouble; that has stayed with me all these years."

John and Stella Morton circa 1970

Peter Morton and cows in the 1980s

Over the years there have been several key workers at the farm including Ted Price in the 1940s and Joe Wilkins in the 1950s and 1960s.

Joe Wilkins with a young John Morton (son of Peter) in 1970

Peter Morton

Michael Morton

In 1982 some Friesian beef cattle belonging to Peter and Michael Morton were loaned to Cynthia Hall (from Stevens Farm in North Marston) to put on display at Stoneleigh with her own Horwood Herd of Friesians.

*Stan Bone, cowman to the Horwood Herd, talking to HRH Princess Anne
(The Mortons' farm sign can be seen above their heads)*

In 1988 the Morton family had a great surprise when one of their cows fetched a record price at Banbury market. Ten years later they gained another award, this time for their sheep!

Record price for Mortons' cow at Banbury Market

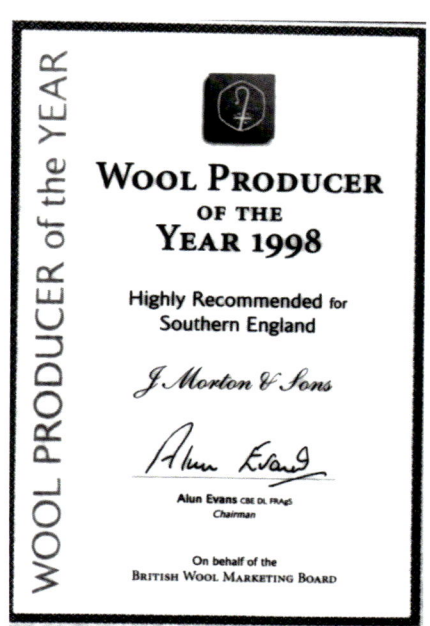

Wool Producer of the Year Award

HILL FARM

The original Hill Farmhouse today

Houses on the site of the old farmyard at Hill Farm

An aerial view of Hill Farm in the 1950s

Hill Farm field map

Hill Farm buildings are visible in the centre of this photograph taken in the early 1960s after the new Dutch barn had been erected on the site

Hill Farm was situated in the centre of the village on the east side of the High Street. It comprised fifty-four acres, a farmyard and a farmhouse. In the 1980s the farm buildings were demolished to make way for new housing. The old farmhouse has been a private residence since 1968.

The house is very unusual as it is divided down the middle into two distinct types of architecture. The orchard behind the house possibly dates back four hundred years on the basis of one foot of coppice stool diameter being equal to one century. The fields extended from the farmyard to behind the school and on to Townsend (Marstonfields Road). One of the fields behind the farm was very much ridge and furrow. Hill Farm is built on such an incline that, when it rained, the water would often gush in torrents through the yard.

In the early 1900s the farm was owned and run by **James Anstiss** and, when he died in 1911, **Bert**, **John** and, possibly, **William** took over the running of it. The Anstiss brothers were quite 'characters' as Clifford Cheshire relates:

"The story goes that two brothers were working together up the fields when one of them picked up his brother's hay fork and started to use it instead of his own; the brothers didn't speak to each other for years after that!"

During the 1920s the Anstiss brothers had a lodger at Hill Farm named Hubert Clifford. Mr Clifford was an architect by profession but was known for encouraging the tailors of the village (working at H J Holden's) to join him in the pub after their working day had finished. He would treat them to some drinks but needless to say, much of their own precious wage would be wasted in there too, and their wives were not happy when they returned home inebriated on a regular basis! The Anstiss brothers were looked after by a resident housekeeper, Miss Legg, who worked for them for years.

Hubert Clifford who lodged at Hill Farm in the 1920s

Another story about the Anstiss brothers goes that, during the Second World War, an American was staying at Hill Farm who had the first sheet music to the "Hokey-Cokey". As the Anstisses could play several musical instruments, they performed this music at a dance in the village hall and (according to the American) it had not been played anywhere else in this country before then! John Anstiss died at Hill Farm in 1942, William in 1952 and Bert in 1963. After their sister, Jane, died in 1968 Hill Farmhouse and its contents were sold.

After the Anstiss brothers retired, **St John Elmer** from Home Farm (on the other side of the High Street) took on the tenancy of Hill Farm. He mainly reared sheep on this land. On his death in 1960 his daughter, **Pauline Elmer**, continued with the tenancy until it was taken over by **Graham Ward** in 1962. As the farmhouse was not part of the tenancy agreement (Miss Anstiss and Miss Legg still lived in it), Graham and his family lived first at Camden Villas in Schorne Lane and then the Red House in the High Street.

Graham tells the story of his first year at the farm:

"It was such a cold winter in 1962/63 that the pipes froze under the concrete. Then the following summer was really wet and the hay crop, no matter how many times I turned it, just wouldn't dry out and was rubbish. I baled it up and stacked it along Townsend (Marstonfields Road) and some boys set light to it which did me a real favour as the insurance company paid out a lot more than it was worth!"

Graham started up the "Northmarston Herd" of Pedigree British Friesians at Hill Farm. These cows were to go on to win prizes nationally. He tells of how he first started off with a few non-pedigree cows in the early 1960s but then William Hall at Stevens Farm persuaded him to buy a few pedigree animals and his prize-winning herd took off from there.

At one point Graham decided to try rearing sheep:

"I once decided to venture into sheep and bought some Cluns; I nurtured them in an old hovel round the back of Anstiss' house and not one of the lambs died so I was really pleased, but as soon as I put them out to graze in the fields they caught 'sheep sickness' and a lot of the lambs died. I think that Elmers had grazed their sheep on the land for so many years that it had become infected. I never bothered with sheep again after that!"

"Afie 2", one of Graham's early prize winners

Graham Ward with prize-winning cow ,"Rita 4", family and friends at the Bucks Show in 1974

As with the other farmers in the village, Graham had village people to help him on the farm:

"I was helped at the week-ends by Chib Harwood who was a great asset to me when it came to gate-hanging, fencing and other odd jobs around the farm. Chib was never interested in tractor driving or milking but helped me out in every other way and I relied on him a lot. When it came to the milking, I was helped out by Mary Essex, Stuart Chaplin and Malcolm Garrett, whilst Robert and Mark Gurney, and Simon Church, also used to come to the farm and do jobs for me."

Robert remembers leaving Archie Higgins's along Granborough Road to earn pocket money at Graham's instead:

"I was then lured away (by not having to travel quite so far!) to Hill Farm run by Graham Ward at the bottom of the High Street. I was probably fourteen or fifteen by then and, not only was it less of a commute but I got higher wages. Whereas Archie paid you what he thought was right – perhaps ten shillings here or a pound there – Graham paid an hourly rate and I meticulously wrote them all down. I had many a happy time there feeding calves, helping with milking and general jobs. I stayed with Graham for three years until I 'ran away to sea' so I was about seventeen then.

In 1975 Graham left North Marston and moved his herd of British Friesians to Wardens Farm in Padbury where it continued to have great success.

HOME FARM

Home Farm today

Home Farm field map

Home Farm circa 1900
(The people in the photograph are likely to be relatives of Denchfield Baker)

Home Farm (on the right) circa 1910

Home Farm stands at the bottom of the High Street in North Marston. It is a timber framed structure, formerly thatched, and was built in the 1600s, making it one of the oldest buildings in the village. At different times it has comprised one, two or three dwellings. In a document dated 1823 it is described as: *"Two cottages….. formerly one cottage."* However, fifty years later it was described as: *"……formerly one cottage and afterwards divided into three tenements."*

In addition to the house being sub-divided over the years the land was sub-let a number of times. Because the farmhouse was built years before the parish's fields were enclosed (*see Chapter Seven*), only a small "close" of land was originally attached to it. At that time, the principle land belonging to the owner of the property was in the numerous strips in the open fields around the parish which are recorded in detail in the earliest of the deeds. No farming has taken place from Home Farm since 1989.

In the photograph above showing Home Farm around 1900, the farmhouse comprised a cottage area (*seen on the left of the picture*) and a barn area (*on the right*), with a vegetable garden at the front. The area on the right where two men can be seen leaning on their forks in the garden was not converted into a dwelling area until the 1940s. The family pictured are highly likely to be relatives of **Denchfield Baker** who owned the house at that time.

For much of the twentieth century the land at Home Farm was farmed by the Elmer family, **Henry (Harry) Elmer**, his son **St John Elmer** and grand-daughter, **Pauline Elmer**.

Henry Elmer

St John Elmer is known to have acquired the farm from his aunt, Emily Ann Cheshire, in 1931 but he rented out the farmhouse and continued to live with his wife, Kathleen, and father, Henry, in Melba Cottage a few doors away. He and his father worked together on the farm and it is said that Harry was a really hard worker who wore the same old clothes day in and day out!

During the 1940s St John had the house at Home Farm completely renovated, combining the cottage and the large feed-barn area into one dwelling again. Sadly his wife, Kathleen, died in 1949 before they could move in, but St John, along with his father and daughters, Pauline and Gillian, lived in it together thereafter. The girls were looked after by Eleanor Cheshire (whose cottage, today named "Eleanor's Cottage", stands next door to the farmhouse).

The Elmers had sheep and cattle (Red Polls, Lincoln Reds and Shorthorns). In the mid 1900s they took on land at Hill Farm over the road (when the Anstiss brothers retired) and it was there that they milked their cows. They also rented land along the Granborough Road near the old allotments.

St John Elmer in the 1950s

Rowland Linnell worked for St John for many years and his daughter Susan Cobbold relates:

"My father used to work for St. John Elmer when I was a young child in the 1950s. St John had a daughter, Pauline, and they lived at Home Farm in the High Street but my dad worked mainly in their farm buildings over the road at Hill Farm. Dad would do the milking early morning and then walk home for breakfast carrying a can of fresh milk. I remember him doing the hay-making as well in 'Three-Corner Piece' along Granborough Road near where the allotments were. I believe my dad worked there until St. John died in 1960; he may have carried on working for Pauline for a while but he left and went to Calvert Brickworks after that."

Rowland Linnell in the 1950s

Pauline Elmer

Jim Tattam has some amusing memories of St John Elmer:

"Old St John Elmer from Home Farm opposite would often come over and watch the horse-racing on TV with my dad, having previously

placed their bets with Malcolm Holden at the garage, and on one particular day when they were doing this, my dad told St John he could see a man walking down his path. St John rushed out and on his return told dad that it was the electricity man come to cut off the supply. When my dad asked him if that meant he hadn't paid his bill, St John replied that he always waited until they came round to cut him off before he paid because it saved him the postage stamp!"

When St John Elmer died in 1960 his daughter Pauline Elmer continued to run the farm but on her death in 1989 all farming there came to an end. Her sister, Gillian, lived in the old farmhouse for several years but the land was dispersed and the house itself finally sold on. Elmers Meadow, in Granborough Road bears the family name though the field on which it was built did not belong to the Elmer family: the close was simply named in remembrance of Pauline.

---------------- JERSEY FARM ----------------

Jersey Farm field map

Jersey Farm is situated near Granborough and lies within its parish. However, for a large part of the twentieth century the land was farmed by North Marston residents (hence the inclusion in this chapter).

For many years leading up to 1953 Jersey Farm was tenanted by **William Peasland Buckingham** who lived in North Marston at 5 School Hill. William Buckingham used heavy horses on his small-holding and he would walk from School Hill twice daily to milk his cows, except on a Sunday when his farmhand, Meyrick Cox, would do it for him. (Meyrick also lived in School Hill and was the village sweep).

William Buckingham was a pillar of the Primitive Methodist Church in Quainton Road and often on a Sunday he would walk to Quainton to take a morning service, and then go on to Kingswood for an evening service before walking home to North Marston. He would never have considered working on the Sabbath Day; Sunday was the "Lord's Day" and was to be respected. Once a neighbour asked him on a Sunday if he could borrow a piece of farm machinery at some stage and was told firmly by William that he would not discuss the matter until the next day!

William once sold some sacks of corn to a dealer who complained that he would 'have a job' to make any profit on the deal so William offered him an extra shilling as he did not want him to be out of pocket! During the war William had land-girls to help him, one of whom, Rosie, married a local man and lived in Granborough.

In 1953 his son-in-law, **Eric Harwood**, (who had been working with him for many years), took over the tenancy of Jersey Farm.

Previous to this, Eric had also tenanted two fields opposite Jersey Farm (Hart Hill and Mill Hill) owned by the Ecclesiastical Commission but in 1951 these were sold to William Hall and the tenancy had to be relinquished. Eric had sheep and milking cows at Jersey Farm whilst his wife, Mabel, kept chickens back at home along the Marstonfields Road (then called Townsend) together with Christmas turkeys. Eric also grew a small amount of corn, and the threshing and baling would be done by Tom Hunt (from the village), Victor Alderman (from Stonehill Farm), John Parrot (from Church Farm in Oving) or Tom Rickard (from Wings Farm in Granborough). The lovely old threshing barn is still standing today.

Eric Harwood with Jennifer Harwood and Ann Smith in 1957

Eric and Jennifer Harwood in the 1960s

In 1969 Jersey Farm went back to be farmed by the Dancer family and a new farmhouse was built there for **Glyn Dancer** and his family. Glyn farmed this until his death in 2001 after which the house was sold as a private dwelling.

Glyn Dancer

------------ MANOR FARM (ST JOHN'S LANE) ------------

The new house at Manor Farm

An aerial view taken in the 1980s of the new buildings at Manor Farm

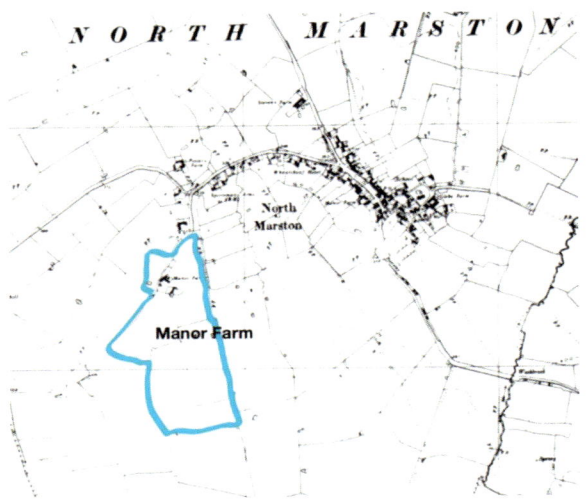
Manor Farm field map

Manor Farm comprises two hundred and thirty acres. In 1973, fields previously belonging to St John's Manor Farm, were re-amalgamated and a new farmhouse and farm buildings were erected. The development costs were covered by the EEC Amalgamation Grant plus the proceeds from the sale of the old St John's Manor farmhouse, its redundant farm buildings and four acres of land (*see also St John's Manor Farm*).

The land on which the new farmhouse and buildings were to be built was simply a green field site. Peter Horn from Devon and Franklins from Old Stratford did the main building work, and most of the fields had to be re-seeded. The buildings were designed to house a dairy herd. Today the farm has commercial sheep, a few beef cattle and horses. **Geoff Cheshire** has a life-long tenancy of the farm.

In 1975 Geoff Cheshire, on his horse, and accompanied by his two dogs, drove his ninety-six British Friesian cows along the road from his previous farm at Hogshaw with his wife, Esme, driving the Landrover in front.

Geoff and Esme had many successes with their Shipptonlea Herd of Pedigree British Friesians: the herd won the Bucks Herd Championship for five successive years and also won Supreme Championship at the Bucks Show.

Geoff Cheshire

As well as the dairy herd, Geoff also established a beef herd of Aberdeen Angus/Limousin cross, and had a flock of two hundred and fifty Scotch half-bred sheep. Geoff's son, Richard, ran a pedigree flock of Texel sheep for both breeding and fattening whilst his younger son, Tom, started his pedigree herd of Limousin cattle at Manor Farm before moving to Cumbria and then France where, today, he is a successful breeder.

At one Bucks County Show, Geoff won seven cups in one day for his dairy cows, beef cattle, sheep and the carcase compettion.

Stock bulls were used from the famous Horwood Herd in the village, owned by William Hall. The herd was dispersed in 2000 and one hundred and seventy were sold at Beeston Castle in Cheshire.

John Turner worked for Geoff Cheshire for thirty-two years and "Ant" Carter for twenty years. Geoff and Esme's children, George, Richard, David, Tom and Jennifer, all helped on the farm too.

John Turner with one of Geoff's prize-winning cows

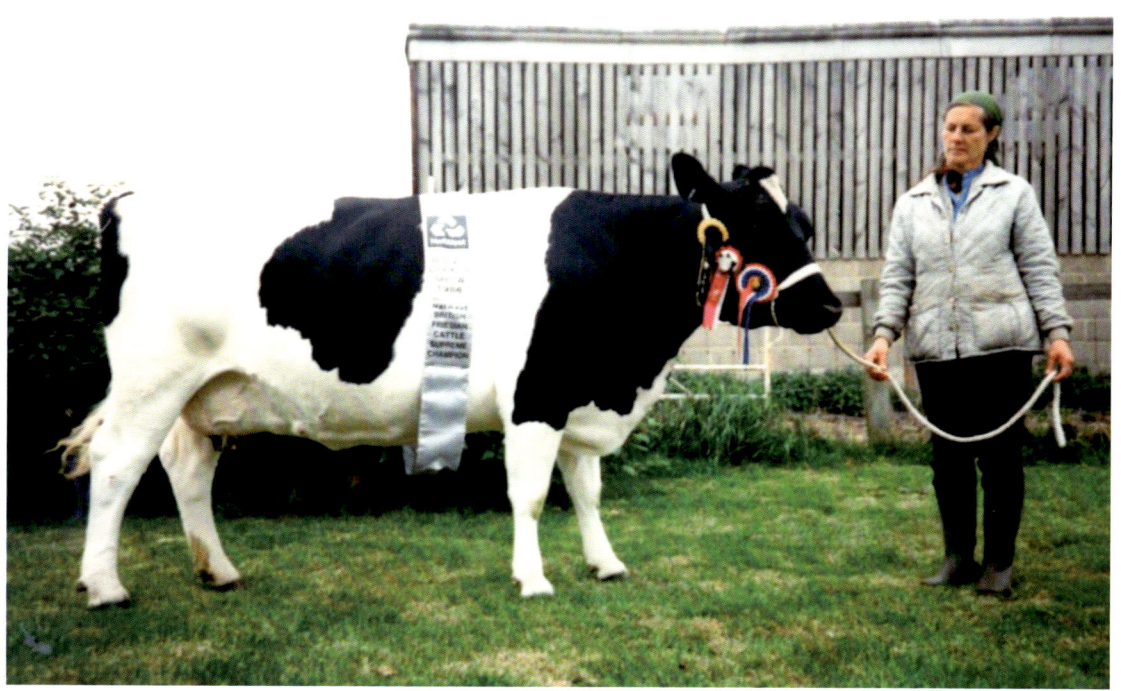

Esme Cheshire and the Supreme British Champion at the Bucks Show in 1986

MANOR FARM, HIGH STREET

Manor Farm, High Street, today

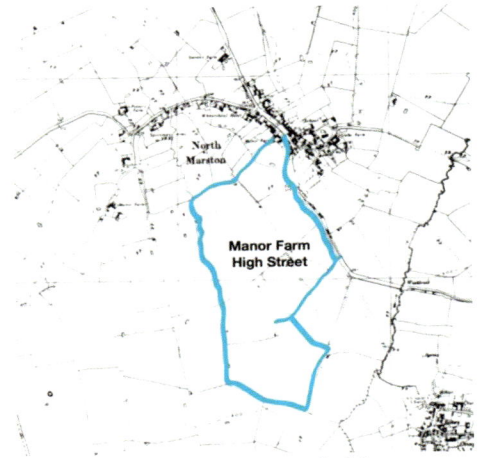
Manor Farm field map

Manor Farm, High Street, in 1959

An aerial view of Manor Farm, High Street, in 1987

It would appear that on the site of Manor Farm there was originally a stone-built 'mansion' which was demolished in the eighteenth century, though part of the offices (servants' quarters) were converted into a farmhouse which is possibly the house we see today. It was probably on this site in 1705 that the Great Fire of North Marston began (*see Chapter Six*).

As a working farm it comprised one hundred and one acres (situated to the right of Portway on leaving the village). For a large part of the twentieth century it was farmed by the Franklin family. The house was sold privately in 2010; the farm buildings are no longer operational and some have been converted for residential use.

At the end of the nineteenth century, the tenant at Manor Farm was **Ralph Chapman** and, although we know nothing of his farming skills or interests, we *do* know that he was very keen on village sport, often providing the football team with a field to play on and sponsoring the team 'strip' (*see Chapter Twenty-two*)! When the farm was sold in the early 1900s the land realised eighty-five pounds an acre.

On 5th July 1920 the farm was sold (*see below*) and it was bought by a **Mr & Mrs Nicholson** and the tenant was **Albert Line**.

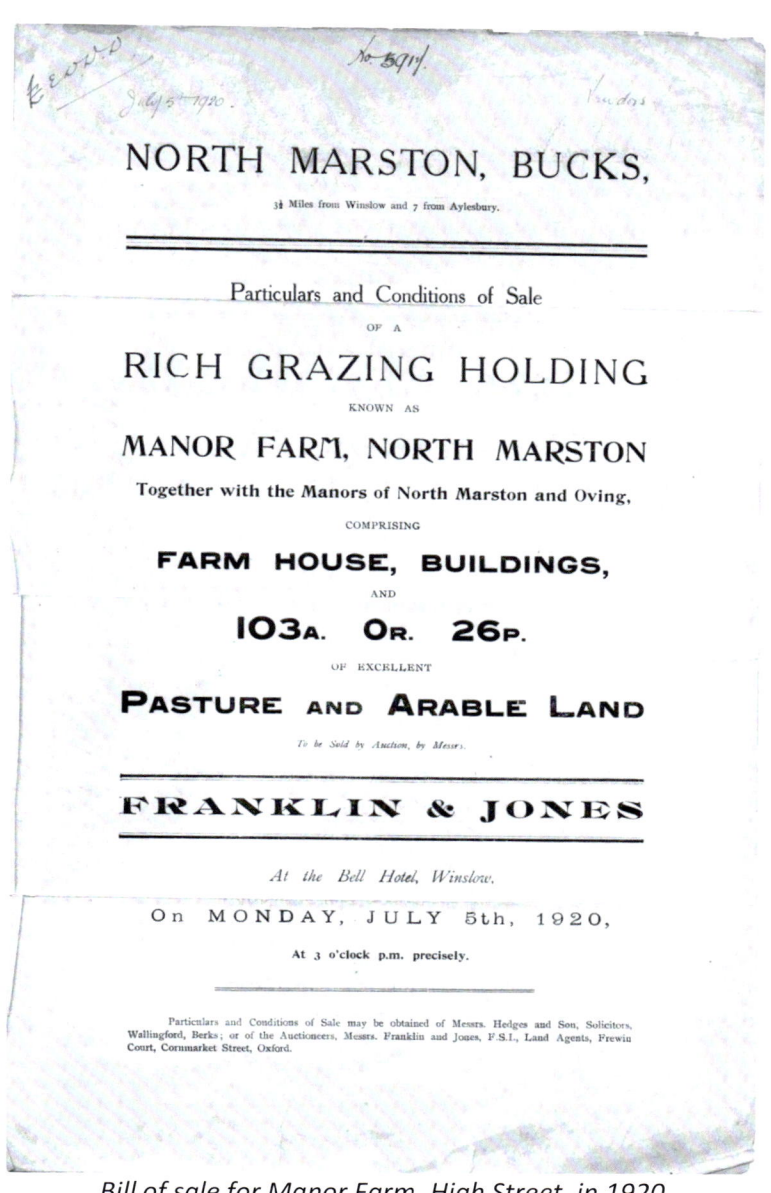

Bill of sale for Manor Farm, High Street, in 1920

In 1934, **Albert Franklin**, then in his twenties, became a tenant of the one hundred and one acres of land and a few of the buildings. He lived in Willowdene in Portway at this time. (Albert was the son of A J Franklin who started up Franklin's Stores in the village). When the farm was sold to a **Mrs Wise**, Albert was able to rent the house and the rest of the buildings and moved in to the farmhouse with his wife, Kathleen, in 1938.

During the 1930s and 1940s the milking was done by hand in small cow sheds which were in fields away from the farm. Eight cows were milked in a shed in Hill Field and about ten cows in another in a field called Gorbroads. The milk was then brought down by pony and trap to the farm where it was cooled ready for transportation to Winslow station. Some cows were also milked at the farm. During the war the farm was home to a number of evacuees; and an Italian prisoner-of-war helped on Manor Farm until the late 1940s.

Kath Franklin driving a horse pulling a hay-turner

During the 1950s Albert Franklin purchased an extra thirty-three acres of land from Jim Buckingham. The buildings around the farmyard were mainly timber with tin roofs but in 1950 the main cow shed was rebuilt with a brick and asbestos roof. As Graham Ward (Albert's nephew) recalls: *"Albert Franklin milked cows at Manor Farm in the High Street and the milking seemed to go on forever, it was so laid back!"* The work was done by heavy horses (Dolly, Punch, Flower and Duke) and Graham also recalls:

"A very early memory of mine is of Uncle Albert mowing with two shire horses, Flower and Dolly who were grey and bay. During hay-making the elevator which took the hay up onto the rick was driven by a horse walking round in circles. There were huge sheets on poles over the ricks to keep them dry and we boys used to play under there. It was really hot!"

Albert Franklin with two of his heavy horses

The farm was mainly dairy and sheep with some arable but it was also home to a number of other livestock, including horses, pigs and pheasants. Security was maintained by a gaggle of geese, headed by George, a one-legged gander who lived to the ripe old age of forty-three! In the early days many men from the village helped on the farm full-time or part-time. The full-time workers in 1945 were "Chib" Harwood, Lionel Linnell and Will Ward.

During the Second World War, Chib Harwood, as cowman, was awarded a Certificate from the Agricultural Commission for the largest yield of milk per acre during the winter of 1943-44. (In fact, the farm was responsible for Chib meeting his future wife, Olive Price, as she helped in the house!)

Olive and Chib Harwood's wedding in 1946

Chib Harwood

At hay making and harvest times many men from the village, young and old, would help with the work: Leonard Harwood, Eric Harwood, Archie Higgins, Terry Linnell, John Wilkins, Ted Tattam, Leslie Ward, Walter Carter, Robin Harwood, Will Ward and, of course, Albert's two sons, Tony and Keith.

Later on, in the 1950s and 1960s, the full-time workers were Harold Harwood, Will Ward, and Tony and Keith Franklin. One of these workers once exchanged a chicken for some silk ties which a 'foreign' gentleman was trying to sell door-to-door. What the gentleman did not know was that the chicken had died some days before and been slung on the dung heap but he evidently went away happy!

Will Ward

The local drover, "Glory" Smith, used to visit Albert and Kath to sit in the kitchen by the large, warm Rayburn and have a meal. In return he would give them a cabbage or other kind of vegetable. He lived in a little black hut on the road between Oving and Whitchurch and drove farmers' cattle to market.

"Glory" Smith

During very cold winters the farm hosted local skaters on the frozen pond on the front lawn.

Albert and Kath Franklin

When Albert Franklin retired due to ill-health in 1968 he and Kathleen moved back to Willowdene and his sons, **Keith and Tony Franklin**, then bought the farm from Mr Wise. Tony and Mary Franklin moved into the farmhouse in the High Street whilst Keith and Diane Franklin moved to a new house built in Home Close. Tony and Keith continued to milk cows and between 1968 and 1970 had a new modern milking parlour with a bulk tank installed. The open yard was covered by a new barn of concrete and asbestos.

However, in 1974, they realised that milking was not going to support two families and bought the village milk-round from Nancy Carter.

Tony and Keith Franklin

Some of the old farm buildings were converted to bed and breakfast units in 1990 and this business continued until about 2008.

Tony Franklin has many fond memories of life at Manor Farm:

"Although the majority of the time was pure hard work, my fondest memories were based around hearty meal-times when we all stopped and got together: for example, hay-making picnics and huge fry-ups at 10pm cooked by my mother, Kathleen. Much of the food was sourced from the farm garden, including some very strong home-made wine!"

Tony and Mary moved from Manor Farm in 2010.

An old hand-cart used at Manor Farm

---------------- MARSTON FIELDS FARM ----------------

The original farmhouse at Marston Fields

Marston Fields field map

The farmhouse circa 1900

Marston Fields Farm in 1959

Marston Fields farm lies at the very end of the Marstonfields Road. It comprises two hundred and eight acres. The farmhouse dates back to 1779 and was built after the "Inclosure" Award on land that was ridge and furrow. In 1994 the original farmhouse was sold as a private residence and, by 1998, all the farmyard buildings had been converted into housing. A new farmhouse was built in Bewkers Fields in 1990.

In the 1980s Marston Fields was established as the first "Link Farm" in Britain encouraging conservation (*see Part One of this chapter*). Today the farm still has arable land and sees the rearing of sheep. It is also home to the Tuckett Brothers Model T Ford Specialists.

During the late Victorian period, Marston Fields Farm was owned by Lord Cottesloe of Swanbourne but the tenant was **Thomas Biggs** who was a very influential man in the village: Chairman of the Parish Council, District Councillor, Justice of the Peace, School Manager, Churchwarden, Trustee of the Clockland and Poors Piece Charities, and Overseer of the Poor.

Due to his importance, he often came into conflict with the somewhat domineering rector of the parish, Rev James (*see Chapter Eleven and Part One of this chapter*). Thomas Biggs had eleven children, of whom two, **William** and **Francis**, would follow him as tenants. Then the Biggs family bought Marston Fields Farm in the 1920s and owned it right through to the early 1970s. Thomas Biggs himself moved to Stevens Farm in Granborough Road sometime between 1875 and 1891, though moved back to Marston Fields to live out his final years.

The Biggs family in the late 1800s

During his younger days, Thomas Biggs rode in steeplechase races on the Aylesbury Race Course and hunted regularly with Lord Rothschild's staghounds. In 1859 he had married Mary Biggs, daughter of Joseph Biggs who owned Stevens Farm, and when, fifty years later in August 1909, they celebrated their Golden Wedding Anniversary the whole village was invited to the celebrations at Marston Fields with over four hundred people attending. It was very tragic that, just five months later, Thomas collapsed and died at a Unionist meeting in Oving just after he had given a speech and proposed a vote of confidence in favour of the candidate, Mr Lionel de Rothschild. It was the middle of winter and his body was taken back home to Marston Fields on a horse and cart.

During the late 1920s the tenant at Marston Fields was **Aubrey Bull** and in about 1930 a very young Robin Harwood, aged six years old, would travel from Marston Fields in a horse and cart with his brother Dick (who worked there) to Winslow Station to pick up cattle which had come down from Yorkshire on the train. These cattle would then be driven back to North Marston along Winslow High Street, stopping off for water from the tanks at the Crooked Billet and The Boot (both no longer pubs). Robin can also remember riding on the cart from Marston Fields with the milk churns to deposit on the churn stand outside Glebe Farm by the church. Whilst there he and Dick would go into the churchyard, where the old Schorne College (*see Chapter Twelve*) was being demolished, and pick up a cart load of bricks to throw down on the road back to the farm. (Marstonfields Road in those days was just a track).

Between 1941 and 1943, **Sid and Margaret Dickins** were the tenants at Marston Fields.

When **Charles (Charlie) Brazier** and his wife, **Doris**, subsequently took over the tenancy, an era began at Marston Fields which has left its imprint in the memories of a very large number of village people.

Charlie kept sheep and a herd of milking cows and, like all farmers in those days, still relied on heavy horses to help him in the fields. Doris would drive the shire horses (sometimes in tandem) and throughout her life took an active part on the farm with her husband.

Thomas Biggs

Mary Biggs, wife of Thomas

Charlie Brazier at Marston Fields in 1957

Charlie Brazier and his prize rams in the 1950s

The Braziers in Marston Fields kitchen in 1956
L-R: *Michael, Doris, Minnie (Charlie's mother), Charlie and Frank (his brother from Brook Farm)*

All those who knew Charles and Doris Brazier describe them as lovely people. Village youngsters gravitated to their farm at Marston Fields because they were made so welcome:

"Marston Fields was like home to me. There was always lots of bread and dripping. Connie Seaton worked in the house in the 1940s. When we were working down the fields she used to send us very welcome bottles of cold tea and she made sandwiches two inches thick! I remember once when Mr Brazier was sitting at the table, a mouse ran along his collar!" (Chris Holden)

In 1958 Eveline Parker started working in the house at Marston Fields. She cooked a hot meal every day for lunch with huge helpings of pudding; there were sometimes sixteen people round the table! When fish was served, Mrs Brazier would insist on everyone having "tartan" (tartare) sauce. Pat Brazier (nee Holden) remembers:

"I spent much of my teenage spare time down at Marston Fields Farm with Charlie and Doris Brazier. They were wonderful days that I still look back on with fondness. I also remember the wonderful meals we had there (many, I am sure, would break just about all the dietary rules of today!) Mrs Parker used to help in the house and I learnt many of my cooking skills from her."

Many local people worked there throughout these years: Chris Holden, Will Pipkin, "Woggy" Cox and Henry Mills to name just a few. In the winter of 1962 to 1963 the snow was so deep that the only way to get to Marston Fields Farm was by tractor or by walking over the tops of the hedges; the road was totally blocked.

Charlie and Doris Brazier with Queenie standing next to their churn-stand in 1962

In the 1960s the huge kitchen at Marston Fields contained a beautiful old rocking horse, an extremely long high-backed settle, a wooden airer suspended from the very high ceiling and a huge table. There were layers of "coconut matting" on the floor. Whenever it needed replacing, another lot was just placed on top – it was about six inches deep! Mrs Brazier often cleaned out the chickens in the kitchen sink and it would be swimming with intestines. There was always a smell of singeing where she burnt off the spikes left on their skins after they'd been plucked. A tiny open wooden staircase led from the kitchen up to a small attic room (perhaps once a servant's room) which contained budgerigars in cages. The long corridor leading from the kitchen up a few steps had stuffed foxes' heads with staring eyes fixed along its length! Big wide stone steps led down from the kitchen to the cellar and the smell of rotting apples hit you as you descended; a solitary meat safe stood in the corner surrounded by old boots discarded over the years. There was a bathroom next to the sitting room with a bath in the distant corner and a small wash-basin, but the rest of the room was full of all sorts of junk. The hot water tap ran so slowly that the water was cold by the time there was enough in the bath to sit in, so you had to run back and forth to the kitchen to top it up with kettles!

Doris Brazier was an indomitable character and everyone who knew her has tales to tell! She always wore jodhpurs in the daytime and a sheepskin jacket when going out. Eveline Parker joked: *"Fred Gowin mended these items so often that he reckoned there was nothing left of the original garments!"*

Marston Fields farmyard in 1962

Eveline's daughter, Susan (now Chaplin), spent every school holiday at Marston Fields with her mother and, like others who have visited there, tells of Mrs Brazier's 'knack' of getting everyone to do jobs!

"Right from the start Mrs Brazier got me doing jobs! I had to collect the eggs, feed the chickens, feed the cats (lots of sludgy bread and milk mostly), brush her suede boots, clean out the bird cages, sweep the yard, do the shepherding, bring in the wood and do all sorts of housework to help my mum. I never minded though – she certainly instilled a work ethic in me! She was the same with everyone, though; people were always given a task even if they were only on a social call."

One relief cowman evidently used to sit in his van at the top of Gog Hill until the very minute he had to start work because he knew he would get the job of fetching in the wood or coal if he got there early!

Doris Brazier

Doris Brazier was such a slow driver that the double-decker bus once overtook her. Whenever anyone went past her (which was most of the time) she would raise her fist at them and say, "Go on you mad thing, you!"

Charlie and Doris Brazier in the early 1960s

There were always a huge number of feral cats running around the farmyard and Stuart Chaplin (who did relief milking at the farm) remembers one hilarious incident involving the cats:

"Mrs Brazier asked the RSPCA to come in to collect them. It took us hours to round up the wretched things and we finally got them shut in one of the outhouses. When the RSPCA arrived Mrs Brazier opened the door only to find an empty shed: the cats had all escaped down the drain in the corner!"

In 1967 Charlie Brazier died and his son, **Michael Brazier**, along with his mother, continued to run the farm until 1975, milking cows and rearing sheep and a few beef cattle.

Michael Brazier in 1974

Marston Fields Farm was bought by **John and Sally Robinson** who spent a few years renovating it and finally moved there in 1979. Around 1980, arable farming was introduced and by 1986 the cattle rearing ceased.

John and Sally Robinson (left) pictured with family members at the back door of Marston Fields in the 1980s

In the 1980s Marston Fields became the first "Link Farm" to be established in Britain. This was a joint venture between the Farming Wildlife Advisory Group and the Countryside Commission, and was opened by Sir Ralph Verney on 1st May 1984.

Sir Ralph Verney at Marston Fields in 1984

The aim of a "Link Farm" was to show how nature and landscape conservation can co-exist and thrive with modern farming and to demonstrate how landscape and wildlife can be protected and enhanced amidst commercially viable farming practices.

New plantations of broad-leaved trees were established to provide suitable conditions for many species of birds (many mature oaks were felled for the Second World War effort and all the elms died of Dutch Elm disease in the 1970s). All the ponds on the farm were conserved. The plentiful hedgerows were maintained and nest boxes were erected to encourage kestrels and owls. Pastures have never been sprayed with herbicides and the use of artificial fertilisers has been limited to encourage the development of traditional pastures.

As a consequence there is much wildlife to be seen and seventy species of birds have been spotted. English partridges have been bred over the last twenty years and are now re-established in the area.

The conservation work on the farm continues to today.

In 1982 the Robinsons' daughter, **Mary**, had married **Neil Tuckett** and in 1990 they built themselves a new farmhouse in Bewkers Field in which to live. The original farmhouse was sold in 1994 and the farm buildings round the old farmyard were converted into residences.

The new house named "Marstonfields" which was built in 1990

Marston Fields farm is well known these days as the headquarters of Tuckett Brothers Model T Specialists and has been featured many times on television. In 2011 Neil Tuckett and others made national news headlines when a 1911 Model T Ford was driven and carried to the top of Ben Nevis to celebrate the one hundredth anniversary of the original drive (having been driven from North Marston to Fort William in a single day: four hundred and seventy miles in seventeen hours).

Mary and Neil Tuckett in front of the 2012 Olympic beacon on the farm

Neil Tuckett pictured in 2004 in a 1911 Ford Model T which he restored for a Channel 4 TV programme

---------------- STEVENS FARM ----------------

Stevens Farmhouse circa 1900

Stevens Farmhouse in 1948

An aerial view of Stevens Farm in 1959

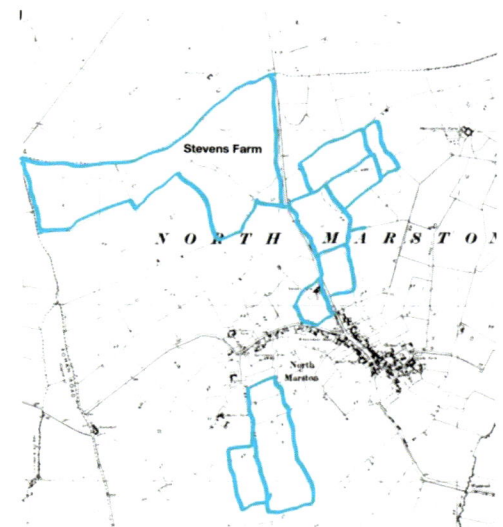
The land to the south of the map was sold to St John's Manor in 1989

Stevens Farm is situated in Granborough Road. In the 1800s, and before, it was always known as Stevens Farm but at the turn of the nineteenth century the owners referred to it as Marston Gate (as it stood close to one of the gates still across the road on entering the village). The farm buildings were converted to dwellings in 2000 and the original farmhouse is now a private residence.

Joseph Biggs farmed Stevens Farm from the 1830s and one of his daughters, Mary, married Thomas Biggs from Marston Fields Farm. By 1891, we know that **Thomas Biggs** and Mary were themselves living at Stevens Farm (renamed "Marston Gate") with five of their children (whilst his son, William, had taken over the tenancy at Marston Fields from his father). Thomas Biggs was a very influential man in North Marston (*see Chapter Eleven, Part One of this chapter and Marston Fields Farm*).

At the time of his death aged seventy-five in 1910, Thomas Biggs was living back at Marston Fields Farm and his son, **Thomas Bertram Biggs** had taken over the running of Stevens Farm. In the 1920s Thomas Biggs (junior) married Winifred ("Winnie") Kimble and they farmed there until they eventually retired to live at Windways (in Portway) in 1935.

Thomas Bertram Biggs

Winifred Biggs

The farm was then purchased by **Albert Line** with his wife Martha ("Tilly"). Previous to this he had tenanted farmland at Manor Farm in the High Street. Not much is known about life on this farm during Albert Line's time but after 1948, when he sold Stevens Farm to **William Hall,** it was to become known worldwide.

Bill and Gladys Hall

William (Bill) Hall, his wife, Gladys, and children, Arthur and Cynthia, moved to Stevens Farm in 1949 from Fulbrook Farm, Hogshaw. During the Second World War, William Hall was ARP Warden for Hogshaw. Whilst still at Fulbrook during the war, Bill ploughed up land for many farmers in the area (including Bert Line) who did not have a tractor. Bert mentioned to Bill at the time that he hoped one day he would succeed him at Stevens Farm and, when the time came for the farm to be sold, he evidently made sure that Bill got it!

Bill had already established his Horwood Herd of Friesians in 1934 (later he was to introduce Holsteins to the herd). In the early years, pigs, poultry, sheep and corn were also farmed. In 1950 he was the founding member of the Central Counties Holstein Club and was its President and Chairman for five years.

The Horwood Herd became so renowned that not only were the cows sold all over the British Isles but they were also exported to Japan, Colombia and Jamaica. Over the years, animals from this herd won many awards at local, county and national level, at shows all over England, both breed and interbreed. Also, as a herd, many successes were achieved including, in the interbreed National Dairy Herds Competition, The Bradfield Trophy for bull and progeny (which was won with a homebred bull, "Horwood Janrol") and the Alec Steel Young Stock Section which was won three times.

Cynthia Hall receiving the Bradfield Cup in 1959

Bill Hall in the early 1960s

Bill Hall with prize-winning bull, "Horwood Janrol", in 1959

Cynthia with her father and her favourite cow, "Babs 21", in the early 1970s

Thousands of visitors in coach-loads from all over the world came to North Marston to view the herd at Stevens Farm.

As **Cynthia Hall** grew up she herself developed a keen interest in the herd and took part in many competitions, primary stock judging all over the country and winning the highest placed junior at the London Dairy Show in 1973. She was also an active member of the Aylesbury Young Farmers and has held most of the posts there. Cynthia was put on the Holstein Society judging panel when she was twenty-six years old and has judged at all the major shows in the British Isles over the years.

She was an active member of the Central Counties Holstein Club and, after acting as Vice Chairman and Chairman, became its President in 1987. In 1988 she had the honour of being made President of the Holstein Society, having served on its board and committees for many years, and was the Holstein Friesian Society's final president.

A herd of the size and importance of the Horwood Herd needed to have first-rate herdsman to look after it: in the 1960s Johnny Woolley (whose sister, Nora, had looked after Cynthia as a baby) was herdsman, to be followed in the late 1960s by Bob Gale and around 1970 by Stan Bone whose son Harold (known as "H") worked alongside his father. They worked on the farm for thirty years. When the Horwood Herd was sold in 1999, the following statement appeared in the sale catalogue: *"Ably assisted by his son, Harold, Stan has been the cornerstone on which the present day herd has been built; working with Cynthia, they have together become a formidable, respected and very successful team".*

Other farm helpers over the years have been Jim Smith, John Woolley (Snr), Geoff Ayres and John Holden (many helping out with hay-making, harvest and other odd jobs).

Cynthia Hall

Johnny Woolley in 1962

Bob Gale in 1967

L-R: *Stan Bone, Cynthia and Arthur Hall at Oxford Show in 1971*

Stan Bone with "Dulcie 4" at the Bucks Show

Stan Bone teaching a cow to lead in 1988

"H" Bone and Cynthia Hall at the Bucks Show

After William Hall died in 1975, Cynthia continued to run the farm and the herd. At its dispersal sale in 1999, the Horwood Herd was quoted as being "one of this country's most respected herds of Holstein cattle".

Further land had been purchased by Stevens Farm over the years: from the Church Commissioners; from Messrs Stilgoe in 1975 (and later sold); from Bucks County Council in 1989 of Archie Higgins's smallholding at Hagditch).

In 1989 planning permission was granted for conversion of the old farm buildings and the herd was sold at Crewe on 20th May 1999, followed by the farm sale in June after which the demolitions and conversions commenced, finishing in late 2000. Cynthia herself moved into a newly-built bungalow on her farm and the old farmhouse became a private residence.

Stevens Farm in June 2001 after conversion

ST JOHN'S MANOR FARM

St John's Manor today

St John's Manor viewed across the old farmyard

Son and Win Brazier at the front of St John's Manor in the 1940s

The old farmyard at Manor Farm (date unknown)

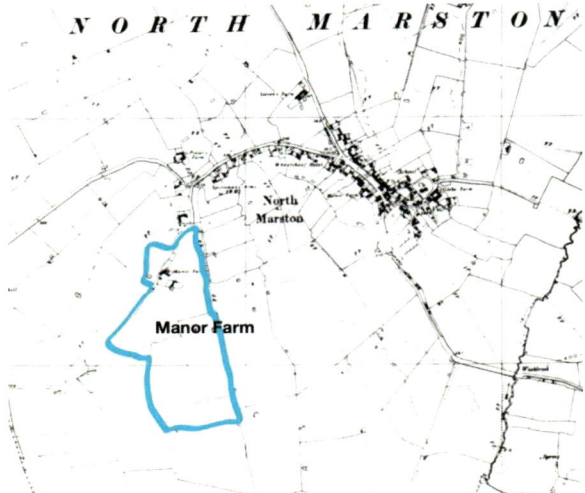

Land farmed by Son Brazier in the mid 1900s

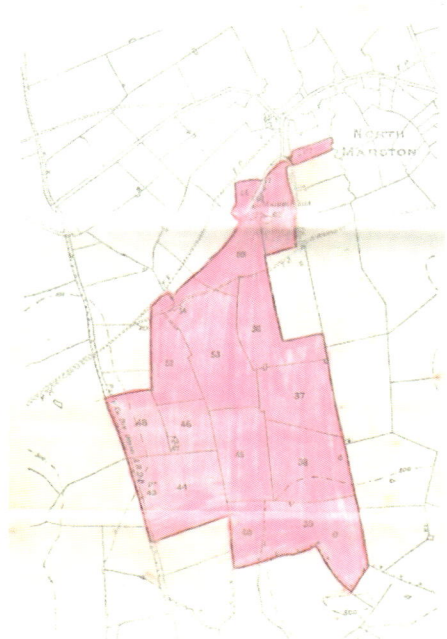

A map showing the land belonging to St John's Manor after Enclosure in 1778

St John's Manor is situated in St John's Lane and dates back to the fourteenth century. It was the farmhouse for the land which, from about 1260, provided income for St John's Hospice in Oxford but in 1456 the land was conveyed to Magdalen College Oxford (built on the site of St John's Hospice). St John's Manor Farm was later known as Manor Farm. The building is a T-plan and one of the earliest in the parish with the rear wing being the oldest part of the house. In 1913 the two hundred and twenty acre Manor Farm was sold by Magdalen College, Oxford, to Bucks County Council and divided into four holdings one of which was St John's Manor Farmhouse, its buildings and seventy acres. The farmhouse and its buildings were sold as a private residence in 1974 along with four acres of land; the remaining fields were amalgamated into the 'new' Manor Farm which was built by Bucks County Council on adjacent land, south of the old farmhouse.

In the late 1800s the tenant of St John's Manor was **John Clarke** (who died in 1894) and he was succeeded by his son, **Harry Clarke**. Around 1913, **Isaac Clarke** (not a son of Harry's) took over the tenancy with his wife, **Emma**.

Emma and Isaac Clarke circa 1913

Isaac with his pony and trap

The farmyard at St John's Manor circa 1913

In the 1930s **John Edwin Brazier** (known as "Son") took on the tenancy at Manor Farm. His brother, Ron, also lived there until Son got married in 1938 to Winifred Tattam (from the Red House in the High Street). In 1939 their daughter, Josephine (known as "Poppet") was born and she worked on the farm with her father until her marriage in 1960.

Poppet Brazier in 1957

Son Brazier in the hayfield

Son Brazier milked no more than a dozen cows and had a few sheep and cattle. He also grew beans and a little corn; like most of the other farmers in the village he would call on Victor Alderman's threshing machine at harvest time.

Arthur and Jack Price helping Son Brazier

The field on the opposite side of the lane to St John's Manor is called "Champions", and is possibly named after "Robert le Chaumpiun" of North Marston in the thirteenth century.

Champion Tree

Poppet Brazier remembers:

"Champions saw quite a few village events, Bonfire night especially. Dad delighted in making many mangold faces with candles in and hanging them on Champion tree. Champion pond was full of Crucian carp, roach and rudd. Many came to catch the elusive fish. Anything caught bigger than a tiddler was put in the yard tank for people to see and to ponder who had caught the biggest. Then the fish were returned to the pond".

Son Brazier

Win Brazier

Looking at fish in the tank at St John's Manor in the 1950s

Jack Price, Will Ward and Rowland Linnell from the village all worked for Son Brazier at times. Jack did the vegetable garden which, according to Poppet, was huge.

Rowland Linnell in the 1950s

It is interesting to note that Son Brazier also had Gibbings Close in Granborough Road until it was used by the council for housing in the early 1950s. After his sudden death in 1969, Manor Farm would never again be a working farm, becoming a private dwelling in 1974.

Two of the fields behind St John's Manor farmhouse (Cats Brains and Lower Shotshill) were originally part of the St John's Manor estate but were separated off in 1913 and considered to be worthy of a smallholding; they were subsequently tenanted to Bill

Pipkin in the 1920s, who milked nine cows there, followed in the 1930s by **Fred Tattam**.

In 1973 the land around St John's Manor (which had been split into four separate holdings in 1913 and farmed by Son Brazier, Fred Tattam, Vic Alderman and Joe Midwinter) was recombined into one holding and a new house and farm buildings were erected south of the old St John's Manor farmhouse.

The development costs for this new farm (*see Manor Farm, St John's Lane*) were covered by EEC grants together with the proceeds from the sale of the old St John's Manor farmhouse, its redundant farm buildings and four acres of land. These were sold to Michael and Alison Finnemore in 1974 in a derelict condition without water.

The Finnemores and their two children camped out in the building for their first year in residence and worked hard for several years to make the house habitable and to repair all the buildings. Michael and Alison bought extra land to increase their holding to sixty-one acres. It is now reduced to fifty-five acres. The land starts at the wooden gate opposite the entrance to the farmyard at Dancers Farm and includes the green lane and fields on the left and right of the lane and the thirty acre field (Bancroft), at the end of the lane, which still shows the ridge and furrow strips used at the time of the open fields prior to "Inclosure" in 1778.

Michael and Alison kept a flock of pedigree Suffolk sheep, selling rams to other sheep farmers and selling fat lambs through the markets or for the freezer. The fifty-five acres of grass is now let to other farmers for grazing.

Michael and Alison Finnemore

SHOTSHILL

Shotshill field map

Jones John Midwinter with his wife, Emily, outside their home in Bowling Alley, Oving

Shotshill was a smallholding of fifty-six acres created from land previously belonging to Manor Farm (St John's Manor) and which was sold to Bucks County Council in 1913. It is situated along the Roman road we know as Carters Lane. It comprised three fields named Upper Shotshill, The Ploughing and The Meadow, together with a few outbuildings. The land was farmed as a smallholding by the Midwinter family (from Oving) from 1913 until 1974 after which the land was returned to Manor Farm now in the tenure of Geoff Cheshire in St John's Lane.

In 1913, after the Smallholders Act had come into being, there was a smallholding of fifty-six acres left over from the division of land belonging to Manor Farm (St John's Manor) in St John's Lane. As everyone in North Marston at the time had been allocated what they wanted, **Jones John Midwinter** from Oving put in for this and was successful.

David Midwinter recalls:

"My grandfather remembered seeing army manoeuvres on Shotshill before the First World War; there was a gun carriage being pulled by a team of horses galloping all over – goodness knows what damage they did to the hedges, fences and fields! In those days there was no barbed wire fencing though; many fences were made out of willow branches."

Jones John Midwinter on an old mowing machine

After the war, Jones John's son, **Joseph Midwinter**, returned to help run the farm and they milked nine cows at Shotshill at that time. His son, David, tells how his father would leave home very early in the morning to get to North Marston and he knew he was late if the Oving church clock had passed five o'clock! Joseph took his milk to Waddesdon Manor Station. He would do the milking, then get the pony out of the field, hitch it up to the loaded cart and arrive at Waddesdon for the 8.20am train. David Midwinter also tells the following amusing story:

"When my father got to Waddesdon Manor station he would chat with everyone there and pick up on all the latest news. He had read in the Daily Mail at one time that Prince Edward had broken his arm whilst out hunting with Lord Rothschild and the Whaddon Chase but he was corrected by a porter who said, " Be b........ed for a tale, he broke his b.........y arm chasing a chambermaid down the stairs!" !

Joseph Midwinter haymaking at Shotshill

We have the following interesting anecdote about freak weather in the inter-war years:

"Sometime during the 1920s there was a freak rain-storm. My father couldn't get out of his cow-house at Shotshill to come home along Carters Lane because of the floods and Victor Alderman and his men who'd been threshing near Waddesdon could only get back from there by pushing their bikes along underwater. The water came up to their chests. Then in 1932, so I'm told, there was such a heat-wave that the older farm-workers had to go home as it was too hot in the hay-fields and several of them suffered minor strokes. That said, they were probably wearing heavy clothing with leather gaiters and shirts and ties!"

After the agricultural depression of the 1920s, Joe Midwinter stopped milking cows at Shotshill but he continued to keep beef cattle and sheep there. He also did a small amount of arable farming and his neighbour, Victor Alderman, did the threshing for him right up to 1963 (*see Part One of this chapter*).

Another very interesting thing happened during the Second World War: an army tank became stuck in a pond in a field next to Shotshill. This tank had evidently been on manoeuvres, come across the fields from Pitchcott and got wedged solid in the pond! The army tried to pull it out with jeeps but to no avail, and, in the end, they had to get another tank as well as jeeps to yank it out.

A very young David Midwinter on a Fordson tractor harrowing at Shotshill in the early 1950s

In 1964 Joe's son, **David Midwinter**, was granted the tenancy at Shotshill (although Joe continued to work on the farm until he was quite old) and continued to keep beef cattle and sheep there until he relinquished the tenancy in 1974. David had worked with his father for many years before he took over the tenancy at Shotshill. In 1956 he had started up a milking herd again at their other smallholding in Oving. It is interesting to note that, although Shotshill came with no farmhouse, the Midwinter family gave that name to their home in Bowling Alley in Oving.

David Midwinter

STONEHILL FARM

Stonehill Farmhouse today

Stonehill Farm was situated in the south of the parish and comprised forty-eight acres. It was bought, in 1913, by the Alderman family who also took on extra land at the same time which they rented from Bucks County Council. They farmed it until it was sold in 2000.

Benjamin Alderman moved to Stonehill Farm with his young family from the Mill in Whitchurch in about 1898. It is believed that the house was almost new at the time and had been intended as a hostelry for passing travellers. There was also a cottage near the corner to Deadman's Lane though this was soon demolished and the stone used to build the cattle sheds around the yard.

Stonehill Farm was owned at the time by Mr Dancer of Pitchcott Hill Farm some three miles away across the fields. In about 1913 the farm was purchased from the landlord for one thousand three hundred pounds.

Benjamin's son, **Victor Alderman** married Constance Butler (known as "Connie" or "Congo") in 1918. Connie came from Edgecott (where her family ran the Fox Inn) but was in service at Glebe Farm, North Marston, for the Kibble family. Victor lived at Stonehill all his life, as did his brother Lewis who never married. In 1921 **Gordon Alderman**, Victor's son, was born.

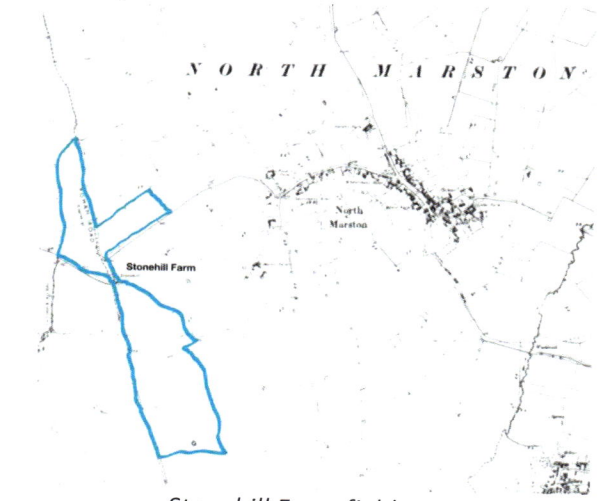

Stonehill Farm field map

Victor, Gordon and Constance Alderman

"Vic" Alderman (as he was always known) was an Agricultural Contractor, as were his cousins in Whitchurch (at the Mill and the Quaker Barn) with whom he continued to work closely. During World War Two, arable farming became a vital part of the farming industry and Victor and Gordon would be working from farm to farm for nine months of the year. His threshing machine was in particularly high demand at harvest time and he did the threshing for a large number of farms in the village (*see Part One of this chapter*). Memories abound of the Aldermans' threshing machine. Chris Holden remembers:

"Aldermans had a threshing box run by a steam engine and it had a chaff cutter. There'd be a fine wire mesh round a stack of corn to stop the rats escaping and we boys enjoyed catching the rats. Once, I remember, a weasel ran out and no rats!"

Vic Alderman's tractor-driven threshing box

Stonehill has always been predominantly grass and, for many years, carried a small herd of dairy cows, though it was later used for grazing beef and sheep.

Victor and Connie Alderman at Stonehill in the 1960s

Connie Alderman sitting on the old milk churn stand in Carters Lane (with Vic in background)

In 1951 Gordon married Edna Porter from Whitchurch after which he moved to Oving but he continued to work on the farm at Stonehill. He was a very good cricketer, acting as wicket-keeper for the North Marston champion side in the 1950s (*see Chapter Twenty-two*) and also for Winslow and Bucks. He helped to build the original pavilion at the village ground. During the Second World War, Gordon, being a farmer and therefore in a reserved occupation, was in the Home Guard (though he referred to it as "War Ag."). One of his duties was to help guard the railway bridge at Bicester against air raids for which he was armed with one grenade! David Rawlings from the village helped the Aldermans on the farm at this time.

Gordon and Edna had three children: Christopher, Lyndsey and Alan. As a youngster, Chris took a keen interest in the farm.

Victor, Gordon and Chris Alderman in the 1960s

Chris Alderman winning awards in 1965

Gordon, Edna, Chris and Lyndsey in 1964

The farmyard in 1969

The cows leaving the yard and crossing over Carters Lane after milking

By the late 1970s, William Price had given up his council smallholding at Fulbrook (which he had held since 1933) and, with the newly available land, Bucks County Council built a new farm called **STEART FARM** just opposite Stone Hill Farm in the Hogshaw Road. Gordon and Edna Alderman moved there in 1980, and Gordon farmed both Stonehill Farm and Steart Farm aided by his eldest son, **Christopher**, who had now moved into Stonehill.

After the death of his wife Edna in 1992 Gordon moved back to Stone Hill Farm (Christopher having by now moved to Devon) and Steart Farm was taken over by Gordon's son, **Alan Alderman**, who farmed it with his wife, Janet, for several years.

Whilst at Steart Farm, Alan's wife gave birth to a son which made the headlines in the local paper as Alan delivered his new baby, Joanne, on the farm office floor!

The newspaper article from April 1994

Victor Alderman had died in 1980 but Connie lived to one hundred and two, having lived in Stonehill Farm for eighty years! After Connie's death Stone Hill Farm was sold and Gordon moved into North Marston village spending the remainder of his life at Garfield House in the High Street.

Connie Alderman celebrates her 100th birthday with her son Gordon

BROOK (POTTERS) FARM

The original farmhouse at Brook (Potters) Farm

The new Brook Farmhouse

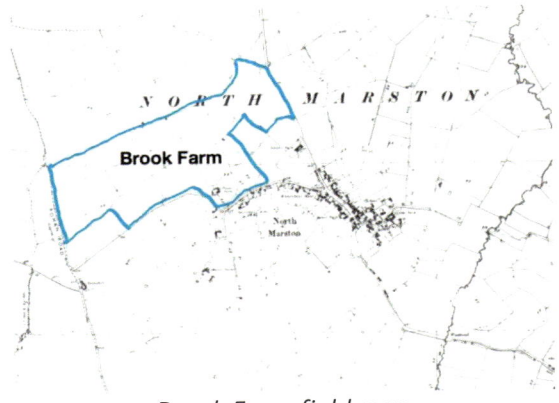
Brook Farm field map

The new buildings at Brook Farm viewed across a field of rape

The original Brook Farm covered an area between the Quainton and Granborough roads. The original farmhouse (now sold into private ownership and re-named Potters Farm) is situated at the very bottom of Quainton Road.

However, since 1923, when purchased by Bucks County Council, the land with it had been divided into small-holdings.

During the 1970s Jack Selmes rented several of the fields and small-holdings until in 1980 the modern Brook Farm was created from an amalgamation under the FAMS EEC scheme. Today, he and his wife, Janet, live in a new farmhouse a little further along the road from the original.

We know that the original farmhouse was updated in the late 1890s, the rear wing being much older. In 1879, the farm was called "Potter's Farm" (after a previous tenant a hundred years before) and it still had that name in the Census of 1901. During the mid-twentieth century the locals always referred to it as "Brook Farm". When the new Brook Farm was created in 1980, the former farmhouse was sold into private ownership and reverted to its earlier name of "Potters Farm".

In the early years of the twentieth century the farm was tenanted by **William Holden** followed by **Samuel Hodges**. In 1923 **Charles Ashley Brazier** (always known as "Ashley") became the tenant.

One evening, during the Second World War, Ashley and his wife, Minnie, heard the back door open and went out to find a British Airman standing in the kitchen. He had baled out from his plane and the rest of the crew were found, alive, in nearby fields.

Clifford Cheshire remembers:

"There was a practice bombing range near Granborough and I was down the field one day with Ashley Brazier stooking up corn when we found a small white smoke-bomb. It was close to the practice ground and I suppose it was one well wide of its target."

Ashley and Minnie Brazier

When Ashley Brazier still farmed from Brook Farmhouse, his son, Frank (who had married his first cousin Dorothy), lived in a cottage and had a smallholding one field over. His other son, Charlie, lived in a wattle and daub cottage on the farm with his wife, Doris, until they moved to Marston Fields Farm in the mid-1940s.

Both had helped their father on the farm but in the 1950s **Frank Brazier** took over the tenancy from his father and moved to the Brook Farmhouse. He farmed mainly sheep. As the name of the farm suggests, it was very close to a brook and Robert Gurney remembers:

"Frank and Son Brazier both farmed down Quainton Road and Frank's place was often under water when I delivered the papers there on my round. Frank would be sitting at the kitchen table reading the paper with water lapping round his feet because the brook had come up."

The holding opposite the Primitive Methodist Chapel, tenanted by **Leonard Harwood** (*see Part One of this chapter*) was called "Brook Farm" in its own right. Leonard lived in Schorne Lane. Like several other small-holders in the village, he had many diverse jobs: hedge-laying, hay-tying, rick thatching, shearing and mowing with a horse for other farmers. He also took a turn at chimney sweeping, running a bookmakers and baking bread for Tom Seaton at the bakery in the High Street!

Leonard Harwood and Frank Brazier at the kitchen table in the farmhouse in 1956

Ern Seaton was another of the smallholders of land at Brook Farm (*see Part One of this chapter*). He had buildings and two fields in Stone Hill plus a part of Hagditch. Ern lived in Church Street with his sister, Connie (though they never spoke to each other!)

Ern Seaton

Ern Seaton's old sheds which are now part of the new house at Brook Farm

Jack and Janet Selmes

William Selmes (left) with a home-bred show beast

Jack Selmes moved from Church Hill Farm to live at Brook Farm in 1982 when all the fields were amalgamated into one unit under the FAMS EEC Scheme. By 1984 all the new buildings were complete.

Today Jack is a beef and arable farmer. His son, William, is continuing the farming tradition.

COX'S SMALL-HOLDING

"Tom Cox's" is situated to the north of the parish, on the left when travelling towards Granborough.

Alfred Cox and his son, **Tom**, lived at the top of School Hill in North Marston next to the village school. In fact, Alfred's wife was nicknamed "Splitter" Cox because she always cut balls in two if they happened to come over the school fence into her garden! Between them Arthur and Tom farmed this piece of land for many years. People can remember Tom Cox riding to work on his bicycle with his little dog under his arm.

The Coxes kept land for many years. They kept hundreds of chickens, all with different-coloured rings on their legs for identification.

Tom Cox's field map

They were kept in chicken runs spread in rows all the way up the hill where the field is situated.

HAGDITCH SMALLHOLDING

The old Hagditch buildings today

Hagditch field map

Hagditch field, which has already been mentioned under Brook Farm, lies to the north-east of the village (on the left of the Granborough Road as you exit the village). Ern Seaton and Leonard Harwood had, at various times, the tenancy of part of Hagditch field (nearest to the present sports field) but the far end of Hagditch field nearer Granborough housed the smallholding tenanted by **Archie Higgins** and owned by Bucks County Council.

Archie Higgins's farm buildings (*see above*) are still visible from the Granborough Road. He also farmed part of Hart Hill Field and The Slad. After Archie's death the land was purchased by **W A Hall Herds Ltd**, followed, in 2000, by **George Cheshire**.

Robert Gurney has clear memories of helping Archie Higgins at Hagditch in the 1960s:

"Aged twelve, I did odd jobs for Archie Higgins at his smallholding, Hagditch Farm, down Granborough Road. I fed chickens, mucked out the cowshed and fed the calves. My first pay 'cheque' was ten shillings for the week. This was in 1966. Archie had milking cows and he also did hay-making; the milk was put in churns on the milk-stand and collected by a lorry. He had his own tractors, a Standard Fordson, and later a Major with a six-cylinder Perkins diesel engine.

I remember hay-making in the summer with Archie and one year (aged about thirteen) I did the whole lot on my own. He'd say, 'If it looks fit, mow it; if it looks fit, turn it; if it looks fit, bale it'. Archie was often not there – he loved going to the races. He had all his own machines including a Massey Ferguson baler which had its own JAP air-cooled engine on the top so you didn't have to power it through the PTO shaft. This baler was always causing problems though. We'd build the hay into a rick and that would feed the animals throughout the winter.

I have a vivid memory of falling off the top of one rick. The old brick barn which was the milking parlour is still there; there was a stall of two; then the feed room; then three stalls of two; then the dairy; then behind that was the engine shed and a lean-to called the `ovel with another stall for cows in there. The cows were milked by a machine into buckets."

Archie Higgins in 1952

Twenty-five
THE SCHOOL 1835-1968
Sue Chaplin

The old school building which dated from 1835

Prior to 1968 when the new school building at North Marston opened its doors, the children of this village and (after 1944) of Granborough too, were educated in the old school, now demolished, which stood on the site of the current playground.

We are extremely fortunate that the school's *Log Books* dating from 1899 and the *Attendance Register 1902-1965* have survived, as these, together with the memories of former pupils and extracts from *The Northmarston Magazine* and *The Schornian* (both published in the village during the late 1800s), have helped to give us a valuable insight into the life and workings of the village school for nearly one hundred and fifty years.

---------------- BEFORE 1835 ----------------

In the early 1800s formal education for ordinary folk was not considered important and did not enter their lives. In 1807 the Tory MP, Davies Giddy, was quoted as saying:

"...giving education to the labouring classes of the poor...would be prejudicial to their morals and happiness; it would teach them to despise their lot in life instead of making them good servants in agriculture and other laborious employments to which their rank in society has destined them".

Boys from wealthier backgrounds were often sent to boarding school whilst the girls would, more often than not, have been educated at home by their mother or, in some cases, by a governess.

In 1715 a Rev Richard Purchas conducted a small private school in North Marston in the Priest Room above the church vestry where he taught at least five private male 'scholars' but these are unlikely to have been from the labouring classes.

The more fortunate of the ordinary village children might have been given some arbitrary instruction from a better-educated family member, or attended a charity school or Sunday school. At some stage during the 1800s the Wesleyan Methodists established a small 'school' in North Marston, though we do not know where this was based. In 1811, the Church of England's National Society was formed with the intention of providing a National School in every parish, run by a trained teacher and based on the teachings of the Church of England. The sites (often given by local benefactors) were usually adjacent to the parish church, with the vicar and churchwardens as trustees. From 1833, the state began to pay annual grants to the National Schools which were subject to inspections.

---------------- 1835-1870 ----------------

The National School

On 24th July 1835 the first National School was opened in North Marston near the church at the top of School Hill. The owner of this site at the time is unknown but the school was built by Messrs John White and F Ward during the Incumbency of Rev John Pigott (Rector 1826-1836), and the main contributions towards it came from the Chapter of Windsor (twenty pounds), Sir Thomas Aubrey (five pounds), the National Society (thirty-five pounds) and the Committee of the Privy Council (sixty pounds). The Rev Pigott himself must also have paid a fair amount towards the school as he is quoted as saying, *"I have had to pay above the sum collected a good deal more than I could afford."*

As well as the government grant, pupils were required to make a small payment called *School Pence* towards their education, and voluntary contributions were exacted from village rate-payers who in return were allowed to nominate a pupil born in *lawful wedlock* to attend the school for free.

The School Committee comprised the vicar, churchwardens, sidesmen and every annual subscriber, so it is clear to see that the school was run very much by the church.

Education was not compulsory, however, and it appears that the National School did not fare too well in its early years, resulting in its temporary closure. After it had re-opened, Rev Knight of North Marston wrote the following letter to the Dean of Windsor in June 1854 asking for further financial help:

"I take the liberty of stating that the National School here, having been closed for some years, has just been restored and opened with the aid of a donation from Her Majesty the Queen, as the possessor of the property left by the late J C Neild Esq. But the expenses incurred in re-opening the School have exceeded Her Majesty's generous donation of £100 by about £30. I, as the clergyman of the parish, am responsible for the payment of that excess, as well as for the deficiency in the Master's stipend as a consequence of the children's pence. I respectfully request the aid of yourself and the Canons of Windsor."

Rev Knight wrote twice more to the Dean of Windsor with the same request but there is no evidence that he was ever reimbursed for his costs! Many years later, in 1871, it is interesting to note that Rev Samuel James insisted that a motion be passed relieving him and his Anglican successors from *all* financial liabilities regarding the school.

In 1861, a Susannah Knight was the mistress of the National School but little is recorded of the curriculum and daily life of the school during these years.

1870-1900

Board School v Church School

In 1870 the Forster Education Act was designed to make good the gaps in the church system by providing "Board Schools" to supplement the National Schools. Board Schools were much more state-controlled and some state funding was provided (about fifty per cent of the costs).

The committees, called "School Boards", were elected by local rate-payers who, themselves, were obliged to pay a compulsory charge on their rates (possibly one to two shillings in the pound) to support the school. The Boards could make their own by-laws allowing them to charge fees or let children in free.

It was a source of much concern to Rev Samuel James that North Marston National School might now become a Board School, thus disrupting the *status quo* and resulting in him losing some of his control over the running of the school. He argued that, as the original school in 1835 had been largely sponsored by Rev Pigott, it was a *church* school and therefore should remain as such. He believed that the responsibility for running the school lay squarely with the church (ie himself!).

At a meeting in 1870 it was reported that considerable difficulty had arisen about the ownership of the school *"which was built by public and parochial subscription and seemed to belong in about equal proportions to the parish of North Marston (territorially) and to the Church of England (ecclesiastically)."*

Although the Board Schools were not, by law, supposed to impose any religious education other than simple bible readings, it was not *that* issue which lay at the heart of Rev James's opposition! It appears that he primarily had his own interests at heart. In 1870 he won his argument and a School Board was declined for the time being.

In 1873, the issue continued to be a topic of debate with Rev James arguing ever more forcefully against the proposed changes:

*"A School Board would (1) shut up schools such as Mrs Faulkner's *(2) compel all children to attend school (3) put the parish to some heavy expenses in the event of further alterations in the Education Act (4) never be able to be shaken off or got rid of."* (*This is likely to have been run from her home premises).

However, the village National School was not without its problems and in 1871 Rev James pleaded with his parishioners to keep their children at school to make up attendances to satisfy the Inspector. In 1875 he received the following letter from the Sub-Inspector of Factories who had visited the village:

"I was very sorry to find that your once very prosperous School had so sadly fallen off. There are a large number of little lace-makers in the village whose education I am bound to look after and report upon. In respect to these I am rather in a dilemma....Am I justified in ordering these children to attend a School when there is no proper teacher?"

Rev James, in his reply, agreed that the school which he had *"raised from its ruins to a promising state of efficiency"* was deteriorating but that it was not his fault; it was simply that he had not exercised *"his unquestionable powers and rights"* for some time!

The issue of whether North Marston School would be better off being a Board School hung in the air right up to the end of the century; in 1887 Ralph Tattam, a rate-payer, said that *"so long as balls and things of that nature were held in the schoolroom the reluctance would continue."* (So much for education being the priority!)

In 1892 the matter was finally laid to rest when it was agreed that the majority of villagers were happier for it to remain as a *Church* School and were willing to pay a voluntary rate so as to avoid a "much higher" compulsory School Board rate. In 1896 (when the school had received a favourable report after its Religious Knowledge Inspection) Rev James, still proud of the fact that he staved off the issue of the Board School, wrote:

"Had there been a Board School we might have been saddled with a busy-body, upsetting, anti-church and anti-everything that is good and wholesome."

Subscriptions, Grants and Salaries

As already discussed, every rate-payer in the village was required to pay a subscription towards the upkeep of the village school. Rev James even asked Queen Victoria if she would contribute an *annual* subscription as she had inherited money from John Camden Neild but she declined!

The subscriptions ranged from one guinea (twenty-one shillings) to half a guinea (ten shillings and sixpence) and were collected on Midsummer Day by the Schoolmaster (for which he was allowed to keep, as a bonus, five percent of whatever he collected). In *The Northmarston Magazine* (March 1870) Rev James wrote:

"We hope our friends will understand and not be offended by our attacks upon their pockets."

THE SCHOOLS. 1.—The following Subscriptions have been promised.

	£	s.	d.		£	s.	d.
Mr. Anstess	1	1	0	Rev. S. B. James	1	1	0
Mr. Archer	0	5	0	Mr. Keen	1	1	0
Mr. Biggs, sen.	0	10	6	Mr. Kibble	1	1	0
Mr. James Biggs	0	10	6	Mr. Josiah Mayho	1	1	0
Mr. Thomas Biggs	1	1	0	*Servants* (Vicarage)	1	1	0
Col. Cartwright	1	1	0	*Penny Readings*	2	2	0
Mr. Chapman	0	10	6	Mr. Price (builder)	0	10	6
Mrs. Dancer	1	1	0	Mr. Tattam	1	1	0
Miss Dancer	1	1	0	Mr. Ralph Tattam	0	10	6
Mr. Dancer	1	1	0	E. Terry, Esq.	0	10	0
Mr. John Holden	0	10	6	Rev J. G. Viller (donation)	2	0	0
J. G. Hubberd, Esq. (don.)	5	0	0	Thomas Ward (Vicarage)	0	10	6
Mr. Ingram	0	5	0	Mr. Watkins	1	1	0
Mrs. James	1	1	0	Mr. John White	0	10	6
				Mr. W. Wood	1	1	0

2.—Subscriptions are due and are collected by the Schoolmaster (for which he is allowed five per cent. on as much as he collects) on or about Midsummer Day in each year, and are considered to cover the year from January 1st, to December 31st. Subscribers whose names are printed in italics have already paid their subscriptions for the year.

3.—The School Committee consists of the Vicar, Churchwardens, Sidesmen if ever elected, and every Annual Subscriber of one guinea.

4.—Every Annual Subscriber of one guinea is also, by virtue of such subscription, entitled to nominate one boy, or one girl, born in lawful wedlock, duly baptised, and not now nor at the time of nominating attending the schools, to attend the school gratis.

5.—Every Annual Subscriber of 10s. 6d. is, by virtue of such subscription, entitled to nominate one boy under six years old (born &c. as before), or one girl (born &c. as before), under twelve years old (age of both boy and girl reckoned at the time of nomination), to attend the school gratis.

6.—Only one nomination in the year is allowed, however soon the nominee may discontinue attendance.

7.—Nominations for the current year (1870) will cease to be in force after Dec. 31st, but it will be open to subscribers to re-nominate the same child, provided the stated age shall not, in the meanwhile, have been exceeded.

Subscribers to North Marston School in 1870

The fees (*School Pence*) which were paid by the pupils ranged from one penny for boys under six years to six-pence for boys over fourteen years. Girls noticeably paid less (only two-pence if over twelve years old) but children from neighbouring parishes were obliged to pay twenty-five per cent more. The issue was sometimes raised that farmers should pay higher school fees than the poor for their children`s education, a matter with which Rev James was in full agreement!

As can be seen above, some children had their fees paid:

"Every Annual Subscriber of one guinea is also...entitled to nominate one boy, or one girl, born in lawful wedlock, duly baptised...to attend the school gratis. Every Annual Subscriber of 10s 6d is...entitled to nominate one boy under six years old or one girl under twelve years old (born as before) to attend the school gratis."

In 1871 the income amounted to £27 17s 6d from rate-payers' subscriptions, £25 12s 1d from the pupils' fees and £41 13s 0d from the government grant.

The headmaster was paid forty pounds a year plus half of the government grant and half the total of School Pence collected from pupils. He was also provided with a house (at the cost of about seven pounds a year) which, in the 1870s, was rented from a Mr Josiah Mayho.

Some funding assistance from the state was based on "Payment by Results" following an inspection by Her Majesty's Inspector. In 1874 the grant awarded was only thirty pounds, much to the dismay of Rev James who wrote: *"The results of the examination are very unsatisfactory especially in spelling."*

In 1875 the *Northmarston Magazine* recorded another *"bad report"* which blamed neglect of past years. As the new headmaster Mr Read could not (it was felt) be held accountable for this, a collection was taken among his friends to express their goodwill and sympathy!

Grants were even given for singing; in 1895 part of it was withheld as the *"note-singing"* was not good. However, the grant for that year totalled eighty-two pounds and three shillings which, added to attendance, gave a total of one hundred and twenty-five pounds.

Schoolgirls circa 1888

Renovation of the School in the 1890s

By the late nineteenth century the school premises were becoming inadequate and the first mention of this was at a School Meeting in November 1892:

"The present building has been patched and added to and is still unacceptable to the Inspectors; and if it is patched and added to again the money will be thrown away as it is sure to be condemned again eventually."

The following month it was agreed to buy "twenty poles of ground" for the enlargement of the premises as required by the Education Department.

Good progress was made and it was reported in *The Schornian* in April 1893 that *"the parish school enlargement goes on apace and by the time of the Inspector's visit will perhaps be completed."*

In 1894 a new playground was completed (*"a capital bit of field"*) and in 1895 Rev James reported that a *"cause for thankfulness"* was now *"an enlarged and altogether improved Parish School, new playground, and unequivocal Church management without injustice to nonconformist parents."*

The final mention of improvements came in September 1897 when the District Council *"at last gravelled the very disgracefully neglected road called School Hill up and down which 100 poor children pass every day."*

Pupils in 1897

L-R Front row: Glad Carter, Annie Carter, Cis Cheshire, Syd Carter, Will Pipkin, Bob Walker, Ewart Carter, Gilbert Cheshire; **L-R Second row**: Nell Tattam, Lucy Cheshire, Darrie Guthrie, Edie Cheshire, Syb Cheshire, Violet Carter, Daisy Carter; **L-R Third row**: Alice Walker, Nell Walker, Ern Tattam, Maurice Carter, Fred Walker, Win Cheshire, Gus Carter, John Walker; **L-R Back row**: Frank Carter, Vic Carter, Dennie Tattam, Harry Smith, Ellen Walker, Mabel Carter, Ted Tattam

> <u>Mixed School.</u> "The school has come on so well, and the scheme of instruction is so good of its kind that the higher grants may now be recommended. The order is admirable and the children's interest in their work is most satisfactory. The Staff as at present arranged is sufficient and suitable."
>
> <u>Infants' Class.</u> "The infants' division is also in very creditable order and deserves a place in the front rank of such classes."

An extract from the Inspector's Report of 1900

The renovation of the school in the 1890s appeared to have worked wonders in every way as, in May 1900, following the Report by Her Majesty's Inspector, the school received the highest government grant.

Rev James writing in *The Schornian* in 1900 gave much credit to Mr & Mrs Farrar, Miss Reynolds and Miss Buckingham "...*for the school`s great advance and exemplary efficiency.*" He went on to say:

"*Mr Farrar is a schoolmaster of a thousand and we are glad to have such a man among us as a very useful, conscientious parishioner and sharer in all good works.*"

The Headmasters

During the years between 1870 and 1900 we know of nine headmasters at North Marston School: Mr Martin, Mr Hooper, Mr Read, Mr Batchelor, Mr Mackenzie, Mr Burton, Mr Rogers, Mr Guthrie and Mr Arthur Farrar.

Mr Burton with pupils circa 1883

Mr Rogers, Headmaster (left) with Miss Rogers, Sewing Mistress (right) circa 1890

Pupils with Mr Guthrie in 1898

Headmaster, Mr Arthur Farrar (right) and Temporary Monitress, Alice Holden (left) in 1900

---------------- 1900-1931 ----------------

From July 1899 the head teachers at North Marston were required to complete a Log Book at the end of each *week "or at such other times as occasion may require"*. We are extremely fortunate today that these Log Books have been preserved, providing us with the entertaining (and often amusing) minutiae of the life of the school right from the start of the twentieth century.

The School House

It was common for a husband and wife to take up positions as Headmaster and (usually) Infant Mistress in a village school. In April 1893 *The Schornian* had reported:

"By the first of July a new master and mistress will have been elected by the Committee who offer £100 and house to combined master and mistress."

The Red House on the village green was assigned as the "School House".

Mr and Mrs Guthrie had been the first to reside there in 1893, followed in 1898 by Arthur Farrar and his wife, Henrietta; then, on their departure in 1902, the new headmaster, Thomas Pyle, and his wife, Sarah, moved in.

Mrs Pyle on the front steps of the Red House circa 1902

Thomas Pyle and pupils circa 1904

Thomas Pyle was paid £1 8s 6d a week salary. When Mr Pyle became ill in 1904 and left his post, he and his wife (who stayed on as Infant Mistress) nevertheless continued to live at the Red House so the new headmaster, Percival Bridgewater, had to live elsewhere.

It was not until Mrs Emily Dudley became headmistress late in 1907 that the Red House ceased to be linked to the school, as Mrs Dudley was living comfortably in The Gables in the High Street which her husband Ted Dudley, the village builder and undertaker, had built in 1902 a year before their marriage.

School Staff

As well as the headmaster and his wife there was an Assistant Mistress together with a "Pupil Teacher" or "Monitress", the latter post filled in turn by Gertrude Buckingham, Alice Holden and Cissie Cheshire between 1900 and 1907.

Miss Gertie Buckingham, Monitress

In the early twentieth century, a pupil who showed promise in his or her schooling could, after the leaving age of twelve, stay on at the school as a probationer to help with the teaching of younger pupils. After two years as a probationer they would spend another three years learning the job before taking a final exam which, if they passed, entitled them to go to training college to become a qualified teacher.

It appears that the head teacher was partly responsible for tutoring the Monitress. In 1902 Thomas Pyle wrote:

"I commenced evening's lessons with the Monitress, Cissie Cheshire, in my private residence."

When Percival Bridgewater took over as headmaster from Mr Pyle in 1906 there was considerable friction between him and Mrs Pyle, wife of the former headmaster, who was still teaching the Infants. Mr Bridgewater wrote of her:

"After giving three lessons on plasticine modelling she finds she is unable to continue as there is no suitable place for the children to wash their hands."

But things were to get worse! In April 1907 Mr Bridgewater wrote:

"This afternoon the Infants Mistress refused to let me have the number of children present in her room and when I went to investigate the matter I found the door of the Infants Room locked. The Mistress informed me that she should not in future let me know the number of children in her room until Friday as it was a 'piece of officialdom' on my part."

In November, he wrote:

"I have to complain that the Registers of the Infants mistress were incorrect in both totals on November 1st. This is not the first time it has happened."

> 1907
> Oct. 25th This afternoon, the Infants Mistress, Mrs. Pyle, refused to let me have her Register, consequently, I am unable to send the Attendance return to the Attendance Officer for the past month. Mrs. Pyle said she would send the register in when she thought she would.

An entry in the School Log book by the headmaster, Percival Bridgewater, complaining about the Infants' teacher, Mrs Pyle

Percival Bridgewater (right) and Gertie Buckingham (left) with pupils in 1907

After Mrs Dudley became headmistress in November 1907 Mrs Pyle was only ever mentioned in a *positive* light, however, and continued to work with Mrs Dudley for the next ten years. Mrs Dudley herself was to remain in the post of headmistress until December 1930 when she took retirement.

After Mrs Pyle left in 1917 a seventeen year-old girl, Dora Holden (a former pupil who had been a monitress in the school for two years), was appointed as Infants' teacher in her place. Miss Holden (who became Mrs Jack Ayres in 1925) was to remain in that post for the next forty years.

Dora Holden as a young girl

Emily Dudley

Miss Dora Holden (left) and Mrs Emily Dudley (right) with pupils on the school field in 1924

Miss Dora Holden (left) and Mrs Dudley (right) with pupils circa 1923

The School Governors

Just as today, North Marston School had several managers (governors) between 1900 and 1931, notably Thomas Biggs, Edwin Kibble, Henry John Holden, Henry Cheshire and the vicar. One would carry the title of "School Correspondent" and one would be responsible for checking the school registers at least *"once a quarter"*. They were also responsible for ensuring necessary repairs to the building were carried out and they sometimes initiated fund-raising:

"Money was obtained through school children and friends to buy a new football and posts for 13s 10d." (Edwin Kibble 1900)

Mr Henry John Holden and his family also saw themselves as benefactors; they visited the school quite regularly to bestow gifts on the children. At Christmas he, his wife and daughter would distribute oranges and Christmas cards (Mr & Mrs Biggs did the same) and in January 1911 we read that he asked the children to learn a psalm and a hymn, offering prizes to the two best.

Pupil Numbers

After the abolition of school fees in 1891 the government paid out, in their place, a grant to each school which was reckoned according to the average attendance of pupils, so absenteeism was a matter taken very seriously. An Attendance Officer would visit the school every six months to check the registers.

In 1899 we know that one hundred and twenty-four children attended North Marston School and, since 1893 when the school had been enlarged, these had been housed in two rooms: the Long Room measuring 40ft x 20ft and the Infants Room measuring 24ft x 20ft. At the start of the century sixty infants were taught in the smaller of the two rooms (an astonishing number!) though there is evidence that this room contained a "gallery" to help accommodate them.

The marking of the registers was very important and prone to a little 'fraud' at times! In May 1902 the headmaster Thomas Pyle found himself in deep water and it was recorded in the Log Book by Mr Kibble, one of the Managers:

"Mr Shaw, Sub-Inspector...found that the registers had been marked incorrectly, 61 being marked present whereas 57 were actually present. It is clear...that the Master was perfectly well aware of this because it was a surreptitious endeavour on his part to amend the registers on seeing Mr Shaw that drew Mr Shaw`s attention to the matter. It seems an act of deliberate falsification. I am to enquire whether the teacher receives a fixed salary and whether his salary varies with the amount of Annual Fee Grant paid to the school in each year."

From the one hundred and twenty-four pupils in 1899, the numbers decreased each year: by 1914 seventy-six pupils were registered at the school; by 1925 there were fifty on roll (of which the headmistress taught thirty-seven and the Infants` teacher thirteen); by 1930 there were just thirty-seven pupils. The head teacher meticulously recorded the average attendance in the Log Book each week and despaired over any absences, many of which were, of course, unavoidable if linked to illness or the weather. In February 1900 Mr Farrar wrote:

"The snow is still falling and fearing the nine children present at 9 o'clock might take cold, the managers sanctioned their dismissal."

In January 1922 Mrs Dudley recorded:

"The snowy weather has affected the attendance unfavourably this week. There are nine children who have to walk a good distance to school through fields. Some of these have been absent all week."

Of course it was not just the snow which affected those children walking to school; Mr Pyle noted in August 1903 that *"considering the very heavy rain falling from 8.30 am to 9.15 am the attendance was praiseworthy."*

Truancy

The reasons for unauthorised absence were very varied. In May 1899 and in 1902 we read:

"The low state of attendance is accounted for by the beautiful grounds at Waddesdon being thrown open to the public – it resulting in a general holiday in the surrounding villages."

"Today we have the smallest attendance of the year. This is accounted for by a picnic held at Aston Clinton by the primitive Methodist Chapel members".

The head teachers became somewhat resigned to the fact that children would take time off and Thomas Pyle was quite heartened in November 1904 when:

"Although there was a travelling menagerie in the village...Violet, John and Basil Carter were the only children absent."

What headmaster Arthur Farrar found the most irksome above all else, however, was pupil absence due to Lord Rothschild's Stag Hounds meeting in the village which, in those days, caused considerable excitement and interest. A "carted stag" would be brought to Well Leys Field (behind the present Schorne Lane) and released. After it had been chased for a few hours by the staghounds it would be rounded up and put back into the cart.

"At mid-day Lord Rothschild's hounds were in the village....twelve children were away in consequence. The last time the hounds were in the neighbourhood there were thirty-three children absent...Six boys out of the twelve were amongst those who were spoken to on the last occasion. I therefore judiciously administered punishment for disobedience and truancy."

However, on his appointment as headmaster in 1902, Thomas Pyle initially took a different view of the Stag Hunt:

"School opened this morning at 8.30......This change from the ordinary routine enabled the children to attend a meet of Leopold Rothschild Esq's Stag Hounds ....Consequent upon the excitement in connection with the above it was deemed advisable to close the school for the remainder of the day."

He did not always feel this way however! In 1903 he deprived twenty-two boys of their playtime for two weeks *"in lieu of corporal punishment"* for following the hunt and later in the month he inflicted corporal punishment upon several children. In 1905 it was noted in the school's Log Book that King Edward VII himself passed through North Marston with Lord Rothschild's Hunt.

Other very common reasons for absence from school were potato-picking and blackberrying, the latter causing the headteachers particular distress, such as Thomas Pyle in 1902:

"Attendance is about 88.5%. This is lower than usual owing to blackberrying by several scholars notably Carters who were reported. I gave a <u>little</u> and proper correction to Ewart Carter for showing temper and afterwards insubordination. His father sent me a most impudent and threatening letter which I returned with advice."

Problems with Parents!

A hundred years ago, parents felt it their right to question teachers' authority. Another disagreement between Mr Pyle and John Carter occurred in 1902, as reported by Thomas Pyle:

"On leaving school yesterday afternoon I was accosted by John Carter and accused of having struck his boy to the ground, and in the most gross and abusive language challenged to fight. Unless he had been held and restrained by his wife and Mr Thomas Tattam he would have assaulted me."

Even the pupils' mothers sometimes lost their temper with Mr Pyle:

"Mrs Young brought her children to school this morning but because she was abusive her children were sent home again with her."

When Edward Lambourne took himself off home one morning because he had been punished during the second lesson, his mother flatly refused Mr Pyle`s request to send him back again!

Days Off, Outings and Treats

Despite the high importance given to attendance, it is remarkable that, in the early twentieth century, absence from school was tolerated for reasons that we today would find unusual, and the school would close completely for a variety of events.

In January 1910 the school closed for the afternoon for the funeral of Thomas Biggs and in May 1913, when the whole village celebrated the Golden Wedding of Mr & Mrs H J Holden, the school pupils were given a day's holiday as the school was used for the celebrations.

Royal events would also result in a day's closure: the funeral of Edward VII (1910), the wedding of Princess Mary (1922), and the marriage of the Duke of York (1923).

As there was no Village Hall until 1924, the school premises were frequently in use for village functions. The Rummage Sale and the Harvest Tea warranted full-day closures as did the preparation for any evening concert and the fete. In July 1926 the school was shut all day for the Village Sweet Pea Show, only to be closed all day again the following month for the Flower Show. General elections were always held in the school.

As they attended a *church* school, pupils would go to an early service on Ascension Day and Ash Wednesday and the rest of the day would be free. Confirmation services were deemed very important and between the years 1904 and 1925, any Confirmation Service held in the local vicinity resulted in a day off, as below in 1904:

"A holiday was given to the school today to enable the teachers and some of the older pupils to attend the Confirmation Service at Grandboro'."

The whole school was also given a half-day holiday when some of the pupils took part in the Winslow and District Annual Athletic Sports. In 1908 Mrs Dudley reported that they were driven there in conveyances *"kindly lent by Mr Biggs, Mr Watkins and Mr R Chapman."*

One very surprising closure took place on 6th April 1905:

"Half-day holiday given today in accordance with Article 64 of the Education Committee's Regulations - Aylesbury Hunt Races."

The school was also closed (or attendance dramatically reduced) when large numbers of pupils went on an outing arranged by another body, such as the annual outing of the Primitive Methodists to Wendover Hills (attended by nearly thirty pupils) or the trips organised by the Church Lads' Brigade. In May 1914 Mrs Dudley reported:

"The children of the Wesleyan Sunday School were taken for a drive this afternoon and in consequence the attendance fell to 77%".

In those days there were obviously no supply teachers as there are today and, in 1924, the school had to shut because *"the older scholars went to Wembley Stadium with the two teachers"*.

One of the earliest outings recorded by Thomas Pyle in 1902 is delightful and involved no motor vehicle. It reports how pupils from Standards IV –VII (nine to thirteen year-olds) walked to Claydon House observing the wonders of nature en route:

"....left school this morning in company with the master and walked to Claydon House through the fields. On the way out convenient opportunity presented itself to converse with the class upon the Life Habits of the Skylark, Peewit or Lapwing, Woodpigeons, Moorhens, Robins and Cuckoos. The birds were seen and heard, and in some cases their nests were discovered. The black and white swans were an interesting novelty in Claydon Park, and were pleasantly watched during luncheon time."

Christmas brought its own treats, as in 1902:

"A Christmas treat was given to the whole school this afternoon in the schoolroom. The children were regaled with Tea, Cake, Fruit and Sweets. The remainder of the evening was happily spent in games. Mr Henry White also entertained them with a number of records on a fine Phonograph, and at the conclusion each child was presented with a fancy toy."

Just as today, pupils would put on entertainments for their parents and the other villagers to watch. On 2nd May 1912 lessons were suspended for the day for a special concert in which some of the pupils dressed as lace-makers:

A group of dancing girls in 1912

Louie Buckingham, Emily Baker and Dorothy Cheshire in lace-makers' costumes

The Band of Hope and the Temperance Movement

An outing which was considered to be of extreme importance, and for which the school always closed for the day, was the one organised by "The Band of Hope" (*see also Chapter Twenty-one*). This outing is recorded in the school's Log Books every year from 1907 to 1937. London Zoo was a popular place to visit:

"The Village Band of Hope Temperance Society paid a visit to the Zoological gardens, London today. As over 30 of the children were to be absent a General Holiday was given." (June 1904)

Two months later, yet another General Holiday was given so the children could attend the *'Demonstration of Temperance Lodges in Granborough'*.

The consumption of alcohol was considered by the Temperance Movement to be a blight on society, and most villages had a Band of Hope organisation whose members abstained from drinking alcohol and tried to persuade others to follow in their footsteps. So serious was the threat of alcoholism considered to be that lessons on its dangers even entered the curriculum. In April 1902 the following was recorded:

"Two lessons of this afternoon's work were devoted to a Lime Light Lantern lesson to the school on 'Alcohol and the Human Body' followed by an Illustrated Reading of the ever popular story of the Temperance Society entitled 'Buy Your Own Cherries'. The lesson on Alcohol was given under the following syllabus: Alcohol a Poison: Alcohol not a Food: Alcohol Lessens Muscular Power: Alcohol Lessens Mental and Moral Power: Alcohol Interferes with Growth: Alcohol Interferes with Digestion: Alcohol Overworks the Heart: Alcohol Leads to Disease and Death."

It was a serious business!

School Terms and Holidays

These days, a new School Year starts in September but, until 1929, it always began on 1st April regardless of whether or not this was mid-week or mid-term. It was on this day that children were given promotion to the next year group (if deemed of adequate ability) and any new timetables or syllabuses were introduced.

There were the familiar three terms during the year (Autumn, Spring and Summer) but until 1908 the Summer Term would finish towards the end of June, and the Autumn term begin at the end of July, resulting in a very long run-up to Christmas! This was alleviated only by time off for the Village "Feast Week" which was usually held near the start of September. From 1908 onwards, however, the Autumn term began in September *after* Feast Week.

There was no half-term break during the Spring term and, in the Summer, only a day or two off to celebrate Whitsun at the end of May.

In June 1911 the pupils, however, must have been delighted to have been given a whole week`s holiday *"in honour of the Coronation of His Majesty King George V"*. After this it became the norm to have a week's break for summer half-term.

During the First World War some major changes to holidays were introduced during the summer months. On 4th May 1915 Mrs Dudley wrote:

"The Correspondent has informed me that the Summer Holidays are to commence from the 18th June. This is because of the shortage of labour caused by the war, so that the boys may go hay-making."

It is also interesting to note that in 1919, one year after the First World War had ended, the school children were given a week's holiday from 17th to 22nd October as *Peace Week*. This holiday, thereafter, became the October half-term which we still have today.

Pupil Health

Even in the early twentieth century, pupils were subject to school medical inspections. There was a regular examination each year by the school doctor of the "leavers" and any other "special cases". Occasionally a machine was sent to the school for the head teacher to measure pupils' heights and weights; this was then passed on to Granborough School. Also, in 1909, Mrs Dudley noted:

"During the week I have been testing the eyesight of all the children on the roll, according to instructions received, taking from twenty to thirty minutes each morning."

From about 1918 the school nurse visited regularly, mainly to 'check heads'. The headmistress exasperatedly wrote in 1928:

"Nurse visited. One girl excluded. This family is always the one blot on an otherwise clean school."

Just a few years later children were availed of the opportunity of dental treatment:

"Mrs Ayres….took five children to Oving School for teeth extraction. She left on the 1.15 bus and returned at 2.30pm."

The school dentist was obviously a quick worker!

The school's Log Books for the years 1900 to 1931 give us an insight into the types of illness, disease and infection rife at the time: scarlatina, measles, chicken-pox, scarlet fever, ringworm, mumps and whooping cough were all recorded. If a large number of pupils were absent due to illness it was the responsibility of the head teacher to report the matter to the Medical Officer of Health who, in turn, would occasionally shut down the school.

In December 1900 the school closed for a week when half the pupils were absent due to measles, and the effects of a particularly virulent outbreak of scarlet fever in September 1913 lingered until the following March, resulting in seven weeks of closure on and off. During this period two school pupils died. On January 6th 1914 Mrs Dudley wrote:

"George Ward (5yrs old) died yesterday from dropsy following Scarlet Fever. This is a very sad case as eight children and the mother have had the fever at the same time."

In July 1914 the epidemic broke out again, resulting in further school closure of one week.

Some entries in the Log Book at this time mention hospital treatments available: in 1905, after a particularly boisterous playtime *"Alfred Wilkins' thigh bone was broken, necessitating his being sent immediately to the Bucks Hospital at Aylesbury."*

Others, however, are very sad, such as the death in Aylesbury Infirmary of thirteen year-old Renee Harwood from "paralysis".

Maintenance of the Premises

It is a little difficult to imagine the school premises as they were in the early 1900s. Although many improvements had been made in the 1890s, the facilities would have been extremely primitive compared with today, especially the sanitation.

There was no mains water connected to the building so it was impossible for the children to wash their hands, and the outside lavatories were simple earth privies (called "offices"). It is unsurprising that successive head teachers were constantly complaining to the School Governors. In 1903 Thomas Pyle was determined that *"the approaches to the boys and girls offices must be kept separate from each other absolutely."* In 1907 her Majesty's Inspector took up the case:

"There should be no further delay in providing proper lavatory accommodation, there is most urgent need of it. A paved brick path to the boys' offices is also necessary. In wet weather they can only be reached at present by wading through an expanse of mud."

The following year in 1908 things had not improved much according to the Inspector:

"The playground is a quagmire in wet weather and the boys' offices unapproachable. The wooden fence of privacy which screens the approach to the girls' offices has great gaps in it owing to several of the boards having fallen out. The holes in the seats of two of the girls' closets are absurdly small. There is no urinal for the infant boys. The older boys' urinal offers a wall surface of only 3 feet."

Being earth closets the contents needed frequent emptying but this did not always happen. Again, six years on in 1914 the Inspector wrote:

"The offices must really receive more frequent attention. The pails should be emptied at least once a week."

The lack of sinks on the premises caused problems: in April 1905 Bernard Cheshire, Fred Cox and Thomas Pipkin were sent home to wash their hands prior to the Drawing Lesson but Thomas did not return! In 1907 a *"simple washing apparatus was installed for the use of the scholars"* (but we do not know what this was).

In fact mains water was not to be connected to the school until 1945.

Another major problem and constant source of irritation to the head teachers were the two stoves in each classroom, fuelled by coal, coke and wood, which had to be lit every morning. In 1901 Arthur Farrar wrote:

"School fires are a source of trouble...As the fires were only just lighted at 9 o'clock the children were kept at play for half an hour to prevent them taking further colds."

Then, to make matters worse, later in the year he recorded:

"Another surprise visit was made at 10 o'clock by a new Government Inspector. I have ALWAYS been compelled to tell the boys to come early to school winter mornings to light the fires. This morning the boys could not get the infants' fire to go. I went into the classroom and was eventually successful in getting a fire. Previously I had sent for water but before the boys returned with it, time had elapsed and the Inspector appeared. He noticed my unfit state for TEACHING but said nothing."

An Inspection in 1902 criticised the fact that the young boys were lighting the fires unsupervised and highlighted the need for a proper caretaker:

"The rooms are not swept daily and they are scoured but once a year. A responsible person should be appointed to do the cleaning of the school...and to light the fires."

Nothing changed however and the problems continued:

"The stove pipe being so choked today with soot, no fire was lit in it. Children were unable to sit in the choking smoke." (1905)

During the early years of last century, the School Managers were bombarded with requests from the head teachers for general maintenance to be carried out, be it on the leaking, loose skylights, the muddy surface of the playground or the plaster dropping off the dirty walls.

In 1908 much more space was made in the infants' classroom by the removal of the gallery (the wooden raised platform round the edge of the room on which many of the desks were situated) and by 1909 it appears that many of the improvements elsewhere had at last been carried out.

By the late 1920s a regular caretaker, Mrs Lily Young, had been appointed and her daughters, Eveline and Kathleen, would help her in the evenings to dust, clear out ashes and bring in the coke for the stoves next day.

Mrs Lily Young

Year Groups

The schoolchildren were divided between two rooms: the smaller Infant Room and the larger Junior Room.

The infants would usually join the school after their fifth birthday and would remain in the Infants until they turned seven. They would then enter Standard 1, moving thereafter to the next Standard at the start of each new School Year, eventually reaching Standard VII at the age of thirteen.

Girls from the Seventh Standard on the front school steps in May 1923

Pupils could choose to leave earlier if they passed an examination to get a "Labour Certificate". Some older pupils were given "Half-time Labour Certificates" on the grounds of five years' good attendance. These were sometimes abused, however, as can be seen from Thomas Pyle's comments in 1902:

"Sent warning to the parents of Victor Carter, half-timer, that he must not be kept at home to follow hunting parties but when not at school must be beneficially employed."

The school leaving age was raised to fourteen in 1923.

Quite often the head teacher would decide not to promote a pupil at the start of a new School Year. In 1902 Thomas Pyle wrote:

"After careful observation of Mary......and Louisa......I find they are mentally incapable of making a corresponding progress with even the average child in their respective class."

Mrs Dudley often kept children 'back' as they were *"of very slow intellect"* or *"badly nourished and backward"* and would not hesitate to apportion blame:

"Harry......would not only be a drag on Standard 1. He lives at Fulbrook and has to stay away in bad weather. The doctor classed him a few weeks ago as 'mentally backward-hereditary'."

Of another pupil she wrote:

"His home life does not help him in any way with regard to instruction or intelligence."

Very early in the century the Head would sometimes recommend not attending school at all:

"William...is in my opinion idiotic and unable to learn and it is inadvisable to force his attendance at school." (Thomas Pyle 1903)

The Curriculum, Examinations and Inspections

The curriculum between the years of 1900 to 1931 was considerably wide and varied but subject to continuous scrutiny and examination.

The children worked to strict timetables which had to be submitted for approval to Her Majesty`s Inspector, with any daily changes to routine recorded in the school's Log Book.

Until 1903 the pupils wrote on slates instead of paper but Her Majesty`s Inspector that year reported:

"The infant classes are quite strong enough to be promoted to paper. The general abolition of slates is greatly to be desired."

He was also surprised that *"backs are not yet fitted to the forms in the infant class."* (It had always been considered better for the children to sit up straight-backed of their own accord with no support).

As North Marston was a Church School a Diocesan Inspection took place every year, so the teaching of Scripture was a vital part of the curriculum. The outcome of this report was considered of high importance and focused solely on the children's knowledge of the bible, passages of scripture, psalms, the Book of Common Prayer and hymns. The Diocesan Examination was again held in 1900 and the head teacher recorded the Inspector's findings in the Log Book (*see following picture*).

Extract from the school's Log Book of November 1900

By 1931 little had changed:

"Bright and intelligent answers were given to questions on Our Heavenly Father. The written work on Our Lord's Temptation was very good but the help it is meant to afford us in our lives was not well understood."

Those children showing excellent knowledge of the Bible and Prayer Book were awarded prizes and certificates (*see the picture on the right*).

Naturally much emphasis was put on the teaching of Arithmetic, and the following extract from 1903 shows the level of skill expected of a nine or ten year-old when carrying out long multiplication:

"To my intense surprise the III and IV Standards were without exception unable to work correctly such sums as the following: 590 x 150, 902 x 307, 4205 x 2300, 5003 x 3002. The 0s in the multiplier quite puzzled them."

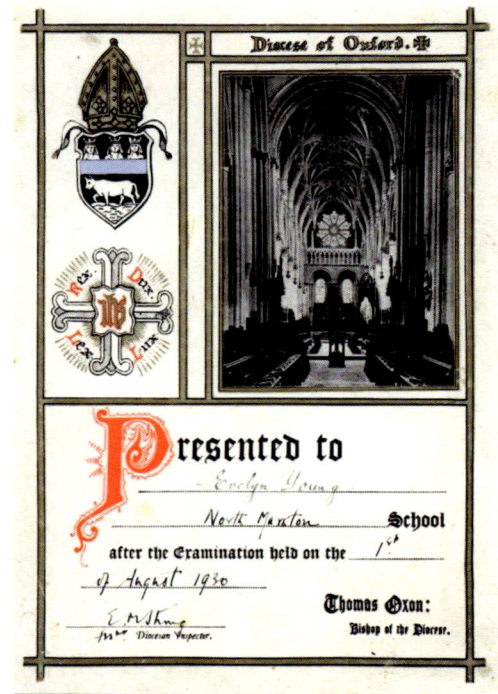

Eveline Young's Diocesan Certificate 1930

It is interesting to note that the elementary principles of the Metric System were also being explained to the ten year-olds in 1902.

As well as the regular lessons in Writing, Spelling, Hand-writing and Reading, a wide variety of other subjects were fitted in to the school week: Recitation, Singing, Map-colouring, Composition, Poetry, History, Geography, Drawing, Elementary Science, Handwork, Domestic Economy (girls), PE and Gardening.

Lessons in PE (called "Drill") were rather irregular in the early years of the twentieth century and very much depended on the clemency of the weather! Specific exercises were followed, when possible, in the school yard. Boys occasionally had the opportunity to play a football match against another school (eg Winslow High School in 1902) but more often as a treat than as part of the curriculum. In 1928 Mrs Dudley wrote:

"This afternoon the boys were allowed time for a football match (1 ½ hrs) as a reward for 6 weeks' excellent attendance."

The Winslow and District School Sports were an annual event in which a selected few took part. By the end of the First World War visiting teachers would come yearly to inspect the Drill and issue a report as in 1925:

"Running in file has improved, but running in breaks and games is still heavy and clumsy. Standing and starting positions require correcting. Marching has improved but running should be lighter."

The PE Inspector had therefore even observed the children's physical movements whilst at play! Playtimes brought the usual scrapes and mishaps as in 1915:

"I am sorry to say two windows have been badly cracked today by boys with their whip-tops."

Needlework and Handicraft also commanded regular inspection and were considered highly important. In 1903 it was noted that every girl in the Upper Standards was sewing on buttons incorrectly! Twenty years or so later we read :

"Needlework and knitting are well arranged and carried out. Patching is taught in connection with other stitches in a practical manner."

163
1925.

The work and finish is very good.
Lower Group. - The work of these younger children is very pleasing, especially the manipulation of the hems on the pinafores. Stitches and knitting very satisfactory.

In the 1920s the older girls were given weekly instruction in Housewifery and Cookery at Winslow.

In 1904, Drawing had been made a compulsory subject for every child in the school and again was inspected. Lessons called "Object Lessons" (where pupils looked in detail at a variety of subjects ranging from "Cups and Saucers" to "The Weasel Family") were a popular part of the curriculum, especially for the younger children and lent themselves to the inclusion of free-hand drawing which was considered so important. In 1902 we read:

"A live bat having been brought to school by one of the Upper Standard boys, advantage was taken to give today's Object Lesson on Bats."

The school was inspected by Her Majesty's Inspector every year and a full report written not only on the academic achievements of the pupils but also the fabric of the building (the latter usually being quite scathing).

As well as the huge number of inspections to which the children were subjected, they also took school exams at the end of the Spring and Summer terms. Some pupils were also entered for Scholarships and, as early as 1918, Annie Buckingham gained a place at Aylesbury Grammar School while the following year Albert Franklin and Alan Cheshire won places at the Royal Latin School in Buckingham.

One very enjoyable day in the year that was neither inspected nor examined, however, was the celebration of Empire Day on 24th May. The day would be spent in school singing rousing patriotic songs, 'raising the flag' and playing games. In 1933 the King's and Queen's speeches were even read to the children. The last recorded celebration of this in the Log Book is in 1933.

During the First World War

The first reference to military action is made in the Log Book on 19th September 1913 when the headmistress wrote:

"School closed today by order of the Managers on account of the Army Manoeuvres, the soldiers being in the immediate neighbourhood."

The immediate effect on the school was, as already mentioned, an earlier start to the summer holidays (ie in June) to allow the children to work in the hay-fields as there was a shortage of labour because the men of the village had gone off to fight.

On the first Empire Day (24th May 1915) during the war, a collection was made:

"...to send comforts to our soldiers and sailors. The nice sum of 14s was realised which will be forwarded to the Secretary of the Overseas Penny Fund."

This collection was subsequently made every Empire Day during the duration of the war; in 1918 the sum of £1 16s 11d was divided between the funds of the Red Cross and the Overseas Club.

In November 1915 Miss Buckingham, the Supplementary teacher had to cease work as the Education Committee reduced the staff for purposes of economy.

During the war much attention was paid in school to the production and preparation of food: in 1915 eight of the older girls were given cookery lessons from 9.30 to 11.00 in connection with the "Cheap Food Campaign Week". These took place in the Headmistress's own kitchen and she noted:

"Each day a dinner (two-course) had been cooked for six people according to Circular 58 issued by the Education Committee."

The girls continued to have lessons on other food-related topics in accordance with the Food Campaign Scheme of the County Council. The boys, on the other hand, were busy in the school gardens. In 1917 it was recorded:

"The boys have been digging the small plots in the playground in order to plant them with potatoes etc. in view of the shortage. Work done in gardens one hour in the morning, one

hour in the afternoon, digging and picking up potatoes.......work continued on measuring, calculating and sharing."

The children named their garden "The Victory Potato Plot" and in 1917 their five pecks of seed resulted in twelve and a half bushels of potatoes from seven poles of ground. The school also closed for nine half-days to enable the pupils to pick blackberries - six hundred and seventy three and a half pounds in total weight! They collected two hundred and twenty eggs for the "wounded" and their monetary contributions for the Overseas Penny Fund, the John Cornwell Fund, the Lord Kitchener National Memorial Fund and the Red Cross throughout the war amounted to £3 17s 11d. Coal was also in short supply and in October 1917 Mrs Dudley was very grateful to Mr H J Buckingham, one of the managers, for lending them some coal for the school stoves.

War was taking its toll on the young men. In October 1916 Mrs Dudley noted that the school closed in the afternoon on account of a *"military funeral in the village"* and in December 1917 *"Miss Holden received the sad news of the death of her soldier brother."* When the war ended in 1918, Mrs Dudley listed in the Log Book the sixty names of all former pupils of the village school who had served in the army and navy.

---------------- 1931-1949 ----------------

The Head Teachers

Between 1931 and 1940 the head teacher was Mrs Dorothy Richardson. After her departure in October 1940, the post was filled by Mrs Irene Lewis who continued to live in the School House in Schorne Lane. In October 1943 her successor, Miss Lucy Funnell, resided at Manor Farm. Between July 1946 (Miss Funnell`s departure) and July 1949 there were no fewer than three Acting Heads (Phyllis Cubbage, Henrietta Harrison and Chrystabel Curtis) which created a period of considerable instability for the school in the post-war years.

Mrs Dorothy Richardson

In January of 1931 Mrs Emily Dudley retired after twenty-four years as headmistress at North Marston School and, after a short interregnum during which a Mrs Walter took temporary charge, Mrs Dorothy Richardson took up her post as the new headmistress in September of that year.

Mrs Richardson stayed for nine years, assisted during that time by Mrs Ayres in the Infants' classroom, leaving eventually in 1940 to become head teacher at Kimble (after which Mrs Irene Lewis took charge until 1949).

Mrs Richardson was very different in her approach to life from Mrs Dudley: she was married with a four year-old daughter for whom she immediately hired a young fifteen year-old girl from the village (Eveline Young) as a nanny; within six months she was to become pregnant with her second child, taking just ten weeks off work before resuming her duties; and, throughout her time at the school, she was often away on professional courses to further her career. Her younger daughter, Valerie, reflects on her mother's determination:

"Looking back on things, I realise that my mother must have been quite progressive to go back to work just a month after I was born. She always wanted to better herself and getting that job at North Marston was an achievement. She had put herself through college and, to get the money to do so, had played the piano in 'silent movie' cinemas during the 1920s!"

Mrs Richardson was provided with a "School House" at 14 Schorne Lane which had just been newly built by the council (though still without any mains water).

Mrs Dorothy Richardson

The School House at 14 Schorne Lane

By all accounts, Mrs Richardson was very strict but, as Robin Harwood recalls:

"Mrs Richardson found it hard to control us boys. She used to keep her cane in a tank of rain water round the side of the school. Someone (not me) cut the cane up with a penknife but I got the blame for it."

School Days

Although in many ways forward thinking for her time, Mrs Richardson was, nevertheless, obliged to continue very much with the curriculum and methods already set out by the Education Committee, though it is interesting to note that, soon after her arrival, she wrote:

"The lessons marked on the timetable were reversed to enable the Senior Boys to make a Doll's House with the help of the Headmistress' husband."

Regular, rigorous Inspections were made by outside parties of the Teaching of Drill, Handwork, Cookery, Needlework and Music; and there remained the annual Diocesan Inspection (still as detailed as ever) as well as the visit by Her Majesty`s Inspector who wrote in December 1936:

"Under the present Headmistress the satisfactory standard of conduct and attainment which is usual at this school is being very well maintained. The children are sturdy and vigorous bodily and are mentally alert, though there is a sharp contrast between the willing and accurate response of the boys and the extreme diffidence of all but a few of the girls."

Arithmetic, Composition, History, Geography, Art and Reading remained core subjects and the older girls travelled to Aylesbury every Tuesday for a Domestic Science Course. Scholarship examinations continued to be taken for Aylesbury Grammar School and Wolverton Technical School, where success often resulted in a fee-paying place being awarded. In 1945 the school closed for the day when these exams took place even though they were being held in High Wycombe and Wolverton.

It is interesting to note that from the 1930s onwards, fewer 'days off' were awarded to the children than in the previous decades. Royal events such as the funeral of George V and the Silver Wedding of George VI and Queen Elizabeth plus some religious festivals (Ascension Day and Ash Wednesday) still warranted a day's closure, as did a school outing or a special celebration such as VE Day. However, since the opening of the Memorial Hall in 1924 the school premises were not in such high demand.

The events of the agricultural year still impacted on the villagers during this time as shown by the following entry in the Log book in July 1934:

"So many children want to take teas to the men in the hayfields and wish to leave early that the managers have decided the afternoon session should close at 3.30pm until the hay harvest is over." (School usually closed at 4.00pm)

The children's health continued to be monitored regularly during the 1930s and 1940s. The school doctor and dentist visited at least once a year and the nurse every four months. The Infants' classroom would often be set aside as a 'surgery' on such visits, thus disrupting the day's timetable!

School Premises and Innovations

The School Log Books from 1931 to 1949 read, in some ways, exactly as those from earlier times when it came to problems with the fabric of the building and the facilities: the old coke stoves were still *"smoking very badly"* in 1943 and as for the lavatories...!

On 16th June 1938, Mrs Richardson wrote that *"the offensive condition of the lavatories has been reported to the Correspondent."* Action was in fact taken the very next day as she recorded that a bottle of disinfectant had been received!

The problem of emptying the lavatories became very acute in 1943 and 1944 when they were sometimes not emptied for two weeks at a time. Both Robin Harwood and Chris Holden, who were pupils in those days, remember these old outside privies and in the 1930s it was evidently the job of "Barthie the Sweep" to do the emptying when Lily Young the caretaker notified him that they were full.

The structure of these outside privies appeared to lead to much mischief as Robin Harwood relates:

"Sam Lambourne wanted to sting Dorothy Walker's bottom as she sat on the outside privy (you could creep up behind) but he stung Mrs Ayres the Infants' teacher instead!"

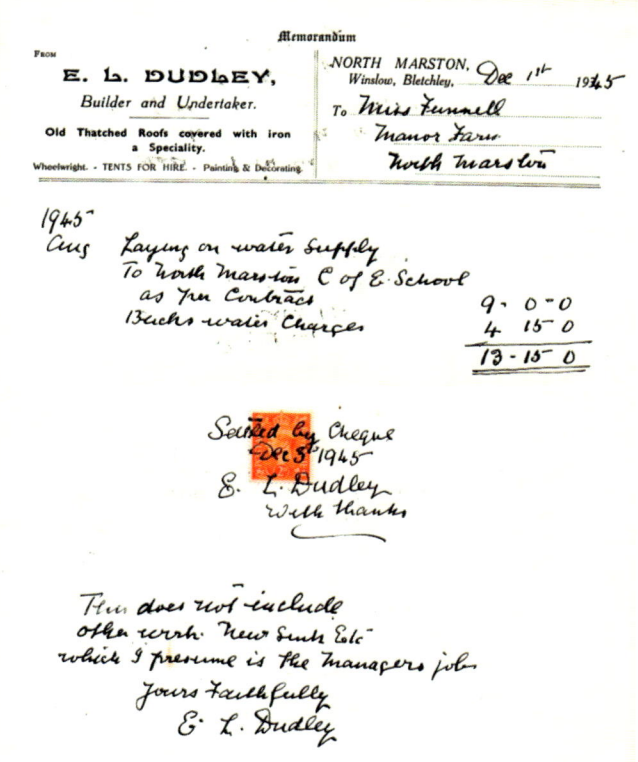

Invoice, dated 1945, from Ted Dudley for laying on the school's water supply

At last in 1945, a water supply was finally laid on to the school by Ted Dudley, the village builder (*see invoice on previous page*) but this did not extend to flush toilets which were not introduced until August 1959. Mr Dudley sent his invoice for £13 15s directly to the headmistress, Miss Funnell (who appeared to be lodging at Manor Farm at the time). The new water supply was paid for out of the school's Gardening Fund and School Fund.

North Marston School benefited from several other innovations in the 1930s and 40s. In January 1938 electricity was connected for the first time, paid for from the Electricity Fund which had raised money at various school social events. In May of that year a wireless was also installed, the children tuning in on the first day to the "BBC singers" and "The Opening of the Empire Exhibition at Glasgow".

In 1945 plans were afoot to supply hot meals to the school, though these did not actually materialise until January 1949 when they were brought from Whitchurch by Mr Luker.

During the Second World War

Surprisingly, the first reference to a possible future conflict was made in the school's Log Book in September 1938 when Mrs Richardson reported that the vicar from Granborough *"called at the school today and fitted teachers and children with gas masks"*.

North Marston School was affected greatly by the onset of World War Two in September 1939, mainly due to the large numbers of evacuees from London who were suddenly billeted in the village (*see Chapter Twenty-three*).

Fifty new pupils arrived in September 1939, accompanied by a Miss Gibbs of North Paddington Central School. With a pupil roll suddenly totalling ninety, space inside the building was at a premium and extra furniture was borrowed from places such as the Village Hall. The head teacher reported: *"Timetable and syllabus not followed – the main object of the week being to discover what the children can do."*

By November some evacuees returned to London as, no German bombs having yet been dropped on the city, it was considered safe to do so. Miss Gibbs was loaned to Oving School. However in October 1940, due to the Blitz, forty evacuees came back to the village and one hundred pupils were recorded on roll! Mrs Richardson wrote:

"It is impossible to teach adequately. The number of children in the Head Teacher's charge is 70, ranging from young children of 7 years of age to boys and girls of 13 years of age."

Mrs Ayres, the Infants' teacher taught the other thirty. According to the Admissions Register, some of the little ones evacuated from their homes were only four and five years old.

With large numbers of evacuee children living in North Marston, the school teachers took it in turns to organise activities *"of a recreational nature"* during school holidays, an average of twenty-three pupils attending each day.

During the height of this crisis, Mrs Richardson took up her new post at Great Kimble School and Mrs Lewis, the newly appointed head teacher, arrived along with an extra teacher, Miss Payne, from West Ham.

In 1944, the decision was taken to close Granborough School and on 3rd July 1944, fifteen pupils from there (of whom thirteen were evacuees) joined North Marston.

Tommy Gray who was evacuated to North Marston from London in 1941

Evacuees, varying in number, attended North Marston School during the duration of the war, the last one returning to London in July 1945, though some, such as Tommy Gray (*pictured in 2011 on previous page*) and his family, remained in the area for the rest of their lives.

As soon as war had been declared, the school gardens became very active (as in World War One) to support the "Dig for Victory" Campaign. A former pupil, Clifford Cheshire, remembers the extensive area of gardens which were cultivated and says:

"We seemed to do an awful lot of digging."

In October, ten hoes, five spades and four forks were delivered to the school and in April 1940 three hundred-weight of seed potatoes were received.

Growing vegetables was not the only activity carried out by the school to support the war effort: in May 1941 War Weapons Week saw the pupils raise £5 2s 6d at a rummage sale in aid of the Spitfire Fund; in February 1942 Washing Week raised £223 2s 6d which was put into the school's National Savings; Wings for Victory Week in June 1942 realised £166 6s; and in May 1944 Salute the Soldier Week raised the staggering total of £628 from the school's programme of events which included a Doll and Flower Show, a Pet Show, Sports and Fancy Dress.

Blackberrying (which had caused earlier head teachers such anguish when pupils played truant) was now positively encouraged. In late 1941 all the pupils, including the Infants, were given a total of five afternoons off school to pick blackberries to raise money.

In May 1941 Mrs Lewis wrote:

"The Milk Scheme is commenced in the school. Mr Gould, North Marston, is the supplier. Thirty-six children are taking one-third of a pint each at the cost of one half-penny per day."

At the beginning, the milk would have been ladled out of a large container using a measure; one-third of a pint milk *bottles* were introduced many years later in September 1949.

---------------- 1950-1965 ----------------

School fancy dress parade in the playground on Coronation Day 1953

Miss Sheila Ingram's Years

At the start of 1950 there were thirty-eight pupils on roll. During the 1960s the number increased and totalled seventy-four by 1965. Having arrived in September 1949 simply to cover as Temporary Head Teacher, Miss Sheila Ingram, who resided in Winslow, was in fact to stay on as headmistress of North Marston School until December 1965. As with all the head teachers who had preceded her, Miss Ingram taught the junior pupils (aged seven to eleven years) together in the "Big Room". It was not until 1963 that a folding partition was installed to enable the younger juniors to be taught separately.

Miss Ingram and pupils in 1949

L-R Front row: Simon Carter, Raymond Clark, David Holden, Keith Franklin, Rosemary Woodford (behind) Colin Hunt, Jim Tattam, Barry Heritage, David Keys; **L-R Second row**: Janet Gowin, Martin Newman, Fiona Batson, Ann Newman, Jennifer Harwood, Pat Hall, Barbara Sargest, Fay Linnell, Claire Eilfort, Alan Butt, Jean Hall; **L-R Third row**: Gillian Elmer, June Harwood, Monica Butt, Barbara Geall, Tony Franklin, Jennifer Howlett, Margaret Keen, Kathleen Tattam, Valerie Norwood; **L-R Back row**: John Clarke, Poppet Brazier, Jean Trentham, Margaret Carter, Bligh Barnes, Carol Butt, Henny Eilfort, Edith Clark, Peter Newell

School Pupils in 1958

L-R Front row: Roy Tattam, Malcolm Newman, Philip Goodsell, Trevor Bonsor, Gillian Price, Ann Rawlings **L-R Second row**: Linda Harwood, William Daubney, Nicola Carter, Terence Holden, Josephine Lawes, Lynette Driver, Arthur Smith, Ann Russell, Philip Brazier, Susan Linnell, Robert Ayres, Janet Ecob **L-R Third row**: Shirley Barton, Jean Daubney, Linda Hilsdon, Diana Brazier, Michael Dench, Julie Packham, Valerie Henley, Neil Bevan, Susan Griffin, Deidre Batson **L-R Back row**: Clara Rose, Steven Lamb, Paul Young, Alan Dench, Patrick Lawes, Peter Russell, David Smith, Christopher Driver, Michael Laws, Susan Goodsell

Susan Chaplin (nee Parker) remembers her school lessons from the early 1960s:

"Every morning we would spend an hour and a half before and after playtime on Composition and Arithmetic including long division of the following: pounds, shillings and pence; tons, hundredweights, quarters, stones; miles, furlongs and chains; and bushels, pecks and gallons. Miss Ingram would mark all this work thoroughly with each individual at her desk every lesson. No spelling, grammar or computation mistakes went unnoticed! And, of course, when we were seven years old we all wrote with a fountain pen.* In the afternoons there would be knitting and sewing (we made shift dresses and skirts with elasticated waists – all the rage!) and Miss Ingram was terribly proud of the new sewing cabinet she had been allowed to buy for the school."

*In 1953, Miss Ingram was the first head teacher ever to use 'biro' instead of a fountain pen when filling in the school's Log Book.

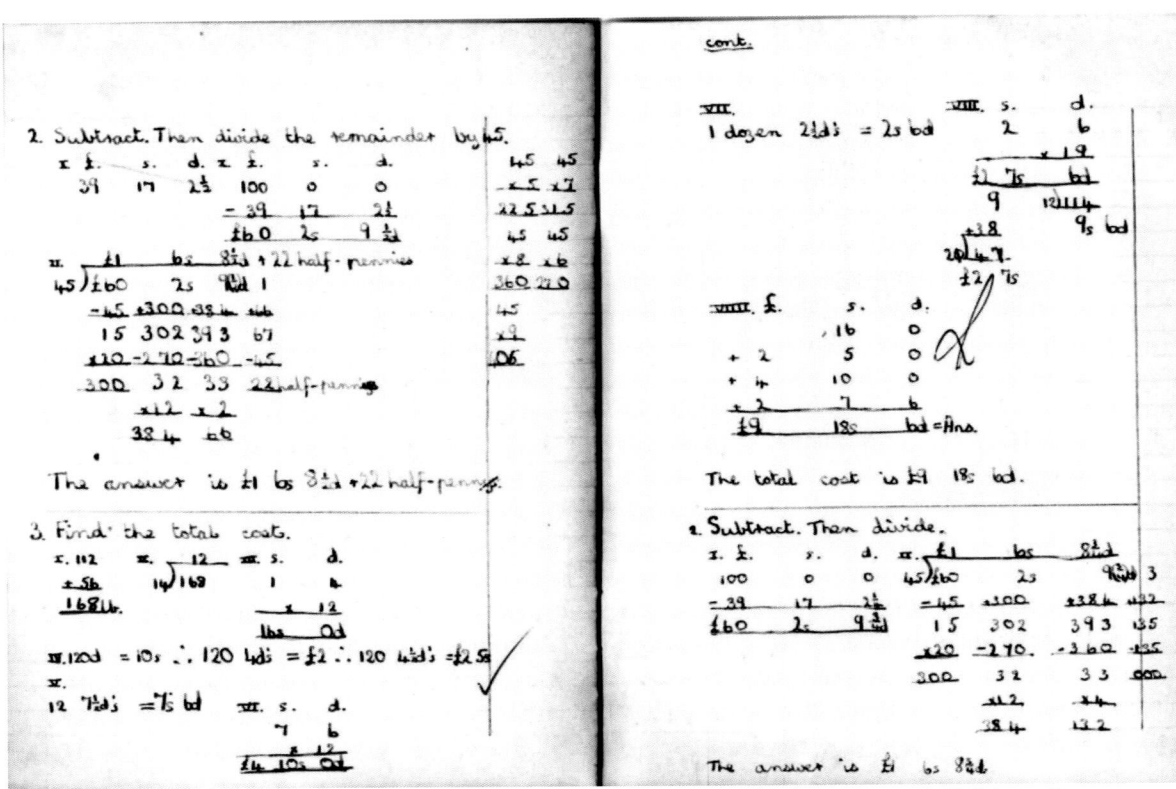
A nine-year old pupil's arithmetic book in 1963 showing long multiplication and division of money

There was not a great deal of organised sport but in the 1960s PE lessons took place with black rubber mats and a spring-board. In the summer the Claydon District Sports were attended.

In 1958 a large metal climbing frame was installed on the tarmac playground and there were no restrictions on its use. Two former pupils at that time recall:

"In the school playground was a climbing frame on hard concrete and I remember thinking as a child how high it was, but in later life wondered what all the fuss was about! It had three bars – low, medium and high – and we could go on this totally unsupervised: there were no playground monitors in those days. After all we were country children and were used to falling out of trees. No-one 'carted' us to school then either; we walked there ourselves." (Robert Gurney)

"Favourite games for the girls at playtimes were hula-hooping and skipping with a long rope held by a person at each end. The school field (on which the new school was eventually built) had gardens which were all tended in the summer. In the winter the heap of mud on the other side of the field by the wall next to Church House would freeze over and it would make the most fantastic slide. We often crashed into the wall to stop! There were also lots of 'Nature Walks' and every summer an outing in Bill French's coach (from Winslow)." (Susan Chaplin nee Parker)

Miss Ingram was a very good pianist, accompanying the hymns at the daily morning assembly in the Big Room, and in 1958 she was delighted to receive an amplifier and speaker for the wireless set so that the BBC music programmes (such as *Singing Together*) could be enjoyed. Other radio programmes also became a regular feature of lessons and the radio could even be plugged through to the Infants for them to do their *Music and Movement* – progress indeed!

Pamphlets of radio programmes from the 1960s

Religious Education continued to be taught and, whilst rigorous examination of pupils no longer took place as in the past, prizes were still awarded for knowledge of the Scriptures. Both Jennifer Heffer (nee Harwood) and Susan Cobbold (nee Linnell) recall winning the Bishop's Prize. In 1954 Jennifer received a Book of Common Prayer and in 1963 Susan was given a New Testament Bible.

At the end of each school year certificates would be awarded for all subjects as well as for Attendance. Jennifer Harwood attended school for five years between 1950 and 1954 without missing a single day (*see certificate below*).

Miss Ingram finally retired from teaching in December 1965.

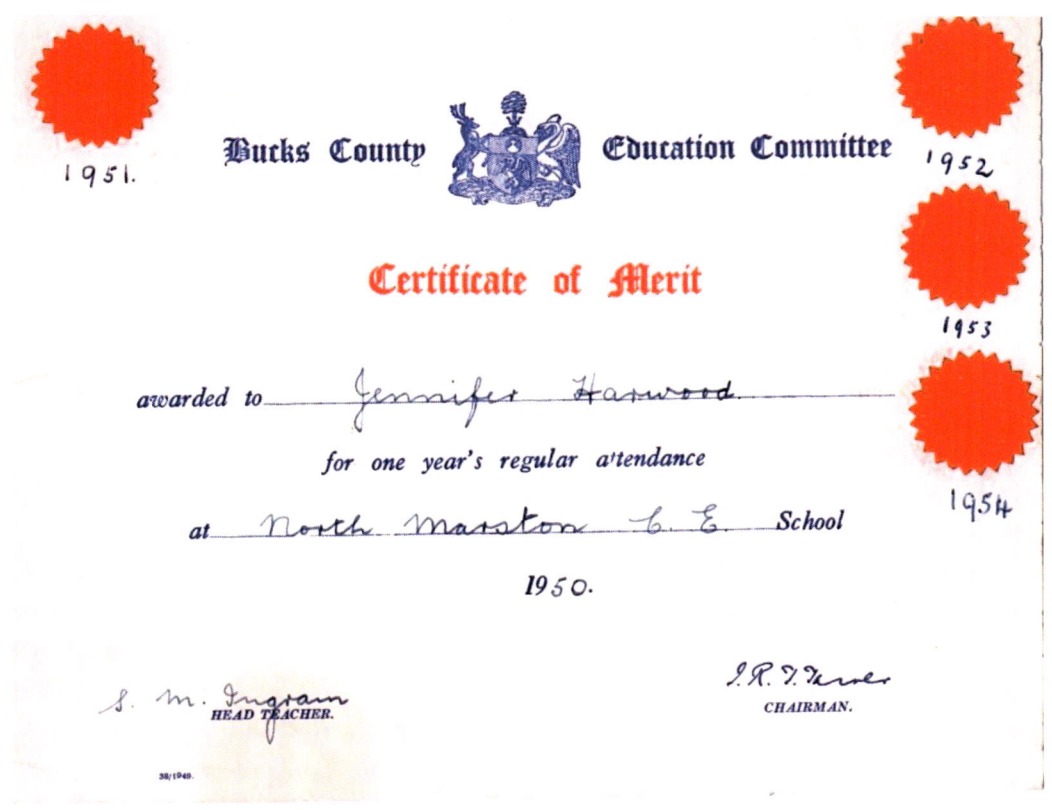

Miss Ingram with the top year group in July 1965 **L-R Front row**: *Roy Tattam, Ann Holden, Miss Ingram, Susan Parker, Janet Linnell* **L-R Back row**: *Hugh Bevan, Robert Mansfield, Malcolm Newman, Robert Gurney, Richard Jacobs*

Mrs Dora Ayres and Mrs Yvonne White

As already mentioned, Mrs Dora Ayres had joined North Marston School (as a young Miss Dora Holden) in 1917 and she continued to teach the Infants until 1959, when she retired after forty-two years unbroken service. She would have taught three generations of the same families during her time at the village school, and she also took the church Sunday school for many years.

Mrs Yvonne White, on her arrival in September 1959, only intended staying for a week as temporary cover in the Infants' class but ended up leaving twenty years later in 1979! She and Miss Ingram would travel to and from school on Bill French's coach from Winslow, picking up the Granborough children en route. The pupils were dropped off and collected outside The Bell (now The Pilgrim). Mrs White set about trying to cheer up what she considered to be gloomy surroundings by getting the walls painted yellow, sticking up artwork with sellotape (as there were no pinboards in those days) and making a Wendy House. She used successful traditional methods in her teaching of reading and arithmetic, totally disapproving of "new-fangled ways".

Mrs Yvonne White

Mrs Dora Ayres on her retirement

The Janet and John Reading Scheme from the 1950s and 1960s

An example of the text from the Janet and John books

Mrs White had a wonderful sense of humour and in 2011, aged over ninety, she still remembered the funny side of life at North Marston School:

"One particular child joined my class and was uncontrollable! At the end of the first day when her mother came to pick her up she asked me how she'd got on. When I told her how awful she'd been her mother replied, 'Well, she has picked up bad habits quickly!'"

Miss Constance Chapman

In 1963, Miss Constance Chapman (also from Winslow) was employed to teach the younger Juniors after the installation of the partition across the 'Big Room'. This was the first time the pupils had ever been divided into three classes. She chose to drive *herself* to school in her Riley Elf– quite an innovation!

Stoves, Milk and Bloomers

It is quite amazing that, given the numerous complaints about the school stoves by all the headteachers over the years, one of the last entries made by Miss Ingram in the Log Book before her retirement in 1965 read:

"The fumes from the coke stove in the Infants Room were so bad that the room could not be used and the children of this class were sent home."

Most pupils remember being warned to stay off the piles of coke outside the far end of the building. The original open fire in the Infants Room in the early 1950s was the subject of the following amusing anecdote from Rosemary Woodford:

"School days came and Infants were taught by the truly gifted Dora Ayres. In the winter our break-time milk would be arranged around the fire to thaw, a soggy coat or two steaming on the guard. Mrs Ayres would gravitate from her desk until she was backed up to the fireguard; then she would carefully gather up her skirt until her voluminous pink 'directoires' (bloomers) were exposed to the maximum heat effect."

Some of the most common memories of past pupils, such as Susan Cobbold, relate to the school milk:

"Every day we were given milk to drink in one-third pint bottles and in the winter it would be frozen solid, so it was brought in and stood next to the coke stoves to thaw out and it was awful! I'd rather have drunk it frozen!

School Dinners

Although many of the village children in the early 1950s still went home for lunch, about twenty-five stayed at school for their meal. It was becoming quite clear, however that the school premises were rather inadequate for this purpose and in 1953 Her Majesty's Inspector highlighted the need for basins to be provided so that the children could wash their hands before lunch and the plates could be warmed in them during the season when the stoves were not alight. She also went on to say:

"The water heater which stands in the cloakroom, also used as a scullery, is a potential source of danger. It would be wise to shield it from the children."

This cloakroom stood between the two classrooms and, from it, food was served through a hatch into Miss Chapman's classroom where the children ate, causing Miss Chapman to complain constantly about the invasive smell of cabbage!

Since 1949 when school meals were first introduced, Mrs Kathleen Lambourne had worked from mid-day, preparing the tables for lunch (often to Miss Chapman's great annoyance as she would start 'clattering about' before the lessons had finished!) and then serving the food and clearing away afterwards. Mrs Lambourne was to remain in this post until 1968.

Mrs Kathleen Lambourne

The caretaker at this time was Miss Violet Carter and a big dispute arose when Miss Carter accused Mrs Lambourne of not cleaning *her* side of the cloakroom. The outcome was that, during the school holidays, Miss Carter painted a black line down the middle of the cloakroom to show where she thought Mrs Lambourne's responsibility for cleaning finished. Miss Ingram could not believe her eyes but the line stayed and, from then on, both ladies cleaned *to* the line but the line *itself* was never touched and gathered dust as years went by! Violet Carter continued to work as the school caretaker until she was eighty years old.

Miss Violet Carter

Renovations before Final Closure

By the mid fifties North Marston School was in need of much renovation and in 1957 architects visited with a view to building an extension. Nothing was to come of this, however.

During August 1959 there was one very major improvement to the facilities as Miss Ingram reported: *"During the summer holiday water-borne sanitation was installed in the existing out-buildings"* – the first flush lavatories!

One other big development was the installation of the telephone in September 1960 with the number "North Marston 286".

Very little else in the way of renovation was ever carried out in the old school building.

1965-1968

Mr John Aldridge

After Miss Ingram's departure, the new headmaster, John Aldridge, took up his post in January 1966 (the first male head teacher since 1907) and two years later he was to oversee the transition of the village school into its new premises.

On 17th April 1967 the builders moved onto the school field which was the site for the new school.

The next eighteen months were very difficult for staff and pupils alike, the noise and the mud adding to the existing restraints of the old premises. Her Majesty's Inspector wrote in June 1967:

"The 73 children work in three rooms with total floor space of less than 1,300 square feet. There is not a single window set low enough for any child to see the world outside. Overflow classes are taught in a small kitchen smelling heavily of rotting wood, with a descant from a plumbing system so noisy that there is a ban on using the lavatories when medical inspections are held in this room."

In order to reach the outside lavatories the Infants had to walk across a plank over a large trench which had been dug alongside the old school walls. Mrs White had to leave her class to escort each child across the plank then wait for them to come back!

In May 1968 John Aldridge reported that, as the temperature in the Infants' classroom was only forty-seven degrees, he had gathered some wood together and lit a fire in the old stove!

Finally, in September 1968, the new school opened: it had its own kitchen (with Mrs Bevan in charge assisted by Mrs Louie Price); Mrs Hall was the playground supervisor; new gymnasium equipment was provided for the first time; there were bright, airy classrooms; but above all, **it had inside lavatories and no coke stoves!**

The old school prior to its demolition in September 1968 with the new school just visible on the right

The new school nearing completion in 1968

The photos on the following page show headmaster, John Aldridge, and class teacher, Miss Garton, with their classes in 1971, a few years after the school opened.

The 'new' North Marston School continues to flourish and has itself seen many changes and renovations over the years..... but that is another story.

Classes of schoolchildren in 1971 with Mr Aldridge (top) and Miss Garton (bottom) outside the new school building

Twenty-six
GYPSIES ON THE DOORSTEP
John Spargo

Introduction

Until recent times, and for generations before that, the north Buckinghamshire village of North Marston had a gypsy encampment on its parish boundary. Over the centuries the two communities co-existed. The gravestone of a *King of the Gypsies* stands to this day at the side of the lane leading to the village, the lane itself once known as Gypsy Lane.

Why did the Romanies choose North Marston in the first place? What was it that drew them to establish a base here from which, as musicians and itinerate tradesmen, they travelled throughout the Midlands?

"Gypsies on the Doorstep" offers an intriguing proposition that North Marston has had vagrants living on its doorstep for longer than people might have realised.

Hogshaw

Originally called *Hocsaga* (signifying marshy or sedgy ground) Hogshaw was a Saxon village encompassing about one thousand acres and working the open fields that surrounded a small settlement comprising numerous dwellings and the church of St John the Baptist. However, the most significant feature of Hogshaw was that it was the site of a commandery of the *Knights Hospitallers*.

Knights Hospitallers

The Order of St John of Jerusalem, otherwise known as the Knights Hospitallers, was founded in the early eleventh century bound by oath to serve pilgrims and other travellers during the crusades in Jerusalem. They prospered through gifts and became well established throughout England. When the Knights Templar order fell into disgrace in the early 1300s the Hospitallers gained many of their possessions.

In addition to a number of hospitals across the country (essentially these were hostels and places of rest for pilgrims and travellers) the Order also had commanderies such as the one at Hogshaw. Their function was as a "branch house" to manage income-generating estates, through labouring tenants, on behalf of the Order. The commandery controlled the land and churches gifted to them by wealthy benefactors, and was originally endowed with the churches of Cholesbury, Hogshaw, Oving, Addington, Creslow and Ludgershall. Later acquisitions included the churches at Quainton and North Marston.

The commandery of Hogshaw was probably founded during the reign of Henry II (1133-1189) on lands given by a local baron but the income from its estates and churches never achieved great wealth. According to the *Victoria County History*:

"The commandery was never an important one. There was a survey taken of its lands, income, expenses, etc. in 1338 when there was a preceptor in residence with one other knight. It had then all the ordinary accessories of a small monastery: a court, garden, mill and dove house, with arable land and pastures attached. The chaplain serving Hogshaw Church, with the chaplain who served the house, and a certain Thomas Fitz Neel, who held a knight's corrody, sat at table with the preceptor and his brother. There were the usual servants in the house, an attendant squire, a porter, a cook, a pistor, and two grooms for the preceptor."

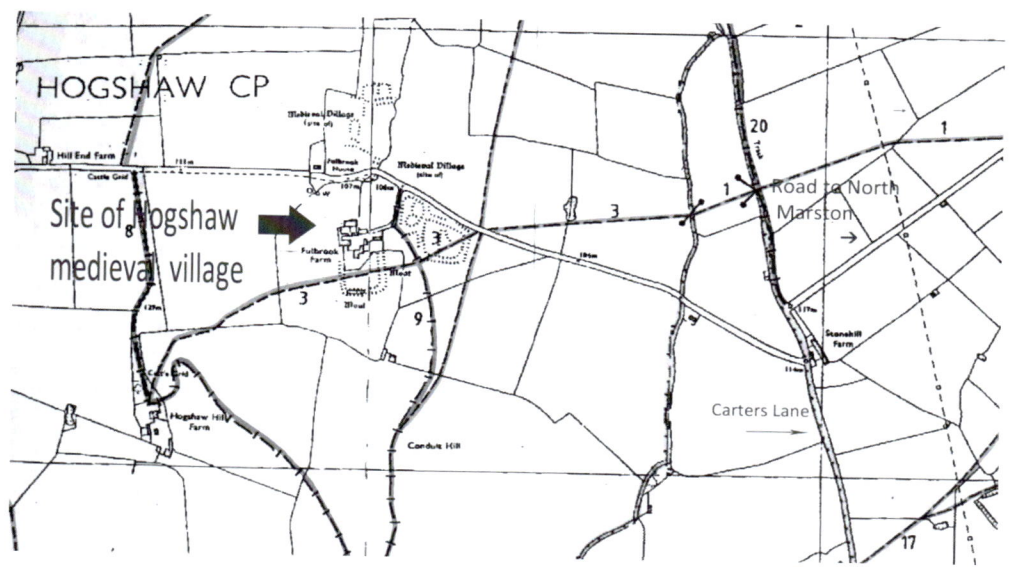

Modern maps showing the site of the medieval village of Hogshaw straggling Steart Lane at Fulbrook Farm

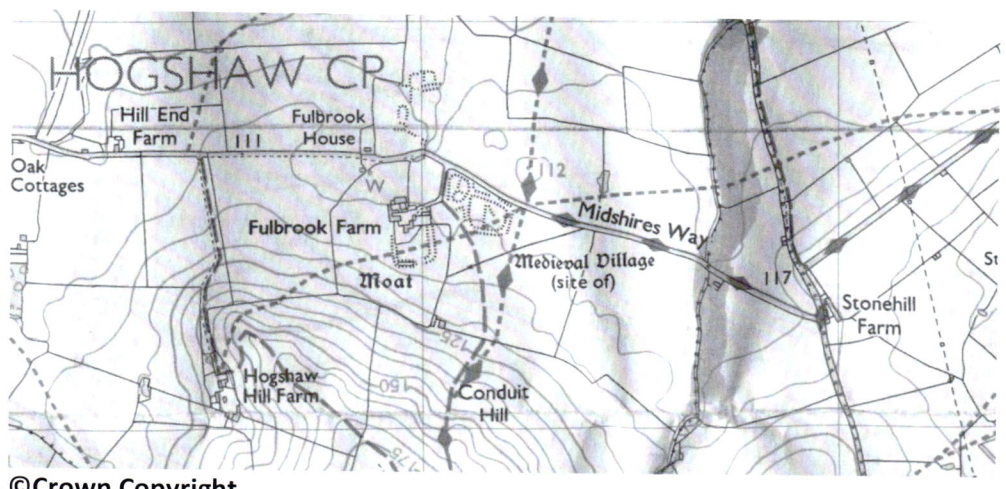

©Crown Copyright

By the late fifteenth century, and struggling to generate an income, the commandery decided to turn their land over to sheep; the booming wool trade was far more lucrative than arable farming on the poor quality soil at Hogshaw. Wool had become the backbone and driving force of the medieval English economy between the late thirteenth century and late fifteenth century.

Unfortunately for the tenants at Hogshaw, this shift to pastural farming required the enclosure of the village and its open fields and, furthermore, the order no longer needed as many labouring tenants.

The Hospitallers undertook the wholesale clearance of Hogshaw between 1485 and 1517. They enclosed three hundred and ninety acres of arable land and five hundred and sixty-nine acres of pasture all surrounded with a ditch, part of which remains visible to this day. Some of the evicted tenants may have joined the bands of displaced vagrants roaming the countryside to the great consternation of local settlements. But many will have remained very close by, clustered in a small vagrant community on the border between Hogshaw and North Marston.

Why did the evicted villagers stay close by?

The main reason for villagers wanting to stay in the area was likely to have been associated with a sense of belonging and a deep-rooted attachment to the church and the community around it. The village of Hogshaw had been home to them and their ancestors since Saxon times. It was the place of the birth, marriage and where hundreds of their forebears were buried.

It is probable the villagers would have salvaged what building materials and domestic goods they could from their former dwellings to create and furnish make-shift shelters; this meant they had to find somewhere not too far away to carry their material.

The commandery would have continued to need a few labourers from those who knew the land; it was advantageous for the able-bodied to stay close so as to be available for work. Generations of inter-marriages with neighbouring communities will have created familial ties with North Marston, Pitchcott, Oving, Granborough, East Claydon and Quainton so there were family-related reasons to remain in the area.

Records show Hogshaw church remained a place of worship until 1650. It was in decay when surveyed in 1636 and, although the ruined church building was destroyed in the English Civil War by the regicide Cornelius Holland, people were still being buried at Hogshaw up to the year 1683. The former parish of Hogshaw was consolidated with that of East Claydon.

Where would the displaced Hogshaw residents have gone?

On Hogshaw's eastern boundary with North Marston is a Roman road, (now known as Carters Lane) for centuries used as a drovers' road on which cattle were driven south from Buckingham to Aylesbury and which cut through an area of common land marked on maps as *North Marston Common*. This Common ran from the site of the present Stonehill Farm (which was formerly a cattle-drovers' hostel) and extended southwards down Carters Lane to the Quainton boundary. Sited a couple of miles from other settlements such as Pitchcott, North Marston and Quainton, and so not infringing any of them, a vagrant community established near the road as it cut through the common would have been within walking distance of Hogshaw church. It would also have been close enough to the abandoned village to enable the transport of domestic goods, livestock and salvaged material.

The vagrant community lay within the North Marston parish, probably only a short distance south of the present Stonehill Farm, from where the evicted residents may have been able to see Hogshaw church, just over a mile away across the pasture to the west. Unlike the visible indications of building

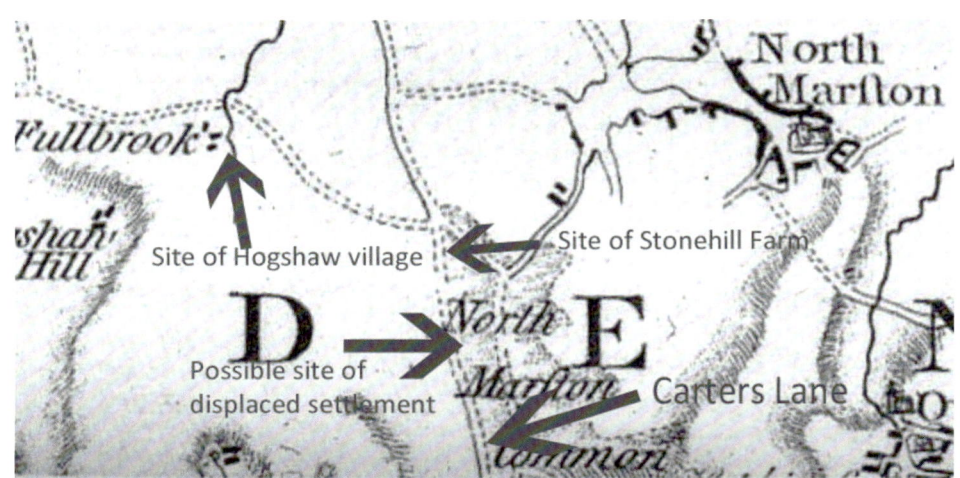

A map drawn in 1760 showing North Marston Common which stretched south along the side of Carters Lane

foundations and roadways (which can still be seen at the site of the medieval village of Hogshaw) this make-shift settlement left no discernable traces on the landscape; this is no wonder as, since then, the common has been enclosed and farmed for two hundred and thirty-five years.

The evicted villagers would not have been welcomed by neighbouring settlements, themselves struggling with poverty. North Marston, for years a centre of pilgrimage, was witnessing a dip in its fortunes following the removal of John Schorne's relics and lucrative shrine to Windsor in 1478. Attitudes to paupers were hostile so it would have been safer for those evicted from Hogshaw to remain as a self-supporting, isolated community rather than fall prey to the harsh penalties for *vagrancy*.

Vagrancy and the Law

Vagrants had always been perceived as a major social and economic problem leading to a series of statutes designed to deter and control vagrancy in the years following the Black Death.

In 1495, and during the period of eviction from Hogshaw, a draconian statute was passed that stated:

"Vagabonds, idle and suspected persons shall be set in the stocks for three days and three nights and have none other sustenance but bread and water and then shall be put out of Town. Every beggar suitable to work shall resort to the Hundred where he last dwelled, is best known, or was born and there remain upon the pain aforesaid."

The homeless villagers would not have been prepared to run the risk of falling foul of this; their sense of isolation would further have been compounded in 1531 when another statute directed that *"....an able-bodied beggar was to be whipped, and sworn to return to the place where he was born, or last dwelt for the space of three years, and there put himself to labour."*

Clearly, there was little incentive for the displaced families to seek charity from neighbouring communities, a situation further compounded in 1547 when a bill was passed *"which subjected vagrants to some of the more extreme provisions of the criminal law, namely two years servitude and branding with a "V" as the penalty for the first offence and death for the second."*

The same legislation also demanded that cattle drovers should have a licence displayed on their left arm, should be over thirty years of age, married, and a respectable householder, presumably as measures against *vagrant* cattle rustlers.

The isolated little community near the drovers' road may have been tolerated because it was a source of itinerant labour and also as it occupied only a small part of a large area of common land on the fringes of the parishes of North Marston, Quainton and Pitchcott.

Doubtless, many of the North Marston "commoners" using the common to graze stock or gather fuel will have empathised with the plight of the small homeless community, some of whom they may have known before their eviction, thinking to themselves "there but for the grace of God..."

Over time, some of the young from the displaced community would have married and moved away, reducing the size of the settlement on the common. However, it is likely this small *community of vagrants* living on the common would eventually have been joined by other itinerants….**Gypsies**.

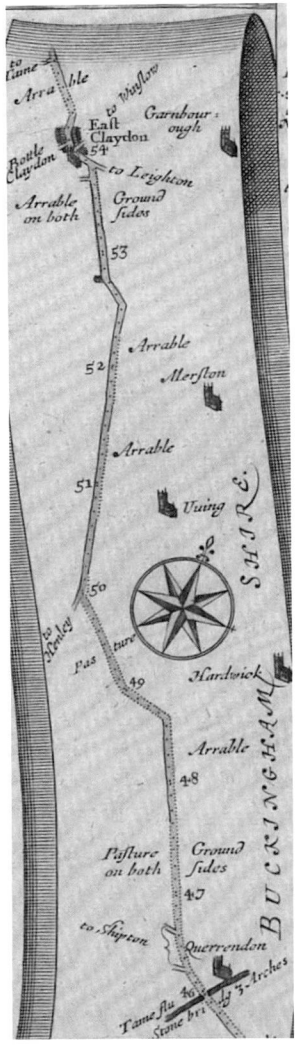

On the left can be seen a section from John Ogilby's Map (London to Buckingham) of 1675 which shows that the main route ran north from Quarrendon, skirted to the west of Oving and North Marston, and passed through East Claydon. This road pre-dates the A421 and A413 and followed the roads which today are known as Carters Lane and Deadman's Lane. This would have been the route taken by cattle drovers heading south from Buckingham to Aylesbury.

The map below dates from 1825 and shows a road to "Fullbrook" called Stewart Lane (now Steart Lane) and the disappearance of North Marston Common.

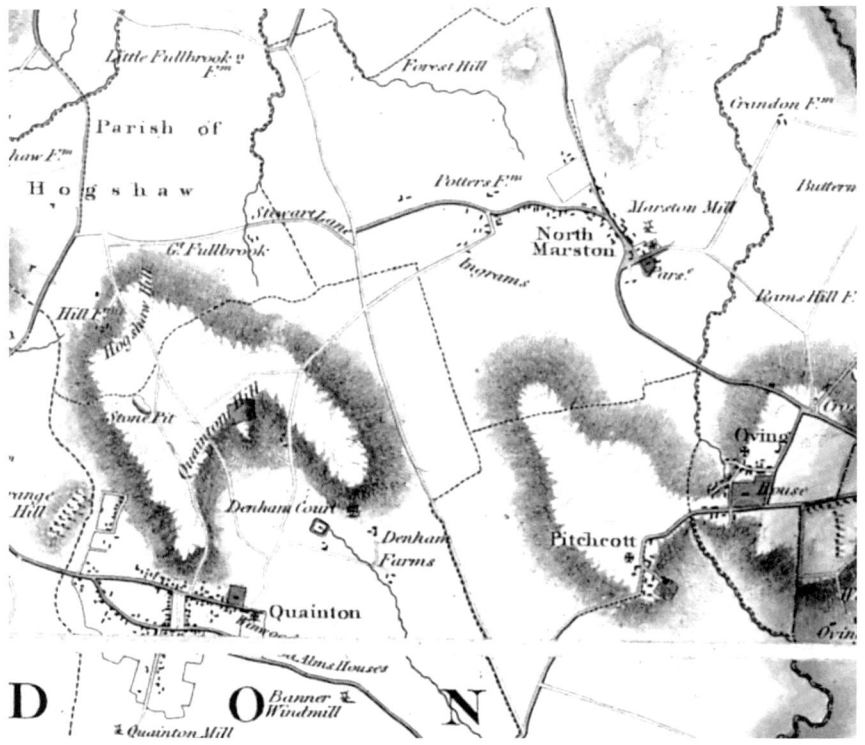

Gypsies

We do not know when people known as *Gypsies* first joined the vagrant community on North Marston Common. They were certainly there by the early 1600s as we have the well-documented story of Edward Bozwell, the so-called *King of the Gypsies*. He is introduced in a very atmospheric way by Alison Uttley in her book about Buckinghamshire published in 1950:

"An old road which the country people call a Roman road, although it is probably an early British track, runs under Quainton Hill to Dedham's Lane or Deadman's Lane. This is Carters Lane, sometimes called Gipsy Lane, a way that is very lonely, a haunted road, as I have been told by people in different parts of the county who know it. It is gipsy land, where the gipsies have lived for generations. Now it is not so easy for them to stay anywhere, but the lane usually has a few of them. They alone know its secrets and they are secluded there. On one side are open fields, bounded by a ditch, and on the other a hedge of trees so rough and wild that until lately the lane was almost hidden and impenetrable. It has been cleared up and changed, but the loneliness remains.

In the ditch among the wild flowers and nettles there stands a large, rough-hewn block of stone, fashioned like a monument, which is said to be the gravestone of the King of the Gipsies who was buried here centuries ago. Scratched deeply in its face is the date 1641. The figure 4 is reversed, in the way a child or illiterate person writes it.

This stone lay in the ditch for many years, known to the country people who always called it the Gipsy's Grave. Recently it has been set upright by the road. Even now it is difficult to find among the deep grasses and thick undergrowth of the tangled lane.

Others have told me of this haunted lane, along which they will not go at night. It was notoriously bad a hundred years ago and dangerous on account of the lawless tribes who lived there."

The *Gypsy* Stone as it became known was later more thoroughly researched by the Quainton historian and former chairman of Quainton Parish Council, the late "Roddy" Rodwell who wrote:

Execution of Quainton's Gypsy King

"Edward Bozwell, a strolling Gypsy and called the King of the Gypsies, was executed on Fryday the 20th[h] March 1640 for Horse Stealing."
Thus reads an entry in the Register of St. Mary's Church, Aylesbury. The gallows were on the Bicester Road, at the corner of Griffin Lane, formerly Gallows Road, before they were removed to County Hall as 'the new drop' in 1740. Bozwell was joined on the scaffold by two other gypsies, Tynimere and Edward Smyth, who were convicted for horse stealing and highway robbery.

At the side of Carters Lane, formerly Gypsy Lane, on the eastern boundary of Quainton parish, is a stone reputed to be that of a gypsy king. It bore a carved crown and an inscription which is now illegible but on old photographs clearly shows the date of burial to be 25 March 1641.

At this time the New Year began on Lady Day, 25th March, according to the Julian calendar, so that 20th March 1640 and 25th March 1641 were just a few days apart. Carter's Lane was traditionally the site of a gypsy encampment, so it would not be unreasonable for the body to be brought there for burial, bearing in mind that as an executed prisoner he could not be buried in the churchyard."

Rodwell's interest in the Gypsy Stone extended to him seeking to have it listed as an ancient monument in 1992, as the following Bucks Herald article of the time reports:

New light is shed on stone's past

A LUMP of stone said to mark the burial place of a one-time King of the Gipsies could become an official ancient monument, following a chance discovery by Quainton Parish Council chairman, Gordon Rodwell.

The stone, which sits on the verge of Carter's Lane, the old Roman road to Hogshaw, had apparently been refused listed monument status a few years ago because there was no documentation to prove how old it was.

But when Mr Rodwell recently went through some old parish papers he discovered a mention of it in 1705.

He said: "I happened to notice that they (the papers) mentioned a turning point near the stone. There is a turning point near the stone so it must have existed in 1705."

Apparently the stone used to sport the date 1642 on its weathered flanks but this has faded away with time.

Over the years gipsies have been seen visiting the stone.

Quainton Parish Council will discuss the possibility of seeking to have the unusual stone listed at its meeting tonight (Thursday).

The original location of the Gypsy Stone is not known for certain. The *current* location lies just inside the parish of Quainton. The fact that Rodwell found reference to the stone in *parish papers* of 1705 (by which we assume he refers to the parish of Quainton) suggests, perhaps, that it was originally placed close to where it stands to this day in the verge of Carters Lane, a short distance north of the entrance to Quainton Dairy and a short distance inside Quainton's parish boundary (*see map below*).

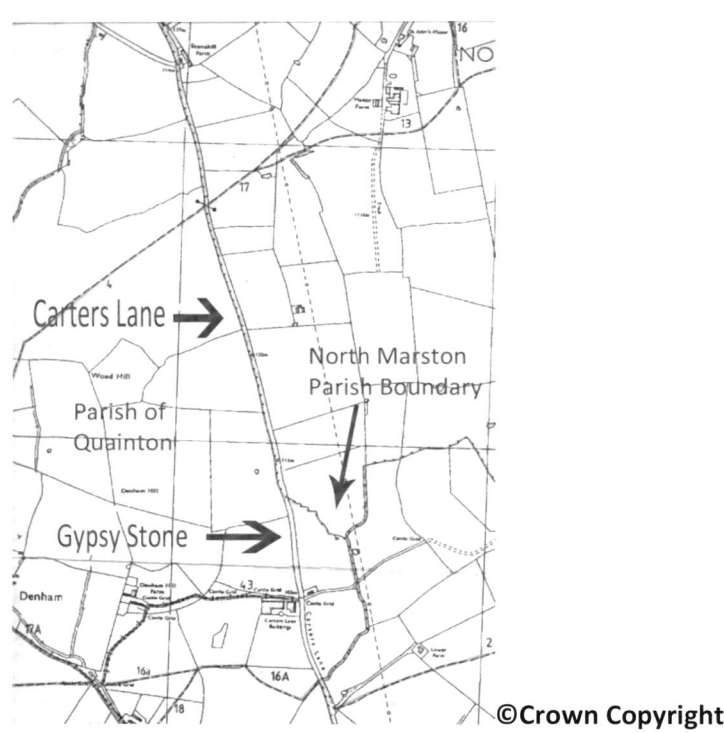

A modern map showing the road-side location of the Gypsy Stone

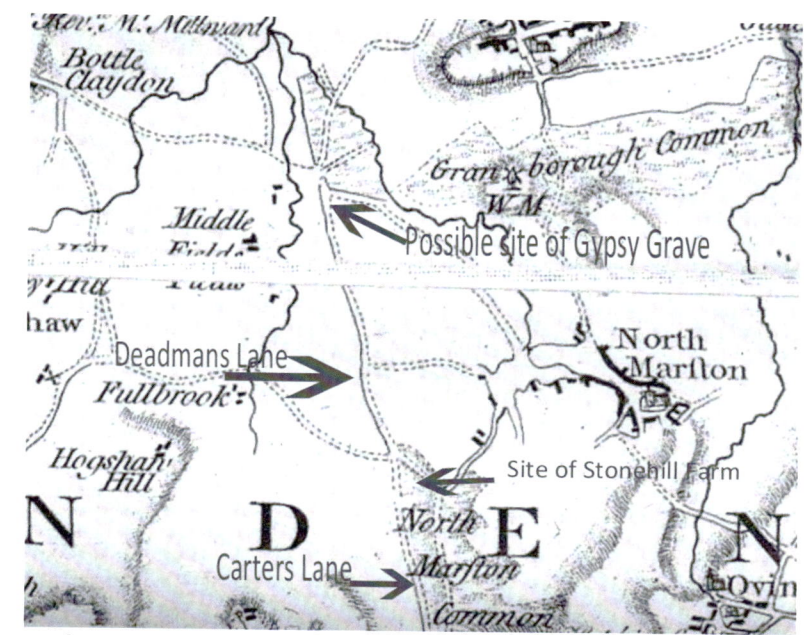
Map of 1760 showing the roads to the north of North Marston Common

However, an *alternative* location is prompted by the fact that beyond Stonehill Farm (where Carters Lane bears sharply to the right towards North Marston) the old road continued northwards and this lane has always been known as *Deadman's Lane* (Uttley referred to it in the earlier passage about the Gypsies). The field at the bottom of Deadman's Lane on the right hand side is known as *Deadman's Ground* and the point where Deadman's Lane meets the Hogshaw Road from Granborough is known as *Deadman's Gate*.

This might be a coincidence or it might indicate the "Gypsy King" might actually have been laid to rest there, within the parish of North Marston and a couple of miles from where the Gypsy Stone now stands. The "turning point" mentioned in the 1705 papers discovered by Roddy Rodwell could have been at the end of Deadman's Lane where the drovers' road forked left and then, shortly after crossing a brook, turned right towards East Claydon (see map from 1760).

To put Edward Bozwell in context: for centuries the Bozwells (or Boswells) were one of England's largest and most important gypsy families. The title *King of the Gypsies* has been claimed or given over the centuries to many different people. It is both culturally and geographically specific. It may be inherited, acquired by acclamation or action, or simply claimed. The extent of the power associated with the title varied; it might be limited to a small group in a specific place, or many people over large areas. Unsurprisingly, for centuries, there have been many examples of Boswells being described as *King of the Gypsies.*

By the time of Bozwell's execution in 1641, *Gypsies* had become widely spread across Britain; in fact the first authenticated records of a gypsy presence go back to 1514 in England.

The English term *Gypsy* (or *Gipsy*) originates from *gypcian*, short for *Egipcien*. It was once believed that the Romanies originated in Egypt. It appears that English-born gypsies were broadly tolerated but immigrant gypsies less so. In 1554 a law was passed which made being an immigrant gypsy a crime punishable by death. In 1596 one hundred and six men and women were condemned to death at York just for being gypsies, but only nine were executed. The others proved they were born in England. Romany gypsies under English statute were given special privileges that other wanderers lacked.

It seems the small gypsy community on the edge of North Marston from which Boswell's followers originated became a fixture, although their exact location in Carters Lane/Gypsy Lane/Deadman's Lane is not known, and indeed it may have moved over the years.

A romanticised view of a gypsy encampment in the 1700s

After the enclosure of North Marston in 1778, the land that had been North Marston Common became part of allocated land-holdings; any residual vagrant community would have had to move or face prosecution. The wide verges of the drovers' road offered a solution and it is reasonable to assume the encampment moved from place to place along the verges, perhaps dictated by the seasons.

The next mention of North Marston gypsies (or *vagrants* as they would have been described in official records) is found in the baptismal records of North Marston church in 1715 where on 13th April Mary, daughter of Mary Davis, *vagrant*, was baptised. In all, there are twelve references to the baptism of children of *vagrants* from 1715 to 1855, and four burials between 1673 and 1735.

To some it might seem strange that an ethnic group now more commonly associated with Catholicism in England should choose to have a child baptised in an Anglican church, but Romanies often adopted the dominant religion of their host country in the event that a ceremony associated with a formal religious institution is necessary, such as a baptism or funeral.

These North Marston "vagrants" were Romanies as is evidenced by the names they chose for their children that included *Jasper*, *Absolom* and *Fido*. These were all children of Thomas and Sarah Smith and research undertaken by their descendants suggests North Marston may be a link into a widespread Smith family inhabiting Buckinghamshire and Northamptonshire. Jasper became known as the *King of the Fiddlers* and died in Banbury in 1838 aged eighty-nine. His death certificate listed his occupation as "Gypsy".

A gypsy fiddler in the late 1700s

Gypsies at a camp in 1895

The gypsy name for smith or farrier, as it is often used in its Romany form, is *Petulengro* (which literally means *"horse-shoe man"*). Throughout the nineteenth century, a romanticized picture of the Romany culture gained popularity. The vicar at North Marston during the latter part of the nineteenth century, Rev Samuel James, had a gypsy god-daughter called Esmerelda Zingara, a wild-spirited girl who, he claimed, was "descended from the Boswells".

Gypsies continued to camp in the area of Gypsy Lane through the nineteenth, twentieth and into the twenty-first century. There are numerous references to gypsies in the oral histories of village residents. They were a source of itinerant labour for local farmers and the competence of the village policemen was sometimes judged by his ability to 'manage' local gypsies. It was an accepted fact that there had *always* been gypsies living on the edge of the parish.

The last North Marston gypsy link was the Smith family who lived in a caravan in Deadman's Lane for over forty years until the death of their patriarch, Ivor, in 2007. When that family ceased to live there, it ended the tradition of vagrants on the parish boundary that I believe can be traced back to the eviction of the Hogshaw villagers over five hundred years ago.

Twenty-seven
A WALK THROUGH THE VILLAGE IN 1901
John Spargo

Hello, my name is Jane Smith. I am seven years of age and I live in North Marston. The house where we live is called Garfield House and my father is the village police constable with the County Constabulary.

Garfield House, the village police house

My family moved here from Marsh Gibbon last year, all except my baby sister Helen, who was born here six months ago. With all of us children and a house to keep clean, my mother is always busy so we often help by running errands, perhaps to one of the village shops, like Mr Baker's or Mr Henley's although our meat, bread, milk and cheese are delivered to the house by Mr Tattam the butcher or Mr Watkins the baker. We have a well in our back-yard so, unlike our neighbours, we don't have to fetch water from the pump in Quainton Road; carrying water is heavy work so we're pleased about that!

A woman fetches water from the pump in Quainton Road

As a policeman, my dad doesn't have a lot of trouble to deal with in the village: perhaps a young man who has had 'one too many' at The Wheatsheaf or The Sportsman, or one of Mr Holden's tailors getting a bit worse for wear in The Bell. There are never any problems at The Armed Yeoman though: the landlord there, Mr Anstiss, won't stand for it.

For most of the time, the village is very quiet. In fact, if you stand in front of my house and listen carefully, you can hear Mr White, the blacksmith, striking horseshoes at the forge at the top of the High Street. There is the occasional cart rattling past: perhaps one of the village carriers like Mr Gregory or Mr Carter, or a coal-cart from Winslow. Some days, sheep and cattle are driven through the village to fresh pasture or to be sold at Winslow Market. In most of the cottage gardens around the village you'll see a few hens and, in one or two, a pig being fattened for winter.

Mr John White, the village blacksmith

Some of the boys and girls in my class are the children of tailors but most of the children's fathers are farmworkers. My best friend is Emily Wilkins and her dad is a tailor; I have another friend called Ella Baker and her dad drives a farm wagon. At certain times of the year, such as haymaking, the school is closed so that village children can help in the fields because North Marston is a farming village.

If I take you for a walk through my village I'll describe to you what we can see.

Let's cross the road from my front gate. Here is Hill Farm that is owned by Mr Anstiss who has six sons. That thatched cottage facing my house belongs to Mr Tattam. His son, Ernest, delivers milk every morning from a little cart and his sister, Nellie, is in my class at school.

Mr Tattam's cottage

The tiny little cottage next door as we walk up the High Street is where Mr Ward lives. It used to be a shop years ago. Mr Ward is a carpenter and makes coffins in his back yard. I've heard that he sometimes takes a nap in one of his coffins!

Next we come to a very grand looking house built of brick and called The Red House. It's where my school-master and mistress (Mr and Mrs Farrar) live.

The Red House

As we walk up the High Street we pass lots of small cottages. Mr Carter lives in that one: he's a carrier and is always taking folk to and from the railway station at Granborough Road. The next house along is The Mill House with the remains of a windmill in the garden which fell down in a bad storm, so they say.

Looking around you, there are many little cottages dotted about, some without an upstairs and all with a thatched roof; if it's sunny you sometimes see women sitting outside their cottages making lace.

Lace-makers outside a cottage in the Granborough Road

There used to be lots of lace-makers in this village but now there are only a few left. Some of the girls at my school know how to make lace and I've seen photographs of girls dressed in lace-makers costume for a school concert.

Schoolchildren dressed up in lace-makers' costume

This bigger house is called Gordon Cottage and it's where the blacksmith, Mr White, lives.

Gordon Cottage

Next to Gordon Cottage is The Bell which is run by Mr and Mrs Garner. Mr Garner is also a boot-maker who makes and mends the boots for the boys at Schorne College that we shall see later. Can you hear the little tapping sound coming from Mr Garner's hammer in his shop?

The Bell Inn with Mr Garner's bootmaker's shop on the right

Now look in front of you at Mr Holden's big building that you can see here at the top of the High Street; it's called Shakespeare House and lots of tailors work there. Mr Holden is rich and very strict and my dad says his young apprentices are scared of him. And, look! If you peep through the open doorway into the court-yard you can see rolls of material being unloaded from a cart for Mr Holden's cutting rooms; soon it will be sewn into trousers or hunting jackets.

The open doorway to the loading yard at Holden's

Walking up the narrow street beside Mr Holden's we come to Mr Cheshire's Post Office. You can hear the clatter of the telegraph machine operated by Jane, Mr Cheshire's daughter. She's probably receiving a message for Mr Holden or for the Vicar. And there's Mr Cheshire's son, Alfred, standing at the Post Office gate, smartly dressed in his post-man's uniform!

Alfred Cheshire

The next cottage along belongs to Tom Cheshire; he's a butcher and slaughter-man. I can see his little son, Clarence, playing in the front garden.

Tom Cheshire

Next we come to Mrs Price's house. It's called Flora Villa, and it's set back from the road with a lovely front garden. It was built by her late husband, Mr John Price; he built many places in the village, including Schorne College, but his son Albert has taken over the business now. The house next door is Yew Tree Cottage and that's where Mr Baker, the shopkeeper, lives.

Yew Tree Cottage at the bottom of School Hill

And now we are standing at the bottom of School Hill leading up to my school, although the vicar, Dr James, says we should call it "College Hill" because of Schorne College which is at the top of the hill, right opposite my school. Most people still call it "School Hill" though, as that's what it has been called for years.

Can you smell fruit and wine? That's coming from Mrs Carter's little cottage at the bottom of School Hill; she makes and sells all sorts of things including shilling bottles of wine. My dad isn't too happy about that but he says there isn't much he can do about it. Mrs Carter's husband works for Rev James, the vicar, and drives his family about in their carriage.

Let's walk up School Hill. It's quite steep isn't it? That cottage on the left is where my friend Alice Buckingham lives. She goes to my school and my Sunday-school. Her dad's a farmer.

And now we've reached my school. It's quite a small building and there are only two class-rooms. But if you look over the road towards the church you can see a much bigger school: this is Schorne College which was built by the vicar, Dr James. Only boys are allowed to go to Schorne College and my dad says there aren't many people who can afford to send their sons there.

Schorne College as seen from the Church

Let's walk down this little footpath that runs alongside the college and the church. Can you see it's brought us out by the church gates?

The church gates and footpath
(Schorne College can be seen just behind to the left)

Over to our left is Glebe Farm where Mr Kibble lives. Doesn't it look smart? It was re-built a few years ago; and on our right is Vine Cottage that Dr James has re-named "The Matronage" as it is where the youngest college boys, or those who are unwell, stay and are looked after by the College Matron.

The Matronage (Vine Cottage)

If we cross the lane we can see the Vicarage down the drive-way. Watch out! There's a horse and carriage coming out of the vicarage gates driven by John Carter. He's wearing a top hat and he's the vicar's groom. The old gentleman sitting in the carriage was Dr James himself, and the thin young woman in black sitting next to him was his daughter, Susan. I expect they're off to visit Dr James's son who is Vicar at Oving. Miss James is in charge of the Sunday school at the church and she also arranges the London Children's Holidays in the village when each year twenty or thirty London children come to North Marston to stay with families. Some of the boys are scallywags and my dad is kept busy while they're here.

Dr Samuel James

We'll walk down Church Street. Look over there and you can see Abbotts Cottage and Camden Villas. Look at those boys sitting on those piles of road-stones.

Boys sitting on road-stones in Church Street

Let's walk down that lane running along past Camden Villas which is called Schorne Lane. A man called John Schorne was a vicar here centuries ago and it is said he performed miracles, including discovering water one day when there was a terrible drought. It was said that the water had miraculous healing powers and people came here from all over the country to be cured, and to drink from his holy well. Some people call Schorne Lane "Well Lane" or "Holy Well Lane".

As we walk down the lane, we come to the Wesleyan Methodist Church where lots of my friends go to Sunday school, but I go to the other chapel down Quainton Road.

The Wesleyan Methodist Church

Then, the next thing we see is the water pump and pump-house. This is where the Holy Well used to be but they had to cover it over after a woman drowned in it. This pump is where everyone in this part of the village gets their water.

The water pump on the site of Schorne's Well

If we turn and walk back to Church Street the big field on our left is called Fuller's Croft. In front of us, on the other side of Church Street is The Armed Yeoman owned by Mr Henry Anstiss.

Mr Henry Anstiss on the steps of the Armed Yeoman

There are some very old buildings in this part of Church Street like Burnaby House and Cromwell Cottage.

Burnaby House and Cromwell Cottage on the left of the picture

Opposite Cromwell Cottage is Bankside. The front gardens are very pretty aren't they?

Church Street with Bankside on the right

If we carry on down Church Street we can see a big house opposite called The Elms where old Mrs Buckingham lives.

The Elms on the left, looking up Church Street

Here are some heavy horses from Marston Fields Farm, coming down Church Street on their way to be shod by Mr White at The Forge. The lead horse has stopped at Winkfield House on the corner. That looks like young Fred Price walking along behind them.

Farm horses outside Winkfield House

We have reached the bottom of Church Street and this is where the High Street becomes Portway. The cottages we can see to the left are called Chapman's Cottages. Jim Chapman is a tailor and he lives there with his wife, Amy, and little son, Harold, who is four years old.

Entering Portway (Oving Road) with Chapman's Cottages on the left

There are one or two little cottages beyond Jim Chapman's, but this is virtually the edge of the village on the road to Oving. However, I'd like to walk a little way along Portway to see if Mr or Mrs Gregory are in their garden as they always have a chat with me if I'm passing. Mr Gregory is a farmer and he has a son called Albert.

Mr & Mrs Gregory in Portway

I'm now going to turn back along Portway and walk towards the High Street.

Portway (Oving Road) looking towards the village (Church Street off to the right)

We soon reach the forge on our right. Can you feel the heat from Mr White's furnace inside? He's getting the horse-shoes ready for those farm horses I expect. Next to the forge is Baker's Stores and Forge Cottage. Look, there's Sarah Rayner the Vicar's housekeeper going into Baker's Stores to buy some groceries. Mr Baker has two young daughters, Emily and Vida. Mr Baker's father is called Denchfield Baker and he lives at Home Farm, next door to our house. We think it's funny that his name is Baker because he's a butcher!

Forge Cottage and Baker's Stores (The Forge can be seen on the right)

The pretty house opposite Baker's Stores is called The Laurels and it's where Arthur Holden lives. He's in my class at school and he's always smartly dressed because he is one of the tailoring family. His older sister, Alice, is a pupil-teacher at my school. The tiny cottage next door to The Laurels is called Rose Cottage and that's where yet another tailor lives called Mr Gowin: his son George is also in my class. He's very small for his age.

Rose Cottage nestling beside The Laurels

As you will have realised, there are lots of tailors in the village all working for Mr Holden at Shakespeare House.

Holden's tailoring shop in the High Street

As well as the tailors working inside the building, Mr Holden has a shop here on the High Street, opposite Rose Cottage. I can see the shop now; it has a big awning that stretches out over the pavement on sunny days. This is quite a busy place with the comings and goings of customers to Mr Holden's shop or the boys and their parents on their way to or from Schorne College.

As we continue along the High Street we come to Marston House where old Mrs Tattam lives with her daughter Lucy. The village blacksmith, Mr White, made that iron gate for her. If he looks out of his window from where he lives at Gordon Cottage (on the opposite side of the road) he can see it.

Marston House

Have you noticed that lovely smell of fresh bread? It's coming from the bakery. Can you see the big chimney rising from the ovens at the back? Look, there's Mr Watkins, the baker, loading up his cart with dozens of loaves of bread to deliver to his customers.

Mr James Watkins, the baker

The younger man helping him is Henry Cheshire who is also a Sunday school teacher. My dad often pulls Henry's leg about having more daughters than he has.

Henry Cheshire prepares for a bread delivery

"..hardly anything comes down the road."

As you can see, there are lots of children playing in the street. It's quite safe because hardly anything comes down the road although we have to watch out for Mr Rothschild's Stag Hunt. When that comes through the village nothing must get in its way! It causes quite a stir and children chase after it towards Granborough, but they can't keep up with the horses and stag-hounds. Most of the huntsmen, including Lord Rothschild from Waddesdon Manor, buy their smart hunting jackets and breeches from Mr Holden; they say even the Prince of Wales is one of his customers!

Lord Rothschild's Hunt at the Mill House (looking down towards the High Street)

You remember that, earlier, I mentioned Denchfield Baker, the butcher, and said he lived next door to us at Home Farm? Well, here's Home Farm. It's actually two houses; haven't they got some lovely vegetables in their front garden?

The Baker family at Home Farm

If we continue past my house and turn into Quainton Road, we can see there are more cottages down here than in all the rest of the village; they are mainly small cottages built higgledy-piggledy wherever space could be found.

A cottage in Quainton Road

There's the water pump I mentioned, and over the hedge you can see Mr Pipkin working in the garden of his pub, The Wheatsheaf.

The Wheatsheaf

On the left now we come to old Mr Dudley's cottage and his yard and garden.

Mr Henry Dudley

Ted Dudley, his son, is a builder and is a friend of my father's; my dad says he is very clever with his hands. Ted is a bell-ringer and a trumpet player in our village band. Ted's father, Henry Dudley, owns the farm at the back of the Wheatsheaf. Here's Ted now driving his sister, Rosanna, in a pony and trap. She must be visiting her family for the day, as she doesn't live here any more since she got a job in service working for Lord Rothschild on his estate at Halton.

Ted Dudley and his sister, Rosanna

And now here's Mr Cox's Prune Cottage, named after the plum trees growing in the garden.

If you walk further down Quainton Road you pass the Parish Barn on the right where farmers thresh grain at harvest time. Now we can just see the Primitive Methodist Church on the left hand side where I go to Sunday school. The person in charge of my Sunday school is Mr Mark Price, the brother of the builder at Flora Villa.

The Primitive Methodist Church in Quainton Road

Quainton Road is always busy with people walking up and down. If you go to the end, past Mr Henley's grocery shop, and Mr Gregory's pub (the Sportsman's Arms) it joins Carters Lane.

The Sportsman's Arms

When you reach Carters Lane, if you turn right, it leads to Brook Farm and beyond that is Stonehill Farm. As children, we are told never to go this far out of the village because of the gypsies who live further down Carters Lane or Deadman's Lane. Some of the gypsy boys chase us and throw stones. If you turn left at the end of Quainton Road it leads up to St John's Manor Farm which is empty at the moment; people say it is haunted but my father says that's rubbish.

Not many people live in Granborough Road; there are just a few cottages which mainly have thatched roofs.

Because my dad is a Police Constable, we don't live in one place for long and so the County Constabulary will be moving us to another village in a year or so. I will be sad to leave North Marston as I like it here and I have made lots of friends. When I am older I might come back here to live.

Jane Smith

Modern Street Name	Former Name(s)	Origin of Modern Name
High Street	Broad Street	The main thoroughfare through the village, the distance between opposite properties being greater than anywhere else in the village
Portway		A road name found in many villages from the Roman meaning "entrance to the settlement"
School Hill	College Hill, Church Ring (at the top), Church Hill	Location of the village school and, for a while, Schorne College. (The loop at the top end around the east end of the churchyard and down to Parsnip Pond was once called *Church Ring)*. It appears as Church Hill on deeds from the mid-19th century until about 1910
Quainton Road	Hogshaw Road, Lower Road, Lower End, Quainton Street, Hogshaw Street	Road leads to Quainton and Hogshaw. People living in this road were described as *"down-towners"* in Victorian times. For years it was the most populous road in the village
St John's Lane	Carters Lane	The oldest property in the lane is St John's Manor
Carters Lane	(Adjacent to Stonehill Farm it was once called Hogshaw Turn)	*Probably* named after the main users, the carters and carriers. Colloquially known as Gypsy Lane in the past due to a gypsy site half way along Carters Lane towards Quainton Dairy
Carters Meadow (1995)		Named after a local woman called *Alice Carter* who once owned the site upon which the estate is built
Elmers Meadow (1993)		*Elmer* was a village farming family name
Gibbings Close (c1950)	Gibbons Close	Named after a former land-holder on this site. Two hundred years ago the field on this site was called Gibbons Close

Shepperds Close (mid 1980s)		Named after a former land-holder on this site
Dudley Close (1994)		Named after a village builder and undertaker, *Ted Dudley*, whose family home and business were on this site
Morton Close (1977)		Built on land formerly farmed by *John Morton* of Glebe Farm and Burnaby Farm and named after him by the parish council in recognition of his contribution to the village
Deadman's Lane		*Probably* acquired this name colloquially because of the gibbet that is said to have stood at the bottom end of the lane (at the boundary of three parishes)
Schorne Lane	Holy Well Lane, Well Lane	Named after the fourteenth century rector, *John Schorne,* who 'discovered' a spring that became a holy well that is sited in this lane. The well and his shrine at the church attracted thousands of pilgrims over nearly two centuries
Marstonfields Road	North Marston Fields, Townsend	Named after an area called *Marston's Fields*, to which it leads, that formed part of the large open fields worked by villagers prior to Enclosure in 1778. The name distinguished the area from the neighbouring open fields belonging to Oving parish, which would have been *Oving's Fields*
Church Street	Vicarage Rise, Church Lane (at the top end)	
Hill Farm		Named after the farm formerly on this site
Steart Lane	Stewart Lane	Marked as such on Bryant's County Map of 1825

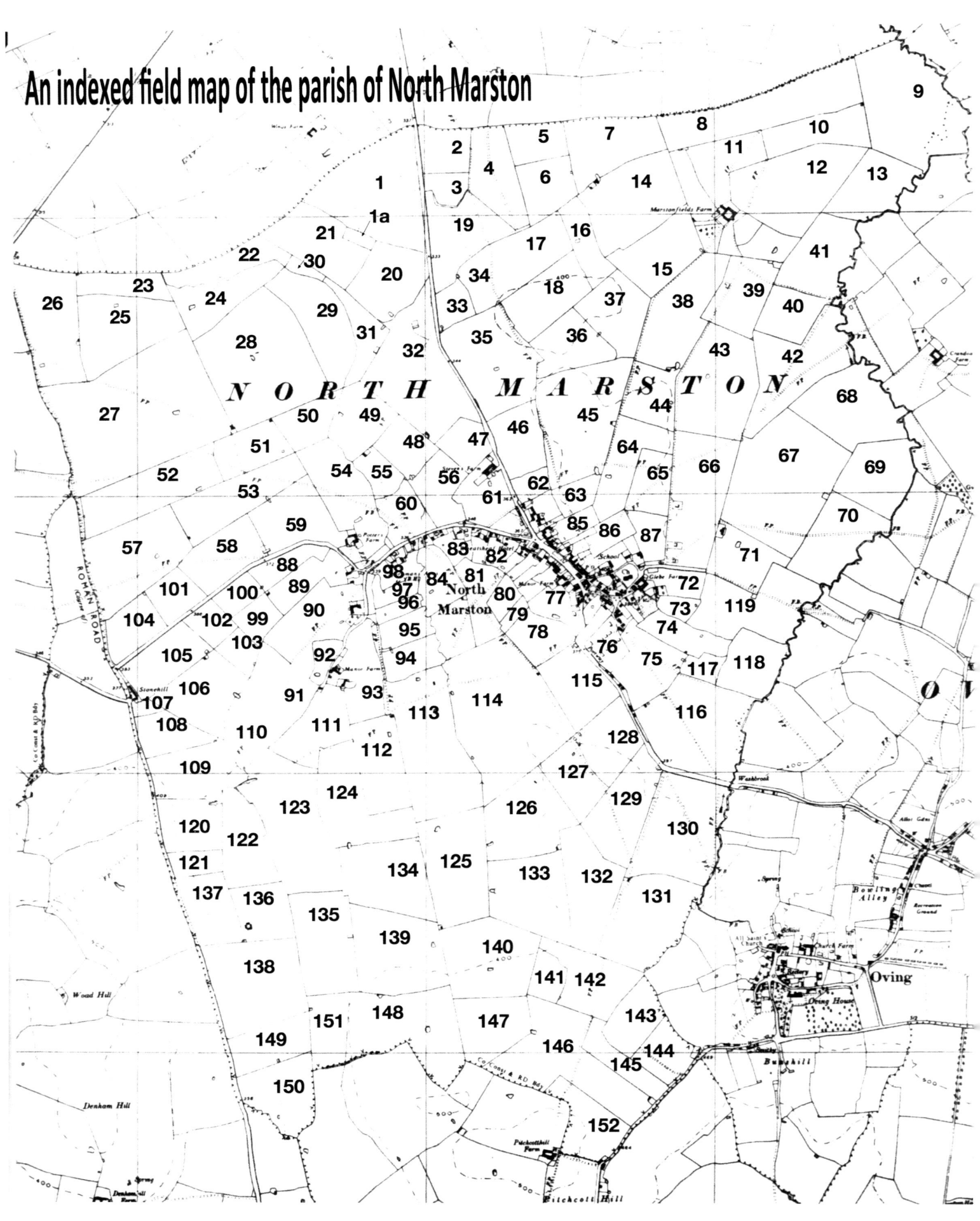

FIELD NO. (2013 MAP)	CURRENT NAME	LAMBOURNE'S MAP	OTHER NAMES
1	Mill Hill/Tom Cox's	Tom Cox's	
1a		Little Mill Hill	
2		Pool Field	
3		The Pool	
4		Poors Piece	
5		Little Field	
6		Little Field	
7		Thistly Field	
8		Old Ploughing	
9		The Meadow	
10		Seed Piece	
11		Big Common	
12		Home Close	
13	Town Meadow	Town Meadow	
14		Old Field	
15		Long Litmore	
16	Barnets Ley	Barnets Leys	
17	Lower Thornton	Lower Thornton Hill	
18	Upper Thornton Hill	Town Meadow	
19		Clock Land	
20	Hearts Hill/Hart Hill	Hart Hill	
21	Wind Mill/Mill Hill	Mill Hill	
22	Water Meadow	The Slough	
23	Long Breach Meadow	Long Breach Meadow	
24	Water Meadow	The Slough	
25	Long Breach Ground	Long Breach Ground	
26	Deadman's Ground	Deadman's Ground	
27		Great Ground	
28		Middle Ground	
29		The Slad	
30		The Slad	
31		The Slad	
32	Hagditch	Hagditch	
33		Four Corner Piece	
34	Lower Thornton	Lower Thornton Hill	
35	Grunhill	Great Grunhill	
36	Fullers Ley(s)	Fullers Leys	
37	Far Field/Hill	Far Hill	
38		Lower Barley Ground	
39		Bewkers	
40	Little Ploughing	Little Mill Ditch	Little Mill Ditch (deeds)
41	Big Ploughing	Mill Ditch	Ploughed Mill Ditch (deeds)
42	Dick Tom	Dicks Tarn	Dick Town (deeds)
43		The Gog	
44		Upper Barley Ground	
45	Big Hill	Big Hill	
46	Home Close	Home Close	
47		Little Hagditch	
48		The Green	
49	Slade	Big Field	
50		Big Field	
51	Slade Part	Eight Acres	

FIELD NO. (2013 MAP)	CURRENT NAME	LAMBOURNE'S MAP	OTHER NAMES
52	Deadman's Lane	Keens Lower Ground	
53	Lower Meadow	Long Meadow	
54	Brook Field	Home Field	
55	Chapel Green	Chapel Green	
56		Stevens Green	
57		Great Lower Ground	
58	Ern Seaton's	Seed Rise	
59	Ern Seaton's	Langlands	
60		Chapel Green	
61	The Green	The Green	
62		Gibbons	
63	Little Hill	Upper Churchill	
64	Gravel Pits	Gravel Pits	
65		Old Ploughed Piece	
66		Town's End	
67	White Piece	White Piece	
68	Ploughed Piece	Old Ploughed Piece	Old Ploughed Piece (deeds)
69	Far Broad Oaks	Far Broad Oaks	
70	Broad Oaks	Broad Oaks	
71	White Piece	(No Name)	
72	Home Close	Glebe Close	
73		Church Close	
74	Wells Close	Well Close	
75	Well Leys	Well Leys	
76		Fullers Croft	
77		Home Close	
78		Home Close	
79		Paddock Close	
80		Watkins	
81		Andrew's Oaks	Anders Oaks (colloquial)
82		Wheatsheaf	
83		Sheppards Close	
84	Ansties	Lower Franklins	
85		Home Close	
86		Churchill	
87		Little Town's End	
88	Prices Hill	Prices Piece	
89	Prices Hill	Prices Piece	
90	Home Ground	Home Ground	
91	Big Windmill Hill	The Big Hill	
92	Champions	Champions	
93	Nine Acres	Home Close	
94	2nd Woods Close	2nd Wools Close	
95	1st Woods Close	1st Wools Close	
96		Cottage Close	
97	Coopers Close	Coopers Close	
98		Sportsmans	
99	Prices Piece	Prices Piece	
100	Prices Piece	Top Shafters	
101		Old Ploughing	
102	Top Staffords	Middle Shafters	
103	Bottom Staffords	Bottom Shafters	

FIELD NO. (2013 MAP)	CURRENT NAME	LAMBOURNE'S MAP	OTHER NAMES
104		Stonehill Field	
105	Stonehill	Stonehill	
106	Middle Ground	Middle Ground	
107		Close	
108		Seven Acres	
109		Big Field	
110	Big Windmill Hill	Little Windmill Hill	
111	The Home Field	Lammas Close	
112	The Pool Field/Leycroft	Leycroft	
113	Bancroft	Bancroft	
114		The Hill Field	
115		Generals Piece	
116	Great Ground	Great Ground	
117	Pightle	Pightle	
118	Bell Close	Bell Close	
119	Fallow Close	Fallow Close	Pasture Field (deeds)
120	Nine Acres	Nine Acres	
121		Little Field	
122	The Pool Field	Pool Common	
123		New Pond Leys	
124	Tom Cox's	Ley Croft	
125	Lower Mead	Lower Mead	
126		Lower Gorbroad	
127		Haynhill	
128		Portway Piece	
129	Turners Piece	Turners Piece	
130	Washbrook	Wash Brook Ground	
131	Tattams	Tattams Far Ground	
132		Ploughed Piece	
133		Upper Gorbroad	
134	Cats Brains	Cats Brain	
135		Lang Plough Piece	
136	Barn Common	Barn Common	
137	Road Common	Road Common	
138	The Ploughing	Carters Lane Ground	
139	Lower Shotshill	Lower Shots Hill	
140	Middle Mead	Upper Mead	
141	Best Grove	Four Acres	
142	Eight Acres	Eight Acres	
143	Poors Piece	Poors Piece	
144		Allotments	
145	Brickhill Piece	Brickhill	
146	Big Grove	The Big Grove	
147	Ingrams	Ingrams Hill	
148	Shotshill	Upper Shotshill	
149		Lower Field	
150		Ten Acres	
151	The Meadow	Lang Field	
152		The Grove	

BIBLIOGRAPHY

A Late Medieval Pilgrimage Cult: Master John Schorne of North Marston and Windsor by Richard Marks (British Archaeological Association 2002)

Benjamin Keach and a Monument to Liberty by Kenneth Dix (Fauconberg Press 1985)

Buckinghamshire in the 1760s and 1820s: The County Maps of Jefferys and Bryant (Buckinghamshire Archaeological Society 2000)

Buckinghamshire Parish Registers: North Marston, St Mary (Buckinghamshire Family History Society 2005)

History and Antiquities of the County of Buckingham by George Lipscomb (Self published 1847)

History and Topography of Buckinghamsire by J Sheahan (Longman 1861)

Kelly's Directory 1899

Memories Shared Volumes 1-6 (North Marston History Club 2011)

Robson's Commercial Directory 1839

The County Books Series: Buckinghamshire by Alison Uttley (Robert Hale Ltd 1950)

The Northmarston Magazine 1870-1876 (Edited by Rev S B James)

The Poor Relations of the Late Miser Neild by John Wright (1855)

The Schornian 1878-1903 (Edited by Rev S B James)

The Vestry Book 1863-1894

The Victoria History of the Counties of England, edited by William Page (London, Constable & Co. 1905)

Tis the Far Famous Vale by Ken and Margaret Morley (The Book Castle 2007)

<u>Other Source Material</u>

Family documents and correspondence (loaned by the family)

National Census 1841-1911

North Marston Parish Church Records of Baptisms, Marriages and Deaths

North Marston Parish Magazines 1940-2000

North Marston School Admissions Register 1902-1965

North Marston School Log Books 1899-1968

Register of Baptisms in the Parish of North Marston 1911-2011

Unpublished notes on Windmills by Stanley Freese (The Centre for Buckinghamshire Studies)

Unpublished notes on Windmills by John Wright of North Marston

Wesleyan Methodist Church Sunday School Attendance Register